# Greece
## a country study

Foreign Area Studies
The American University
Edited by
Rinn S. Shinn
Research completed
April 1985

On the cover: Discobolus (Discus Thrower) by Myron, ca. 450 B.C., survived only in Roman marble copies.

Third Edition, 1986; First Printing, 1986

**Library of Congress Cataloging-in-Publication Data**

Greece  : a country study.

    (DA pam  ; 550–87)
    Rev. ed. of: Area handbook for Greece / Eugene K.
Keefe.  2nd ed. 1977.
    Bibliography: p.
    Includes index.
    1. Shinn, Rinn-Sup.    II. Keefe, Eugene K.    Area
handbook for Greece.    III. American University
(Washington, D.C.). Foreign Area Studies.    IV. Series.

DF717.G78    1985          949.5          86–1231


Headquarters, Department of the Army
DA Pam 550-87

# Foreword

This volume is one of a continuing series of books prepared by Foreign Area Studies, The American University, under the Country Studies/Area Handbook Program. The last page of this book provides a listing of other published studies. Each book in the series deals with a particular foreign country, describing and analyzing its economic, national security, political, and social systems and institutions and examining the interrelationships of those systems and institutions and the ways that they are shaped by cultural factors. Each study is written by a multidisciplinary team of social scientists. The authors seek to provide a basic insight and understanding of the society under observation, striving for a dynamic rather than a static portrayal of it. The study focuses on historical antecedents and on the cultural, political, and socioeconomic characteristics that contribute to cohesion and cleavage within the society. Particular attention is given to the origins and traditions of the people who make up the society, their dominant beliefs and values, their community of interests and the issues on which they are divided, the nature and extent of their involvement with the national institutions, and their attitudes toward each other and toward the social system and political order within which they live.

The contents of the book represent the views, opinions, and findings of Foreign Area Studies and should not be construed as an official Department of the Army position, policy, or decision, unless so designated by other official documentation. The authors have sought to adhere to accepted standards of scholarly objectivity. Such corrections, additions, and suggestions for factual or other changes that readers may have will be welcomed for use in future new editions.

The Director
Foreign Area Studies
The American University
5010 Wisconsin Ave., NW
Washington, D.C. 20016

# Acknowledgments

The authors are grateful to a number of individuals in the agencies of the United States government and in international, diplomatic, and private organizations in Washington, D.C., who gave of their time, research materials, data, and suggestions to make this study possible. Without associating any of these individuals with the contents of this study, including errors or omissions, the authors are indebted also to Dr. Michael Herzfeld of Indiana University for helpful advice and suggestions concerning Chapter 2 of this volume, to Dr. Demetrios G. Papademetriou of Population Associates International for providing unpublished papers as well as bibliographical and other assistance on migration; and Ellen Laipson of the Congressional Research Service, who reviewed and provided valuable comments on Chapters 4 and 5.

Special thanks are owed also to members of the Foreign Area Studies staff who contributed directly to the preparation of this volume. These include Stephen B. Wickman, who coordinated the early stage of this project; Andrea T. Merrill and Denise R. Barber, who edited the manuscript and the accompanying figures and tables; Harriett R. Blood, who prepared the graphics along with Gustavo Adolfo Mendoza, who designed the cover and the illustrations for the title page of each chapter; Gilda V. Nimer and Lynn W. Dorn, librarians; Margaret Quinn and Beverly A. Johnson, who photoset the text and tabular material; and Charlotte Benton Pochel, who assisted in other areas of manuscript preparation. The assistance of Ernest A. Will, publications manager, and Eloise W. Brandt and Wayne W. Olsen, administrative assistants, is also appreciated. The book was indexed by William A. Ragland.

Chapter 4 in this study reflects the collaboration of Rita Moore-Robinson, who wrote the sections on "Political Development, 1981–85" and "Political Parties" (except "Other Parties"); Peter J. Kassander, who drafted a portion of "Turkey"; and Millicent H. Schwenk, who contributed the section on "Western Europe and Regionalism." The rest of the chapter was written by Rinn S. Shinn. Appendix B was written by Stephen B. Wickman; Appendix C was written by Peter J. Kassander.

# Contents

## List of Figures

# Preface

This volume replaces the *Area Handbook for Greece*, originally published in 1969, revised in 1977, and reprinted in 1983 as *Greece: A Country Study*. In the years after the completion of the 1977 edition, the most significant political development was the rise to power of a socialist party through a landslide victory in the October 1981 general elections. The Panhellenic Socialist Movement (Panhellinion Socialistiko Kinima—PASOK) formed the first left-wing administration in Greece and followed up on its campaign promises for sweeping domestic and foreign policy reforms. The Socialist initiatives represented varying shades of departures from the conservative, pro-Western policies of the center-right governments of the preceding decades.

The purpose of this study is to present an objective and concise account of the dominant social, economic, political, and national security concerns of contemporary Greece. Sources of information include scholarly journals and monographs, official reports of governmental and international organizations, foreign and domestic newspapers and periodicals, and interviews with individuals who have special knowledge of Greek affairs. Brief comments on some of the more useful, readily accessible English-language sources appear at the end of each chapter. Full references to these and other sources used by the authors are listed in the Bibliography.

The contemporary place-names used in this study are generally those approved by the United States Board on Geographical Names, as set forth in the official gazetteer published in 1960; however, names of persons and places that have acquired a familiar spelling or a conventional form in the West are given in that form. The reader will therefore find Constantine rather than Konstantinos or Athens and Crete rather than Athinai and Kriti. The dictionary used was *Webster's Ninth New Collegiate Dictionary*.

Measurements are given in the metric system; a conversion table is provided to assist those who are unfamiliar with metric indicators (see table 1, Appendix A). Appendix A provides other tabular material on social, economic, and security matters. A Glossary is also included, as is a chronology of important historical events (see table A, Preface).

## Table A. Chronology of Important Events

| Date | Description |
|---|---|
| ca. 3000-1400 B.C. . . . . | Minoan civilization in Crete |
| ca. 1400-1100 B.C. . . . . | Dominance of Mycenae |
| ca. 1100-800 B.C. . . . . . | Dorian invasion; destruction of Mycenaean cities; "dark ages" in Greece |
| ca. 800-700 B.C. . . . . . . | Monarchies overthrown and landed oligarchies established throughout Greece, except in Sparta, where military-totalitarian system is created |
| ca. 700-600 B.C. . . . . . . | Greek city-states colonize European shores of the Mediterranean; aristocratic oligarchies replaced by tyrannies—the rule of one tyrant—a link between oligarchy and democracy |
| 499-78 B.C. . . . . . . . . | War with Persians |
| 478-58 B.C. . . . . . . . . | Athens transforms Delian League into an Athenian empire |
| 460-45 B.C. . . . . . . . . | War between Athens and Sparta (first Peloponnesian war) |
| 446-31 B.C. . . . . . . . . | Golden Age of Pericles; consolidation of the Athenian empire and greatest cultural flowering of antiquity in Athens |
| 431-04 B.C. . . . . . . . . | Second Peloponnesian war |
| 360-36 B.C. . . . . . . . . | Establishment of Macedonian Empire under Philip II |
| 336-23 B.C. . . . . . . . . | Rise of Alexander the Great of Macedonia; extension of Macedonian Empire from Mediterranean to India |
| 215-168 B.C. . . . . . . . | Macedonian wars; various alliances fail to resist Roman infiltration |
| 168-46 B.C. . . . . . . . . | Greece and Macedonia become Roman provinces |
| 148 B.C.-A.D. 300 . . . . . | Period of Roman rule |
| A.D. 285 . . . . . . . . . . | Roman Empire divided into western and eastern halves |
| 330 . . . . . . . . . . . . . | Emperor Constantine transfers capital of Roman Empire to Byzantium (renamed Constantinople); Christianity becomes state religion |
| 330-1453 . . . . . . . . . . | Byzantine Empire |
| 395-477 . . . . . . . . . . . | Intermittent raids into Greece by Goths and Vandals |
| 577 . . . . . . . . . . . . . | Beginning of continued invasions by Avars and Slavs |
| 1054 . . . . . . . . . . . . . | Schism between Roman and Greek Christian churches |
| 1453 . . . . . . . . . . . . . | Constantinople falls to Ottoman Turks |
| 1453-1821 . . . . . . . . . . | Greece part of Ottoman Empire |
| 1821-29 . . . . . . . . . . . | War of independence |
| 1831 . . . . . . . . . . . . . | Great Powers recognize Greek independence |
| 1831-62 . . . . . . . . . . . | Prince Otto of Bavaria rules as king of Greece with sanction of Great Powers; period of frequent intervention by foreign powers, especially Britain, into Greek affairs |

| Date | Description |
|---|---|
| 1863-1913 . . . . . . . . . . | After deposition of Otto, Prince George of Demark rules as "King of the Hellenes" |
| 1897 . . . . . . . . . . . . . . | War with Ottoman Empire over Greek claims to Crete and Thessaly; Greece soundly defeated, but Crete given substantial self-government |
| 1909 . . . . . . . . . . . . . . | Military coup imposes economic and social reforms and reorganizes military; Eleutherios Venizelos appointed prime minister; pattern set for military intervention in politics |
| 1912-13 . . . . . . . . . . . . | Balkan wars; Greece doubles in size as result of war gains; assassination of George I; succession of his son, Constantine |
| 1914-18 . . . . . . . . . . . . | Question of Greece's entry into World War I provokes virtual civil war, with rival governments led by Venizelos and King Constantine I; Constantine forced into exile by the Allies; Alexander, his son, becomes king, and Greece enters war on Allied side |
| 1920 . . . . . . . . . . . . . . | Alexander dies; Constantine's return to throne is overwhelmingly approved in plebiscite |
| 1921-22 . . . . . . . . . . . . | War with Turkey ends disastrously with cession of Anatolia; exchange of population increases Greece's population by 20 percent |
| 1922-35 . . . . . . . . . . . . | Period of unstable governments and frequent military interventions revolving around choice between a monarchy and a republic; Constantine abdicates and is succeeded by son, George II; brief period of military dictatorship; Greece declared a republic (1927-35) |
| 1935 . . . . . . . . . . . . . . | Monarchy restored |
| 1936-40 . . . . . . . . . . . . | Dictatorship of John Metaxas |
| 1941-44 . . . . . . . . . . . . | Italian-German-Bulgarian occupation of Greece during World War II; resistance forces in Greece led by Communists |
| 1944-45 . . . . . . . . . . . . | Communist uprising in Athens crushed by British troops |
| 1946-49 . . . . . . . . . . . . | Civil War; under Truman Doctrine, United States supports government forces against Communist rebels |
| 1949-63 . . . . . . . . . . . . | Period of recovery under right-wing leadership; North Atlantic Treaty Organization (NATO) membership; beginning of Greek industrialization and rapid social change |
| 1959 . . . . . . . . . . . . . . | Greece applies as associate member of European Economic Community (EEC) |
| 1961-62 . . . . . . . . . . . . | EEC membership agreement signed in 1961; becomes effective in 1962 |

*Table A.—Continued.*

| Date | Description |
|---|---|
| 1963-67 . . . . . . . . . . . . | Monopoly of power by conservative forces ends but is followed by period of unstable governments and political controversy |
| 1967-74 . . . . . . . . . . . . | Right-wing military dictatorship imposes harsh rule with many human rights abuses; monarchy ends; Turkish invasion of Cyprus precipitates collapse of junta and theatens to provoke war |
| 1974 . . . . . . . . . . . . . . | Democracy restored under Constantine Karamanlis; end of monarchy confirmed by plebiscite |
| 1980 . . . . . . . . . . . . . . | Karamanlis elected president |
| 1981 . . . . . . . . . . . . . . | Election of socialist government led by Andreas Papandreou; full membership in EEC; beginning of three-year economic recession |
| 1985 . . . . . . . . . . . . . . | Socialist government refuses to nominate Karamanlis to second term as president; Christos Sartzetakis elected new president; general elections scheduled for June 2 |

# Country Profile

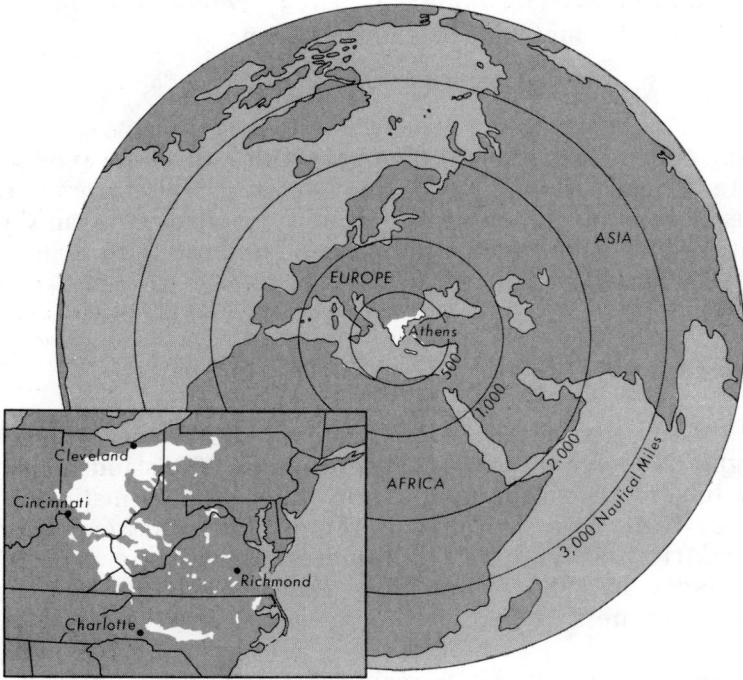

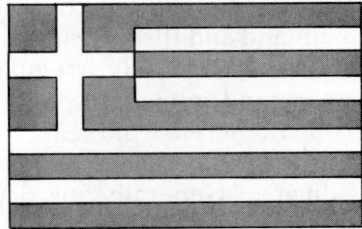

## Country

**Formal Name:**  Hellenic Republic.

**Short Form:**  Greece.

**Term for Citizens:**  Greek(s).

**Earlier Political Status:** Greece achieved independence from Ottoman Empire after 1821-29 war. Technically a monarchy until 1973 when military junta replaced it with republic. Referendum on December 8, 1974, rejected return to monarchy after junta had been overthrown.

**Capital:** Athens.

**Flag:** Nine horizontal bars of equal width—five blue and four white, placed alternately. In blue canton is white cross with arms of equal width and length. Blue symbolizes Grecian sky; white cross symbolizes Christianity and dedication to struggle for freedom.

## Geography

**Size:** Land area nearly 132,608 square kilometers, of which roughly 20 percent consists of more than 2,000 islands, about 170 inhabited; islands range from small rock formations to Crete, fifth largest island in Mediterranean Sea. Land boundaries only 1,170 kilometers; coastline 15,000 kilometers. In 1985 continued to claim six nautical miles of territorial waters.

**Topography:** About 80 percent of territory mountainous. Nine geographical and historically defined regions (six mainland and three insular). Most extensive lowlands are plains of Thessaly. Highly irregular coastline marked by many bays, coves, and inlets. No point on mainland peninsula more than 100 kilometers from sea.

**Climate:** Generally hot, dry summers and damp, cold winters. In northernmost regions and center of mainland, continental influences cause more severe winters. Considerable local variation in rainfall and temperature because of altitude and proximity to sea.

## Society

**Population:** In July 1984 estimated at nearly 10 million; average annual growth rate 0.9 percent. About 86 percent of population lives on mainland peninsula. Two largest urban centers—Greater Athens and Greater Thessaloniki (Salonika)—account for two-fifths of total population.

**Religion:** Orthodox Christianity, professed by over 96 percent of population, official state religion. About 1.5 percent Muslim, mainly from Turkish community. Small numbers of Roman and Greek Catholics and Jews.

**Ethnic Groups and Languages:** Ethnically and linguistically homogeneous. Population unofficially estimated as 97 percent Greek-speaking. Turkish-speaking minority centered in Thrace constitutes about 1 percent of population; remainder scattered among Vlachs, Slavs, and Albanians. Form of Greek used by schools and government standard modern Greek.

**Education:** Nine years of education, free and complusory for children up to age 15. In early 1980s roughly 82 percent of age-group 12 to 17 in secondary school; 17 percent of 20 to 24 age-group in higher education. Literacy rate in 1981 about 80 percent.

**Health and Welfare:** Complicated system of social security— almost 650 carriers for old-age, survivor, and disability pensions; financed through employer and employee contributions and government subsidy. National health service being established. In 1982 life expectancy 72 for men, 76 for women.

## Economy

**Gross National Product (GNP):** Estimated US$34.9 billion at current prices and exchange rates in 1983. National income per capita approximately US$3,560 in 1983. Rapid GNP growth compared with European Economic Community (EEC) partners up to 1980 followed by three-year period of stagnation. First signs of feeble recovery in 1984. Bumper agricultural production largely responsible for projected 2.2- to 2.5-percent increase in GNP in 1985.

**Resources:** Oil imports met 63 percent of energy demand in 1983. Energy plans promote greater reliance on domestic resources. Modest offshore oil reserves and abundant lignite . Mining represented only 1.3 percent of GNP in 1983, but considerable mineral wealth to be exploited, particularly bauxite, ferronickle ores, and magnesite.

**Industry:** Estimated 28.9 percent of GNP and 29.2 percent of employment in 1983. Characterized by small, family-owned enterprises. A few large, modern establishments dominated fields such as mineral processing, oil refining, chemicals, engineering, and shipbuilding and repair. Construction vital branch of industrial activity.

**Agriculture:** Estimated 17.3 percent of GNP and 28.8 percent of employment in 1983. Largely self-sufficient except for red meat, dairy products, and animal feed stuffs. In 1981-84 sector exposed to serious competition from EEC members. Handicapped by geographic limitations and fragmented structure of small farms. Panhellenic Socialist Movement (Panhellinion Socialistiko Kinima—PASOK) policy sought to strengthen processing and marketing through cooperative movement.

**Exports:** Merchandise exports US$4.1 billion in 1983. Basic manufactures—primarily textiles, cement, metals and metal articles, aluminum and alumina, chemcials, and pharmaceuticals—46 percent of total; traditional exports, such as food, beverages, tobacco, raw materials, and ores, 33 percent; and petroleum products, 18 percent. Major markets: Federal Republic of Germany (West Germany), Italy, France, Saudi Arabia, and United States.

**Imports:** Merchandise imports US$9.5 billion in 1983. Mineral fuels 28 percent of total; foodstuffs 13 percent; manufactured consumer goods, capital goods, and intermediate manufactures plus raw materials each around one-fifth of imports. Major suppliers: West Germany, Saudi Arabia, Italy, France, and Japan.

**Balance of Payments:** Structural deficit on current account balance fluctuated between 3 and 8.3 percent of gross domestic product over 1970-84 period. In 1982-84 deficit stabilized at high level—around $1.9 billion. Invisible receipts, mostly from shipping, tourism, and emigrant remittances, offset large share of yearly trade deficit, but their performance weakened after 1979 owing to unfavorable international economic conditions. Rapid buildup of foreign debt between 1979 and 1984. Debt service 17 percent of foreign exchange earnings in 1983.

**Exchange Rate:** Dr129.3 to US$1 in January 1985 (for value of the drachma—see Glossary). Steady depreciation in 1980-84 period, exacerbating domestic inflationary pressures. Inflation averaged 18.5 percent in 1984, down from 24.5 percent in 1981.

## Transportation and Communications

**Roads:** Dominant form of inland transportation, covering over 80 percent of intercity passenger and freight transport; 8,777 kilometers of national highways in 1984, supplemented by 28,639 kilometers of provincial highways. Plans to construct national roadway between ports of Igoumenitsa and Volos and upgrade other vital linkages.

**Shipping and Ports:** One of world leaders in international shipping. Merchant fleet flying Greek flag totaled 3,082 vessels with 34.7 million registered tons in May 1984, third largest in world. Well-developed interisland maritime links with seven major ports. Imports shipbuilding and repair industry. Modernization of Igoumenitsa and Volos ports planned to promote country's role as crossroads between EEC and Middle East.

**Railroads:** 2,478 kilometers of track in 1984. Use limited by narrow-gauge track and obsolete equipment. Operated by state monopoly, Hellenic Railways. Priority given to electrification and double tracking of Athens-Thessaloniki-Yugoslavia line by 1987.

**Airports:** Domestic and international service provided by state monopoly, Olympic Airways. Regular service to some 30 domestic airports. In 1985 government considering construction of new Athens airport at Spata.

**Telecommunications:** Practically all telephone communications connected with automatic trunk-line network. State-owned Hellenic Telecommunications Organization investing heavily in modernization of system and satellite connections.

# Government and Politics

**Government:**  Parliamentary system with separation of powers. Unicameral legislature elects president of the republic (head of state), who appoints prime minister (head of government), representing majority of legislature. Government must maintain confidence of legislature. Government based on Constitution of 1975 and highly centralized. Efforts under way since 1981 to decentralize decisionmaking. Judicial system consists of civil and criminal and administrative courts. Highest civil and criminal court is Supreme Court.

**Politics:**  Highly competitive political setting marked by two major political parties—PASOK and New Democracy (Nea Demokratia—ND)—and distant third party, Communist Party of Greece—Exterior (Kommunistikon Komma Ellados—KKE-Exterior). PASOK won October 1981 parlimentary elections and was led in mid-1985 by Andreas Papandreou. Principal opposition came from ND and KKE—Exterior. Other minor parties remained on periphery of party system.

**Administrative Subdivisions:**  Nine regions of geographic and historical but little administrative significance divided into 51 provinces (*nomói*; Sing., *nomós*), primary administrative units. Within each province are municipalities and smaller communes, both of which have locally elected officials. Despite talks of decentralization under PASOK administration, central government continued to wield strong influence at local government level.

**Foreign Relations:**  Member of North Atlantic Treaty Organization (NATO) and EEC. Close relations with most countries in world. Major foreign policy disputes are with Turkey over Cyprus and Aegean Sea. Relations with United States close bilaterally but marked by some philosophical differences on international issues.

# National Security

**Armed Forces:**  In 1985 total personnel on active duty, approximately 178,000: army, 135,000; navy, 19,500; and air force, 23,500 total reserve, 405,000.

**Units:** In 1985 army had one armored division, one mechanized division, 11 infantry divisions, one special forces division, three armored brigades, one mechanized brigade, four armored reconnaissance brigades, six tank battalions, four motorized infantry battalions and reconnaissance battalions, 13 forward artillery battalions, seven antiaircraft artillery battalions, two surface-to-surface missile battalions, three army aviation battalions, and one independent aviation company. Air force organized into three commands: Tactical Air Command, Air Matérial Command for Transport and Supply, and Air Training Command.

**Equipment:** Navy had 10 submarines, 14 destroyers, seven frigates, 29 missile patrol boats, two coastal minelayers, 14 coastal minesweepers, and variety of small landing craft. Air force had eight fighter and ground-attack squadrons, one rescue squadron, three transport squadrons, and one surface-to-air missile wing. Most equipment of United States, French, or British design. Some manufacture and repair of equipment done under licensing agreements. Developing local defense industry.

**Budget:** Expenditures represented Dr247.7 billion, or approximately 25 percent of total governmental budget in 1984.

**Foreign Military Treaties:** North Atlantic Treaty Organization, 1952.

**Police Forces:** Security corps staffed by 25,000 City Police and Gendarmerie. City Police in cities of Athens, Piraeus, Patrai, and island of Corfu. Gendarmerie in rest of country. Gendarmerie performs investigative functions. All police under unified command structure and civilian control.

Drama 4

5 Kilkis Xanthi 2 1

7 6 Serrai Komotini

Edhessa 12 Kavala Alexandroupolis

8 Florina Thessaloniki 13

Veroia 11 14

Kastoria Kozani Poliyiros Mount

9 15 Katerini Athos

17 10

Grevena 16

18 Larisa

Ioannina 23 51

Kerkira Igoumenitsa Trikala

19 20 Kardhitsa Volos 25 Mitilini

22 24

21 Arta 27

Preveza Lamia

Levkas Karpenision

29 28 26 50 Khios

Mesolongion 31 Amfissa

30 32 Levadhia Khalkis 33

Patrai 34

37 36 Athens Samos

Argostolion Corinth Piraeus 48

Zakinthos Pirgos 41 Navplion

39 38 Tripolis 35 Ermoupolis

40 49

Kalamai Sparta

42 47 Rodhos

Khania 43 Rethimnon 44 Iraklion

Ayios Nikolaos 46

———— Provincial boundary
⊛ National capital
● Provincial capital

| | | | | | | |
|---|---|---|---|---|---|---|
| 1 | Evros | *14 | Khalkidhiki | 27 | Evritania | 40 | Messinia |
| 2 | Rodhopi | 15 | Pieria | 28 | Aitolia and Akarnania | 41 | Arkadhia |
| 3 | Xanthi | 16 | Larisa | 29 | Levkas | 42 | Lakonia |
| 4 | Drama | 17 | Grevena | 30 | Kefallinia | 43 | Khania |
| 5 | Serrai | 18 | Ioannina | 31 | Fokis | 44 | Rethimni |
| 6 | Kilkis | 19 | Kerkira | 32 | Voiotia | 45 | Iraklion |
| 7 | Pella | 20 | Thesprotia | 33 | Evvoia | 46 | Lasithi |
| 8 | Florina | 21 | Preveza | 34 | Attica | 47 | Dhodhekanisos |
| 9 | Kastoria | 22 | Arta | 35 | Argolis | 48 | Samos |
| 10 | Kozani | 23 | Trikala | 36 | Korinthia | 49 | Kikladhes |
| 11 | Imathia | 24 | Kardhitsa | 37 | Akhaia | 50 | Khios |
| 12 | Thessaloniki | 25 | Magnisia | 38 | Ilia | 51 | Lesvos |
| 13 | Kavala | 26 | Fthiotis | 39 | Zakinthos | | |

*Includes the
autonomous
area Mount Athos

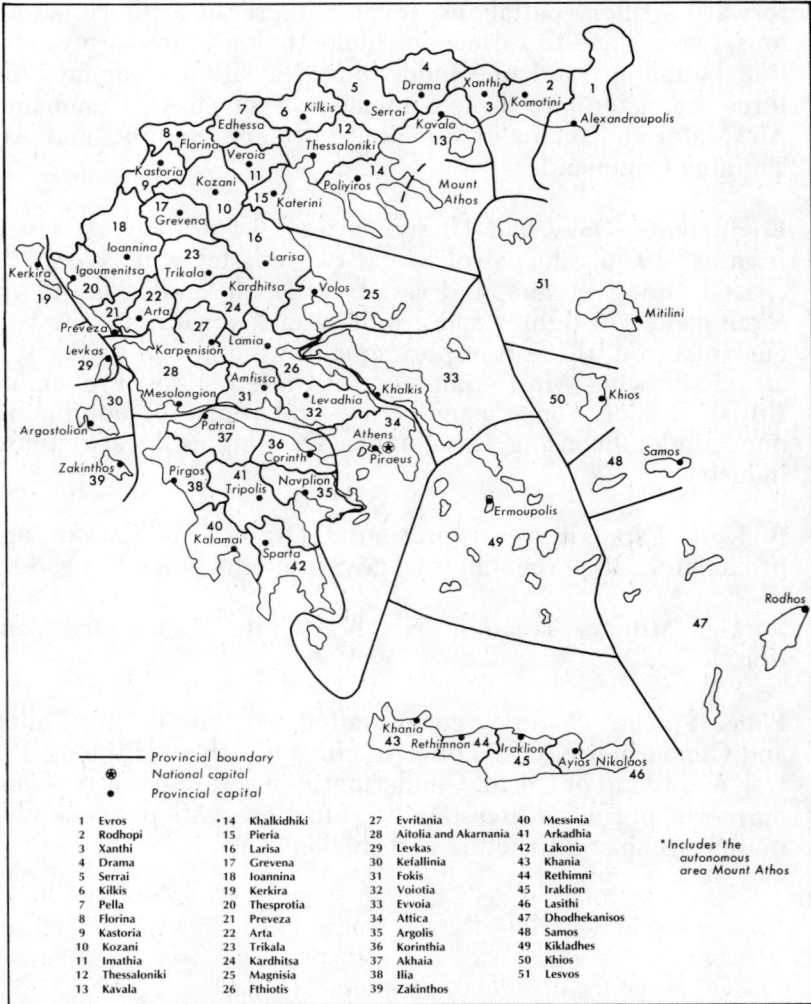

*Figure 1. Greece, 1985*

# Introduction

"A TRULY GREAT VICTORY for the people and a great defeat for both the foreign and local reactionaries," declared Andreas Papandreou, exulting at his first press conference after the general election of June 2, 1985. The 66-year-old charismatic founder/leader of the left-wing Panhellenic Socialist Movement (Panhellinion Socialistiko Kinima—PASOK) was successful in his bid for a second four-year mandate (1985-89) in what he called "the most significant political showdown in our country's recent political history." In that confrontation, or "the showdown between the forces of progress, democracy, and change and those of reaction, dependence, and authoritarianism," as he put it, PASOK overcame the challenges from numerous political groups representing the full range of the ideological spectrum. The most serious threat came from the center/right-wing New Democracy (Nea Demokratia—ND), which had ruled the nation after the collapse of the colonels' dictatorship (1967-74) until it was deposed by PASOK in the October 1981 election.

The 1985 campaign, as in 1977 and 1981, was essentially a two-party contest between PASOK and the ND. The two parties received a combined 87 percent of the vote—45.8 percent for the Socialists and 40.9 percent for the ND—as compared with 12 percent for the distant third political grouping, the Communist Party of Greece (Kommunistikon Komma Ellados—KKE), which was split into a pro-Moscow (KKE-Exterior) and a Eurocommunist (KKE-Interior) faction. Thus the 1985 election reinforced the virtual two-party system that had been in place since 1977.

The election took place in a sharply polarized political atmosphere in which both contestants were more interested in denouncing the other than in debating real issues and programs for the future. The ND sought to portray PASOK as a Marxist party with totalitarian strivings, committed to the creation of a one-party state at the expense of Greece's pluralist democracy. PASOK contended that a victory for the ND would mean the reimposition of a heavy-handed, authoritarian right-wing rule characteristic of the 1950s and early 1960s. Implicit in its contention was the message that many left-wing activists would likely face persecution or exile in the event of a conservative return to power.

Preelection polls showed the two parties in a dead heat. During the intense three-week electioneering, PASOK maintained that a second term of office was needed to complete its programs for economic recovery and modernization, social welfare reforms, governmental reorganization, and full independence in foreign affairs. It did acknowledge that its economic performance fell short of expectations but that much of the blame should be placed on what it called the mistakes of previous conservative governments and the sluggish international economic environment.

For its part, the ND hammered away at the dismal state of the economy, which was beset by inflation, unemployment, heavy taxation, and inadequate investment capital. Its economic alternative called for the lessening of the traditionally large state role in the economy and for the promotion of private initiative, market forces, and favorable conditions for investment. In foreign affairs the opposition cited the danger of Greece's isolation from its Western allies, claiming that Papandreou's erratic independent foreign policy showed a pro-Soviet bias. A notable aspect of the opposition's strategy was an intense effort to project a refurbished image as a centrist, liberal, and progressive party. Obviously this was considered important in countering PASOK's charges that the ND was run by reactionaries.

PASOK loyalists were quick to embellish the election results as an affirmative verdict on Greece's first experiment in socialism, whereas the ND partisans sought to portray the results as something of a moral victory for themselves if for no other reason than because the opposition group actually increased the number of its parliamentary seats—at PASOK's expense—from 115 in 1981 to 126 in the 300-member parliament. The ND leader, Constantine Mitsotakis, opined that the election outcome would have been different if the campaign period had been longer and if the opposition had had the benefit of full access to the state-controlled television.

Despite their victory the Socialists had a reason for soul-searching. PASOK's 1985 performance was solid but far from spectacular, as was its landslide victory in 1981. It lost ground in urban constituencies, where some of its middle-income supporters voted for the ND in protest against the Socialist failure to turn the economy around and to reduce big government. The Socialists' loss was more than offset, however, by gains in the rural areas, where their social welfare programs and infrastructure projects, as well as subsidies from the European Economic Community (EEC), considerably benefitted farmers.

Some observers commented that PASOK did not win as much as the ND lost because the 1985 results could be seen more as a negative vote against the conservatives than as an expression of faith in Papandreou's socialism. Their reasoning was buttressed by the view that the margin of PASOK victory would have been much slimmer had not a sizable number of Communist voters swung to PASOK—to keep the ND out of power. Harilaos Florakis, general secretary of the pro-Moscow Communist Party of Greece-Exterior, was probably mindful of such a swing vote when in his first postelection speech he accused PASOK of seducing "a number of left-wing voters" through fear-mongering and "schemes for political blackmail."

Whatever the real reasons, PASOK formed a one-party government, thereby laying to rest the preelection fear held by many observers that its narrow win would almost certainly result in a weak and unstable government—and worse yet, leave the Communists holding the balance of power in the politics of coalition building. It was generally known that the Communist price for participation in coalition rule would have been, inter alia, the severance of Greek ties with the North Atlantic Treaty Organization (NATO).

Unlike the previous elections, foreign affairs played a relatively muted role in 1985. This was not because external affairs were any less intractable than previously. On the contrary, foreign policy problems remained a volatile issue, but it was played down during the campaign because the voters were much more concerned with bread-and-butter matters.

The impact of geography on the country's international affairs remains far-reaching. Greece's strategic location on the southern tip of the Balkan Peninsula jutting into the Mediterranean Sea—not to mention its own military weakness and internal schisms—has made it historically susceptible to foreign influence and intervention. For example, the country's independence from the Turks in 1831 had to be internationally guaranteed by Britain, Russia, and France, all of which had strategic interests in the Balkan region. This guarantee proved highly tenuous, though, because of intense British and Russian rivalry for spheres of influence in Greece. This rivalry culminated in the emergence of Britain as the paramount power in the mid-nineteenth century, a status that remained unchallenged—except for a German interlude during World War

II—until 1947, when the United States became the principal power able to help the Greeks preserve their independence and territorial integrity.

Greece's accession to NATO in 1952 underlined its abiding concern for external security at a time when the world was rapidly becoming polarized and when a threat was perceived to be emanating principally from the Soviet Union and such East European countries as Albania, Bulgaria, and Yugoslavia, with which Greece shared common borders. In the years after the Cyprus crisis of 1974, however, Athens added Turkey as another potentially hostile country. In fact, Turkey was perceived to be the principal threat to Greece's security, especially under the Papandreou administration.

The accident of geography is also responsible for the country's receptivity to emigration. Greece has few natural resources; therefore, since antiquity Greeks have been enthusiastic emigrants, seeking fortunes and establishing colonies in foreign lands. In the modern period they have ranged far and wide, spreading to distant points in Australia, Canada, South America, and the United States. In recent decades Greek job seekers have headed for cities of Western Europe in great numbers. These young men and women, sons and daughters of farmers, pastoralists, and fishermen, are setting the pace, upon their return to homeland, for rapid social change in a nation of proud, ancient culture, inhabited in the 1980s by about 10 million people, all but 3 percent of them being Greek-speaking.

Greek history can be traced to as early as 3000 B.C., when various tribal peoples emigrated into the southern Balkan Peninsula in successive waves from Asia Minor. In ensuing centuries these settlers fashioned the Minoan and Mycenaean cultures on the Aegean Sea. After the Mycenaeans were overwhelmed around 1100 B.C. by primitive Hellenic tribes from the north, there followed the 300-year-long Greek "dark ages." It was during this time of chaos and turmoil that many Greek city-states emerged, the two most prominent being Athens and Sparta. Although alternately warring and forming alliances among themselves, these city-states were generally united by a common, though tenuous, identity as Hellenes. Such identity provided a common rallying ground for the Greek defeat of the Persian Empire and set the stage for Greece's classical period, or "golden age," which spanned roughly from the sixth to the fourth centuries B.C.

The golden age saw the full flowering of Hellenic civilization. Greek philosophers, dramatists, and poets laid the foundation for the cultural, intellectual, and spiritual development of succeeding European civilizations. Aeschylus, Aristophanes, and Aristotle only begin the long list of the greatest figures of the age. In the plastic arts sculptural masterpieces were created—conceptions of the idealized human in form and content. In architecture the Acropolis in Athens and other sites provided models that would endure for centuries.

Despite the wars and conquests in which Greece subsequently became embroiled, the growth and spread of Greek art and learning continued apace. Alexander the Great, son of King Philip of Macedonia and conqueror of Greek city-states, brought Greek culture to all corners of the lands he occupied. In the second century B.C. the Romans, who had subdued the Macedonians and made Greece a Roman province, adopted the mantle of Greek civilization. When the Roman Empire was later divided, the ruling elite of the eastern portion—the Byzantine Empire (330-1453)—eagerly embraced the Greek language, literature, and culture. Constantinople (present-day Istanbul, Turkey), the capital of the Byzantine Empire, became the flourishing center of Greco-Roman culture.

The 1,000-year reign of the Byzantines came to an end in 1453, when Constantinople fell to the Ottoman Turks. For more than 350 years thereafter the Greeks would languish in obscurity under the Ottomans, while retaining a social and cultural identity of their own by adhering to their Orthodox Christianity; in time this identification provided the basis for the Greek concept of motherland and nationalistic stirrings.

Contemporary Greece remains predominantly Orthodox, its established religion under the Constitution being defined as the Easter Orthodox Church of Christ. The church and the state are separate, nonetheless. The church, which depends on the state for financial and legal support, is the most important social institution, and orthodoxy permeates the life of the people in varying degrees of religiosity, despite gradual tendencies toward secularization. Attendance at services in both rural and urban parishes has been declining, limited largely to women, children, and older men.

Greece is linguistically homogeneous; however, throughout the twentieth century the country has been rent by disputes over the various forms of Greek to be used for different purposes. School-children were bedeviled by the necessity of learning one form of Greek for everyday speech and reading, another for learned discourse and classical literature, a third for reading newspapers, and yet another for understanding the church liturgy. As part of long-standing efforts to resolve the language question, it was decreed in 1977 that the use of *katharevousa*, the language of officialdom, education, and classical literature for 150 years (as recently as 1974) would be replaced by demotic, for centuries the language used in colloquial speech and in popular literature. Authorities hoped that with some adjustment and amalgamation the demotic form would in time develop the necessary range of expression for juridical, scientific, and technical purposes. The switch did not affect the church, which in the 1980s has continued to use *koine*, historically the liturgical language.

For all their ethnic cohesion and their patriotism, Greeks are pluralistic and are easily given to factional quarreling. Within the Greek resistance against the German occupation of World War II, royalists and communists battled one another. After World War II ended, civil war raged throughout the country, bringing untold suffering, until 1949. The issue of whether a monarchy or a republic was better for the country divided the Greeks for 150 years until it was resolved by a referendum in 1974.

In the 1980s the pervasiveness of familial-interest politics and of patron-client relationships was being moderated somewhat in the social and political life of the people. There was growing public awareness that the traditional way of social and political interactions should be placed on a more rational and systematized footing, but this perception was not reflected in reality. For Greek villagers and urbanites alike, loyalty to the family remained unsurpassed. The family has traditionally been the focus and repository of virtue and responsibility. Leaving the village did not deprive the migrant of this loyalty or, for that matter, attachment to the village in which he and his parents were born. As a result, socioeconomic and political behavior continued to center on family-related and personal—as opposed to impersonal, organizational—connections.

The emphasis on family ties had economic ramifications well into the 1980s, reflected not only in the nature of business enterprises and distaste for the impersonality of large corporate organizations but also in the slow acceptance of cooperative ventures in agriculture. Businesses were run on the conviction that it is more profitable and more secure to keep them within the family as well as on the strong sense of obligation to provide for and accommodate the interests of immediate family members and their relatives. Thus there was a reluctance to expand an enterprise if to do so would mean seeking outside capital or putting outsiders in positions of trust and authority. An individual would be unlikely to invest capital in enterprises in which there were no family connections. Not surprisingly, the securities market remains poorly developed, and even the biggest commercial or industrial firms have tended to remain family companies.

By the mid-1980s Greece had reached a stage of economic development far above that of developing countries but remained near the bottom of most socioeconomic indicators in the 24-nation Organisation for Economic Co-operation and Development (OECD—see Glossary), which comprises all the noncommunist industrial nations, including Greece. In recent decades the state of the economy has been a major concern of successive governments. As recently as August 1985 Papandreou himself described the Greek economy as "underdeveloped" and went on to emphasize that "modernization was and remains the primary prerequisite for our country's development."

The economy was structurally weak, characterized as it was by a declining and sluggish agricultural sector, a fragmented and dualistic industrial sector, a considerable technological gap separating Greece from other industrial nations, stagnant productive investment, a large services sector, and a heavy reliance on imports, tourism, and shipping. Attempts to rectify these characteristics through developmental strategies, which began in the 1950s, had mixed results at best. They were hampered by a dearth of readily exploitable natural resources, by short-sighted economic policies geared to political clientelism rather than to rigorous economic criteria, by the lack of an entrepreneurial class willing to make risky industrial investments, by political instability, and by an inefficient bureaucracy.

On top of these factors the PASOK government inherited an economy burdened with such problems as high inflation and unemployment, a widening public sector deficit, deterioration in the balance of payments, numerous insolvent industrial enterprises, an overconcentration of development in Athens, and an international economic milieu beset by recession. Mismanagement by the Socialist government further complicated the problems.

In late 1985 it was unclear whether the PASOK government could appreciably improve its economic performance by 1989, the final year of its second term in office. Among the notable steps taken since 1981 by the Socialist administration have been those aimed at popular mobilization—specifically, decentralized planning, workers' participation in corporate affairs, promotion of agricultural cooperatives, and more efficient bureaucratic procedures. These steps have been taken concurrently with efforts to improve social infrastructure, redefine a state role in directing investment activity into productive enterprises, and restructure overindebted firms. Paradoxically, these effort have been contrary to the government policy of making substantial cuts in public expenditures.

The economic challenges facing the government were formidable in late 1985. The Socialist leadership was realistic in acknowledging that it needed "the support and active help of all productive classes," as well as the acquisition by Greek investors of "a modern development mentality." The Socialists were also mindful that some prospective investors, domestic and foreign, were still hesitant to place full confidence in the PASOK administration, which they appeared to distrust not only because of its penchant for controversial foreign policy posturing—particularly with regard to the United States—but also because of its reputation, rightly or wrongly, for being biased against big businesses.

A significant aspect of the economic picture in the mid-1980s was the large defense spending evident in the years after the Turkish invasion of Cyprus in 1974. Greece continued to devote around 7 percent of its gross national product—the highest of all NATO countries—to military expenditure. Its perceived need to be prepared for any possible conflict with Turkey was a function of unresolved issues over Greek-Turkish relations, which also complicated Athens' ties to NATO (of which Turkey was also a member). Earlier in the year Turkish prime minister Turgut Ozal had proposed to sign a friendship, good neighbor, conciliation, and cooperation agreement with Greece as a step toward the settlement of all existing differences, indicating at the same time his readiness to meet with his Greek counterpart anytime, anywhere. In expressing his own eagerness to live in peace with Turkey, Papandreou reiterated his conditions for a dialogue with Turkey. These conditions included the withdrawal of Turkish forces from Cyprus and Turkey's unqualified recognition of the principles and rights advocated by Greece with regard to the the Aegean.

September 30, 1985                                    Rinn S. Shinn

# Chapter 1. Historical Setting

*Funeral mask from the royal tombs of Mycenae, ca. 1500 B.C., of beaten gold, approximately 0.3. meter*

BY ONE HISTORICAL yardstick Greece is a relatively young country. Its history as a nation-state begins only in the 1820s and 1830s. The greater part of the territory occupied by contemporary Greece was acquired in the last 100 years. By another important yardstick—the one by which Greeks and most Westerners measure the country's past—Greece was the seat of Europe's earliest civilization, and its classical period (the sixth to the fourth centuries B.C.) was the archetype for the cultural, intellectual, and spiritual development of later civilizations.

After the fall of the Roman Empire in the fifth century A.D., the classical age was largely forgotten as the territory underwent successive invasions and occupations by the Albanians, Franks, Slavs, and Turks, producing a racial, cultural, and linguistic mix. As a result, under the Byzantine Empire and the Ottoman occupation, membership in the Greek nation was determined not by geography or language but by adherence to the Orthodox Christian religion.

In the seventeenth and especially the eighteenth centuries, however, intellectual influence from Western Europe helped spark a revival of interest in Greece's ancient cultural and territorial heritage. The burgeoning cult of classicism gradually developed into a nationalist movement established on the romantic idea of Hellenism—a commitment to the platonic ideal of a secular and purely human excellence achieved through the self-conscious construction of a civil and social order based on rationalism. These ideas derived more from a western European (especially Italian) interpretation of classical thought than from the Hellenes themselves, but the ideas nevertheless proved to be remarkably potent symbols around which resistance to the Ottoman Turks coalesced. A war of independence finally broke out in 1821 and was successfully concluded in 1829 only with the intervention of the Great Powers—Britain, France, and Russia.

A sovereign state was created in 1831 with the approval of the Great Powers, but the price of European recognition was high. Greece's important strategic position in the eastern Mediterranean made it the object of fierce competition between Britain and Russia, which vied for the right to "protect" the new state, that its, to use it to promote their own geopolitical interests in the area. After Russia's defeat in the Crimean War

(1854–56) Britain's domination of Greece was unchallenged except for a brief period during World War I when the king and some of his supporters promoted Germany as a possible replacement. The British remained in control until 1947, when they yielded the role of protector to the United States.

Because the area was no longer locked up by the Ottoman Empire after 1831, the stability of the regional balance of power was the paramount concern for the British. The size of the new Greek state was limited to a small portion of "historic Greece" and left almost 80 percent of those who identified themselves as Greek outside its borders. Irredentism was thus a unifying element in Greek domestic politics and the enduring goal of foreign policy. By the mid-twentieth century, Greece had grown to approximately twice its size at independence. The effort to "redeem" Greek territory suffered several spectacular disasters, however, especially in the second war with Turkey (1921–22). In addition, the unrelenting pursuit of the irredentist dream ravaged the economy.

To ensure the new state's compliance with the needs of the European powers, and a European monarch and a European-style parliament were imposed on Greece. The monarchy never fit in comfortably with traditional Greek society and political practices. It was a source of intense resentment among many Greeks, and within a decade opposition arose to the monarch's authority. By the end of the nineteenth century there was a considerable sentiment in favor of abolishing the monarchy and establishing a republic. The battle between monarchists and republicans thereafter dominated the political debate and often became violent. The king was deposed and reinstated no fewer than four times. This constitutional issue was finally and definitively settled by a referendum in 1974 when almost 70 percent of the electorate voted to abolish the monarchy.

The parliamentary system imposed by the Europeans was equally inappropriate. European-style parliamentary politics presupposes European-style political parties having coherent ideologies and policy programs, hierarchical organizational structures, internal discipline, and national memberships. The political "parties" that developed in the Greek context, however, had none of these qualities. They were, instead, localized factions surrounding strong and persuasive personalities, tied together in a network of relationships between patrons and clients that were based on mutual benefit rather than on ideas.

A small oligarchy of political leaders (*tzakia*) ruled Greece through patronage and the spoils system.

Patronage employment in the civil service became the principal path to upward mobility, resulting in a state bureaucracy far out of proportion to its European counterparts. Competition among the political factions revolved around control of this bureaucracy, rather than around policy programs. At the same time, because it was integral to the patronage system, the civil service never developed norms of apolitical professionalism. Tenure in a position was not fixed and depended on the success of one's patron, not on one's qualifications. It therefore behooved the temporary holder of the office to use that office to make as much money as possible in a short time.

At the turn of the twentieth century the military became a second route to upward mobility. And, as in the civil service, patronage rather than military skill determined one's career. The political factions in civilian life were replicated within the military, destroying its professional and institutional coherence and creating factions competing with each other for promotions and pensions and with other sectors for a portion of the budget. But the military, especially the army, quickly realized that it had a natural advantage over other interest groups—its weapons—and proceeded to use them to great effect, actively intervening in the political process by means of frequent coups (at least 12 major coups, both successful and unsuccessful, and innumerable mini-coups) and military dictatorships. The competition among factions within the armed forces brought with it an unfortunate reliance on violence in political debates, often with tragic results.

The importance of the state as employer was in large part owing to Greece's weak economy. A small minority, commonly known as the oligarchy, amassed fortunes in trade, shipping and, to a lesser extent, land while the vast majority of the population languished in rural wastelands. This conservative economic elite benefited from the retention of traditional economic and social structures and joined forces with the political elite to stifle reform. Throughout the nineteenth century, economic development was slow and decidedly uneven; small-scale agriculture and precapitalist modes were dominant into the twentieth century, and industrialization was barely evident until the 1960s. Thus a vicious circle of underdevelopment evolved. The state, the major employer by default, devoured a huge proportion of the national wealth in unproductive services, leaving less capital available for productive investment and reinforcing economic stagnation.

Between 1909 and 1935 there was an attempt to overturn the oligarchy. Eleutherios Venizelos, perhaps Greece's most influential and popular political figure thus far in the twentieth century, supported by a dedicated faction within the army, attempted to make a bourgeois revolution overturn the stagnant socioeconomic system and create a new, dynamic economy controlled by the middle class. He forged a coalition of entrepreneurs, industrialists, workers, and immigrants committed to modernizing the economy and effecting social progress.

The political-economic oligarchy launched a counterattack, enlisting its own army faction and the king, and civil war seemed imminent. During the 1920s, however, the conflict degenerated into a battle between the army factions for control of the army itself. The social reform program was lost in the process as the Venizelists instead concentrated on establishing a republic by deposing the king, who had allied with their rivals. The Antivenizelists, for their part, rallied around the symbol of the monarchy. Thus, the revolutionary movement collapsed before any substantial reform of the economy, the society, or the political system could be effected. The only remnant of the conflict was a bitter division between republicans and monarchists that came to symbolize a more general difference in ideological orientation—the republicans representing a somewhat reformist left wing and the monarchists representing the conservative oligarchy.

A republican coup was attempted in 1935 but failed miserably and was followed within a year by a fascistic military dictatorship that immediately purged the military of republican tendencies and imposed strict ideological conformity. The right remained in power for the next 46 years, imposing a "guided democracy." During that time the pattern of political alignments was transformed by the emergence of the Communist Party of Greece as a major political movement. The left wing of the political spectrum was now inhabited by the Communists, displacing the republicans, who took the center position. During the World War II and the Civil War (1946–49), the Communists made an unsuccessful bid for power, leading to their expulsion from the system and a further strengthening of the right, which was increasingly identified with the military. Any criticism of the socioeconomic status quo was labeled "unpatriotic" and made illegal. Thus, although three political

blocs could be discerned in the 1950s, the left was disen-
franchised, and the center was artificially restricted to a narrow range of issues. The right exercised overwhelming domination of the political system.

Underneath this cap, however, a slow social transformation was taking shape as a result of unusually strong economic
growth beginning in the mid-1950s. Government policies to
encourage industrial development, together with an infusion
of foreign capital, created expanding industrial and service
sectors in the major cities. This led to a rural migration to
urban centers and a rapid increase in the ranks of the petite
bourgeoisie, or small merchants, and salaried workers. This
migration disrupted the old clientelist networks, and by the
mid-1960s a new mass electorate had emerged that was susceptible to the appeals of a modern mass party. Andreas Papandreou, a charismatic and controversial figure with a penchant
for leftist rhetoric, began to pull together a novel coalition of
forces among this mass electorate and challenged the traditional parties, especially those of the center.

The evolution of this new center was interrupted, but not
stopped, by a military dictatorship from 1967 to 1974. The
junta tried, brutally but ultimately unsuccessfully, to reimpose
the conservative dogma on the political system and halt the
social changes. After the junta's collapse in 1974 and the restoration of democracy, the process of change picked up where it
had left off. Although a moderate conservative party under
Constantine Karamanlis governed for the next seven years, it
was evident that the political environment had changed. The
Communist Party of Greece was legalized in 1974, finally ending the artificial truncation of the political spectrum since the
civil war. More important, it appeared that the whole electorate had shifted to the left, isolating the extreme right and
prompting a scramble to capture the newly defined center.
Andreas Papandreou's Panhellenic Socialist Movement
emerged as a social democratic party that drew its support
from both the center and the left. In the 1981 elections it
swamped the other parties, winning a stunning victory and
ending the right's monopoly of power.

## Ancient Greece

Archaeological evidence suggests that continental Greece
and the Aegean Islands supported a sparse Neolithic popula-

tion as early as the sixth millennium B.C. Sometime before 3000 B.C. bronze-working Helladic (pre-Greek) tribes entered the peninsula overland from Asia, displacing the original inhabitants and spreading to the islands. On Crete the new settlers developed a culturally and technically sophisticated civilization that benefited from its proximity to Egypt and the cultures of the Near East. The Minoans—named for Minos, their legendary king, whose successors ruled from the massive palace complex at Knosos—dominated the Aegean world, relying on sea power to protect their commerce and to defend their unwalled cities.

Helladic development on the mainland was markedly slower. At about the beginning of the second millennium B.C. the Achaeans (proto-Greeks) invaded the peninsula from the north and settled there and on the islands among the Helladic inhabitants. By 1600 B.C. the Minoans had extended their political, economic, and cultural hegemony over the Achaeans, whose tribal kings employed Minoan craftsmen to build places in emulation of their overlords on Crete. The interaction of the Minoan and Achaean cultures gave rise to a new civilization that had its center, Mycenae (Mikinai) in the Peloponnesus (see fig. 2). The process by which the two cultures—that of the patriarchal Achaeans, accompanied by their sky-gods, and that of the Helladic earth-goddess worshipers—were fused was the basis of much classical Greek mythology. The Minoan civilization declined after 1400 B.C., succumbing finally to a combination of natural disasters and conquest by the Mycenaeans.

The period from 1400 to 1100 B.C. was the Mycenaean heroic age that inspired the Homeric epic, *The Iliad*, describing the assault of the Achaeans on Troy, on the coast of Asia Minor in what is now known as Turkey. After 1100 B.C. the steady migration of the Dorians, primitive Hellenic tribesmen from the north, overwhelmed the Mycenaeans and ushered in the 300-year-long Greek "Dark Ages."

The beginnings of the polis, or city-state, are found during this chaotic time when, for security, the people of the countryside moved within the shadow of an acropolis, the fortification of a local lord or tribal chieftain constructed on defensible high ground. Athens, for instance, grew from the villages clustered around one such acropolis in Attica. The polis became the distinctive form of political and social organization in classical Greece. It forms the root of the word "politics," meaning the "business of the city." But the idea of the polis meant more to the Greeks than just a city and its surrounding countryside. It

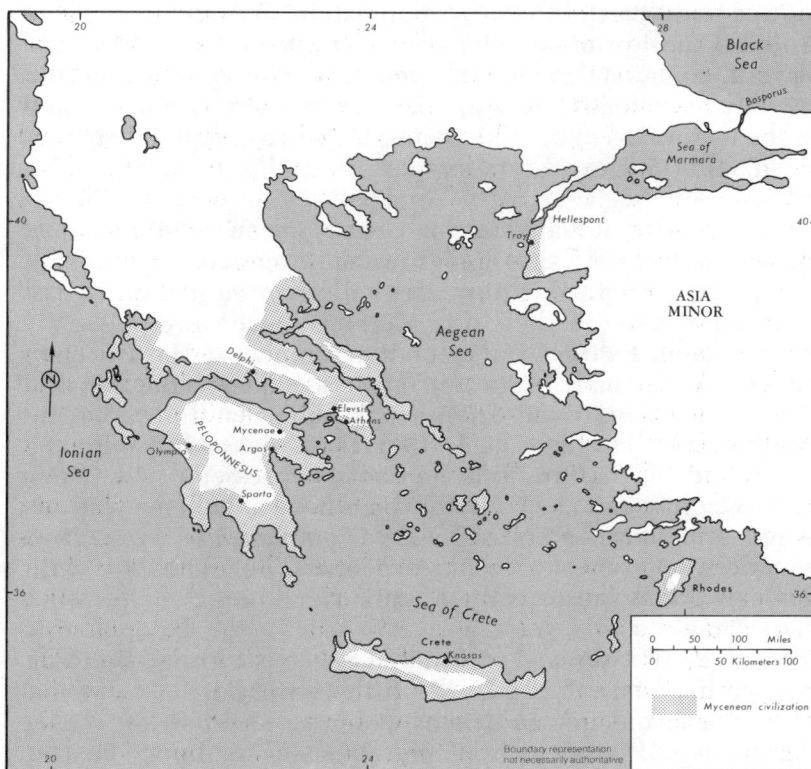

*Figure 2.    Centers of Mycenean Civilization, about 1400 B.C.*

represented as well the way of life, the collective values, and the traditions and institutions peculiar to that city that distinguished its citizens from those of other cities. Classics scholar H.D.F. Kitto has pointed out that "without a clear conception of what the polis was, and what it meant to the Greeks, it is quite impossible to understand properly Greek history, the Greek mind, or the Greek achievement."

Two basic patterns of political development evolved among the city-states and were represented in the rival cities of Athens and Sparta. Athens, which in the popular imagination epitomizes Hellenic civilization, was a direct democracy (from the Greek word *demos*, the people) and a cosmopolitan state—in the words of Pericles, "thrown open to the world." Even in democratic Athens, however, citizenship was restrict-

9

ed to a small part of the city's population. Women, even those from the most prominent families, were denied any rights, and slavery, common throughout Greece, was the basis for most of the city's economic growth. Sparta, authoritarian and isolated in the mountains of the Peloponnesus, was a completely militarized state that existed to support an exclusive caste of warriors.

A shortage of arable land in Greece encouraged individual city-states to establish colonies for the excess population. Although they retained cultural ties with their mother cities, the colonies that ringed the entire Mediterranean were politically independent. Political fragmentation, implicit in the city-state system, led to internecine warfare that plagued the classical Greek world. But even when geography separated them and politics set them against each other, the Greeks were united by their collective cultural consciousness, expressed in the Olympics, which began in 776 B.C., and other Panhellenic festivals at such religious centers as Delphi, Olympia, and Elevsis. They generally felt superior to other peoples, believing that with few exceptions (perhaps the Egyptians) all non-Hellenes were barbarians.

Geographically and culturally Greece is a bridge between Europe and Asia. Early in the fifth century B.C., however, under the leadership of Athens, it served as a barrier against the westward expansion of the Persians under Xerxes II (499–78 B.C.). Athens emerged from the Greek victories at Marathon (490 B.C.), Salamis (480 B.C.), and Plataea (479 B.C.) at the peak of its prosperity and creativity. It was also recognized as the leader of an alliance of Greek city-states known as the Delian League. After Persia's defeat, Greece entered its "Golden Age," which saw the full flowering of Hellenic culture and produced many of the masterworks of art and literature for which the classical period is famous. The playwrights Aeschylus, Sophocles, and Euripides perfected the tragedy, and Aristophanes the comedy, as theatrical forms. Herodotus and Thucydides set standards for historical writing by which modern historians are still judged. The Greeks also excelled in sculpture, developing a dynamic and naturalist style, and in architecture. Peace was short-lived, however, as conflicts between Athens and Sparta over commerce and cultural domination brought about a system of rival alliances comprising practically all of continental and Anatolian Greece. The resulting Peloponnesian wars, which were fought intermittently over half a century (460–45 and 431–04 B.C.), were even-

*Theater at Epidaurus, ca. 340 B.C.*
*Courtesy Peter J. Kassander*

*The Temple of Apollo at Corinth*
*Doric order, ca. sixth century B.C.*
*Courtesy Jean R. Tartter*

tually won by Sparta, but the wars left both Athens and Sparta economically and physically exhausted.

The political turmoil of the next century produced some of the most famous and influential pieces of political philosophy in the works of Plato and Aristotle. But it also ended the hegemony of the traditional centers as Philip II, king of Macedonia—a relatively primitive region in the north that had remained untouch by the wars—invaded the south and quickly subjugated the city-states. After his assassination in 336 B.C. he was succeeded by his son, Alexander the Great. Alexander not only united and centralized Greece under Macedonian control but also created an empire of vast proportions, stretching from Greece and Egypt in the West to the Indus River in the East. Upon his death in Babylon in 323 B.C. at the age of 33, his empire gradually collapsed, but the spread of Greek culture and commerce during this period had enduring consequences on the political and economic development of the Near East and formed the basis for later Greek claims to Anatolia.

Macedonia ruled Greece for the next two centuries, though it never completely succeeded in destroying the independence of the city-states. A long-standing Macedonian alliance with Carthage against Rome during the Punic wars in the second and first centuries B.C. led to four Roman wars against Macedonia. The Romans were welcomed by the Greek city-states as the "protector of Greek freedom." In 148 B.C. Macedonia became a Roman province, followed in short order by the rest of Greece. The English word *Greeks* derives from the Latin; the Greeks themselves use the word Hellenes (Ellenes). A favored part of the empire and revered by the Romans for its art and literature, Greece was prosperous and for the first time peaceful under the mantle of the Pax Romana. Although the city-states had forfeited their political liberty, Greek culture continued to flourish.

## Byzantine Empire

In A.D. 285 Emperor Diocletian reorganized the Roman Empire, dividing jurisdiction between its western, Latin-speaking and eastern, Greek-speaking halves. In 330 Diocletian's successor, Constantine, established his capital at the site of the Greek city of Byzantium as the "New Rome," strategically situated on the European shore of the Bosporus. The city was renamed Constantinople for its founder. For nearly 12 centuries, until its capture by the Ottoman Turks in 1453, Constantinople remained the capital of the Roman Empire, which became known during the Middle Ages as the Byzantine Empire (see fig. 3).

Although Greek in language and culture, the Byzantine Empire was thoroughly Roman in its law and administration. Emperor Justinian's codification of Roman law was compiled— in Latin—in Constantinople in the sixth century. The Byzantine Empire was not considered a specifically Greek state but was ecumenical, intended to encompass all Christian peoples. Its Greek-speaking citizens called themselves Romans, not Hellenes. Absolute and theocratic in principle, the emperor in practice delegated considerable authority in the provinces to a military aristocracy.

Christianity was recognized throughout the Roman Empire as the official state religion before the end of the fourth century, and a patriarchate was established in Constantinople with ecclesiastical jurisdiction over the Greek East. In contrast to the Latin church, whose patriarch in Rome (the pope) asserted the church's independence of secular control, the Greek church was not only identified with, but was subordinated to, the interests of the state. It was not surprising, therefore, that political dissidence within the empire was often expressed in terms of theological heterodoxy. The decisive break between the Latin and Greek churches in the eleventh century (1054) was the result of a reaction by the Greek patriarch against the Roman pope's claim to supreme authority. The Greek church, for its part, maintained that it alone had remained faithful to the Christian orthodoxy taught by the Apostles and the early church councils from which the Latin church had departed (see Religion, ch. 2).

Christian Byzantine culture was hostile to Hellenism and rejected it for its putative paganism. The classical heritage as a moral force was thereby dismissed among medieval Greeks, to whom the Hellenes were simply the people who once occupied Roman provinces that had since become a poor and primitive backwater far removed from the centers of Greek culture and economic development in Constantinople and Asia Minor.

Gradually, as stronger demands were made on imperial resources to defend the empire's southern and eastern flanks against Persians, Arabs and, later, Seljuk Turks, the European provinces were left open to invasion first by Goths and, from the sixth century, by repeated waves of Slavs, who eventually

13

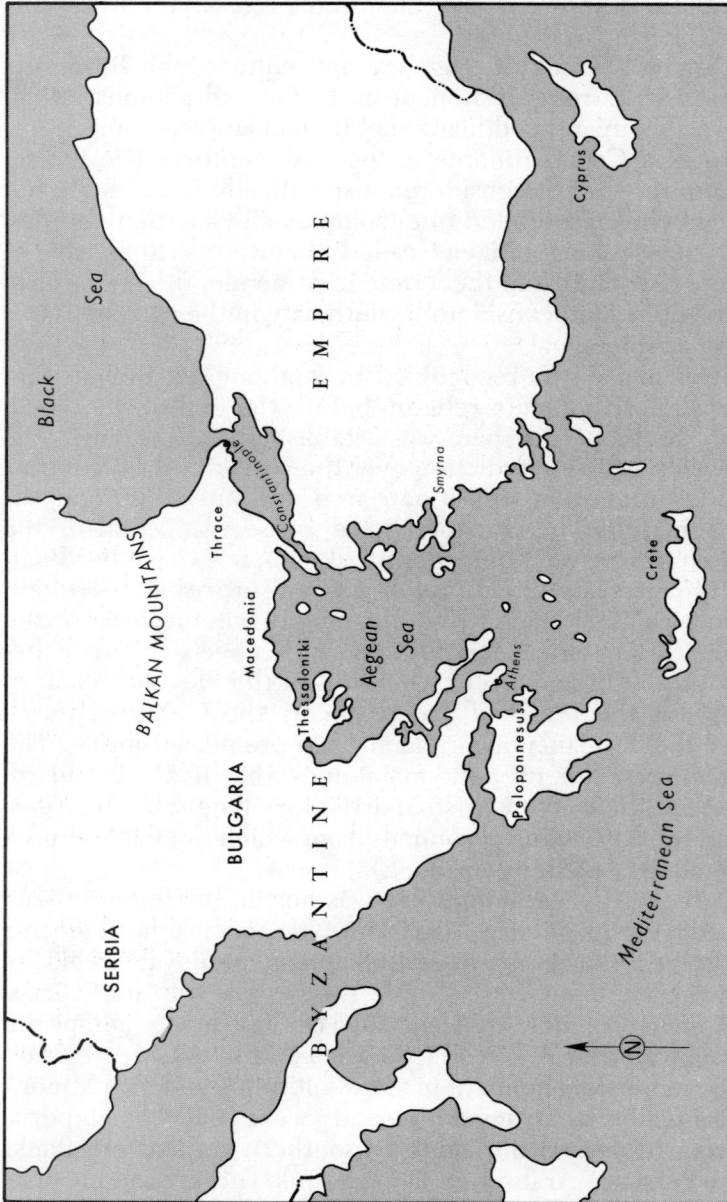

*Figure 3. The Byzantine Empire, Early Eleventh Century*

overran the interior of the peninsula and settled there in such large numbers that Byzantine sources frequently referrred to continental Greece as Slavinia (Slav-land). The church was the means through which the Slavs were gradually assimilated into the Greek population, though enclaves retained their separate identity into the modern era.

West European merchants and adventurers were attracted to the Byzantine Empire both by its wealth and, after a long period of nearly continual internal strife in the late twelfth century, by it relative weakness. In 1204 Constantinopole was sacked, and the Aegean Islands, along with most of the European provinces, fell to the largely French contingents of the Fourth Crusade and their Venetian allies. Count Baldwin of Flanders was installed in Constantinople by the crusaders as emperor of the so-called Latin Empire, and territory conquered from the Greeks was dismembered into a number of tributary feudal states, creating "New France" in Greece where Western political, social, ecclesiastical, and economic institutions were transplanted intact. Large tracts, especially on the islands, were annexed by Venice (also known as the Venetian Republic) and other Italian states or were seized by Catalan and Navarrese mercenaries. The Greeks referred to the Western conquerors collectively as Franks. Independent Greek kingdoms were established in Epirus and at Nicaea and Trebizond from remnant provinces of the Byzantine Empire. Constant warfare pitted Frank against Frank or against Greek, Slav, or Turk, and territory changed hands frequently. In 1205, for instance, the acropolis of Athens became the residence of a Burgundian duke and the Parthenon his church; in 1311 Athens was taken by the Catalans, and in 1388 it passed to the Florentines, in whose hands it remained until conquered in turn by the Turks in 1456.

The Latin Empire lasted for 57 years before Constantinople was retaken by the Greek Palaeologi Dynasty of Nicaea under which the Byzantine Empire was restored. Some of the feudal states survived for 200 years, however, and Italian domination of many Greek islands and mainland enclaves persisted for an even longer time. Venice held Crete until 1669 and still retained the Ionian Islands at the time of the collapse of Venice in 1797.

## The Ottoman Occupation

The fall of Constantinople in 1453 to the Ottoman Turks was the culmination of a gradual dismemberment of the Byzantine Empire. Initially, the Orthodox Greeks welcomed to the Muslim Ottomans, finding them less offensive religiously than the Roman Catholics. However, in contrast to the Venetians, who encouraged cultural development and served as the conduit for influences from the West, the Ottoman occupation closed access to Europe and imposed strict isolation on Greece. For the next 300 years little of note happened while Greece settled into the patterns of subjugation.

Western historians have tended to underrate the severity of the Ottoman occupation. For all but the elite among the Greek population, life was hard, and much of the intense animosity between Greeks and Turks has its origins here. Greece was partitioned by the Turks along military lines. The principal task of the administrators was to oversee the collection of taxes from the sultan's non-Muslim subjects. Greeks kept the use of their land, but they paid a fixed part of the revenue from it (with no dispensation during bad years) for the upkeep of Turkish soldier-landlords. A particularly onerous form of taxation levied by the Turks was the conscription of Christian children for the corps of janissaries, or soldiers. Every four years—until 1676—one out of every five young Christian males in the European provinces was sent to Constantinople to be reared as a Muslim and serve in the sultan's bodyguard.

As early as 1480, armed resistance to these harsh taxes arose in the mountainous areas. Bandits, or klephts, attacked tax collectors and other Ottoman authorities in what a prominent historian, Richard Clogg, has called "a primitive form of national resistance." Their targets were not limited to Turks, however, and in many cases their activities were indistinguishable from common bandits. Nevertheless, their exploits were recorded in ballads and became a part of the folklore, helping to inspire nationalist rebellion in the eighteenth and nineteenth centuries. To combat the klephts, the authorities established irregular troops, the *armatoloi*, recruited from the Greek population. Distinguishing the two groups was difficult from the beginning, for men switched back and forth between them according to their relative profitability; but as the Ottoman Empire slipped into decline, these two armed groups played a central role in the fight for independence.

Signs of decay were apparent as early as the seventeenth

century, probably resulting from the withdrawal of the sultans from direct control of the affairs of the government (known as the Sublime Porte) and the consequent increase in corruption and court intrigue. Most offices were sold at ever more inflated prices, tenure was short, and great effort was expended in amassing as much wealth as possible in a short time. The chronic decay in administration was matched by a steady territorial retreat, starting with the failure of the siege of Vienna in 1683. The gradual decline undermined both the ideological and the economic foundations of the empire, which were based on military expansion and colonization.

During this period a small Greek elite, known as the Phanariots, gained a privileged position within the Porte. As the Ottoman Empire weakened, the sultans found themselves forced to negotiate with the Western powers. They relied on Greek interpreters, the Phanariots, to conduct these negotiations and gradually handed over to them decisionmaking authority in many spheres of foreign policy. By the eighteenth century the Phanariots, drawn originally from 11 families in Constantinople, exerted more and more influence on a broad range of issues and even acquired the post of *hospodar*, or prince, of the Danubian principalities of Moldavia and Wallachia in present-day Romania.

Simultaneously, a large Greek mercantile class developed a commercial network spanning the empire and beyond. Thousands of Greeks migrated in what is known as the diaspora and set up families and businesses throughout Asia Minor, Central Europe, and as far as the Black Sea. By the eighteenth century, Greek traders dominated commerce in the Aegean, and their profits, much of which returned to the mainland, helped to provide funds for education and cultural development in Greece.

Despite centuries of Ottoman rule, a Greek "nation" had survived, but it was difficult to define clearly. Because self-identified Greeks could be found over half the globe, geographic definitions were inadequate. Although the Greek language had not been challenged, many of those who felt themselves Greek no longer spoke Greek, having adopted the language of their new homes. The Orthodox religion, therefore, provided the principal criterion for determining Greek nationality. The Porte allowed a significant amount of local autonomy and often administered through preexisting institutions, the most important of which was the Orthodox Church. Religion and nationality were inextricably tied for both Greeks and Turks. To be an Orthodox Christian was to be a Greek, just as a Greek who converted to Islam thereby became a Turk. The sultan's Orthodox Christian, or Greek, subjects were regarded as a separate nation, or "millet," having a degree of autonomy within the Ottoman Empire. The patriarch of Constantinople was recognized not only as the head of the Orthodox Church but also as the temporal leader of the Orthodox Christian millet. He bore the title "ethnarch" and was responsible for the civil administration of the people through a separate system of courts having distinct laws and customs based on the Roman Law of the Byzantine Empire. Local government operated under the clergy and the landowners, who were the leaders of the Greek communities. Ironically, the Turks referred to the Greek Christian millet as the Roman Nation.

The gradual but steady internal collapse of the Ottoman Empire allowed a nationalist movement to emerge out of these threads by the mid-eighteenth century. Its first stirrings were a cultural revival. The church itself increasingly came under criticism because of its corruption and open collaboration with the Turks. Although dissatisfaction never evolved into full-blown anticlericalism as in Western Europe and the church maintained its influence among the majority of the population, the secularization opened Greece up to new ideas. As education became more widespread, owing to funds donated by prosperous merchants of the diaspora, West European ideas became current. Many of the teachers in the newly created academies had studied in Western Europe and brought with them a reverence for classical Greek history. It came as something of a surprise to the Greeks that their own history, neglected in Greece because of the church's policy, was considered the touchstone of Western civilization. Recapturing the past glories of Greece became an obsession with many intellectuals, and the revitalization of the Greek language was seen as a critical step in awakening a spirit of nationalism in the people. A new language, *katharevousa*, was created to purge Greek of contamination from other languages. The reform served only to complicate matters, and language remained an issue well into the twentieth century (see Language, ch. 2).

The late eighteenth century was a time of revolutionary ferment throughout Europe. The French Revolution, with its slogans of liberty, equality, and fraternity, was especially taken to heart, and many Greeks began to talk openly of rebellion against the Porte. Growing unrest followed Napoleon's capture of the Ionian Islands from Venice, the occupation of Corfu in 1797, and a successful revolt by the Serbs in 1804. For the first time both the Porte and the Greeks took seriously the possibility of revolt.

## The War of Independence, 1821-29

The crucial element in the evolution of a successful rebellion against the Porte was clearly the empire's own internal collapse. Although an independence movement had been growing for sometime, the Greeks considered themselves too weak to take on the Ottoman Empire alone. They tried to coordinate their efforts with revolts by Serbs and Bulgarians. The effort failed, but uprisings in the Peloponnesus coincided with an invasion of the Danubian principalities by the Greek rebel, Alexander Ypsilantis, in the spring of 1821. The rebellion spread rapidly, and on March 25 (Easter Day) Germanos, bishop of Old Patrai, officially proclaimed the revolution, throwing the church's formidable symbolic force on the side of the rebels.

Leaders came from the lower clergy, klephts and *armatoloi*, pirates and merchant captains, and irregular troops all over the mainland. Neither the church, the landowners, nor the merchant class, generally prosperous under the empire, had associated themselves with the independence movement prior to the outbreak of hostilities, but they were moved to join the rebellion because of its obvious popular support.

After the initial rash of violence the war settled into a long, drawn-out contest of endurance. Almost immediately the Greek rebels set up three regional assemblies to govern the liberated areas. And just as quickly internal conflicts between the new institutions and among political factions emerged, plaguing the rebellion for the duration of the war and beyond. A constitution, strongly influenced by the ideals of the French Revolution, was written in 1822, but attempts to establish a central government failed to resolve the factional strife. During much of 1823 and 1824 a virtual civil war undermined the war against the Turks. The situation was extremely complex and confused, and historians still debate what the actual issues were. There were a number of competing groups and ideologies involved, and frequently shifting coalitions among them complicated the political atmosphere.

As in any revolutionary period there were conflicts over the strategy and tactics of fighting the war and over the nature

19

of the postrevolutionary system. To some extent these two sets of issues overlapped. There was a fundamental difference between those who wanted to pursue the war using the traditional klephtic methods of guerrilla war and relying on religious fervor as the motivating force and those, especially those educated in the West, who preferred the European model, using regular armies and set-piece tactics, motivated by a conscious nationalism. The former, known as the "military" party (headed by the klephtic leader Theodore Kolokotronis), also hoped to retain the basic oligarchical structure of society, substituting themselves for the Ottoman authorities while maintaining the central role of the church. The rival "civilian party", or Westernizers, wanted to transform Greece into a secular, liberal, constitutional state. Regional rivalries exacerbated the situation.

The European powers, meanwhile, looked upon the Greek rebellion as a threat to the balance of power, only recently reestablished by the Congress of Vienna after the Napoleonic wars. The demise of the Ottoman Empire would leave a vacuum, and it was obvious that there would be three rivals to fill it: Russia, Britain, and France. Until mid-1823, therefore, the powers maintained strict neutrality. By then the three powers' commercial interests in the region had begun to suffer. Simultaneously, the Greek rebellion caught the imagination of many of the European intellectual elite, who agitated for support of the effort and in many cases went to Greece to fight (most notably British poet Lord Byron, who died of fever in 1824). The rebellion had shown surprising strength, but it was clear that foreign intervention would be required to tip the balance.

Between 1823 and 1825 the three powers maneuvered to place themselves in the best position to guarantee influence beyond the war. As it became increasingly obvious that the powers would eventually intervene, rebel factions, or parties, tied to the powers grew up, further complicating the internal situation. The turning point came in 1825 with the sultan's request for aid from Egypt, a tributary state. Because Egyptian control of the Peloponnesus was unacceptable to the powers, they began the process of negotiating an end to the war, recommending an autonomous status for Greece within the Ottoman Empire. In 1827 when the Turks, flushed with a series of recent military successes, refused mediation, a joint naval force dispatched by the three powers destroyed the Turco-Egyptian fleet in the Bay of Navarino. Tsar Nicholas I of Russia, acting in his self-appointed role as protector of Orthodox

Christians, declared war on Turkey, and a Russian army pushed to the outer defenses of Constantinople. By the 1829 Treaty of Adrianople Russia compelled Turkey to recognize the independence of Greece, but Crete and Thessaly, though claimed by the Greeks, were left in Turkish hands.

To counter Russia's claim to be sole protector of Greece, Britain forced a renegotiation of the border settlement, spelled out in the first London protocol in 1829. Of greater significance, the European powers also gave Greece their formal recognition. Greek leaders protested that 80 percent of the nearly 4 million Greeks in the Ottoman Empire had been left under Turkish rule, and Greece's pro-Russian president, John Kapodistrias, rejected the settlement. Kapodistrias, who had made domestic enemies by his attempts to disarm the kelphts and to centralize the republic's government, was assassinated in 1831, plunging the country into anarchy.

The European powers convened once again and in the second London protocol, agreed to in 1831, declared Greece a monarchy under joint British, French, and Russian protection. It was further decided that a foreign monarch was required to avoid identification of the executive with one of the native factions. Although somewhat rankled by the degree of foreign dominance inherent in these protocols, many Greeks, recalling the violent end of Kapodistrias' presidency, nevertheless yielded to the terms.

## The Kingdom of Greece

### Otto I, 1831–62

The "protecting" powers gave the Greek crown to Otto, the 17-year-old younger son of the king of Bavaria. Until he reached the age of majority, however, the direction of the Greek government fell to a regency council headed by Count Joseph von Armansperg. The Greek Westernizers' vision was put into place. The new state was designed to be thoroughly European, at least in its institutional structure. The regents imposed a complicated judicial code, modeled on that of Bavaria, ignoring a long history of customary law. They replaced the traditional decentralized forms of local government, inherited from the Ottoman period, with a modern, centralized bureaucracy that the Greeks considered alien and unworkable. The Orthodox church was declared to be "autocephalous," or independent, in 1833, though in practice it was firmly subordinated to the state, and the Roman Catholic Otto was named its head. Tax collection was efficient, and the taxes were no less burdensome than they had been under the Turks. The capital was moved from its original site in Navplion to Athens in 1834.

Armed irregulars continued to cause trouble in the early years, and efforts to incorporate them into a Bavarian-style army were disappointing. Many returned to the traditional practice of brigandage and sometimes resorted to violence for political intimidation. Factionalism remained endemic, and parties tied to the foreign powers dominated the political scene until the Crimean War (1854–56). The "English" party favored constitutional rule, which Otto adamantly refused despite the promise of a constitution in 1832 and, above all, maintenance of the Balkan status quo. The "French" party also favored constitutionalism but promoted an irredentist foreign policy. The "Russian" party, however, saw the state domination of the Orthodox church as a direct challenge to Russia's rightful protective role and hoped Otto's abdication would lead to a replacement more solicitous of Russian interests; in short, it hoped to upset the Balkan balance to its own advantage. Otto's position continued to deteriorate as economic crises required increased taxation, and many felt that Otto had betrayed the heroes of the revolution by giving privileged positions not only to Bavarians but also to Greek immigrants (*heterochthons*) who had not participated in the long war of independence. Furthermore, Otto, facing bankruptcy, failed to aid a Cretan revolt against the Turks in 1841, confirming for many the charges of betrayal leveled against him by the opposition. By the 1840s Otto had managed to alienate practically everybody, and in 1843 a broad-based conspiracy developed.

In 1843 leaders of the Russian and English parties brought army officers into the conspiracy, resulting in a bloodless coup, which forced Otto to grant the long-awaited constitution. The March 1844 constitution, patterned after the French constitution of 1830, established a bicameral parliament having a lower house elected by direct ballot (since 1838 any propertied male over the age of 25 had the vote) and a senate, the members of which were appointed for life by the king. The new constitution represented a small opening of the system but in effect left most of the power in the hands of the king, particularly the unlimited authority to appoint and dismiss cabinet ministers at will.

The first election in 1844 left an unfortunate legacy of corruption, patronage, and palace interference that conditioned political life for many years to come. Coherent party organizations did not develop; factions were more common and were based not on ideological or programmatic differences but rather on personalistic and clientelistic networks. Deputies tended to be free agents, eager to support whoever had the most to offer, and increasingly in the 1850s that meant the king. The electorate, undereducated and unorganized, tended to be almost totally submissive to the influence of local bosses. Effective participation was limited to this small oligarchy (*tzakia*; figuratively, "the great houses") who owed their position not to electoral promises but to a reputation of heroism gained during the war or, more commonly, to personal ties with constituents cemented in the practice of ritual kinship (godparenthood) and supplemented by favors (*rousfeti*). The bureaucracy created by the Bavarians quickly became the principal source of employment and upward mobility and grew out of all proportion to the state's population or resources. Patronage again was the key to appointment and promotion, and bribery became institutionalized. Only the military was insulated from the patronage system. The grafting of European parliamentary forms onto the traditional environment failed (see Relations Outside the Household, ch. 2).

Otto tried to use irredentism to offset growing opposition. The "Megali Idea" (Great Idea) of annexing territories inhabited by Greeks outside the borders of the new state had tremendous popular support. During the Crimean War Otto's efforts to annex Thessaly and Epirus–tilting Greek neutrality in Russia's favor—won him popularity but also the undying enmity of the British and the French. The humiliating Anglo-French occupation of the port of Piraeus in 1854 underlined Russia's relative weakness as a patron and transformed the popularity into contempt. Otto's position steadily weakened until in 1862 several popular and military revolts, first in Navplion, then in Athens, emboldened the opposition to depose the king, appoint a provisional government, and call a constitutional convention to write a new constitution and elect a new ruler. Otto left the country, without resistance, on a British ship.

### George I, 1863–1913

Otto's departure was not mourned by anyone, least of all the British, for whom Otto had become a major obstacle. They and the French, insisting on the retention of the monarchy, sought an appropriate, that is, more accommodating, successor. After a short search that included the candidacies of the tsar's nephew and of Queen Victoria's second son, Alfred, they chose a compromise candidate in William George, son of Christian IX of Denmark and brother-in-law of the heirs to both the British and the Russian thrones. The British made it clear that as king, George I would be expected to maintain the status quo in the eastern Mediterranean and to quash the Megali Idea. As consolation the British rewarded Greek cooperation by ceding the Ionian Islands in 1864.

Shortly after George's acceptance the Greek legislature began work on a new constitution. The 1864 charter established a "crowned democracy" by which the royal prerogatives were strictly limited and a unicameral legislature, elected by universal male suffrage, retained all constitutional powers. It was the most liberal constitution in Europe at the time and instituted the broadest suffrage.

Foreign powers, particularly the British, continued to play a central role in Greece's domestic politics. King George accused the British ambassador of being responsible for two of the five cabinet crises in 1866. This intervention merely exacerbated the instability caused by the extreme fragmentation of political forces. Personalistic politics became more widespread in the 1860s as a result of procedural changes within the legislature. Parliamentary politics on the European model, which is dependent on parties and coalition politics, became almost impossible in this environment. The only clear-cut issue was relations with Turkey; some factions argued for an aggressive pursuit of the Megali idea, and others advocated caution and patience. Between 1867 and 1870 there were five different governments. Only the king remained a constant figure in the system, and his personal influence grew steadily.

Nevertheless, the condition of the people remained remarkably unchanged through the 1870s. About 75 percent of the population still lived in villages, engaged in small-scale agriculture. Poverty was widespread, transportation was primitive, public services, such as running water, were practically nonexistent even in the largest cities, and economic development was painfully slow. Commerce was the major sector, and industrialization was not yet apparent; thus the paths to upward mobility were limited to trade (especially in the diaspora), politics, the civil service, or the army. A significant middle class did not yet exist, and the society was split into two groups: a small, wealthy oligarchy made of affluent merchants, shipowners, high-ranking civil servants, a few absentee land-owners, and some senior clergy; and a vast peasant class.

Urbanization increased in the 1880s, and with it a petite bourgeoisie appeared, composed of shopkeepers, middle-level servants, teachers, lawyers, physicians, and military officers. George made significant advances in education, both primary and secondary, and the National Technical University of Athens (commonly called the Polytechnic), founded in 1836, and the University of Athens, founded in 1837, were helping to produce an educated elite in the liberal professions as well as some engineers. Athens had grown to a population of 65,000 by 1882 and was becoming a magnet for ambitious villagers, but job opportunities remained limited.

Economic conditions were clearly hampering progress on all fronts. Greece suffered from chronic balance of payments and debt problems that forced the European powers periodically to take control of its finances. Almost 40 percent of national revenue was devoted solely to servicing the national debt in he early 1880s; therefore, even the meager public services available outstripped the state's ability to pay for them. In 1882 Kharilaos Trikoupis was appointed prime minister and immediately embarked on an ambitious program to promote development and public works. Debt programs again interfered, however, and the development program had to be abandoned within three years, but tremendous progress had been made in a very short time (see Historical Development, ch. 3).

At the same time, Trikoupis tried, with marginal success, to reform the political system by rooting out bribery and routine violence and brigandage, reorganizing the police forces, and ending the traditional spoils system by regularizing civil service appointment procedures. He was particularly incensed at what he called the crisis in Greek politics—the plethora of small, incoherent parties that made ministerial stability impossible to achieve. In an influential article written in 1874, Trikoupis blamed the king's practice of entrusting the government to minority factions that were doomed to be overthrown by competing factions. He contended that a promise by the king to appoint only leaders with avowed majority support in the parliament would ensure greater stability and foster the development of stable party organizations that would be more willing to form lasting coalitions. Trikoupis was thrown in jail for three days for attempting to undermine the constitutional order, but the article provoked public debate on the state of the political system. In 1875 the king agreed to Trikoupis' demand. The salutary effects of the change were obvious when Trikoupis held the office of prime minister uninterrupted for three years, from 1882 to 1885. In the first four decades of constitutional government (1843–83) the average life span for a cabinet had been only about nine months. Between 1864 and 1881 alone there had been nine elections and 17 governments. For the next 20 years something approaching a two-party system appeared, with Trikoupis alternating with Theodore Deliyannis, his arch rival and exact opposite, in the prime minister's post.

## Irredentism: Expansion and Defeat

Irredentism was the most enduring issue in Greek politics. The truncated state erected in 1831 left more than twice as many self-identified Greeks outside its borders as inside. Many Greeks considered the European powers' high-handed intervention as a mortal insult to national honor. John Kolettis, one of the most aggressive advocates of the Megali Idea, announced in 1844:

> The Kingdom of Greece is not Greece. [It] constitutes only one part, the smallest and poorest. A Greek is not only a man who lives within this kingdom but also one who lies in Jannina, in Salonica [Thessaloniki], in Serres, in Adrianople, in Constantinople, in Trebizond, in Crete, in Samos and in any land associated with Greek history or the Greek race. . . . There are two main centers of Hellenism: Athens, the capital of the Greek kingdom, [and] "The City" [Constantinople], the dream and hope of all Greeks.

Almost all Greeks agreed with Kolettis; the only question was how to accomplish the dream and how fast. The more cautious stressed Greece's inadequate resources and unpreparedness to face the inevitable opposition of not only Turkey but also certainly Britain and Russia—the latter having Pan-Slavic dreams of its own for the Balkans. The solution was patient and careful consolidation of the political and economic system and the establishment of a strong military. The militants tended to point out that Greece would remain economically unviable as long as the wealthiest and most productive centers of historic Greece remained outside its boundaries. Greece could not afford to wait. In broad terms, Trikoupis sided with the former, Deliyannis with the latter.

Since independence attention had been focused on Crete, Epirus, and Thessaly. Crete was the scene of continuous revolts by the Greek majority against the Muslim landlords. In 1877 war broke out in the Balkans between Russian and Turkey. There were uprisings by Greeks in other Turkish territories, but the 1878 Treaty of San Stefano, which ended the Russo-Turkish war and provided generously for the aspirations of Serbia and Bulgaria, did not make any concessions to Greek territorial claims. At the Congress of Berlin the next year, German chancellor Otto von Bismarck proposed that the disputed provinces be ceded to Greece, but the suggestions were rejected by the British, who underlined their intransigence on this question by threatening a naval blockade of Greece if the irredentist agitation continued. The issue of these Turkish-held provinces troubled Anglo-Greek relations until 1881, when the British—confident that Russia could gain no advantage from it—obtained the sultan's reluctant agreement to turn over Thessaly and southern Epirus to Greece (see fig. 4).

Crete remained "unredeemed," and sporadic rebellions broke out over the next decade and a half. Reports of a massacre of Greeks on the island whipped up public opinion and forced Deliyannis to declare war on Turkey early in 1897. The well-equipped Turkish army, recently reorganized by German advisers, routed the ill-prepared, poorly led Greek forces in a 30-day campaign in Thessaly. The protecting powers intervened to prevent the Turks from pursuing their victory against the demoralized Greeks. Minor territorial adjustments were made in favor of Turkey, and Greece was required to pay an indemnity. An international commission was created by the powers to manage the bankrupt Greek state's finances. But, despite Greece's defeat, the Cretans gained the substance of their original demands for greater self-government. The second son of George I, Prince George, was named high commissioner of Crete and given a mandate by Britain to organize an autonomous regime there under the Turkish flag.

The humiliating defeat overwhelmed the fragile stability that had been in place for two decades. Political leadership faltered; Trikoupis had died in 1896, Deliyannis was held responsible for the war, and no one of similar stature emerged to take the reins. The political system sank into immobilism and confusion, and public opinion began to sound menacing.

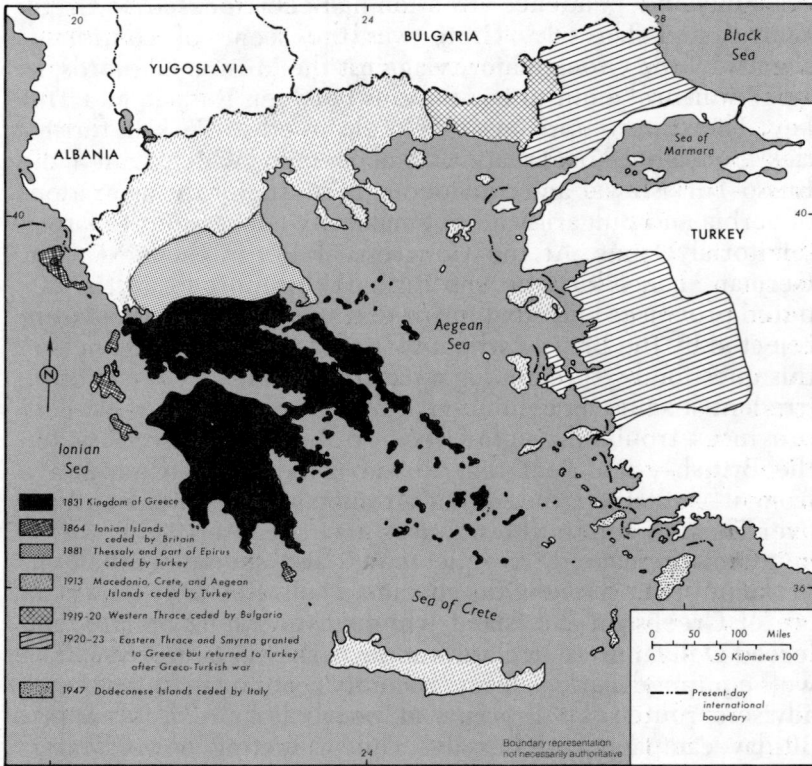

Source: Based on information from Leften S. Stavrianos, *The Balkans since 1453*,
New York 1965, 662.

*Figure 4. Expansion of Modern Greece*

**The Coup of 1909**

The defeat had undeniably shown the weakness of the
army, and a series of steps were taken over the next decade to
improve the military's leadership, organization, training, and
equipment. Although the idea of reorganizing the military had
broad support, the methods used were highly controversial.
The crown prince, Constantine, was named to the newly created post of commander in chief of the army and given full
independence of action in personnel matters, discipline, and

reorganization. Lacking significant military training and having little experience in command—and that only in the disastrous war of 1897—many officers questioned the 32-year-old's qualifications for the post, which would have primary responsibility for the reorganization. At the same time, the reforms threatened the career aspirations of many officers, especially noncommissioned officers.

The military might have been willing to endure this combination of grievances if there had been some obvious improvement in the fighting ability of the army and the navy. Military expenditures had increased, although not without debate, and by 1907 the army and navy were fairly well equipped. But plans to increase the numbers of conscripts were continually postponed because of economic problems. As a result, there was considerable evidence to suggest that the Greek military had actually fallen behind its Balkan neighbors in combat-ready strength. In absolute terms there had been considerable improvement, but in relative terms the Greek military was actually worse off than it had been in 1897.

The failing economy provoked dissatisfaction from all groups, not just the military. Noncommissioned officers, shopkeepers, the educated middle class, workers, and peasants all took to the streets to demand action to address the crisis and, increasingly disgusted with the immobilism of the parliament and the traditional parties, they called for royal intervention to restore order. By 1909 the situation was becoming critical. A secret organization known as the Military League was established. Made up of junior officers, it was inspired by the success of the Young Turks, who had seized power in Turkey in 1908 and had embarked on an ambitious program of social and economic reform.

The league's goals were never systematically laid out. The general thrust of its complaints was that the tinkering in which the parliament constantly indulged was no longer adequate to deal with the multitude of problems facing Greece. More substantial changes, not in personnel but in the very structures of government and the armed services, were necessary. Parliamentary politics had to stop its obsession with petty issues of personality and privilege and take up its role as protector of the nation and the people. There was an element of antiroyalism, but it was rooted in the perception that the crown prince had not earned the right to lead the military and did not prevent the league from blaming the king's passivity for the current immobilism. The league demanded his intervention in politics, despite a constitutional prohibition against it.

Faced with intransigence by the government, the Military League demonstrated its strength on August 28, 1909, with a massive assembly at the military barracks of Goudi on the outskirts of Athens. It was made unmistakably clear that the military could overthrow the government at will, but the leaders of the league preferred to retain an appearance of legality. For the next seven months the parliament was essentially held hostage and legislated the "revolution" demanded by the league. Many of its demands concerned the organization of the military itself, particularly to safeguard its autonomy and professionalism. Other reform proposals were more vague, couched in irreproachable patriotic terms; respect for religion; honest administration; speedy and impartial justice; education based on practical needs of the country and national military requirements; security of life, honor, and property; reorganization of national finances to allow tax cuts; suppression of political waste and corruption; and the immediate buildup of the army and navy.

Initial public response to the coup seemed to be favorable, but within a few weeks spontaneous demonstrations of opposition broke out, focusing on Crown Prince Constantine. In addition, the decision to maintain constitutional forms limited the military's power. The league was dependent on the cooperation of civilian politicians but offered them little incentive to play along, except for the threat of military force. The parliament obliged with an extraordinary amount of legislation but was obviously rankled by its humiliating subordination. Little by little the politicians began to reassert themselves. Finally, factional disputes began to break out within the military, threatening its institutional integrity.

By December 1909 the "revolution" was running out of steam. The league turned for help to the one politician who seemed to them at once untarnished by past experience and ideologically compatible—Eleutherios Venizelos, a dynamic Cretan politician who had come to the attention of Greek reformers several years before. His first act was to call a convention to revise the constitution and make parliamentary government effective. Elections the next year—which were also a referendum on the revised constitution—gave Venizelos' newly formed Liberal Party 300 of the 364 seats in the parliament. The day after the convening of the new legislature, the Military League announced its formal dissolution, although it promised that the army would remain "a vigilant guardian of the national honor and ideals."

The historic importance of this coup revolves around two features. Although the military, particularly the army, had periodically intervened in Greek politics (1843 and 1862), it had never before placed itself in control of the political system. In 1909 the military entered the political arena to save the nation from the corruption and incompetence of the traditional political leadership. It saw itself "as the savior of the nation"—the ultimate guardian of "Greekness" and justice. Since 1909 the Greek military has been a political actor, intervening at least a dozen times throughout the 1920s and 1930s, in a military dictatorship from 1936 to 1940, and again in a military dictatorship from 1967 to 1974. Each time the same exalted justification was used. Its political influence, whether in power or not, has grown steadily since 1909, and its autonomy is considered inviolate by both civilian and military leaders.

The second critical aspect of the 1909 coup was the generational and ideological transformation it brought to Greek politics. Until 1909 the political system had been under the absolute rule of a kind of political aristocracy, whose authority rested not on property or wealth, as in Western Europe, but on control of a clientelistic network. The military's virtual overthrow of that political elite opened the system up to new social forces—the urban middle class, for whom Venizelos became the messiah. He immediately embarked on an ambitious program of economic modernization and social legislation, including agrarian reform, industrial development, restructuring of the bureaucracy, encouragement of labor union organizations and, not surprisingly, enlargement and modernization of the armed forces.

### The Balkans Wars

Irredentism remained a powerful dogma in Greece, and Venizelos, who had long been in the forefront of the fight for the union (enosis) of Crete and Greece, was a militant irredentist. Since the turn of the century, attention focused increasingly on the north, especially Macedonia. The region lacked any specific national character and had become a quiet battleground for Bulgarian and Greek guerrilla groups since at least 1903–04. Serbia also had a claim on the ethnically mixed area. None of these nations could hope to overthrow Turkish rule in the region single-handledly. In 1912, therefore, an alliance of

Serbia, Greece, and Bulgaria was signed; within a few days the first Balkan war broke out. From the beginning the armies fought to position themselves to best advantage after the war. The Treaty of London, signed in May 1913, ended the war and forced Turkey to surrender to the Balkan allies all its European territory except eastern Thrace and Albania, which was granted independence. Within a month the former allies went to war again—this time against each other to divide the spoils.

Serbia and Greece, along with Turkey and Romania, allied against Bulgaria in the second Balkan war. The peace agreement signed at Bucharest in 1913 awarded Crete, the Aegean Islands, and Macedonia (including Thessaloniki), to Greece. As a result of Venizelos' foreign-policy activism, Greece's landmass increased by almost 70 percent, and its population grew from about 2.8 million to 4.8 million. The Balkan triumphs consolidated Venizelos' power and magnified his dynamism as he continued to press for social reform. An unfortunate side effect of the war was King George's assassination in Thessaloniki in 1913. His son, the controversial Constantine, succeeded him.

### World War I: The National Schism

Since 1910 Venizelos had instituted an ambitious program of social and economic modernization and political reform. Through a revision of the 1864 constitution in 1911 he attempted to streamline the legislative process, strengthen the judicial branch, simplify the amendment procedures, and establish guarantees of civil rights. In addition, the parliamentary term was extended to four years from the previous three. He tried to improve rural security and attacked tax evasion and bureaucratic waste and mismanagement. He launched a campaign to end "corruption," though somewhat half-heartedly. Legislation along these lines passed easily in the Liberal-dominated parliament. The net effect of the reforms was a virtual economic and social revolution that severely undermined the position of the oligarchy.

The outbreak of World War I in 1914 interrupted the long period of unusual internal unity and reform but opened the possibility of further territorial gains. From the beginning Venizelos pressed for an alliance with the Triple Entente (Britain, France, and Russia) against the Central Powers (Germany, Austria-Hungary, and Turkey). He strongly believed that Greece's only hope of liberating the remaining "unredeemed"

Greeks in Thrace and Anatolia lay with British cooperation. By openly allying with the entente and actively supporting campaigns in the Balkans, Venizelos hoped to convince the British that Greece was not only loyal and reliable but also strong enough to assume the role of guardian of Britain's interests in the eastern Mediterranean. King Constantine, however, had close personal ties with Germany (his brother-in-law was Kaiser Wilhelm II) and also believed that the Central Powers would win the war. Open alliance with Germany was out of the question, but he insisted on strict neutrality, invoking his royal prerogatives in foreign policy.

By 1915 the conflict between the king and the prime minister had become open and increasingly virulent. Venizelos resigned as prime minister, but an election in May confirmed his popularity in a landslide victory for the Liberal Party. Refusing to accept the outcome, Constantine forced a second resignation, dissolved the parliament, and called a new election for December 1915. No longer a nonpartisan symbol of national unity, the king had become a leader of a faction. The Liberals, saying that the issue had become a constitutional question of parliamentary government versus royal absolutism, boycotted the election. Voter abstention reached almost 65 percent. The nation was increasingly split between supporters of the two rival camps, and over the next two years the battle consumed the nation in a violent clash of personalities and ideas.

Constantine refused to cooperate with the British and French in an evacuation of Serbian troops across Greek territory, and his surrender in May 1916 of a strategic fortress in Macedonia to the Central Powers provided the pretext for an Allied occupation of Thessaloniki to be used as a staging area for operation in the Balkans. On August 30 a group of pro-Venizelos officers in Thessaloniki, encouraged by Britain and France, launched a coup against the government in Athens. In October Venizelos arrived in Thessaloniki and established his own provisional government, which immediately joined the Triple Entente and began to create a private army of the remnants of the Greek army. The Allies, meanwhile, began a blockade of most of the kingdom, relentlessly pressuring Constantine (who was desperate to prevent a Venizelist takeover) into a series of concessions, including the occupation of Athens by the Allies. As French troops entered the city, rumors spread that Venizelists were among them, and riots broke out. The "November Days" followed, during which Constantine's regime set loose an unprecedented wave of persecution and mob violence against suspected Venizelists all over the city.

The battle over entering the war became extraordinarily bitter, developing into a "national schism" that conditioned the political scene for the next 20 years. The degree of passion on both sides cannot be explained simply as a disagreement over alliance partners, although that clearly was an issue. More likely, it was a contest between two visions of Greece: a republic with a modern, capitalist economy run by an entrepreneurial elite, or a constitutional monarchy controlled by a conservative oligarchy presiding over traditional socioeconomic structures. The conflict between the crown and Venizelos over the war issue, therefore, catalyzed the counteroffensive of the traditional elites. The two fundamental conflicts that survived the war were over the regime and the nature of society.

Members of the conservative elite seized upon Constantine as their leader and represented an oligarchy that could best be defined as a political elite rather than an economic class. It comprised a "state bourgeoisie" of politicians, state officials, and lawyers dependent on the state budget as its principal economic base. As such, it constituted the nucleus of a ruling class, which also included the landowners, members of the liberal professions, and the Ionian aristocracy (developed under Venetian rule). In contrast, new social forces—the "new men": a commercial, shipping, and industrial bourgeoisie—developed in the urban areas from around 1880, with the help of the Trikoupis economic programs, and tied themselves to the modernizing tendencies of the 1909 coup. Venizelos captured these entrepreneurs and combined their support with support from other groups—the incipient working class, the newly incorporated Greeks, and even some elements of the peasantry, especially in Thessaly—to create a powerful interclass alliance committed to economic, social, and political regeneration.

Venizelos' ambitious program of social and economic modernization and political reform was clearly aimed at destroying the *tzakia* once and for all. He did not, however, destroy the traditional practice of patronage but used it to his own benefit, parceling out state jobs to his clients and those of his allies. The methods were essentially unchanged, but the beneficiaries were dramatically different. Although the Venizelists were fairly unified, their opponents were internally divided, representing a wide range of socioeconomic groups and ideological tendencies that can best be characterized as Antivenizelism, rather than as a positive program. Some elements, such as the landowners, wanted to subvert land reform; others sought to reverse the socioeconomic and cultural reforms of Venizelos; still others wanted to promote their commercial ties with Germany or Austria-Hungary. The principal paradox of the Antivenizelists was their choice of the king as the rallying point. They had been almost uniformly republican prior to Venizelos' assumption of power, but his success in capturing the democratic mechanisms made the republic not only useless but also dangerous to their larger position. In addition, the king had built up a small but devoted coterie within the military, which now played a major role in the opposition.

The military, continuing its central political role assumed in 1909, was itself split into two warring camps. The army had expanded dramatically and had become democratized since the Balkan wars. Between 1912 and 1918 the number of combat officers tripled, and many of the new officers came from the less privileged classes, ending a brief tradition of elitism in the military academy. In addition, enlisted men increasingly treated the army as a career that offered a reasonable possibility of eventual promotion to the officer corps. The number of reserve officers who were granted regular commissions also mushroomed, and they formed the least stable and professionalized group in the army. Their status within the military was very shaky. They were the first to be forcibly retired whenever the army lists that determined promotion became overcrowded. Conspiracies became commonplace, and employment and promotion in the army depended for the first time not on merit or experience but on the correct choice of military and political patrons. The politicization of the military was institutionalized during the national schism.

Once firmly installed in Athens, the Venizelists avenged themselves on the royalists, exiling 30 prominent Antivenizelists and purging the civil service, the church, and even (for the first time) the judicial system. The army was most severely affected by purges; many royalist officers were forcibly retired, setting a precedent that would be followed throughout the 1920s.

The civil war between the "State of Athens" and the "State of Thessaloniki" lasted until the summer of 1917, when the French and British presented Constantine with an ultimatum: abdication or the bombardment of Athens. Constantine, without formally abdicating, gave the crown to his second son, Alexander. Venizelos returned to Athens as prime minister and in July 1917 brought Greece into the war against the Central Powers. Ten Greek divisions fought on the Macedonian front, and Greek troops were among the Allied contingents that entered Constantinople in 1918.

World War I ended on November 11, 1918. At the Versailles Peace Conference Venizelos lobbied for further territorial gains. Both Greece and Italy shared an interest in Asia Minor, but Greek occupation of the area was more acceptable to Britain. Thus, Venizelos left the conference with permission to occupy Smyrna (Izmir), and Greek troops did so in May 1919. The 1919 Treaty of Neuilly gave Greece almost the whole of eastern and western Thrace (excluding Constantinople) and permission to administer Smyrna and its surrounding areas for five years, after which a plebiscite would be held to determine whether the population wanted union with Greece. In addition, in a separate protocol, Italy agreed to cede the Dodecanese Islands to Greece, and Greek sovereignty over the Aegean Islands, won in the Balkan wars, was recognized. It was a brilliant diplomatic victory, but the treaty was never implemented.

Upon his return to Athens Venizelos called for elections. Despite the happy outcome of the peace conference, the wartime troubles—foreign occupation, blockade, violence, and partisan bitterness—turned the electorate against Venizelos. Apparently, the most telling argument against him was that the territorial gains in Asia Minor could not be held without more war. To vote for Venizelos was to vote for war. The Liberal Party went down to defeat, the proportions of which were exaggerated by the peculiarities of the electoral system. Venizelos himself was defeated and went into self-exile in Paris. At the same time, the royal question reasserted itself. King Alexander died unexpectedly in October of 1920 of infection caused by a monkey bite. In a December plebiscite—the results of which were almost certainly tampered with—the electorate overwhelmingly voted for Constantine's return as king. With Venizelos out and Constantine in, Venizelists throughout the administration were replaced with royalists. Royalists army officers purged in 1917 were reinstated, and Venizelist officers lost their privileged positions.

### The War with Turkey, 1921–22

As the Greek army occupied Smyrna, a Turkish nationalist movement under the leadership of Mustafa Kemal (Atatürk) gained strength and in 1920 set up a rival government in Ankara declaring its independence from the pro-Allied Turkish government in Constantinople. It quickly became apparent that Greece had to choose between remaining in Anatolia and risking war with the Turkish nationalists or giving up the irredentist dream, abandoning 1 million ethnic Greeks to probable reprisals. Politically, there was no choice. Apparently fortified with hints of support from the British, the Greek government, now under Dimitrios Gounaris, launched a preemptive strike, with a fatal lack of preparation. European leaders, disturbed by the surge of Turkish nationalism, leaped to end the fighting by offering Greece a compromise by which it would retain eastern Thrace and Smyrna would be placed under a Christian governor appointed by the League of Nations. Greece in return would have to withdraw from all other parts of Asia Minor. The offer was rejected unanimously by the parliament.

The campaign dragged on with little apparent success, and Atatürk avoided disaster three times in 1921 by strategic retreats. A succession of governments in Athens quibbled over strategy while the Europeans offered one last compromise solution, which was rejected. A coalition government joining all royalist parties took office on May 22, 1922, and decided on a final offensive to take Constantinople. After moving 19 badly needed battalions to eastern Thrace, the Greeks were informed by the Allied powers occupying Constantinople that they would resist any attack. The plan was abandoned. Atatürk lured the overextended Greek army to within 97 kilometers of Ankara before mounting a brilliant counterattack that sent them reeling in a disorderly retreat back to the coast. Within two weeks the Greek army escaped, and Smyrna was captured. The Turkish army went on a rampage, burning the Greek section of the city and killing about 30,000 Greeks while Allied ships sat anchored in the harbor. The 2,500-year Greek presence in Asia Minor was over.

The Treaty of Lausanne, signed in 1923, cancelled Greece's gains at Neuilly and provided for the exchange of Greek and Turkish minorities. More than 1.3 million Greeks were expelled from Asia Minor, and 400,000 Muslims were sent from Greece to Turkey. Greece was faced with a 20-percent population increase overnight.

## The Interwar Period: From Republic to Dictatorship

### The Revolution of 1922

The disaster in Asia Minor inevitably had repercussions on the political scene. Almost immediately after the army's evacuation from Smyrna, a delegation of officers and their units landed in Athens and set up a "revolutionary committee," headed by colonels Stylianos Gonatas and Nicholas Plastiras, which demanded Constantine's ouster. Again, a token civilian government was established, but the military committee, backed with armed force, took control. Constantine abdicated and was replaced by his son, George. Constantine left the country and died a few weeks later.

The coup was conducted in the name of Venizelism, but Venizelos refused to participate in the new government. He did agree to act as diplomatic agent in the negotiations of the Lausanne treaty. To expiate the nation's shame, Gounaris, the prime minister at the start of the war, and seven of his closest associates were tried for high treason by a revolutionary tribunal. Six were found guilty and were executed shortly thereafter. The extreme measures helped to restore discipline in the shattered army but were labeled a "monstrous crime" by the Antivenizelists, who promised revenge. Parliamentary elections were held but were boycotted by the royalists; thus the new parliament was, except for seven members, made up entirely of Venizelists.

Royalist officers launched a countercoup in October 1922 in which the new king was allegedly involved. It was quickly put down, but it gave the initiative to extremist republicans. The army was once again purged of royalists, and the revolutionary committee announced the formation of a constituent assembly to draw up a new constitution. Despite Venizelos' reservations the republic was proclaimed on March 25, 1924, and was ratified in a plebiscite a month later. The popular vote in favor of the change was 70 percent, almost one-third of which came from the "New Greece," the recently incorporated lands and the Anatolian refugees. The republican constitution was not promulgated until 1927.

The early years of the republic were difficult. The vaunted "revolution" of 1922 was no more than the reassertion of Venizelism. It did, however, have lasting significance in two respects. Venizelism was now becoming splintered, especially over the regime issue. Venizelos was once again in self-imposed exile, and the Liberal Party broke up into three separate factions led by rival personalities, only two of which favored the republican constitution. True to tradition, the party failed to be institutionalized into a coherent organization separate from its founder.

The second major impact of the revolution was the obvious autonomy of the military as a political force. The army, itself split into patron-client networks replicating the general Venizelist-Antivenizelist division, increasingly ignored civilian leadership of all stripes and for much of the 1920s dominated policymaking. Ironically, its splintering prevented any institutional takeover of the political system. The frequent conspiracies and coups in the 1920s and early 1930s had limited goals and can be seen as a kind of interest-group politics. The only real difference between the army and other groups as lobbyists was the army's weapons. That gave their desires an automatic salience to the politicians. But the various military factions had little else in common with one another. The issues prompting coups were usually related to promotion lists, pension benefits, pay scale, and retirement. The coups of 1923, 1926, 1933, the 1925–26 military dictatorship under Theodore Pangalos, his overthrow in 1926, and innumerable abortive conspiracies of the period from 1923 to 1935 were fundamentally based on personal grievances. Only the coups of 1909, 1916, 1922, and perhaps 1935 can be seen as ideologically inspired. In each case republican (Venizelist) officers championed the middle-class causes of economic growth and territorial expansion. But despite the army's self-proclaimed position as guardian of the national honor, in none of these coups did the conspirators intend to establish a permanent military government. They did, however, successfully demand their recognition as political actors on a par with politicians.

Finally in 1926, following Pangalos' ouster by his own troops, new elections were held. The Venizelist-Antivenizelist division still held sway, although the Venizelists were split into two independent parties, and the parliament was evenly divided between the two camps. Neither side had the votes to form a viable government; thus they agreed to an "ecumenical cabinet" joining all factions. This highly unusual arrangement lasted until June 1928, producing most notably the new republican constitution in 1927, which created a presidency vested with powers similar to those the monarch had held, and a second chamber, the senate.

## The Second Venizelos Age, 1928–32

Another election was held in 1928 in which the reunited Liberal Party, once more under Venizelos, won 61 percent of the vote. Venizelos again formed a government lasting for four years (1928–32), a period known as the second Golden Age of Venizelism. After the chronic instability of the recent past, the longevity of this government—the third longest in Greek parliamentary history—was a welcome relief and made possible a comprehensive reform using the old Venizelist themes of political, economic, and social modernization.

In the years since the Asia Minor disaster, Greece had undergone substantial social change. The massive influx of refugees strained the resources of the society and the state beyond anyone's imagination. Relocation was the first major problem. Aid from the League of Nations helped, and within a few years about half of the refugees were resettled in rural areas. Urban resettlement remained troublesome even during World War II. Absorbing this new population into the work force, however, created major disequilibrium in the economy. Life in the villages had not changed significantly, and small-scale farming was still the principal source of employment. Venizelos began a program of modernizing agricultural production, shifting from export crops to cereals for domestic consumption. It was hoped that improving agriculture would not only help the chronic balance of payments problems but also stimulate demand for the incipient industrial sector. The state, using foreign loans, started a broad program of land development and public works.

Hints of growing social unrest gave urgency to the economic measures. The lack of upward mobility in Greece caused the emigration of almost 400,000 in the first quarter of the twentieth century, most of them males between 15 and 45 years of age. At the same time, labor strikes, made up largely of disillusioned refugees and encouraged by the Communist Party of Greece (Kommunistikon Komma Ellados—KKE), were becoming dangerously common. In 1928 Venizelos pushed through a special law making illegal agitation against the existing socioeconomic system, marking the official end of Venizelism as an attempted bourgeois revolution.

In foreign policy Venizelos tried to diversify Greece's alliance system, in 1928 normalizing relations with Italy (since 1922 under the fascist leader, Benito Mussolini) and with its Balkan neighbors, Yugoslavia, Bulgaria, and Albania. He even established good relations with Turkey, for the first time in modern Greek history signing a treaty of friendship in 1930. Building on Venizelos' initiatives, Greece, Yugoslavia, Romania, and Turkey eventually agreed to a mutual guarantee of their existing borders.

The impact of the Great Depression, however, destroyed the fragile domestic tranquillity. Greece, whose economy was based primarily on the sale of luxury agricultural goods (tobacco, raisins, and olive oil), was particularly hard hit from 1931. While exports fell to next to nothing, imports, especially of food products like wheat, had to continue. Remittances from Greeks living overseas, a major source of foreign currency, also dropped, and the state was caught in the middle. By 1933 about two-thirds of state expenditures were devoted to servicing the foreign debts contracted by Venizelos and his predecessors. Greece was forced to default (see Historical Development, ch. 3).

## The 1935 Coup and Restoration of the Monarchy

Venizelos' Liberal Party won the election of September 1932, but the margin of victory was too narrow to form a government. The royalist opposition's minority government could not survive, and new elections were held in March 1933. The conservative Populist Party, the principal royalist party, won a decisive majority. Plastiras, former head of the revolutionary committee formed in 1922 and now a general, failed in yet another coup attempt, but once again violence and instability overtook the political system. Purges of the army, now standard operating procedure, and an attempt to assassinate Venizelos prompted public discussion of a restoration of the monarchy as the only hope for reining in the army. On March 1, 1935, Venizelist officers, many of whom had been forced into retirement as a result of the 1933 coup attempt, conspired to restore their own positions and to "save the republic." The relative importance placed on the two goals is somewhat unclear. The coup, considerably more elaborate than other recent attempts, nevertheless failed. Three army officers were executed, and more than 1,000 others (out of a total of 5,000) were purged from the army, the navy, and the fledgling air force in the most extensive purges thus far. Martial law and strict press censorship were imposed while hundreds of Venizelist civil servants were likewise cashiered. Venizelos, who had accepted leadership of the coup probably had not actively participated in its planning, was sent into exile while

41

both he and Plastiras were sentenced to death in absentia. Venizelos, his political career definitively destroyed, died in Paris the following year.

In April the senate, which had from its inception in 1927 been controlled by republicans, was abolished. Elections held in June 1935 were boycotted by Venizelists protesting the continuation of marital law. In October the republic was abolished, a move that was ratified by a plebiscite on November 3, although the results were obviously falsified. Despair over the frequent violence and continual military interventions was such that shortly before his death even Venizelos advocated a "benevolent toleration" of the monarchy as long as his supporters were not persecuted. King George II clearly wanted to end the curse of the national schism and pardoned all participants in the 1935 coup.

The elections held in January 1936 were inconclusive; the royalists, led by the Populist Party, and the Venizelists split the vote (143 seats to 141, respectively), and for the first time left-wing group, the Communist-dominated Popular Front (15 seats), held the balance between them. Some sort of coalition was clearly necessary, and the major parties began negotiations not only with each other but also secretly with the Communists. News of the contacts became public—leaked by the Communists—and caused an uproar. The minister of war, General Alexander Papagos, warned the king that the army would not condone any deals with the Communists. Fearing another coup, the king replaced Papagos with General John Metaxas, who was equally opposed to the Communists but appeared to be more controllable. A coalition was not formed, and many of the leading political figures coincidentally died within a very short period. Having no immediate alternative, George named Metaxas prime minister, and the parliament, anxious to avoid an extended period of immobilism in the face of popular disenchantment, on April 25 agreed to Metaxas' proposal of a temporary adjournment to last five months, until September 30.

### The Metaxas Dictatorship, 1936–40

Metaxas, a conservative royalist, had long been at odds with the activitist republican factions in the military. He had opposed the 1909 coup, being one of the few commanders who took to the field to counter the revolt at Goudi. Since then, as head of the small Free Opinion Party, he had been a leader of Antivenizelism and participated in a number of coups, including the 1923 "counterrevolutionary" coup, for which he had been cashiered and exiled for a time. He openly expressed contempt for the republic and for most politicians but reserved particular animus for Venizelists. In many ways his coming to power was an opportunity to settle old scores against the Venizelists.

Meanwhile, the deepening Great Depression precipitated labor unrest all over the country, culminating in a violent demonstration by tobacco workers in Thessaloniki, eventually embroiling the whole city for three days in May 1936 and resulting in 12 deaths. The tremendous popular outpouring of sympathy for the rioters included a troubling number of police and soldiers who broke ranks and joined the strikers, presenting the haunting specter of a general left-wing uprising. A call by the Communists for a 24-hour general strike on August 5 to protest proposed legislation imposing mandatory arbitration in labor disputes prompted Metaxas to declare a state of emergency. Saying it was necessary to prevent a civil war in Greece similar to that which had recently broken out in Spain, Metaxas suspended key articles of the constitution, mobilized workers to prevent the strike, imposed press censorship, and dissolved the parliament without setting a date for its recall. The parliament was not reinstated for 10 years.

The dictatorship quickly took on the trappings of fascism, in imitation of Mussolini and Hitler, speaking of a "Third Hellenic Civilization" based on order and discipline and creating the National Youth Organization. Political parties and trade unions were abolished, strikes and demonstrations were made illegal, press censorship continued, and an efficient police apparatus arrested and internally exiled opponents, targeting the KKE organization in particular. At the same time, Metaxas moved against the roots of labor disaffection. Pay scales increased, and working conditions improved. For the first time, the social security law, initiated in 1930 by Venizelos, was implemented. Metaxas tried to ease the burden on agriculture by starting public works projects, raising the price of wheat, and absorbing farmers' debts. Paralleling the world economy's slow emergence from the depths of the Great Depression, Greek unemployment gradually fell, and by 1938 per capita income had risen to 45 percent over the levels in the mid-1920s.

Metaxas' dictatorship started a process of undermining the old clientelist parties by removing their raison d'être, patronage. The resulting vacuum was only partially filled by Metaxas' own political organizations, leaving room for new arrangements. At the same time, the gulf between the wealthy minority and the impoverished majority widened steadily. Communist appeals began slowly to develop an audience. Thus ironically, the regime's right-wing extremism helped set the stage for the rapid expansion of the left during World War II.

## The "Terrible Decade": World War II and the Civil War, 1940–49

### World War II

Metaxas reorganized and reequipped the army in preparation for the European war that he believed was inevitable. At best he hoped to keep Greece neutral, but there was no question that if Greece were drawn into war it would side with Britain. On October 28, 1940, the Italian ambassador in Athens demanded that Italian troops be allowed to occupy "certain strategic points" on Greek territory. Metaxas rejected the ultimatum out of hand with a succinct *ochi* (no), an event that has since been celebrated by a national holiday. Metaxas geared the army up for battle, even recalling some republican junior officers who had been dismissed in 1936, albeit severely limiting their authority.

The Italian forces that invaded Greece expected an easy victory. Within a month, however, an inspired Greek army had counterattacked and driven the Italians deep into Albanian territory. Metaxas' death in January 1941, however, deprived the Greek war effort of his determined leadership. In meetings with Mussolini the previous August, Hitler had conceded that "Greece and Yugoslavia belong exclusively to the Italian sphere of interest," but as preparations were made for the invasion of the Soviet Union (scheduled for the spring of 1941), Germany invaded both Yugoslavia and Greece. The British provided naval support and sent 50,000 troops to aid the Greeks, but within three weeks the Allied defense lines were overrun by a combination of air and armored attacks. Faced with an army visibly disintegrating, General Georgios Tsolakoglou, the Greek commander in Epirus, surrendered his army in the field without government approval. Prime Minister Alexander Korysos, who had taken over after Metaxas' death, committed suicide after learning of treason in his cabinet. Athens was occupied on April 27, 1941, and Crete was captured in

June by German airborne units after nine days of fierce fighting. In 53 days the country fell. The king and his government were evacuated to Egypt, where Greek naval units and the remnants of the army were reorganized to continue the war under British command.

The Axis powers occupied Greece for four years. The Germans were interested in holding only the principal communications routes and positions of vital strategic importance, leaving the rest of Greece to the Italians or the Bulgarians. A collaborationist government, headed by Tsolakoglou, directed general administration and security, particularly after the establishment in 1944 of the collaborationist Security Battalions, armed police forces recruited from young villagers and led by Metaxists and often former army officers. During the occupation most Greeks suffered more from hunger and cold than from military action. During the winter of 1941–42 there was mass starvation, especially in Greater Athens, and casualties numbered in the thousands.

### The Resistance

More than 40 years after the end of World War II much of the history of the resistance and of the subsequent Civil War (1946–49) remains controversial. In the mid-1970s and early 1980s many important documents from British, American, and Greek archives were opened to scholars, and a new debate ensured the revelation of much new material. Nevertheless, to a very large degree interpretations of this period depend on ideological and political biases, and it remains difficult to assign an objectively correct history to the period.

What is clear is that spontaneous resistance sprouted almost from the moment of occupation. The first recorded organized subversion occurred in Macedonia in September and October 1941. The remnants of the predominantly royalist Greek armed forces had been evacuated to the Middle East. Many of the officers who had been purged after 1935 remained in Greece but, wedded to the idea of traditional set-piece warfare, were reluctant to take up arms since they were hopelessly outmanned and outgunned. The only organized force willing to shoulder the burden of resistance, therefore, was the KKE.

The communist organization had been mauled under the Metaxas regime, but most of its leaders had escaped or had been inexplicably released from prison by the Germans in the weeks before the invasion of the Soviet Union. They quickly began to rebuild and expand their former network. The KKE had been founded in 1918 and was, like all communist parties of the period, closely tied to the Soviet Union. The ground was not exactly fertile for communist recruitment, for there was no indigenous socialist movement. As territorial expansion proceeded in the north, and particularly after the arrival of the refugees after 1922, the party began to attract members from ethnic and religious minorities (Macedonians, Albanians, Slavs, and Muslims) condemned to an inferior social and economic status. It grew rapidly during the Great Depression, especially after 1935 when the party, following the policy of the Communist International (an organization founded and directed by Moscow, also known as Comintern), abandoned the idea of Macedonian autonomy and actively sought alliance with the mainstream parties; but it remained weak, receiving only 9 percent of the vote at its height in 1935.

The threat of Communist participation in a coalition government in 1935 and their leadership of strikes in 1936 precipitated Metaxas' seizure of power. The KKE had always been unusual among Greek parties because of its classical communist structures—a small, disciplined, and ideologically committed membership hierarchically organized and headed by a strong, united leadership—and Metaxas tried to destroy it from within. He came close to succeeding but, ironically, the period of underground activity during the dictatorship gave it precisely the kind of experience necessary for resistance activities.

The National Liberation Front (Ethnikon Apeleftherotikon Metopon—EAM) was founded in September 1941 as a coalition of five parties, joining Communists, socialists, and some republicans, but it was dominated by the KKE, although this was not generally known at the time. In February 1942 the EAM announced that it was "taking up arms" and formed the National People's Liberation Army (Ethnikos Laikos Apeleftherotikos Stratos—ELAS). ELAS quickly became the largest national resistance organization, eventually fielding an army of over 1.5 million. Although its recruits came from all social classes and regions, republicanism was a common bond. ELAS' connection with the KKE was purposely kept hidden because the EAM (that is, KKE) leadership feared that the communist label would repel many potential resisters. Nevertheless, the EAM-ELAS spoke openly about imposing a new social order after the war and eventually discussed using the resistance against the occupation as the first step in a revolutionary process. Both the nationalist and the revolutionary themes found an eager audience among the educated, white-collar, urban elite, as well as among rural villagers. By December 1944 ELAS and EAM, its parent organization, had the backing of probably two-thirds of the electorate.

By comparison, other resistance movements paled. In September 1941 a rival organization, the National Republican Greek League (Ethnikos Dimokratikos Ellinikos Stratos— EDES), led by Napoleon Zervas and other regular army officers who were victims of the 1935 purges, was founded. The EDES was republican and antiroyalist and, like the other noncommunist forces, was regionally based and tended to consist of old-style personalist and clientelist organizations. The EDES, centered in Epirus, was by far the largest of these groups, claiming 30,000 members, followed by the National and Social Liberation (Ethniki Kai Kinoniki Apeleftherosis— EKKA), numbering about 1,000 members. In all, approximately 110,000 Greeks actively fought in the resistance, of whom about 72 percent were associated with the EAM-ELAS.

The resistance took some time to gain momentum. From the summer of 1942 the resistance began to take on serious dimensions. Britain, which was the only Allied power of any real significance in the eastern Mediterranean until 1944 when the United States and the Soviet Union began to intervene, tried to impose a unified command on resistance forces under British direction in order to coordinate the guerrilla activity in Greece with Allied operations in North Africa. The destruction of a railroad viaduct at Gorgopotomos in November 1942 was the single most important operation of the resistance and also the only time ELAS cooperated with other resistance movements under a single command.

The British Military Mission complained that much of the energy of resistance groups was directed not against the Axis forces but against each other and that their efforts at coordination were largely futile. The internal rivalries were dramatically shown after the Italian surrender in 1943. The EAM-ELAS miscalculated that German forces would be immediately withdrawn from Greece, leaving the way open for a revolutionary offensive. Collecting a windfall in Italian arms and munitions that made it independent of British sources of supply, ELAS conducted a campaign between the summer of 1943 and February 1944 that virtually eliminated some of the noncommunist resistance groups; others survived only after the British, finally alerted to the power and aims of ELAS, intervened to save them. This period has come to be known as the "first round" of the Civil War.

The Greek forces assembled in the Middle East (known as the Middle East Armed Forces-MEAF), meanwhile, suffered from similar internecine conflicts. The old antagonisms dating from the national schism remained of paramount importance within the officer corps. Beginning in 1942 there was some attempt to reinstate the most able republican officers, a move that was bitterly resisted by the largely royalist army and navy. While the officer corps squabbled over old wounds, the rank and file were overwhelming (probably as much as 80 percent) allied with the EAM. The communist position in the enlisted ranks was continually strengthened as news spread of the communist resistance in Greece. Secret extremist organizations of both left and right proliferated, at times destroying the combat effectiveness of the armed forces.

Between 1942 and 1944 there were frequent mutinies and strikes (delicately termed "anomalies"), culminating in the "grand revolt" of spring 1944 by republican and communist soldiers and sailors trying to force the recognition of a government of general national unity under the auspices of the EAM's clandestine provisional government, the Political Committee of National Liberation (Politiki Epitropi Ethnikis Apeleftheroseos—PEEA), set up in March. Only the threat of attack by British forces finally ended the mass mutiny. The British conducted a purge of the Greek forces to root out the communist elements, reducing its size from 15,000 to 3,000. According to recently available evidence, it is almost certain that the EAM-ELAS did not have any direct communication or guidance of the communist groups, although it was generally assumed at the time and for decades after that the troubles in the MEAF had been part of an overall plan for a revolution. The British despaired of the Greek forces' ever becoming combat-ready, given both the unimpressive credentials of most in the bloated officer corps and the chronic politicization of all ranks. In fact, many analysts, believe that the British interference hindered efforts by the more moderate forces to work out an accommodation within the military.

The resistance was from its inception basically antiroyalist, and the restoration of the republic after the war was considered one of its primary goals. Republicans of all stripes, Communists, and even some monarchists pressed the king throughout the war for a pledge that he would not return to Greece until after a postwar plebiscite had been held to decide the fate of the monarchy. George obstinately refused. The British were thoroughly consistent with their long history of intervention in Greek politics and strongly favored the retention of the monarchy as the one stabilizing force in Greek politics. Their principal concern was that the eastern Mediterranean remain both stable and British, considered especially important since the historical Russian challenge to British hegemony in the area seemed to reappear with the rise of the Greek Communist forces (though reliable evidence of Soviet intervention has never been presented). The end of the war was approaching in late 1944, and the Allied powers were already turning their attention to postwar arrangements. The British prime minister, Winston Churchill, went to Moscow to negotiate with Soviet premier Josef Stalin in October and emerged with the "percentages agreement" apportioning spheres of influence in Eastern Europe between the Soviet Union and Britain. Britain was accordingly given a 90-percent controlling interest in Greece, while the Soviet Union reserved only 10 percent. For all intents and purposes, Stalin had washed his hands of Greece. Apparently, the KKE knew nothing of these developments.

The Germans withdrew from Greece in October 1944. Through the Soviet military mission in Athens the KKE was ordered to "avoid opposition" and to participate in the newly arrived coalition government, headed by George Papandreou, a moderate republican. Although the EAM-ELAS had effective control of all of Greece outside the capital, the Communists bowed to Moscow's directive, accepting six relatively unimportant cabinet positions in the British-sanctioned government.

### The Second Round: The Athens Uprising, December 1944

The new government faced the enormous problem of caring for a ravaged population and rebuilding a shattered nation. Economic conditions in Greece worsened in 1945, despite the end of fighting. It was estimated that 8 percent of the population—well over half a million out of roughly 7 million—had been killed in the war or died during the occupation. Of a prewar Jewish community of approximately 76,000, over 60,000 had been killed. The only other Allied power that had suffered more during the war was the Soviet Union. The physical destruction was assessed in 1946 at US$8.5 billion, or well over US$1,000 per person. Some 1,500 villages had been destroyed, leaving 700,000 Greeks homeless. Fruit and tobacco crops, strong prewar export items, were destroyed, and food production was half of what it had been in 1940. Communications and transportation networks were in ruins. Two-thirds of the merchant fleet had been sunk, and the harbors remained clogged with mines and sunken ships (see Historical Development, ch. 3). Crete, the most important island, was under enemy occupation until the German surrender in May 1945.

Nevertheless, prodded by the British, the new government first turned its attention to demobilizing the resistance groups, particularly ELAS. Plans were made to form a unified national army joining ELAS and the EDES with the MEAF. It was a tense accord, and both Communists and the government were highly suspicious and sensitive to any hint of betrayal. Misunderstandings were responsible for the timing of the uprising, but it is probable that some sort of confrontation was inevitable. The opposing forces were too evenly matched—the KKE apparently realized that the goals of the groups were too antithetical to make for a lasting compromise. In November, in the face of what it considered to be threatening moves by the British, the EAM representatives left the government, and ELAS units refused to surrender their arms to the British commanding officer. On December 3, 1944, a demonstration designed to show the EAM's popular strength in Athens could not be controlled by the British forces which fired into the crowd. Estimates of civilian dead ranged from as few as seven to as many as 28, and the wounded from 12 to over 100. The Battle of Athens, the second round of the Civil War, ensued with Communist and government forces (including British troops) fighting in the streets for control of the capital. The battle lasted for 33 days, and the Communist forces were soundly defeated by a British force strengthened by troops taken from the Italian front to oppose the Communist takeover.

During the fighting the British feared that public opinion was dangerously sympathetic to the Communist revolt and deeply resentful of the government's cooperation with collaborationists from the occupation regime. They persuaded the king to appeal to a broader audience by appointing as regent the archbishop of Athens, Damaskinos, a heroic figure during the occupation and respected by both sides. Papandreou resigned as prime minister, and the regent appointed the Liberal hero, Plastiras, in his place.

Although armed revolution had been openly discussed within the KKE since its inception, the Communists were outmanned and outmaneuvered almost immediately after their initial surprise attack. The Varkiza Agreement, the truce signed on February 12, 1945, was relatively generous to the defeated Communist forces. It guaranteed certain of their political demands, including the right to free expression, trade unions, the lifting of martial law, an amnesty for all participants in the rebellion, a plebiscite on the constitution, and parliamentary elections within a year. ELAS was required to demobilize and surrender its weapons (although in fact it gave up only a portion of its arms cache), which included both small arms and heavily artillery.

The Communists suffered more than a military defeat during the second round. Much of the good will they had earned during the war was destroyed by reports of mass executions and other atrocities that became common knowledge. As many as 11,000 had perished in the month of street fighting, and whole sections of Athens, which had survived the German occupation with few scars, were in ruins. In any case, most Greeks had simply had enough of war and recoiled at the idea of another; so by the beginning of 1945 the initiative had swung toward the noncommunist forces. The KKE's wartime allies in the EAM broke away, and the divisions between republicans and royalists were muted for the sake of a national crusade of anticommunism. By the time of the plebiscite in September 1946 it was clear that the voters had largely disowned the Communists. Ninety-four percent of eligible voters turned out, and two-thirds voted in favor of the monarchy, the most visible target of the Communist attacks; the results were the exact obverse of allegiances during the resistance.

### The Third Round

It is difficult to put an exact date on the resumption of fighting. Sporadic and unorganized clashes occurred throughout 1945, but incidents increased in the late summer and fall. The Communists charged that a "White Terror" was being waged by Metaxists and former collaborators and that the remnants of the wartime Security Battalions formed the core of the vigilante bands. The evidence seems to bear out their accusations, and some analysts suggest that until the spring of 1947 there was, in some areas of Greece, a virtual parallel state of fanatical anticommunists. While former members of the resistance were systematically purged from the civil service, no similar efforts were made to root out collaborators. The police were apparently hesitant to investigate charges of crimes by known right-wingers, while zealously pursuing left-wing activists. Metaxists controlled much of the judicial system, and there seem to have been marked discrepancies in the sentences meted out, depending on the ideological affiliations of the accused. The Communists engaged in a terror of their own, but to a much lesser extent.

The government's decision to reverse the schedule agreed to at Varkiza and hold parliamentary elections before holding a plebiscite on the monarchy was considered a provocation by the KKE, which called for a boycott by its supporters. As the March 1946 election approached, violence increased, and the country began a gradual slide back into civil war. The KKE had lost much of its popular support, but its former supporters did not swing to the right either. In the election only 49 percent of the electorate turned out—a remarkably low rate for Greece—and of that only 65 percent voted for right-wing candidates. The Allied Mission for Observing the Greek Elections estimated that the politically motivated, i.e., communist sympathizer, abstention rate did not exceed 9.4 percent. In effect, despite widespread fraud, the right wing won less than one-third of the vote. Unfortunately, there was no center available to fill the vacuum and reconstruct the political equilibrium. The traditional pre-Metaxist parties (primarily the Liberals and the Populists) had been all but destroyed under the dictatorship since they could no longer deliver to their clientelist networks. Many of the former leaders had been sullied by rumors of collaboration or by the events in the Middle East. The Greeks political scene, polarized between two ideological extremes, convulsed in a brutal civil war for the next three years.

Tradition places the decision by the KKE to start an all-out civil war on February 12, 1946, but the party leadership almost certainly remained divided and confused until well into 1946. Markos Vafiades was sent to the mountains in August 1946 to bring together the scattered guerrilla bands, and in December the Democratic Army of Greece (DAG) was created as the successor of ELAS. Action centered in the north, especially in Macedonia and Thrace, where the mountainous terrain was best suited for guerrilla warfare. The communist forces, which never numbered more that 28,000, were overwhelmingly outmanned by the combined National Army and Gendarmerie (the national police force), totaling about

52

265,000 troops and eventually armed and trained by the United States. To partially offset the disadvantage, the DAG received substantial military aid and advice from the communist regimes in Yugoslavia, Bulgaria, and Albania—though apparently none directly from the Soviet Union—and in the first year had an advantage in morale, tactics, terrain and, to some extent, talent. The National Army insisted on waging a static defense that was inappropriate against a guerrilla adversary, and the leadership was often inadequate. Within seven months the DAG claimed to dominate three-quarters of Greece, and the National Army, despite its size advantage, was in disarray.

In December 1947 the KKE announced the formation of the Provisional Democratic Government, prompting the government in Athens to impose martial law and outlaw the KKE. During the Civil War a series of "paraconstitutional" texts were adopted, severely limiting most civil liberties and mandating extremely harsh penalties (including death) for actions against the prevailing social and political order and against the country's integrity. Many of the provisions remained in force after 1949, some until 1975.

The Greek government found itself increasingly pressed by the revolt, and the British, themselves recovering from the war, by 1947 could no longer provide the kind of assistance necessary to forestall a takeover. In March the Truman Doctrine was announced and included Greece within the perimeter of territory considered vital to American national interests. From that point the Greek Civil War was seen by the United States as a critical battlefield in the worldwide struggle against Soviet expansionism. Between 1947 and 1951 United States military and economic aid (through the Marshall Plan) totaled over US$1.5 billion. The massive infusion of funds and military advisers turned the tide in the war. Time was no longer on the side of the Communists, and the DAG changed its tactics. Thus far they had been rather successful using hit-and-run tactics devised by Vafiades, the DAG's commander. From late July, however, Nikos Zakhariades, the head of the KKE, joined the army in the mountains and insisted on more conventional warfare. The KKE was then mortally wounded when Josip Broz Tito of Yugoslavia, eager to improve relations with the West after his break with the Soviet Union, closed his country's borders to the Greek guerrillas in July 1949. Yugoslavia, along with Albania, had provided both arms and, most important, sanctuaries for the DAG. The KKE had truly been abandoned, and morale plummeted.

The National Army's final offensive came in August 1949, and the last Communist stronghold in the mountains fell on the last day of the month. On top of the damage from World War II, Greece had lost another 80,000; countless more were wounded. The bitterness and violence of the conflict reached appalling proportions; atrocities were common to both sides. The final year of the war was particularly brutal. As the DAG became more desperate, they forcibly recruited fighters in the mountains, practically evacuating entire villages, including young women. At the same time, they rounded up approximately 28,000 children (*pedomasoma*) and forcibly evacuated them to various parts of Eastern Europe to be raised as communists. In all, about 700,000 refugees, almost 10 percent of the population, were homeless. The nine years of war wrecked havoc on the economy and on the society. That experience still reverberated in Greek politics into the 1970s.

## Postwar Democracy: A Fragile Stability

Nine years of war had unmistakably changed the social and political environment in Greece. The mass mobilization caused by the resistance and the Civil War had emancipated the masses and given them, for the first time in modern Greek history, a central place in the political process. In response to these social changes, women were granted the right to vote in 1951. The two opposing poles of communism and anticommunism defined the political debate. Having barely survived the Communist assault, the government decreed anticommunism the national duty, and security became a state obsession. Henceforth loyalty oaths and "certificates of social beliefs" would be necessary to obtain employment in a variety of occupations, including vendors. Personalistic and clientelistic allegiances remained important determinants of voting behavior. The political environment, which until 1936 had been fairly evenly divided between reformist liberals and conservatives, became overwhelmingly conservative. Social reform and criticism of the prevailing system were popularly seen as unpatriotic and probably communistic. Thus, although the Liberals remained a major political force, their rhetoric and actions throughout the 1950s were barely distinguishable from the right. The procommunist left presented the principal alternative, and though it consistently polled only around 12 to 14 percent of the vote, it continued to haunt the political scene. A genuinely independent center did not really appear until the 1960s.

Martial law was lifted and democracy restored in February 1950. A proliferation of personalistic parties, none receiving very broad support, joined in a series of short-lived and unstable coalition governments. Between 1946 and 1952 there were 16 different governments, and the parlimentary system once more sank into immobilism. In this situation the army resumed its traditional place as the locus of antiparliamentary sentiment. The military had emerged from the Civil War with enormously increased autonomy from civilian control. After the purges associated with the Metaxas dictatorship, the Middle East "anomalies," and the Civil War, the army, which had in the past reflected the bitter civilian political divisions and which had suffered serious setbacks in 1948 during the Civil War, had become a remarkably homogeneous institution: royalist, fanatically anticommunist, and universally contemptuous of civilian politicians. It was, in short, a new army. In January 1949 Papagos, hero of the Albanian campaign of 1940-41 and former chief of the army general staff under the Metaxas regime, was asked to assume the position of commander in chief of the army. His price for accepting the post was the dissolution of civilian oversight of the army and virtual autonomy of the army from civilian control. The British, who openly intervened in the rebuilding and governance of the Greek army beginning in 1944, approved the action, and the Greek government reluctantly agreed. From this time the military as an institution, with the backing of Britain and later the United States, became the single most powerful force in the Greek political system.

In May 1950 Papagos unexpectedly resigned from the army. Most concluded (erroneously) that he had been forced out by the government. A secret, extreme right-wing organization, the Holy Bond of Greek Officers (Ieros Desmos Ellinon Axiomatikon—IDEA), founded in 1945 but whose origins lay in the MEAF, determined to stage a coup and force Papagos' reinstatement. Papagos himself defused the situation, and shortly thereafter his reason to leave the army became clear. He formed a new royalist political party, the Greek Rally (Ellinikos Synagermos—ES), one month before parliamentary elections in 1951. Modeled after Charles de Gaulle's French Rally, the ES attracted a broad spectrum of supporters, including both the middle class and the peasants. It emerged as the largest party but failed to get a parliamentary majority. The king asked the runner-up, Plastiras, and his new party, the National Progressive Center Union (Ethniki Proodeftiki Kentrum— EPEK), to form a coalition cabinet. Plastiras fell ill three weeks later and hung on for eight months, during which time a new constitution was enacted, by passing the legal amendment process. Finally, in new elections held in November 1952 the ES won 50 percent of the vote and an overwhelming parliamentary majority. The Papagos government initiated an 11-year period of uninterrupted rightist governments.

Papagos' administration, on the basis of its secure parliamentary majority, ended the squabbles within the conservative ranks and began to address the critical economic situation. A successful devaluation of the drachma created a spurt in exports and impressed the United States and other lenders whose capital would be crucial for any serious reconstruction of the economy. But Papagos' most important initiatives were in foreign policy. Greece joined the North Atlantic Treaty Organization (NATO) in 1952 and in 1953 reestablished relations with Yugoslavia and Turkey in the Balkan Pact. The future status of Cyprus, with its 80-percent Greek majority, was the subject of tripartite negotiations among Greece, Britain and, for the first time, Turkey. The talks ended in failure and began a long conflict between Turkey and Greece that remained unresolved in the mid-1980s.

Papagos died in 1955 after a long illness. King Paul appointed as prime minister a relatively unknown conservative politician, Constantine Karamanlis, who, like Papagos, enjoyed United States backing. Karamanlis formed a new party, the National Radical Union (Ethnikiki Rizopastiti Enosis—ERE), which continued the basic policies of the ES but concentrated on economic development, with considerable success. As part of his economic program Karamanlis applied in 1959 for associate membership in the European Economic Community (EEC). In addition to solidifying Greece's cultural and political connection to Western Europe, it was hoped that the EEC would provide a huge potential market, stimulating growth and modernization while also providing some of the necessary capital. Associate status was finally granted on July 9, 1961 and came into effect on November 1, 1962 (see Historical Development, ch. 3; Appendix B).

Again, foreign policy matters occupied much of the government's time. The Cyprus issue became a major focus of attention as the island's Greeks, led by Archbishop Makarios and Colonel George Grivas of the National Organization of

Cypriot Combatants (Ethniki Organosis Kyprion Agoniston—EOKA), demanded enosis and waged a campaign of violence and terror, first against Greeks who did not back the movement and later against Turkish Cypriots and British authorities. Karamanlis, anxious to avoid an escalation of tension both on the island and in Greece, finally agreed to a compromise solution in 1958 that avoided both enosis and partition. Cyprus was declared a sovereign republic led by a Greek Cypriot president and a Turkish Cypriot vice president. Each would have veto power on matters of foreign relations, defense, and security. A parliament was to be divided on a 70 to 30 ratio between the Greek and Turkish communities. It would also have communal assemblies to deal with religious, educational, judicial, and other local matters. The army was to be divided on a 60 to 40 basis, and Britain was granted sovereign rights over an airfield and a military base on the island. The new constitutional arrangements were to be guaranteed by Greece, Turkey, and Britain.

Although the immediate crisis was over, many Greeks were angered by Karamanlis' recognition of Turkish claims to Cyprus. In the 1958 election the ERE lost votes, but, more important, the procommunist United Democratic Left (Eniea Dimokratiki Aristeras—EDA), founded in 1951 as a stalking horse for the outlawed KKE, emerged as the second largest party, garnering 24.4 percent of the vote, roughly double its postwar average. Analysts attributed the dramatic increase in votes as a protest against the Cyprus compromise, but the left's renewed strength caused considerable concern to conservative leaders and the army.

In 1961 Karamanlis asked for new elections. A united opposition, the Center Union (CU), was established by George Papandreou, a veteran Liberal and former prime minister, joining several centrist and liberal parties. The EDA also contested the election. Against all expectations, the ERE not only won but actually increased its votes. The results can probably be explained by Karamanlis' good record and the CU's having only five weeks to prepare for the election. Nevertheless, there was considerable evidence of irregularities, and Papandreou seized the issue, denouncing the vote as "the product of violence and fraud." The most disturbing aspect seemed to be the open complicity of the army and the police in many of the proven instances of vote tampering. Although there was never any conclusive indication of the extent of fraud or indeed of Karamanlis' culpability, for the next two years Papandreou hounded Karamanlis, charging that his government was illegal and unconstitutional and calling the Karamanlis "regime" a police state bordering on fascism. Papandreou even went so far as to call on Greek youth "to terrorize the terrorists." Finally, he called for royal intervention to resolve the issue.

Tensions mounted, and the murder of an EDA deputy, Grigoris Lambrakis (depicted in Costa-Gavras' film, "Z"), in May 1963 crystallized left-wing opposition in Greece and brought forth a barrage of international criticism. Beset on all sides, Karamanlis resigned, using a minor dispute with the king as his excuse. Elections in November showed a sharp but not decisive swing to the CU. Neither the ERE nor the CU had a parliamentary majority, and the EDA held the balance between them. Papandreou was called on to form a government but resigned within weeks rather than rely on EDA support to stay in power. Karamanlis retired from politics and left Greece, consigning the ERE leadership to Panayiotis Kanellopoulos. New general elections in February 1964 gave the CU an absolute parliamentary majority and enabled Papandreou to establish a one-party government. The liberal center, splintered since the war, had finally coalesced to provide a moderate alternative to conservative rule. In addition, Papandreou had emerged as the first genuinely popular political figure since Venizelos. Like Venizelos, however, Papandreou had a domineering and highly personal style of politics that alienated the more independent-minded members of his own parliamentary party and led to a gradually widening breach within the CU.

More than a year after his election, Papandreou revealed the "Pericles Plan," an alleged plot among army officers and police to rig the 1961 election. This was the first concrete evidence he had brought forward to support his allegations of fraud, and the unexplained four-year delay prompted many to charge him with dredging up old news to strengthen his own position. Others suggested that Papandreou had not revealed the plan earlier in order to make necessary changes in key positions in the armed forces. Whatever the reason, it seemed clear that he expected to benefit politically from the show of vigilance.

Unexpectedly, the right wing, supported by disgruntled members of the CU, counterattacked in 1965 with allegations of an officially sanctioned left-wing plot to infiltrate the military, with no other than the prime minister's son, Andreas Papandreou, as a principal instigator. This left-wing organization, known by the acronym ASPIDA (Shield) (Aksiomatikoi

Sosate Patridhan Idhanika Demokratia Aksiokratia—Officers
Save the Country, Democracy, Ideal, Meritocracy), had allegedly originated among officers of the class of 1953 of the
military academy and was first discovered on Cyprus. Colonel
George Papadopoulous, commander of an artillery unit in
Evros, reported "communist sabotage" in his outfit, no doubt
linked to the ASPIDA group. Stories of threats to the monarchy circulated, and fears of a communist takeover of the army,
first broached in 1944, consumed conservative groups. The
CU dismissed the allegations, particularly those of Papadopoulos, as unfounded and the product of either overactive
imaginations or, more likely, an outright conspiracy to undermine the legally constituted government. The very existence
of the organization remains controversial, but most analysts
and politicians give the allegations the benefit of the doubt.
Hardly anyone, however, accepts the notion of Andreas Papandreou's association with any conspiratorial group, though they
acknowledge that he did have informal ties with some of the
younger officers. Professor Nikolaos A. Stavrou of Howard
University has suggested that the alleged conspiracy and the
"sabotage" associated with it were in fact fabricated by
Papadopoulos' own secret army organization, the National
Union of Young Officers (Ethnkiki Enosis Neon Aksioma-
tikon—EENA). In any case, George Papandreou made a crucial error in shielding his son, then minister to the prime minister, from investigation. The whole affair smacked of a cover-
up, and the ASPIDA charges destroyed Papandreou's popular
support. Fifteen months after coming to office, Papandreou
resigned as prime minister.

## The Military Dictatorship, 1967–74

### The Disintegration of the Political System

The political system that had been stable since 1952 and
had seemed well on its way to becoming a robust two-party
democracy in 1964 disintegrated in less than three years. Most
of the controversy that undermined the system can be attributed to a tragic misunderstanding and a personality clash between George Papandreou and King Constantine II, who succeeded to the throne after Paul's death in 1964. The conflict
resembles in many ways the national schism of the early part of
the century and the feud between Venizelos and the first Constantine. Papandreou suspected the king of harboring thoughts

59

of unconstitutional interference in the political process, while Constantine believed that Papandreou was plotting the reestablishment of a republic. What should have been a relatively minor political scandal—the ASPIDA affair and its aftermath—escalated into a major crisis, owing largely to the intransigence and arrogance of the prime minister and the monarch.

Considerable responsibility for the deteriorioation of relations probably rests with Andreas Papandreou. He was a unique character in Greek politics. A former American citizen and resident of the United States for more than 20 years, he was well known as a distinguished professor of economics at the University of California at Berkeley. He returned to Greece in 1959 and became a respected technocrat as head of the Centre of Planning and Economic Research. In 1963 he began a political career with his election to the parliament and quickly emerged as his father's chief aide, minister to the prime minister. It was an open secret that Andreas was being groomed to succeed his father as the leader of the CU. That revelation stirred considerable resentment among many political veterans, and their ire was exacerbated by Andreas' blatant flirtation with left-wing and communist causes.

He had in the space of about five years become a major political figure, propelled into the public eye by a deliberate emphasis on controversial issues, particularly those favored by the left. He openly advocated a remaking of the social and economic structures of Greece and, sensitive to the potential charge of pro-Americanism because of his history, he outdid almost everybody in the vehemence of his anti-Americanism, unambiguously calling for Greek "independence" in foreign policy. No one outside the communist left had talked this way since 1944, and Andreas' outspokenness, combined with his proximity to real power, sent shock waves throughout the conservative community. In this context the ASPIDA accusations merely confirmed for many their suspicions.

Following George Papandreou's resignation in July 1965 the contest with the king became daily more rancorous. New elections would have been the logical solution to the conflict, but the king refused to permit what he believed would be seen as a referendum on the institution of the monarchy. For 18 months a series of governments tried in vain to restore calm. By late 1966 Andreas had practically eclipsed his father in the public consciousness, and the issue was apparently transformed into a battle between the right and the left for control of the government.

The probability of a military coup was openly discussed in cafés and in political circles, but no political party took serious steps to counter any possible action. Andreas and his supporters dismissed the possibility of any action by the military independent of the conservative political parties, and the military's adherence to electoral politics was unquestioned. Furthermore, perhaps unconsciously drawing on the precedent of the national schism, they believed that the political divisions had infiltrated the army, effectively destroying it as a political unit. Finally, they believed that the army was controlled by the top echelon of officers, whose movements could be easily followed, and that lower ranks were not capable of independent action.

As it turned out, Papandreou and his associates were wrong on all three counts. The autonomy of the military as a political actor had been firmly established during the Civil War, and the experience of the following 20 years—particularly its relationship to the United States, which gave it an essentially independent source of funding—had served only to reinforce that autonomy. Ideologically, the military throughout the postwar period remained overwhelmingly unified in its conservative orientation, although some factions distinguished themselves by their right-wing extremism. Finally, they had completely ignored the Greek military's penchant for coups as instruments of political action. The disintegration of the political system at the hands of the politicians themselves was an open invitation to the miltary to fulfill its historical role since 1909 as the "vigilant guardian of the national honor and ideals."

Comparing the situation to that in 1936 when the Metaxas dictatorship had declared the necessity of forestalling an imminent "communist takeover," a group of army officers, led by colonels Papadopoulos and Nikolaos Makarezos and Brigadier Stylianos Pattakos, invoked the Promotheus Plan, a NATO-prepared contingency plan designed to strengthen internal security in the event of a serious external threat. The coup of April 21, 1967, less than one month before elections, surprised everyone, both politicians and generals (who were planning their own coup), and succeeded virtually unopposed.

## The "Revolution of 21 April"

The 12 members of the junta were all middle-ranking army officers and members of Papadopoulos' EENA, and most, if not all, had been members of IDEA, the secret organization that launched an abortive coup in 1951. They all had similar military and personal backgrounds—sons of peasants or petit bourgeois parents. Their formative military experiences had been defeat by the Germans, followed by a mutiny against the collaborationist regime, the battle for Crete, the chaos of the MEAF and, finally, the Civil War. They shared a contempt for politicians, parliamentary politics, the top leadership of the army, and the oligarchy of which it was the representative. In place of the former regime, the junta installed a collective dictatorship through a "revolutionary council" led by a triumvirate, but Papadopoulos was first among equals.

The revolutionary council introduced martial law throughout the country but continued to reorganize the monarchy and a civilian prime minister for the first eight months. Constantine mounted an abortive countercoup on December 13, and his subsequent flight to Rome ended the charade of civilian control, although a regent was appointed to preserve the king's constitutional role.

A new constitution was announced and adopted by plebiscite on October 29, 1968, replacing the 1952 constitution. The "crowned democracy" was preserved, but the king's powers were greatly circumscribed. It provided for the restoration of the multiparty system at some later date, but under strict controls. The most important articles of the constitution and of associated laws concerned the role of the military. The de facto autonomy of the postwar era was institutionalized, not only in the administration of purely military matters (appointments, salary, etc.) but also in all political matters. The armed forces were required to pay allegiance to "the Country, the national ideals and traditions, and [to] serve the Nation," but there was pointedly no mention of allegiance to civilian authorities, who, for their part, were henceforth bound by the constitution and the laws of the country. Thus the role of supreme guardian of the nation, which the army had assumed periodically since 1909, was constitutionally mandated. The International Commission of Jurists described the 1968 constitution as "no more than a legal instrument devised to keep the government in power."

The profoundly conservative nature of the regime was amply demonstrated by the draconian penalties stipulated for discussing or advocating "ideologies aiming at the overthrow or the undermining of the existing political or social order or the corruption of the national convictions of the Greeks." The structures were clearly directed at the left, but through Papadopoulos' statements it was also clear that the "left" included not only the Communists but also most of the center. Civil rights, including the right to vote and express political views, the free press, and numerous civil liberties were severely restricted, and the junta reserved to itself the right to deny these freedoms to individuals it deemed unworthy or dangerous to public order.

The first three years of the junta were characterized by gross human rights violations, well documented by a human rights organization, Amnesty International, and in hearings before the Council of Europe; these violations included illegal arrests, torture, unexplained imprisonments (by late 1967 at least 6,000 political prisoners had been identified), extremely strict censorship, forced exile, and withdrawal of citizenship. Members of the EDA and other known communist supporters were the principal targets, but many members of center parties, including the Papandreous, and even of the ERE, such as Kanellopoulos, the last precoup prime minister, suffered house arrest, imprisonment, or exile. In addition, the junta tried to impose a code of behavior on the country, outlawing certain traditional practices (for example, the ritual breaking of dishes at tavernas) and mandating both religious attendance and a conservative dress code. Gradually, the regime relaxed some of its more controversial restrictions, lifting martial law from rural areas in 1971. After 1972 it was limited to Greater Athens.

The human rights abuses brought forth an uproar in Western Europe and the United States, causing a serious disruption in diplomatic relations. Although no government withheld recognition of the junta, international bodies, including NATO, heard frequent denunciations of the regime's police-state methods. Greece withdrew from the Council of Europe on December 12, 1969, to avoid being suspended. The EEC suspended negotiations about Greece's future status, and on May 7, 1969, the European Parliament reserved its right to reconsider the association agreement altogether if progress was not made to restore a multiparty parliamentary system as had been promised. Nevertheless, despite the protestations, the obligatory provision of the 1962 association agreement, such as tariff reductions, continued to be implemented. The EEC did withhold US$56 million in development loans previously granted to Greece, but the net effect of these actions on the regime was relatively small.

The reaction of the United States to the colonels' coup was somewhat more problematic. At the time of the coup and persisting into the 1980s, rumors of United States complicity gained wide acceptance in Greece. Proof has never been offered to substantiate this claim, although there is reliable evidence that United States embassy officials had been in contact with the generals who were also planning a coup and had requested its postponement—not cancellation—to allow time for a possible political resolution of the crisis. The colonels' action was apparently a complete surprise to the embassy staff. The United States hesitated to grant recognition but continued relations in the first months, stating that the relationship was conducted through the head of state, the king, who accepted the new regime; therefore, as far as the United States was concerned, there had been no change. After the king's departure in December that line of reasoning obviously lost its meaning, but the United States resumed full diplomatic relations with the junta on January 23, 1968.

The position of the United States was difficult; domestic reaction against the junta was very strong, especially after the revelations of widespread human rights violations, but Greece's strategic situation in the eastern Mediterranean and on NATO's southeastern flank made it almost impossible to break off relations. This view was reinforced by the outbreak of the Arab-Israeli June 1967 War and the perceptible buildup of Soviet naval forces in the Mediterranean. There were those within the government, notably Robert McNamara, secretary of defense under President Lyndon B. Johnson, who advocated cutting off or at least substantially reducing military aid to Greece, but others noted that continuing aid would give the United States more leverage over the junta in its effort to promote the early restoration of democracy. A compromise was reached whereby shipments of heavy weapons were suspended, but all other forms of aid were continued. Between 1967 and 1970 there was a decrease in the level of military aid, but apparently it was a result of previous decisions and had no connection with the coup. In 1972 a long-awaited agreement was signed, giving the United States Sixth Fleet permanent port facilities in Greece. In short, except for some relatively intemperate remarks by Vice President Spiro Agnew in a trip to Greece in 1971, United States administrations did not openly embrace the junta, but then neither did they distance themselves from the military regime, and Greco-American relations continued relatively unchanged. In Greek popular opinion, however, the United States aided and abetted the colonels' regime despite knowledge of its many excesses. This perception led to a simmering anti-Americanism that remained widespread into the 1980s.

The years between 1967 and 1973 saw a gradual but steady increase in Papadopoulos' position within the junta. At the time of the coup he served as minster to the office of the Prime Minister, and by November 2, 1967, he had become head of a powerful body for coordinating government policy in defense, security, finance, education, and social welfare and assumed the prime minister's post as well as the stewardship of the Ministry of National Defense. A year later another reorganization of the government apparatus dissolved the revolutionary council and expanded the powers of the prime minister. At the same time, a new cabinet was appointed with a preponderance of Papadopoulos' supporters. In 1970 Papadopoulos added the foreign ministry to his collection of offices, followed by the regency in 1972.

In May 1973 there was a naval mutiny, indicating that despite extensive purges the navy still harbored a significant number of disaffected officers. Papadopoulos claimed that the king was implicated in the plot and on June 1 declared him deposed. He proclaimed the creation of a "presidential parliamentary republic" to be ratified by referendum and promised to restore a multiparty system and to hold elections in 1974. The president was given an eight-year term and wide legislative and executive powers with exclusive control over foreign policy, defense, national security, and public order. The period of the "Revolution of 21 April" was officially declared at an end. The referendum ratified the new constitution in July 1973.

## The Collapse of the Junta, 1973–74

Although Papadopoulos was now at the height of his power, there were signs of growing dissatisfaction. The referendum vote, though favorable (78 percent), was considerably less enthusiastic than was the 1968 plebiscite on the constitution (92 percent). The favorable vote in Athens, where martial law remained in force, was only 51 percent. After five years of high growth, a noticeable downturn in the economy that began in

1972, including a 30-percent inflation rate, took away one of the regime's most important props. Although labor activity was severely restricted, unrest grew in scattered areas, and public opinion palpably shifted from acceptance to mere toleration of the junta. The most serious disturbances were among students, first at the Law Faculty of the University of Athens in March 1973 and then more spectacularly at the Polytechnic in November. Each time, the protests started as small disturbances over academic and professional issues but rapidly escalated to political matters, spreading to student enclaves all over the country. Many of these students had received basic training in demonstration techniques during the student uprisings in Paris and the United States in 1968 and 1969; and they skillfully manipulated clandestine radiobroadcasts to stir up sympathy among the general population. The Polytechnic demonstration was brutally crushed by army troops and tanks, leaving at least 34 students killed, several hundred wounded, and almost 1,000 arrested according to some reports. The relaxation of police controls was reversed and martial law reimposed, but the severity of the junta's response only increased popular discontent.

On November 25, 1973, within days of the Polytechnic debacle, Papadopoulos was deposed in a coup and replaced as president by Lieutenant General Phaedon Ghizikis. The real power, however, was clearly held by Brigadier General Dimitrios Ioannides, the head of the ESA, the military police that had often been charged with gross brutality. The justification for the new coup was that Papdopoulos had deviated from the principles of the "revolution," now reinstated, and was leading the country to an "electoral adventure."

The reconstituted junta continued to suffer from the growing economic problems and, despite a renewed security crackdown, public opinion inexorably moved toward open opposition. The domestic base of support was crumbling, so Ioannides turned to foreign policy to provide the issues that might restore public confidence. In April and May he initiated a saber-rattling incident over the question of possession of oil deposits recently discovered near the island of Thasos in the Aegean Sea. A more serious confrontation over Cyprus brought Greece to the brink of war with Turkey. Relations with Archbishop Makarios, president of the Republic of Cyprus, had become openly hostile as the junta brazenly supported the activities of the EOKA, the terrorist organization dedicated to the union of Cyprus with Greece. An outbreak of

*Entrance to stadium at Olympia,*
*Peloponnesus, ca. third century B.C.*
*Courtesy Jean R. Tartter*

violence by the EOKA against two Turkish Cypriot villages in 1967 had led to American diplomatic intervention, the rationale being that Greece had violated the Zurich and London agreements of 1959 that had laid the foundations of the Republic of Cyprus and set limits on the size of Greek and Turkish contingents. As a result, Greece had to withdraw the 10,000 troops that had been sent to the island by Papandreou in 1963, and Grivas, head of the EOKA, was sent back to Greece.

On July 6, 1974, Makarios charged the government of Athens with plotting the overthrow of the Cyprus republic. Nine days later Greek regular army officers who had been assigned to the Cypriot National Guard mounted a coup against Makarios, soon joined by the Greek army contingent on the island. The consensus was that the coup had been planned and carried out on orders from Athens. Turkey exercised its right as guarantor of the 1960 constitution of Cyprus and intervened on July 20 to preserve the republic.

The junta called for general mobilization of the armed forces, but the effort collapsed in complete disarray. Many

67

commanders refused to carry out the junta's order to retaliate, and the commander of the "C" Army Corps stationed in northern Greece issued an ultimatum to Ghizikis, demanding a return to civilian rule. The armed forces were collapsing from within, and the issue was no longer simply the army's political strength but its survival as an institution. In desparation the junta turned to Karamanlis, who had been living in Paris since 1963, to restore democracy to Greece. On July 24, 1974, a civilian government was sworn in, ending seven years of military dictatorship.

## The Restoration of Democracy, 1974–81

### The Return of Karamanlis

The choice of Karamanlis was worked out in a compromise between civilian political leaders, primarily from the ERE, and the military. Karamanlis was untouched by any hint of collaboration with the junta and had spoken out forcefully against it from Paris, but at the same time, his conservative credentials were impeccable and therefore acceptable to the military. In addition, Karamanlis had enormous personal prestige in Greece, a factor that helped ease the transition to democratic methods.

The goal of the new regime was to heal the historical rifts of the Greek political system that had prevented the evolution of a stable and effective multiparty parliamentary system. The first order of business was to destroy the ideological rigidity of the system that had restricted political power to only one camp, the right, since 1935. The repression of left-wing opposition (broadly defined to include not only communists and socialists but also centrists) had resulted in political instability and chronic violence and, in addition, had made Greece a living anachronism by artificially stifling social change. By legalizing the KKE Karamanlis hoped to finally end the Civil War and begin the healing process.

Elections were held in November 1974, only four months after the fall of the military dictatorship, and four major parties participated. The right was represented by the New Democracy (Nea Demokratia—ND), founded by Karamanlis, whose core was the old ERE. The ND never developed a full program for the election, instead relying on the drawing power of its leader, whose conservative views were well known. Its electoral slogan, "Karamanlis or the tanks," aptly summed up its approach. The old CU was revived under a new label, Center Union-New Forces (Enosis Kendrou-Nees Dynamis—EK–ND). Deprived of a charismatic leader by the death of George Papandreou in 1968, the center became almost indistinguishable from the ND in its program: support of closer ties with the EEC and commitment to a free-enterprise economy. Unlike the ND, which remained neutral on the question of the monarchy, the EK-ND and the other three major parties came out in opposition to restoration.

In 1968 the traditional left had split; a Eurocommunist wing that advocated independence from Moscow and acceptance of parliamentary procedures formed a separate party, the KKE-Interior. For the 1974 election the KKE-Exterior and the KKE-Interior joined forces in an electoral alliance under the name United Left (Enomeni Aristera), which advocated a nonaligned foreign policy and the nationalization of basic sectors of the economy.

The fourth party was entirely new. The Panhellenic Socialist Movement (Panhellinion Socialistiko Kinima—PASOK) was founded in 1974 by Andreas Papandreou, using his Panhellenic Liberation Movement (PAK), one of the major resistance organizations under the junta, as the new party's core. PASOK, echoing the kinds of criticisms of the Greek society and economy that had made Papandreou notorious in the early 1960s, declared its opposition to a restoration of the monarchy and to a continuation of Greece's relationship with the EEC, arguing that Greece should develop links with the nonaligned nations of the Third World.

Karamanlis' ND won an easy victory in the election, receiving over 54 percent of the vote and an overwhelming majority of the seats in the parliament. The center received 20.5 percent of the vote; the United Left, 9.4 percent; and PASOK, only 13.6 percent—far below its expectations.

The second historical issue to be addressed was the status of the monarchy. Since independence, but particularly in the twentieth century, the debate between republicans and monarchists had soured the political scene, often resulting in violence and distorting the evolution of the parliamentary system. In December 1974, for the sixth time in the twentieth century (previously in 1920, 1924, 1935, 1946, and 1973), a referendum was held on the future of the monarchy. In the fairest vote to date, 69 percent of the electorate voted against the restoration of the monarchy. The constitutional issue that had plagued

Greek politics since independence was finally and definitively over.

Karamanlis had been fully aware of the fragility of his hold on power. Just how fragile was dramatically shown in February 1975 by the announcement that an attempted coup (as it turned out, the fourth in six months) had been thwarted. The extent of participation in the plot among the military was chastening, but it provided the opportunity for the long-awaited cleansing of the armed forces and trials of those responsible for the dictatorship. The new government, bolstered by its electoral mandate, proceeded cautiously, and trials resulted in long sentences for most of the principals involved in the junta, particularly for those in the security forces accused of inhumane treatment of prisoners. Members of the original triumvirate—Papadopoulos, Makarezos, and Pattakos—were sentenced to death, but the government commuted the sentence to life imprisonment. Many outside the government denounced the leniency of the punishments, but the government had to balance the need for just retribution with the need to maintain reasonable relations with the military. A more severe attack on the institution would probably have led to a violent reaction, perhaps a coup.

In 1975 a new basic law of the land replaced the 1952 constitution, which had been reinstated at the end of the junta. The new document created a more powerful executive branch led by a president, elected for a five-year term, who is commander in chief of the armed forces and head of state. The president, responsible for choosing the prime minister, is obliged to invite the leader of the majority party in the parliament to form a government, but he is also empowered to dismiss him after consulting the Council of the Republic, a body made up of former presidents, the prime minister, the leader of the primary opposition party, and former prime ministers who have received votes of confidence in the parliament. He has the power to veto legislation (though the veto can be overridden by a simple majority), dissolve the parliament, appeal to the electorate directly in a referendum, declare martial law, and rule by decree for 30 days without parliamentary approval. This sharp shift in the direction of executive power caused an uproar among opposition circles, but Karamanlis contended that these formidable powers of the president should be considered extraordinary, to be used only when necessary to preserve stability in the context of the "Greek reality" of divisive conflict. The presidency was given to Constantine Tsatsos, a longtime associate of Karamanlis, who during his term never invoked the powers of the office, allowing the parliament and the prime minister to remain the active centers of the political system. In 1980 Karamanlis himself assumed the office.

In foreign policy the Cyprus situation continued to dominate relations with Turkey. In February 1975 a Turkish Federated State of Cyprus was declared to exist in the northern half of the island, which had been occupied by Turkish troops since 1974. Although the new state received diplomatic recognition only from Turkey, many states, in particular Britain, granted de facto recognition. Negotiations between Greece and Turkey dragged on through 1975, but substantive progress could not be made because the two nations held diametrically opposed views on how to solve the conflict. Greece maintained that the matter was intracommunal and could be settled only by negotiations between the Turkish Cypriots and the Greek Cypriots themselves; the Turks, whose claim to the island dates only from 1955, contended that Greece and Turkey, as protectors of the island's communities, were responsible for resolving the crisis. In November the United Nations General Assembly, after much prodding by Cypriot president Makarios, called for the withdrawal of foreign troops from Cyprus, but it was small comfort to the Greek Cypriots because no effort was made to enforce the resolution. A number of other issues, including possession of the Aegean oil reserves (which broke out into a major crisis in 1976 over Turkish explorations in the area), air traffic control over the Aegean, and Greek fortification of some of the islands, exacerbated tensions between the two nations.

The continued impasse complicated arrangements with NATO (from whose military arm Greece withdrew in 1974), threatened to postpone Greece's entry into the EEC, and dangerously undermined relations with the United States. Anti-American feelings, which developed under the junta, were reinforced by what was seen as a bias in favor of Turkey evidenced first during the Cyprus crisis in 1974–75 and again in 1976, when the United States agreed to provide US$1 billion worth of military aid over four years in return for installations on Turkish soil. After strong Greek protests, including the recall of the Greek ambassador, the United States agreed to supply US$700 million over four years in return for facilities in Greece. This seven-to-10 ratio between Greek and Turkish aid became an implicit formula for future United States assistance (see Military Assistance, ch. 5).

The ND asked for elections in 1977, one year ahead of schedule, on the grounds that the government needed a renewed mandate to deal with these complicated international issues. The results of the election showed a shift away from the ND. Although it kept its parliamentary majority, its share of the vote decreased by 13 percent, and its representation in the parliament fell by 22 percent. The principal beneficiary of the vote was PASOK, which doubled its vote and became the second largest party in the parliament with 93 seats, an enormous increase over its previous 13. The center, renamed the Union of the Democratic Center (Enosis Demokratikou Kendrou—EDIK), won only 12 percent (down from 20.5 in 1974), and the traditional left slightly increased its vote.

Karamanlis' most important achievement as prime minister between 1974 and 1980 was the installation and apparent consolidation of a functioning democratic system. By a careful balancing of all the conflicting pressures, he hoped to end the tragic cycle of hatred and violence that had characterizied Greek politics in the twentieth century. His efforts to stabilize the economy—undermined by both the 1973–74 oil crisis and the junta's profligate policies—were less successful (see Historical Development, ch. 3).

**The Panhellenic Socialist Movement Comes to Power:**
**The 1981 Election**

Elections held in 1981 resulted in a resounding victory for PASOK—48.1 percent to the ND's 35.9 percent. The ND's fall had been presaged in the 1977 results, but the size of PASOK's win surprised most observers. Only three parties—PASOK, the ND, and the KKE-Exterior—won seats in the parliament, wiping out the minor parties. Many observers believed that the election indicated a fundamental shift to the left of the whole political environment, rejecting the extreme right wing that had ruled Greece for 46 years and replacing the old center with a modern, progressive social democratic party, PASOK. In any case, the young democracy had faced its first and most difficult test, the alternation of ruling parties, and most observers were confident of the regime's stability.

The most important development in the post-junta period was the growing political clout of an upwardly mobile entrepreneurial class and a white-collar group, created by the uneven but sharp economic growth of the postwar period, and the consequent disintegration of the traditional center parties, which first became apparent in 1977 and was complete by 1981. The critical factor, therefore, was which party could attract the centrist voters. Despite Karamanlis' obvious intention, the ND never developed beyond its ERE core. Although it successfully shed its postwar anticommunism and introduced more progressive socioeconomic policy proposals, it failed to develop either a coherent and attractive ideological basis or a well-structured mass organization. The clientelist networks developed under the ERE remained at the center of the ND and frustrated attempts to attract new members. Moreover, the party had little to offer the voter in search of a party. Karamanlis characterized the ND's basic principles as "radical liberalism" but never defined what that meant. The party's performance under Karamanlis' government was creditable, presiding over a marginal economic recovery and reforms in education and banking, but it was not associated with any discernible program. Finally, and perhaps most important, the party was until 1980 indistinguishable from its founder, Karamanlis. When he retired from politics to become president in 1980, the ND lost its center. Within a short time, but especially after the loss in 1981, the party split into its constituent parts, the more conservative elements gaining the upper hand. The ND's attempts to portray itself as a center-right party failed to convince either itself or the voters.

PASOK provided most of the things that the ND did not: a coherent program of progressive socioeconomic legislation, a charismatic leader in Andreas Papandreou, a clear ideology, and a well-defined mass organization. By 1977 PASOK's rhetoric had noticeably moderated, although its basic principles remained intact. It claimed to unify three currents in Greek politics—the wartime EAM, the CU and its center-left faction, and the resistance to the junta—which shared a commitment to national independence, popular sovereignty, and social liberation. PASOK's slogan in 1981, "Allaghi" (Change), was left deliberately vague to appeal to the widest possible audience. Although it was a clear reference to popular sentiment for a change from the last half-century of right-wing rule, there was no clear definition of what it would entail. The party, which characterized itself as a radical socialist organization dedicated to building a socialism different from both the communist and the social democratic models, was greatly helped by the recent rise of moderate socialist governments in Western Europe, especially in France only five months before, which helped to allay fears and make socialism a respectable political program.

Papandreou continued to call for withdrawal from NATO and the EEC and for the removal of American bases from Greece, but the other aspects of his platform—the socialization of the means of production (as distinguished from nationalization), selfmanagement for workers, administrative decentralization, creation of a welfare state, and democratization of the state apparatus—were more symbols of a general orientation than concrete policy proposals. To a large extent, therefore, PASOK's massive popular vote in 1981 might be attributable to a vote against the past rather than a vote for a vaguely defined Greek socialism.

PASOK represented an innovation in Greek politics, both in its ideological orientation and in its organizational structure, and the formula clearly worked. By 1977 the party claimed a membership of 27,000, which grew to more than 60,000 by 1980. It was a broad coalition of classes, including, in Papandreou's words, "farmers, workers, employees, craftsmen and artisans, the youth and all the people who are subject to odious exploitation by modern monopoly capital, local as well as foreign." Like Venizelos 70 years before, Papandreou brought with him a generation of "new men" to reinvigorate the political system. PASOK was an attempt to create a party on the European social democratic model, rejecting the traditions of personalism and clientelism, but there were many signs that Papandreou's personal control of the party undermined many of the procedural innovations (see Political Parties, ch. 4).

*       *       *

The literature in English on modern Greece is relatively limited, concentrating primarily on political history. The best general histories available are D. George Kousoulas' *Modern Greece: Profile of a Nation*; Richard Clogg's *A Short History of Modern Greece*; John Campbell and Philip Sherrard's *Modern Greece*; and David Holden's *Greece Without Columns*. The last two, although dated, are excellent introductions to the cultural bases of modern Greece. The *Journal of the Hellenic Diaspora* publishes articles of consistently high quality on a wide range of historical issues.

Until recently, social and economic history were largely

neglected. George T. Mavrogordatos' *Stillborn Republic: Social Coalitions and Party Strategies in Greece, 1922-1936* is an excellent study of the social bases of political alignments during a critical period in the twentieth century. Nicos P. Mouzelis, especially in his *Modern Greece: Facets of Underdevelopment*, and William H. McNeill's *The Metamorphosis of Greece since World War II* give a broader historical perspective to social and economic development.

The Civil War is perhaps the most studied period in modern Greek history, but the ideological split that developed in Greece also affects the scholarship on events since World War II. R.V. Burks gives a useful overview of the contending schools of thought on the Civil War in his book review, "Hellenic Time of Troubles." The books mentioned in that review, especially *Greece in the 1940s: A Nation in Crisis*, edited by John O. Iatrides, give a full range of interpretations of the events. Nicholas Gage's *Eleni* gives a more personal and dramatic picture of how the wars affected individuals.

Richard Clogg George Yannopoulos' *Greece under Military Rule*, covering the junta up to 1975, and Clogg's *Greece in the 1980s* offer a broad overview of recent history. *Greece at the Polls: The National Elections of 1974 and 1977*, edited by Howard R. Penniman, provides a good background to the 1981 election by analyzing developments in the political parties in the 1970s. (For further information and complete citations, see Bibliography.)

# Chapter 2. The Society and Its Environment

*Typical village architecture*

EXCEPT FOR THE MUSLIM speakers of Turkish in the Dodecanese Islands and the northern mainland, Greece is relatively homogeneous. A vast majority of Greeks have Greek as
their mother language and consider themselves Greek Orthodox, being baptized, married, and buried by the church although they may not attend services regularly. For centuries
the Greek language and the Greek Orthodox church have provided a sense of Greekness. Historically, this sense of Greekness has been important to those dispersed as migrants as well
as to those living inside the country.

A majority of Greece's almost 10 million inhabitants live in
cities, concentrated especially in Athens and Thessaloniki (Salonika). The mountain areas and islands are losing population,
although the rate of urbanization has decreased. Regional divisions have become less important than the rural-urban split.

The first loyalty of Greeks is to their household, usually
composed of members of the nuclear family. It is the household, not the individual, that is the crucial social actor in Greek
society, and identity comes from membership in such a group.
The family's main concerns are provision of inheritance and
dowry for the new generation and defense of the family reputation. Reputation depends on public recognition of material
success and honorable conduct, the latter especially in terms of
male roles of hero or family provider and defender and female
roles of devoted mother and faithful wife. Greeks consider
attainment of good reputation or prosperity the product of the
struggle between households.

Ties of kinship, patronage, and ritual kinship cut across
classes and unite residents in cities and villages. Class, ethnicity, and the rural-urban dichotomy do not polarize Greek society. Social mobility is possible through education, accumulation
of wealth (often through emigration), and rural to urban migration. Since the nineteenth century there has been an ongoing
expansion of the middle strata through education and the
transformation of thrifty workers into self-employed agriculturists and petty bourgeoisie. Villagers have often aimed at
social mobility through the preparation of substantial dowries
so that daughters could marry urbanites or through the education of sons, especially those who could not be accommodated
on family land.

Greece is undergoing social change; the political, economic, and social transitions of the post-World War II era have touched the lives of most Greeks. Sources of actual and potential change have included urbanization, industrialization, and emigration, as well as repatriation, tourism, and an increasing proportion of women in the work force. The momentum of change was formally acknowledged by the Socialist government of Andreas Papandreou, which came to power in 1981. That government has enacted a number of laws with far-reaching implications. These laws were aimed at abolishing the dowry, restructuring family property and authority, liberalizing divorce, and ensuring job equality, but as of mid-1985 the extent and nature of actual changes remained unclear.

## Physical Environment

Located in southeastern Europe on the southern tip of the Balkan Peninsula, Greece occupies 132,608 square kilometers (131,990 according to official Greek sources). It is bounded on the north by Albania, Yugoslavia, and Bulgaria; on the east by Turkey and the Aegean Sea; and on the south and west by the Sea of Crete and the Ionian Sea. About 80 percent of the territory is mountainous, only about 30 percent of the land is arable, and no rivers are navigable. Islands constitute about 20 percent of the land area (see fig. 5).

There is no point on the mainland peninsula more than 100 kilometers from the sea. More than 2,000 islands lie scattered in the surrounding seas, ranging from small, barren rocks to Crete, the fifth largest island in the Mediterranean Sea. About 170 of the islands are inhabited. The total length of the country's land borders is 1,170 kilometers, and its coastlines of 15,000 kilometers are surpassed in distance by only a few countries in the world. Innumerable bays, gulfs, and sounds cut deep into the mainland as well as into many of the islands, creating a series of small peninsulas and capes. The proximity to the sea and the paucity of good, arable land have made the Greeks seafarers since the dawn of Western history, and, conversely, life for the Greek farmers has not been easy for more than 30 centuries.

The mountains are the dominant geographic feature. The name *Balkan* is derived from a Turkish word meaning mountain. The Greek mountains are continuations of the ranges found in Albania, Yugoslavia, and Bulgaria. The topography of the country can best be described as rugged. Although its

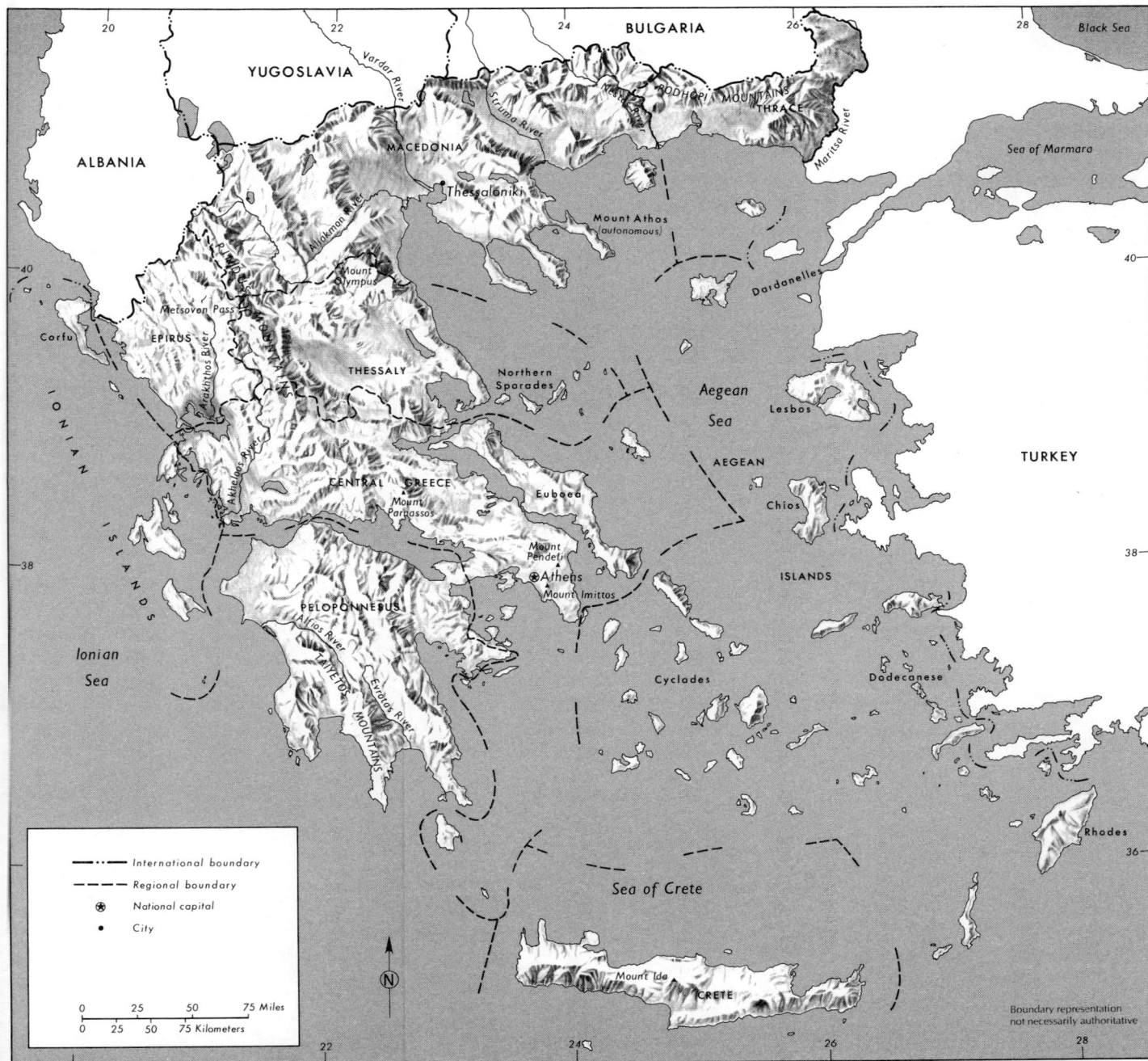

*Figure 5. Topography and Drainage*

mountains are not high when compared with many other European ranges, there are at least 20 peaks over 2,000 meters.

Greece is an area of frequent earthquakes and earth tremors. The famous statue known as the Colossus of Rhodes was toppled by an earthquake in 277 B.C., and in the ninth century A.D. Corinth was destroyed by an earthquake. The most recent serious earthquakes were in June 1978 in Thessaloniki when 50 were killed and 600,000 affected, and in February 1981 in the province of Attica and in the Peloponnesus 65 kilometers from Athens, when 22 were killed and 80,000 affected.

Greece is divided into nine geographic regions—six mainland and three insular. The regions have no administrative bodies or functions, but each has distinctive characteristics and an important heritage. The actual administrative subdivisions of the country are the 51 provinces (*nomói*; sing., *nomós*), but the provinces are habitually grouped by geographic region, and official statistics are conventionally reported by region (see table 2, Appendix A).

The northern tier of regions—Thrace, Macedonia, and Epirus—has common borders with other Balkan countries; from east to west, Thrace borders on Turkey and Bulgaria, Macedonia borders on Bulgaria, Yugoslavia, and Albania, and Epirus borders on Albania. All three regions are Greek portions of formerly larger territories that were divided among the Balkan nation-states after various wars and according to the terms of various treaties. Historically, the Balkan Peninsula has been a hotbed of political intrigue and fractionalization, creating the word *balkanize*.

The remaining mainland regions are Thessaly, Central Greece, and the Peloponnesus. Some of the country's most extensive and most fertile lowlands are in Thessaly. Central Greece contains Athens, not only the capital of the country but also the heart of Greece as a nation-state and as a historical heritage. The Peloponnesus is the odd-shaped peninsula in the south where relics of a 3,000-year-old civilization may be seen in the cities and elsewhere. The insular regions are the Ionian Islands, hugging the western coast from Albania to the Peloponnesus; Crete, a divider between the Aegean and Mediterranean seas; and the Aegean Islands, many of them located just off the Turkish coast but most of them boasting long histories of Greek habitation.

## Thrace

The region of Thrace, located in the northeastern corner, is often referred to as "Western Thrace" or "Greek Thrace" to distinguish it from the much larger Balkan territory known from ancient times by the same name. In the present-day Balkans, Thrace is divided among Bulgaria, Turkey, and Greece. In addition to Turkey and Bulgaria, Greek Thrace borders on the region of Macedonia to the west and the Aegean Sea to the south (see fig. 6). The region measures about 8,578 square kilometers, including the island of Samothrace, which lies in the Aegean Sea southwest of Alexandroupolis, Thrace's major port.

Thrace and northern Macedonia contain the lower courses of main Greek rivers. The river conventionally called the Maritsa rises in western Bulgaria and flows generally south from the Turkish city of Edirne (formerly called Adrianople) to the Aegean, forming the border between Turkey and Greece. The river is known to the Turks as the Meric and to the Greeks as the Evros. That part of the Evros valley located in Greek Thrace is one of the country's important lowlands. The northern border with Bulgaria runs through the Rodhopi Mountains, a barren and sparsely populated area. To the west of the Evros valley the Rodhopi range becomes a wide plateau that reaches south almost to Alexandroupolis, effectively dividing the plains of Greek Thrace. Because of the plateau and the body of water known as Lake Vistonis (actually a lagoon); the plains of Thrace are, in effect, separated into three distinct lowlands. These plains are the key features of the three provinces that make up the region.

The province of Evros has been an important agricultural area for many centuries; the low-lying land, fertile soil, and adequate water from the Evros River and its tributaries have generally ensured good crops, particularly cereals. Thrace was the region in which a Turkish minority was allowed to remain during the massive population exchanges of the 1920s. Most of the residents are Greek, however, many of them having arrived as refugees during the exchanges (see Religion, this ch.). The provinces of Rodhopi and Xanthi are also blessed with fertile plains, with tobacco an important crop. The Muslim minority lives primarily in this area.

Other than the Evros and the Nestos rivers, which are on the region's borders, there are no major rivers in Greek Thrace. Many of the minor rivers and streams of the region have very irregular flow, becoming torrents during the rainy

*Figure 6. Thrace, 1985*

season and trickles during the dry months. All drain toward the Aegean.

The Thracian coastline is generally smooth and uniform, particularly when compared with the highly irregular coast-lines of the rest of the country. The town of Lagos is located at the one major indentation along the Thracian coast, where

85

there is a narrow opening from the Aegean into Lake Vistonis, an important spawning area for many varieties of fish.

The island of Samothrace is administered as part of the province of Evros. The island, located southwest of Alexandroupolis, had a population of 2,871 in 1981. Lacking any good harbors or anchorages—its steep cliffs sometimes rise directly from the sea—Samothrace has not figured prominently in the politics of the Aegean area. The poor soils and mountainous terrain do not favor agriculture; olives have been the major crop. Because of difficult access, fishing has never been important. The name of Samothrace became well known in the nineteenth century when a French expedition to the island found the statue known as the Winged Victory of Samothrace, one of the treasures of the Louvre in Paris.

### Macedonia

Macedonia, which also bears the name of what was historically a much larger area, is the largest Greek geographical region, containing 13 provinces and the small autonomous area of Mount Athos (see fig. 7). In the fourth century B.C., under Alexander the Great, the Macedonian Empire reached into Persia, India, and Egypt but was short-lived; the region was later dominated by Romans, Slavs, and Turks. In 1913, Macedonia was divided between Yugoslavia and Greece.

The Greek portion of Macedonia extends from the Nestos River, the lower course of which divides Macedonia from Thrace, to the Albanian border in the west. Its northern boundary runs through the mountain ranges that Greece shares with Bulgaria and Yugoslavia. Much of the southern boundary is the Aegean coastline, the length of which is greatly extended by the irregular configuration of the Khalkidhiki Peninsula, from which three narrow peninsulas jut into the Aegean. The easternmost peninsula is the location of Mount Athos, the autonomous theocracy where monks from various countries have inhabited monasteries for over 1,000 years (see Religion, this ch.).

Like the rest of the country, Macedonia is very mountainous, but the mountains are interrupted by valleys and coastal plains, and the region has some important agricultural areas. The plain of Drama, the Struma valley, and the Vardar valley are of particular importance to the economy of the entire country as well as of the region. The plain of Drama, located in the province of the same name just west of Thrace, contains

*Figure 7.   Macedonia, 1985*

some of the best tobacco-growing land in Europe. Tobacco is also grown in the Strimon valley; cotton, olives, apples, and peaches are other important crops. The same crops are grown in the fertile valley of the Vardar River.

Thessaloniki is located at the head of the Gulf of Thessaloniki on a natural harbor. As a port, Thessaloniki is second only to the Piraeus complex, and as a city it is second only to Athens. Thessaloniki has become the major city of the north and contains the second largest university in Greece.

Thasos, the island lying near the delta of the Nestos River, is administered by the province of Kavala. The 13,111 (1981 census) inhabitants of the island are mostly engaged in subsistence agriculture. In classical times, about the middle of the first millennium B.C., Thasos had a prosperous community that thrived on the mineral wealth of the island, including gold and fine marble. Such wealth and prosperity attracted invaders like the Athenians, Macedonians, Romans, Genoese, Turks, Egyptians, and Aegean pirates. The island was finally awarded to Greece after the Balkan wars of 1912-13, but the mineral wealth of the island had long been exhausted except for some zinc mines. In the 1970s Thasos became a tourist mecca and a weekend resort for prosperous Macedonians, and other economic hopes were offered by the oil discovered off its shores in 1974 (see Energy, ch. 3).

Although much of Macedonia covers rugged terrain, it is generally well served by transportation, particularly the eastern two-thirds of the area; Thessaloniki is a principal hub of road and rail facilities. In 1985 Greece's main highway and main railroad systems were the Athens-Thessaloniki routes. From Thessaloniki there were two railroads and one road into Bulgaria.

### Epirus

Southwest of Macedonia and south of Albania lies the region of Epirus, once again the Greek portion of a greater Balkan territory divided after the breakup of the Ottoman Empire. The southern limit of Epirus is the same as it has always been—the Gulf of Amvrakikos, the site of Octavian's naval victory at Actium over the fleets of Anthony and Cleopatra in 31 B.C. The islands lying just off the coast of Epirus in the Ionian Sea are a separate geographical region (see fig. 8).

The high peripheral mountains have always hindered communications; until after World War II, Epirus was the most isolated of Greece's mainland regions. Because the mountain ranges run north-south, communication with Albania has traditionally been easier than with other areas of Greece, but that communication was ended by postwar political barriers. There is still only one major east-west pass through the Pindus Mountains—the mountains that run north-south from the border toward the Gulf of Corinth—the Metsovon Pass. Igoumenitsa, a provincial capital, is a terminus for ferry service between Greece and Brindisi in southern Italy.

Epirus has long been known as one of the more backward regions of Greece, partly because of generally poor land, partly because of inadequate farming methods, and partly because of centuries of foreign domination and isolation. Fragmentation of farms and general poverty have caused out-migration.

*Figure 8.   Epirus, Thessaly, and Ionian Islands, 1985*

**Thessaly**

Across the Pindus watershed from Epirus and south of Macedonia is the region of Thessaly, which stretches to the Aegean Sea (see fig. 8). The extensive plains of Thessaly are among the most important agricultural lands in the country. Although the fertile plains of Thessaly have been known as grain-growing areas for many centuries, uncontrolled flooding and poor land use kept farming methods primitive and restricted production. The agrarian system employed by the Turks during their five centuries of domination prevented any modernization or improvement in agriculture. The Greek landlords who replaced the Turks retained the system of large estates until early in the 1920s, when those estates were broken up and some improvements in agriculture were introduced. Between the two world wars flood-control projects initiated by the government (aided by the British) greatly improved the newly diversified agriculture of the plains.

The mechanization of agriculture has helped Thessaly retain its ancient reputation as a granary; it is a major producer of wheat, and olives, tobacco, and some vegetables are also important crops. Thessaly is the leading cattle-raising area, and Vlach shepherds still move great flocks of sheep and goats into the high Pindus areas for summer pasturage and back to lower levels during the winter.

The municipalities of Volos and New Ionia plus six separate communes constitute the urban agglomeration called Greater Volos. Volos is located at the head of the almost land-locked Gulf of Pagasitikos, from which Jason and the Argonauts are said to have sailed in search of the Golden Fleece. Handling the agricultural products of the plains of Thessaly as well as the chromite mined in the mountains has made Volos one of Greece's major ports.

Mount Olympus, which the ancient Greeks believed to be the home of the gods, is located on the northeast corner of Thessaly almost on the Macedonian boundary. Olympus, at 2,917 meters, is the highest mountain in Greece; its peak is usually snow covered and often obscured by clouds.

Several islands of the Northern Sporades archipelago, including Skiathos, Skopelos, and Alonnisos (populations roughly 4,100, 4,500 and 1,500, respectively, in 1981), are administered by the province of Magnisia, the capital of which is Volos. The island of Skiros lying farther to the southeast is also one of the Northern Sporades, but it is included in the province of Evvoia.

## Ionian Islands

The Ionian Islands are grouped as a region more for administrative convenience than for geographic unity. Official sources state that the numerous islands make up about 1.8 percent of Greece's total area, or about 2,387 square kilometers. Many of the islands are uninhabited rocks, but each of the four largest islands and the surrounding satellites constitutes a province. The islands, islets, and rocks are spread along the coast from Albania to the Peloponnesus (see fig. 8).

The northermost and second largest of the islands is Corfu (the province of Kerkira), separated from the mainland of both Greece and Albania by the Corfu Channel. Corfu has a mountain range stretching across its northern and widest area that almost separates the northern coastal plain from the remainder of the island. From north to south the terrain changes from mountainous to hilly to lowland, and much of it is fertile and intensely cultivated. Regular ferry service is maintained between Igoumenitsa on the mainland and the municipality of Kerkira.

Several miles to the south, off the coast of Central Greece, is the island of Levkas. The province and its capital bear the same name as the island. Levkas is the smallest of the four major islands of the region and, with only 21,863 inhabitants in 1981, the smallest province in the country. The center of the island is mountainous, leaving the coastal lowlands as the main agricultural area, but there are upland basins where soils are fertile.

Kefallinia, the largest of the Ionian Islands, is located directly west of the Gulf of Patraikos. The province is very mountainous, and arable land is scarce. The island of Ithaki, lying just to the northeast, is included in this province. Very mountainous also, it has little arable land, but currants and olives are coaxed out of its rocky soil, as they are in Kefallinia. Homer's story of Odysseus, king of Ithaki 30 centuries ago, still lures tourists to the island.

The southernmost province in the region is Zakinthos, and the island, the province, and the capital all bear the same name. Zakinthos lies south of Kefallinia and west of the Peloponnesus. Zakinthos has a wide, fertile plain flanked on the west by low mountains that drop precipitously to the sea; more land is cultivated there than on the other Ionian islands. Currants are grown for export. There is regular ferry service from Zakinthos to Killini on the west coast of the Peloponnesus.

### Central Greece

South of Epirus and Thessaly, stretching from the Ionian Sea to the Aegean Sea and including the elongated island of Euboea, is the region known as Central Greece (see fig. 9). On most maps, Euboea appears to be almost connected to the mainland, but it is actually separated by a waterway that in some places measures 61 meters across.

The region of Central Greece is made up of seven provinces, which bear names that have been used since long before the Christian Era. Attica, Aetolia, Euboea, and Boetia, for example, have designated the same areas since Odysseus sailed to the Trojan War. Athens—located in the province of Attica—is

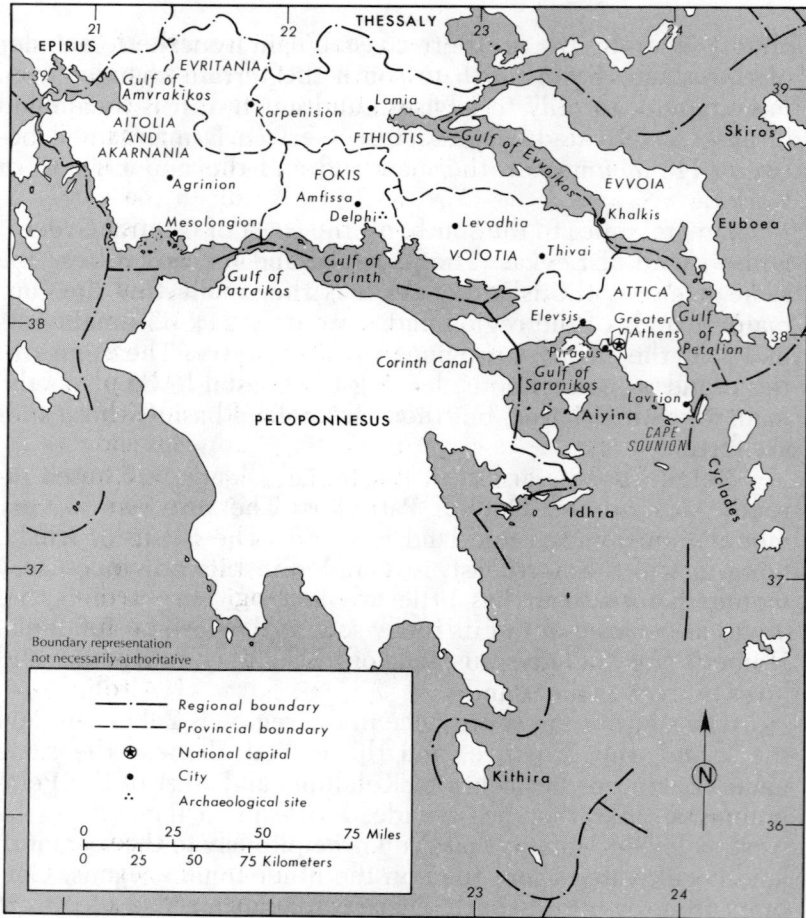

*Figure 9. Central Greece, 1985*

the country's capital. Piraeus, the chief port, is west of Athens. Greater Athens comprised 41 municipalities and 15 communes in 1985, and its population numbered 3,027,331 in 1981. Athens was the hub of Greece's cultural and commercial activity in the late twentieth century, just as it was 25 centuries earlier when ruled by Pericles during its golden age. It is the main terminus for the country's transportation arteries.

Attica has known human settlement since Neolithic times and gave its name to an important dialect of Greek—Attic. The present-day province is mountainous in the north but levels off to plains that extend from Athens to Cape Sounion at the end of the Attic peninsula. The plains near Athens do not compare with those of Thessaly in fertility, but rain and irrigation make the plains arable enough for the production of grains, olives, figs, and cotton. The foothills make good pastures for herds of sheep, goats, and cattle. The area of Lavrion in the extreme southeast near Cape Sounion has long been known as a source of minerals such as silver, lead, zinc, and iron. Bauxite is mined on Mount Parnassos, and marble is quarried at Mount Pendeli and Mount Imittos. Mount Parnassos is better known as the peak sacred to Apollo, the Muses, and Dionysius; the oracle of Delphi was located at the foot of the mountain. The province of Attica administers the islands of Aiyina, Idhra, Kithira, the last lying far to the south between the Peloponnesus and Crete.

Thivai (Thebes) and Levadhia are prosperous mill towns to which cotton farmers of the region deliver their crops. Levadhia is the capital of the province of Voiotia (Boetia). Amfissa, at the head of a plain noted for its fine olives, is the capital of the province of Fokis. Mesolongion, noted as the headquarters of the English poet Lord Byron when he led a group of Greek insurgents during the war of independence (1821-29), is the capital of the province of Aitolia and Akarnania.

### Peloponnesus

The Peloponnesus, a mountainous peninsula, is connected to Attica by an isthmus that is only six kilometers across at its narrowest point (see fig. 10). The Peloponnesus has a smooth west coast, but to the south and east there are fingerlike peninsulas separated by the sea. In the interior is the plateau of Arkadhia. The lowlands include a coastal plain to the north and west in Akhaia and Ilia; enclosed and semienclosed mountain basins watered by springs; river basins; and plains drained underground. The highest elevation is in the Taiyetos Mountains. Some of the place-names are among the most famous in classical Greek history and mythology—Argos, Sparta, and Olympia—home of the Olympic Games.

The Corinth Canal cuts through the isthmus to connect the Gulf of Corinth with the Gulf of Saronikis (also called the Gulf of Aegina), thus shortening the voyage from the Ionian Sea to Piraeus by 325 kilometers. In antiquity ships were beached near Corinth and dragged across the isthmus on a cobblestone road, in preference to a long voyage through pi-

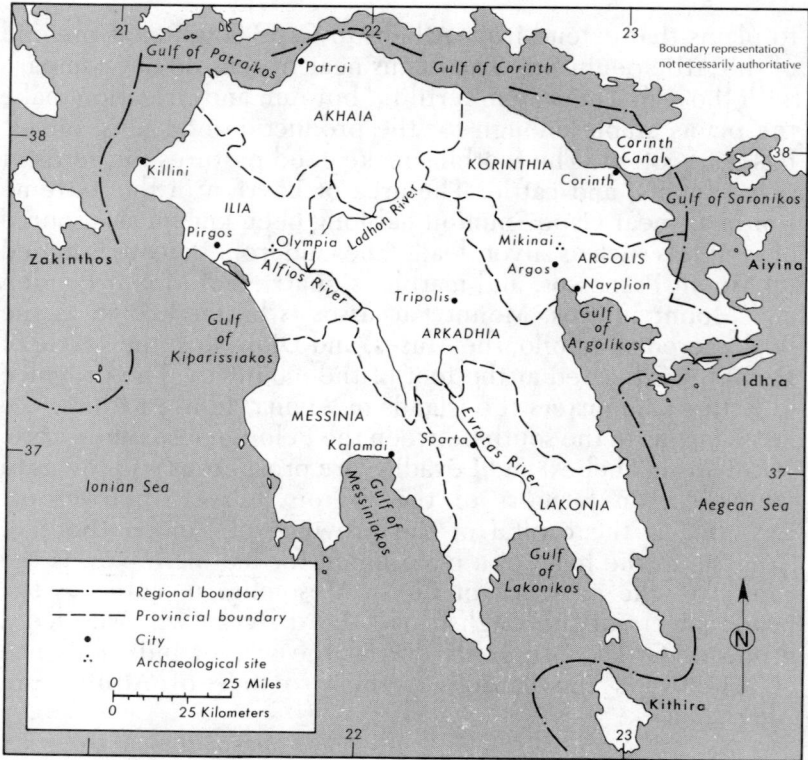

*Figure 10. Peloponnesus, 1985*

rate-infested seas. The possibility of a canal across the isthmus had been discussed many centuries before the time of Christ. During the Roman era, Emperor Nero had ordered the digging of a canal, but the project failed. Finally dug between 1881 and 1893, the canal is 6.3 kilometers long and 24.6 meters wide.

To a great extent the physical geography of the Peloponnesus has determined its settlement patterns; only one municipality, Tripolis, is located in the mountainous interior. Sparta is a municipality several kilometers from the coast at the head of a plain. The other major cities are on the periphery of the peninsula: Patrai, an important industrial and commercial center, the largest Peloponnesian city and one of Greece's major ports; and Kalamai, in the southwestern Peloponnesus, also an industrial and commercial center and a seaport. Co-

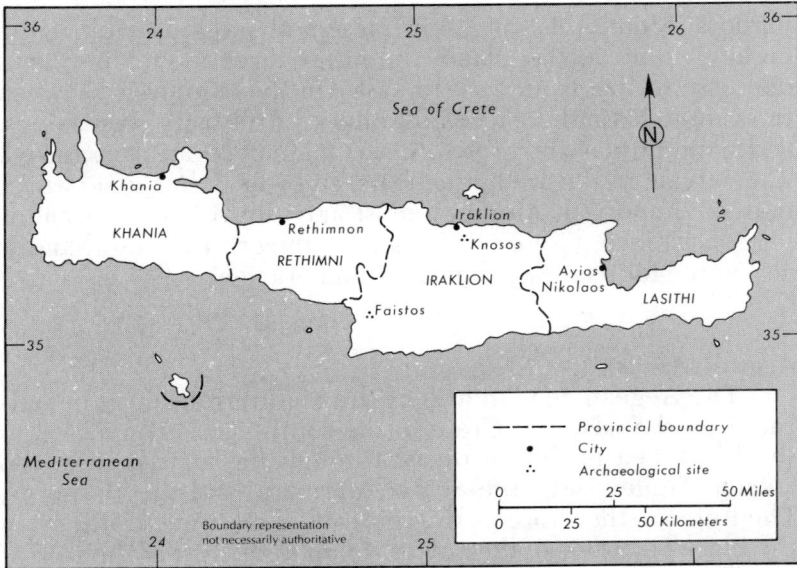

*Figure 11.   Crete, 1985*

rinth, famous in classical times and the source of the word *currant* because it was once the main exporter of that crop, is now relatively unimportant. The alluvial plains—Argolis in the east and Lakonia and Messinia in the south—are fertile but require irrigation. Most of the region's rivers, including the Evrotas and the Alfios, are dry during the summer months, when rainfall is scarce.

## Crete

Crete, the site of the ancient Minoan civilization, is the largest of Greece's islands and the fifth largest island in the Mediterranean Sea (see fig. 11; Ancient Greece, ch. 1). Crete is long, narrow and mountainous. In ancient times copper, iron, lead and zinc were mined on the island, but the veins were exhausted, and the only extractive industry in the 1970s was the quarrying of gypsum and limestone. The northern coast of Crete is heavily indented like much of the mainland and has some fine natural harbors. Along the southern coast, however, the mountains often drop precipitously to the sea as sheer cliffs; the coast is very regular, and there are no natural harbors. Mount Ida, at 2,456 meters above sea level, is the highest point on the island; the other three mountain blocks decrease in size from west to east. On the isthmuses between the mountains and the foothills, olives, citrus fruits, vegetables, and wine grapes are grown. Goats and sheep are also raised. The cereals grown are barley, oats, and wheat, but some wheat must be imported. Although most agriculture on the island is for subsistence, Crete is a major producer of olive oil and is also noted for its raisins, currants, and oranges.

### Aegean Islands

The Aegean Sea, an arm of the Mediterranean, is demarcated by the island of Crete in the south and is connected to the Black Sea in the northeast through the Dardanelles (the ancient Hellespont), the Sea of Marmara, and the Bosporus. The Aegean, therefore, is the route of all maritime traffic from the Black Sea ports of the Soviet Union to the rest of the world.

The term *Aegean Islands* includes Crete and all the islands in the Aegean Sea between Greece and Turkey—the area of the Mediterranean world often referred to as the cradle of Western civilization (see fig. 12). The islands are difficult taskmasters for those who have had to eke out a precarious agricultural existence on the mountain slopes or narrow plains, but the islands have proved to be treasure troves for archaeologists. They also attract tourism, which has brought problems of its own, such as crowding, pollution, water shortages, and unplanned development. A few of the islands belong to Turkey, but most belong to Greece. The population of the Aegean Islands is mainly Greek, but a small Turkish-speaking minority still reside in the Dodecanese. In the early 1980s rights to the seabed and continental shelf and territorial waters were in dispute between Turkey and Greece (see Greek-Turkish Aegean Disputes, ch. 5).

Many of the islands are remnants of a land bridge that once connected Greece and Asia Minor. The islands are actually mountaintops that remained above water when the land bridge subsided millions of years ago. Some of the islands are of volcanic origin; a massive eruption on the island of Thira in the sixteenth century B.C. is held by some scholars to have caused the decline of the Minoan civilization that had spread from Crete throughout the Aegean as well as to parts of the Greek mainland and other areas of the Mediterranean.

The archipelago known as the Cyclades (the province of

*Figure 12.   Aegean Islands, 1985*

Kikladhes) is a group of islands lying southeast of Attica. In Greek mythology the Cyclades rotated around Dhilos, which was revered as the birthplace of Apollo and his twin sister, Artemis. Although uninhabited, Dhilos is an archaeological site and the location of a museum and hence a hub of tourist activity. Most of the other islands of the archipelago are dry, rocky, and infertile, but a few, such as Naxos, the largest, and Siros, site of the capital of the province, grow fruit and vegetables. There is some mining of sulfur, bauxite, and magnesium and some quarrying of marble in the Cyclades, but tourism is an important source of income for the islanders. One of the world's most famous works of art, the Venus de Milo, was found on the volcanic island of Milos in 1820.

East of the Cyclades and just off the coast of Turkey is the Dodecanese archipelago (also known to some geographers as the Southern Sporades; the province name is Dhodhekanisos), which includes 18 uninhabited islands. The Dodecanese were held by Italy from 1912 until 1947. The largest island of the group and the most famous is Rhodes. Rhodes was an important trading center before the Christian Era, and the 320-meter bronze statue of the sun god Helios erected at the entrance to the harbor of Rhodes was one of the seven wonders of the ancient world. A long central ridge runs from one end of Rhodes to the other. The foothills and coastal plains are generally well watered and fertile, and the island is noted for its fruits and vegetables. Other notable islands in the group are Kos, Kalimnos, and Patmos. As in most other areas of Greece, tourism is the fastest growing industry.

The province just north of the Dodecanese is Samos, consisting of the islands of Samos, Ikaria, and the Fournoi group. Samos, home of the mathematician Pythagoras, has named a fishing village in his honor. Samos is covered with trees (a great rarity for Greece), including firs and cypresses that, along with the olive groves and vineyards, give the island a green hue uncommon in the area. The islands of Ikaria and the Fournoi group are not so blessed with fertile land, and most of the population resides on Samos; because economic opportunities are limited, as on other Greek islands, emigration draws off the young people.

The next province to the north is Khios, which includes the island of Chios and a few nearby islets. The island of Chios claims to be the birthplace of Homer, but that honor is also claimed by several other Greek towns. Much of the island is mountainous, but the climate is favorable to the cultivation of citrus fruits, figs, and grapes on the open, fertile plains of the south and east. Since antiquity Chios has been famous for its production of mastic. Sometimes called a natural chewing gum, mastic is produced from shrubs that are cultivated nowhere else in the world and is used in the making of a Greek liqueur and in the manufacture of varnishes and dental adhesives.

The northernmost province in the Aegean Islands region is Lesvos, consisting of the islands of Lesbos, Lemnos, and Ayios Evstratios. After Crete and Euboea, Lesbos is the largest of Greece's islands. Two large gulfs indent the coasts of Lesbos, but both have narrow inlets difficult for shipping. Therefore Mitilini, with its small harbor, is the main commercial port. The terrain is rugged, but the coastal lowlands and lower foot-hills are fertile. Olive oil is the chief export; grain and wine grapes are grown for home consumption. The island of Lemnos supports a decreasing number of inhabitants; with less mountainous terrain than other Aegean islands, scarce water and resources, and searing winds, the island is more suited for raising sheep and goats than agriculture. In recent years Lemnos became a contentious issue between Greece and Turkey.

## Climate

The hot, dry summers and damp, cold winters of the Mediterranean climate generally prevail throughout the country, but in the north and into the center of the mainland, continental influences are also felt. There are many local variations because of altitude and proximity to the sea. The mean July temperature is about 27°C at sea level. Summer heat is moderated along the coasts and on the islands by prevailing northerly winds that blow daily. After the September rain, sea winds become squally and turbulent in contrast to the fine sailing weather provided by these winds in the Aegean summer.

Temperatures in general increase from north to south in Greece, especially in winter. For 1981 the maximum absolute temperature was 41.6°C in Larisa (in Thessaly) in June, and the minimum absolute temperature was minus 12.6°C in Tripolis (in the mountains of the Peloponnesus) in January. Altitude is an important factor, and many of the mountain peaks over 600 meters—even in the southern Peloponnesus and on Crete—are snow covered for several months a year and have over 40 days of frost. It is harder to generalize about rainfall, which may be slightest in the eastern plains and wettest on the coast; Epirus receives more precipitation because it lies on the windward side of the Pindus Mountains and receives prevailing winds off the Ionian Sea.

In addition to the mountainous regions, Greek climatic regions include Attica and the Aegean Islands, the west, and the continental area to he northeast. Attica and the Aegean Islands share monthly average high temperatures. There are periods of drought in the Aegean area, except in southern Crete or where moderated by altitude; the Ionian Islands have fewer problems with rainfall, except in summer. Among both groups of islands, each island may have its own local winds and eddies. In the lowlands of the south and west of Greece, frost is rare, and winter is mild because of the cyclonic depressions. The islands are especially warm into October and November. In the west and south there are sudden rains in the late fall, which is the beginning of the winter rainfall peak.

In the northeast the climate of Macedonia, like that of Thrace (and to a lesser extent the Peloponnesian highlands), is Mediterranean with continental influences, the latter more pronounced away from the coast. The continental influence affects temperature and precipitation. Twenty to 30 days of frost are common, and there is sufficient rainfall to moderate somewhat the dry summers. The Mediterranean climate generally prevails on the plains, both coastal and inland, but in the mountains the colder continental winters are common, and rain occurs in fall and summer. Winds may channel cold air through valleys like those of the Vardar and Struma rivers.

## Population

As of July 1984 the population of Greece was estimated to be 9,984,000. According to the 1981 census, there were 9,740,417 persons. During the 1970-82 period the annual growth rate averaged 1 percent. The 1981 census figure represented an increase of 10.7 percent since 1971 as compared with only a 4.5-percent increase between 1961 and 1971. The 1981 increase was somewhat misleading, however. A careful check reveals that births accounted for only 7.3 percent of the 10.7 percent, the remainder being attributable to a considerable number of repatriated emigrants in the late 1970s.

Using the World Bank's (see Glossary) annual growth rate data, it was estimated that Greece's stationary population would be 12 million in the year 2000, that is, a population with zero growth and a constant age structure. A total fertility rate (the average births per woman surviving to childbearing age) of 2.1 in the early 1980s suggested that the population was close to replacement level already. The difference between births and deaths for 1982 showed an increase of only 51,147.

Birth rates have been falling. Since World War II the number of births per 1,000 inhabitants has dropped from the peak of 20.3 in 1951 to 14.5 in 1981. This rate was still relatively high compared with 13 per 1,000 population in Western Europe in the 1980s. By the early 1960s the drop in the birth rate was related to the limitation of the number of children to two or three and the desire to provide children with a better education and to avoid straining limited housing and income. By the 1970s the drop in birth rates was also associated with urbanization, declining infant mortality, abortions, increased educational level of parents, emigration, and increased numbers of women in the labor force. An early 1980s study by the University of Athens estimated that the approximately 150,000 births annually were balanced by 150,000 abortions annually; other estimates of abortions were as high as 400,000, although the Greek Orthodox church disapproved and a 1978 law had legalized abortions only under particular circumstances, such as rape, incest, an abnormal fetus, or danger to the mother's health. To combat the large numbers of illegal abortions, the Socialist government has begun a network of family planning centers to encourage use of birth control in addition to abortion or condoms.

Life expectancy and infant mortality rates reflected rising living standards. Life expectancy in Greece has risen in the last decade from 67 years for men and 70 years for women in 1960 to 72 years for men and 76 years for women in 1982. The reduction in infant mortality (for children under one year) per 1,000 live births has been particularly dramatic—from 50 in 1960 to 14 in 1982. Although people lived longer, crude death rates increased 19.2 percent, from seven per 1,000 in 1960 to nine per 1,000 in 1982 because of the changing age structure.

The age structure of the Greek population is changing. Age structure is important because of the implications for social security, taxes, the health care system, the work force, and the number of dependents that a wage earner has to support. The absolute number of Greeks over age 65 increased from 514,099 in 1951 to 1,284,002 in 1981. The most productive age-group, 15 to 64 years, accounted for 63 percent of the population in 1981. Those over 65 accounted for 13 percent of

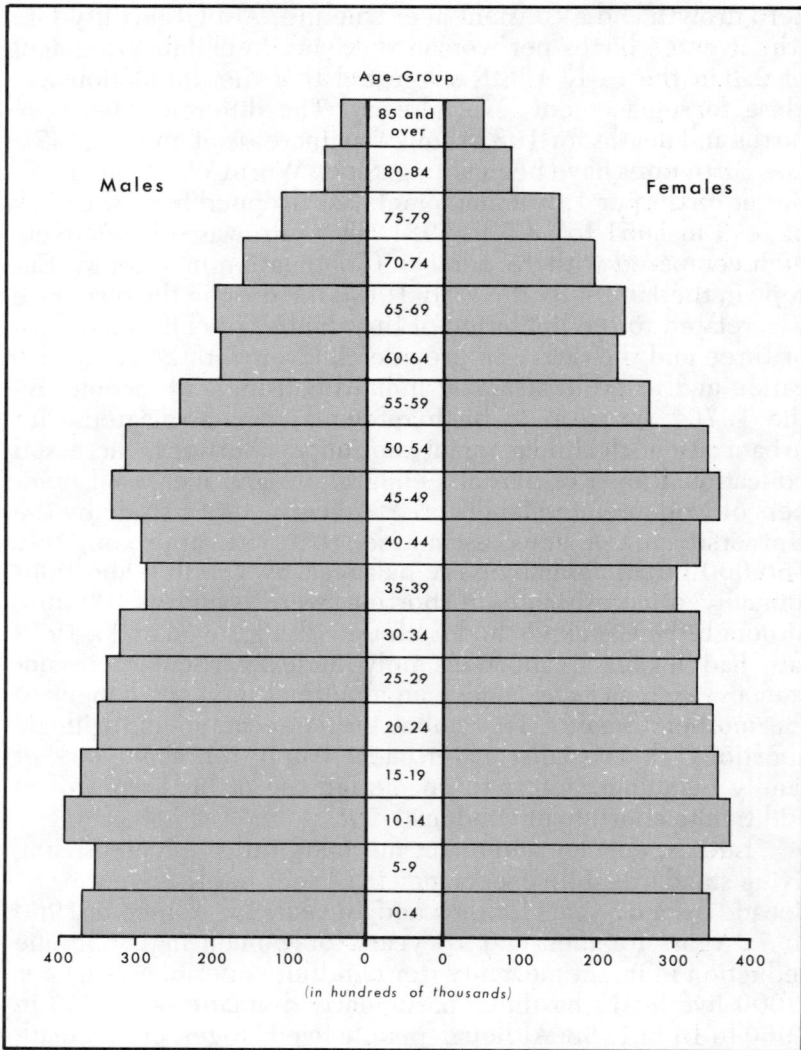

Age-Group

Males

Females

85 and over

80-84

75-79

70-74

65-69

60-64

55-59

50-54

45-49

40-44

35-39

30-34

25-29

20-24

15-19

10-14

5-9

0-4

400  300  200  100   0    0   100  200  300  400

*(in hundreds of thousands)*

Source: Based on information from Greece, National Statistical Service, *Monthly
Statistical Bulletin*, Athens, 29, No. 4, April 1984, 9.

*Figure 13.   Population by Age and Sex, 1981 Census*

the population in 1981. As the number of those aging increased, the proportion of children (up to age 14) decreased
from 32 percent in 1928 to 24 percent in 1981 (see fig. 13).

Migration, by removing the young and active from the rural areas and from Greece as a whole, accentuated this change. Athens, for example, had a large concentration of working-age population in 1981, when 67.1 percent of its population was in the 15 to 64 group and 10.7 percent was over 65 (as opposed to rural areas in which only 59.8 percent was in the 15 to 64 group and 17.2 percent was over 65). The age structure of the Greek population in the early 1980s was not very different from that of the other European Communities (EC) members.

Generally, since 1950 there has been a greater proportion of both sexes' marrying and of marriage at younger ages. For this reason and because of increased life expectancy and a low rate of divorce, the number of married persons is rising. In 1981 there were 7.3 marriages per 1,000 inhabitants (a rate higher than in France, Belgium, or the Federal Republic of Germany [West Germany] but lower than in the United States). Most Greeks married while in their twenties, and women married at a younger age than men (because of family pressures to marry as soon as possible); grooms averaged 27.7 years and brides 22.7 years in 1981. In 1981 there were 6,349 divorces, but this figure dates from before the 1982 law permitting divorce on the ground of common consent or four years of separation; it might be expected that divorces will increase. Earlier marriage has also been linked to earlier, although not increased, childbearing; 65.6 percent of births in 1981 were to mothers between 20 and 29 years of age.

The population in the early 1980s was characterized by its urban concentration and uneven distribution. Data for 1982 showed 64 percent of the population classified as urban— Greater Athens and Greater Thessaloniki together accounting for about two-fifths of the approximately 10 million total inhabitants. The Greater Athens area alone had 3,027,331 persons in 1981, or about 30 percent of all Greeks (see table 3, Appendix A). The average population density was 73.8 persons per square kilometer in 1981, but this figure was meaningless since much of the terrain is mountainous and uninhabitable. About 86 percent of the population lived on the mainland peninsula, the balance being islanders. Over the years the number of islanders decreased steadily, many of them seeking better economic opportunities on the mainland and elsewhere.

It has been reported that Greece is suffering from "runaway urbanization" and "stagnation of the mid-size cities." In the 1960s Athens grew by 37 percent and Thessaloniki by 46 percent. Growth slowed somewhat in the 1970s to 19 and 27 percent, respectively. These two cities overshadowed all others, especially if the Athens-Thessaloniki axis (the two cities and the areas surrounding and connecting them) is considered. Athens tended to attract migrants from southern Greece and the islands, and Thessaloniki attracted those from the north. Other cities lagged behind; even if they showed growth, it was not enough to catch up. Greater Patrai, the third largest city, having 154,596 inhabitants in 1981, grew 16 and 28 percent in the 1960s and 1970s, respectively. Greater Iraklion (110,958 in 1981) and Greater Volos (107,407 in 1981) showed considerable growth—21 and 31 percent for the former and 9 and 22 percent for the latter, respectively, in the 1960s and 1970s.

Urban areas grew at the expense of rural areas. Compared with cities, rural areas offered low economic returns, inadequate services, underemployment, and lower standards of living. Industrialization and growth of the service sector offered economic opportunities to villagers who admired urban values and standards of living; experiences in refugee camps during the Civil War (1946-49) or abroad as labor migrants in the 1960s and 1970s stimulated villagers' desire to move to the city, as did new roads, the mass media, and the example set by relatives and friends. Between 1955 and 1971 roughly 1.5 million farmers left rural areas, 600,000 of them to Greek cities, the remainder abroad; between 1971 and 1981 some 280,000 migrants moved to Athens and Thessaloniki. Rural areas also lost the external migrants who decided to live in cities upon their repatriation. The only rural areas that received migrants were those growing cash crops and employing mechanization. The rural-urban migration appears to have diminished somewhat in the 1980s, partly because of the development of tourism in Crete and the Dodecanese Islands, offering hope to the Aegean and Ionian islands that lost population in the 1951-81 period.

## Emigration

Greece has a long tradition of emigration, a phenomenon not uncommon in the Mediterranean. From the eighth century B.C. Greeks have shown their talent for establishing new communities away from the home base. Participants in the Mediterranean history of seafaring and colonization, the ancient Greeks migrated to the Black Sea, the European shores, and throughout the Aegean in the first phase of Greek outflow. During the spread of the empire of Alexander the Great they migrated as far as the Indus River. After the fall of the Byzantine Empire to the Ottoman Turks, Greeks again migrated outside what is now Greece. The reasons have remained constant over time: overpopulation, the pursuit of a livelihood, and the promotion of commerce, although economic and political circumstances have varied.

The formation of the Greek state during the nineteenth century was complicated by the scattering of ethnic Greeks; they were not concentrated only in the area of the southern Balkan Peninsula and the Aegean Sea. Because the Ottomans were not interested in commerce, by the end of the eighteenth century, Greek merchants, professionals, artisans, and shopkeepers had dominated commerce in the eastern Mediterranean, and their trade extended to cities such as Odessa, Constantinople, and Smyrna and in areas as widespread as southern France, Asia Minor, the Balkans, Central Europe, and the Black Sea. This dispersion, referred to as the diaspora (which in Greek literally means dispersion), persisted into the twentieth century when events in Russia, Turkey, Egypt, Bulgaria, and the British Empire (to which Greeks had turned after the formation of the Balkan states) forced these people to give up the Greek language and identity or return to the Greek state as refugees as late as 1950 (see the Ottoman Occupation, ch. 1).

To some extent creation of Greek communities outside Greece persisted in a somewhat different form until the present. After 1890 migrants went overseas, to the United States in particular until World War II and then increasingly to Canada and Australia. The Greeks in this overseas migration tended to be rural agriculturists who would play more modest economic roles in the host economies than the earlier merchants. In the United States almost 1 million claimed some Greek ancestry in the 1980 census; Greek-American church and political leaders, however, have estimated close to 3 million of Greek descent. In comparison with a total 1984 population of almost 10 million in Greece, this represents a sizable community, especially since only three cities in Greece are larger than the Greek community in the New York City area and only six cities in Greece larger than that in the Chicago area. Communities grew so large because of chain migration, that is, pioneer migrants would encourage kin or compatriots to follow them, who would in turn bring others; the majority of migrants would have someone offering them help with initial orientation, housing, and jobs.

By the mid-twentieth century, migration overseas was overshadowed by the number of Greek guest workers in Western Europe, especially in West Germany. Before 1960 three out of four Greek migrants went overseas, but during the 1960s and early 1970s over two-thirds of long-term emigrants streamed toward Western Europe. After a recruitment agreement was signed by the Greek and West German governments in 1960, between 1960 and 1973 over 80 percent of Greek migrants to Western Europe went to West Germany.

There have been important implications of emigration and repatriation for Greece in the last decades. Labor supply and unemployment have been affected. For example, a Greek labor shortage between 1971 and 1973 was relieved by immigration (much of it illegal) from Pakistan and Egypt. The increase in population between the censuses of 1971 and 1981 reflected the repatriation of Greeks, often of childbearing age, who had been working abroad. The government had expected that the emigrants would receive training while abroad, but the upgrading of skills turned out to be mythical or irrelevant upon their return; migrants themselves had been more interested in working overtime than in taking evening courses.

There is no doubt that thousands of Greeks have benefitted financially from the increased earnings of emigrants. Remittances and savings, upon which much official weight was placed, were not spent on capital investment but on housing (possibly as much as two-thirds of funds), land, and the importation of consumer goods, appliances, furnishings, and clothes. If spent in a manner that would generate employment, such money usually went into agricultural machinery or the service sector (see Other Foreign Exchange Earners, ch. 3). Returnees added to rural depopulation by flocking to Athens and Thessaloniki, for they had become accustomed to urban life and industrial work discipline. Even though they often switched from agriculture, they were reluctant to take what they considered in the Greek context to be ill-paying and low-prestige manufacturing jobs; they preferred to consider reemigration or to join the tertiary sector, frequently using their savings to become self-employed.

Although clearly economically motivated, this emigration had more than economic repercussions, for it delayed marriage and family unity, if not childbearing. It is important not to see emigration as a break with family left behind, because migrants often maintained families at home or pursued family goals, often considering their stint temporary; this mode of maintaining family who remained in poor mountain villages had a conservative motive but possibly revolutionary effects. Whether important values were changed remains to be seen; a 1976 study claimed to find migrants agreeing that husbands should help spouses with housework and married women should work, as well as expressing increased interest in politics and unions. Even if such findings should prove true of all migrants, what people say and do may differ greatly.

There were two important periods of emigration and return in Greece. The early twentieth century migration was paralleled by the large-scale emigration of workers elsewhere in Western Europe in the 1960s and early 1970s. During the beginning of the twentieth century over 400,000 migrants went overseas, mostly to the United States between 1910 and 1929, and during the period of 1950-75 between 312,000 and 600,000 Greeks went to Western Europe. The first wave ended in the 1930s and the second in the mid-1970s as a result of economic reverses in the sites of migration. Indeed, following each of these periods of economic downturn, there was an influx of returnees, in one case not only from overseas sites but also from Asia Minor and in the other largely from West Germany. To give an idea of scale, between 1912 and 1921, there were 151,000 Greek migrants who returned home (as opposed to refugees); in the European migration, there was an estimated return between 1968 and 1977 of 238,000 from all over (of whom 161,000 came mostly from West Germany). In both periods of out-migration Greece lost over one-half of the natural increase in population and one-quarter of those in the most active working ages because young males predominated; the sex ratio of the total Greek population and the proportion of nonworkers was altered.

In neither case of population movement was such an emigration a onetime decision. Over half of those who had emigrated to the United States in the 1910-29 period returned to Greece, often for the duration of the Great Depression, returning to the United States later. From 1930 to 1949 there was no net outflow, first because of return, then because of war. Similarly, the net migration balance reached more than five (into Greece) per 1,000 population in 1975-77. Moreover, during the course of a 1980 survey of returnees, it was discovered that one-fifth of the total of 574 migrants had returned at least once to Greece and reemigrated; of those interviewed, 53 percent would return to West Germany if they could.

The two periods of emigration do differ in certain important ways. The destinations in Western Europe were much closer and were cheaper and easier to reach and return from; as a result, guest workers, as opposed to overseas migrants, less often waited until retirement to return. West Germany did not seem eager to encourage assimilation, and few Greeks became citizens. The migration to Europe grew rapidly, despite periods of economic crisis. The migration had a strong family character because the sex ratio was almost equal and 27.4 percent of Greeks in West Germany were under age 15 in 1977. Traditional migration had drawn on the southern mainland and the islands, while recruitment to West Germany drew on northern and central Greece. Migrants did not retain occupations pursued in Greece but were turned into members of the industrial proletariat, at least for the duration of their stay.

Overall, the emigrants represented some of Greece's most productive citizens, perhaps because of the selection at the time of application and again at the time of renewal of contracts. In the 1970s the overall average age was 28 for men and 25 for women; European emigrants averaged three years older. In the first stage of both overseas and European migration emigrants included mostly men; in a second stage emigrants included more women (most of whom went to work) accompanying husbands and relatives (most aged 15 to 44 and few over age 65). Once emigration began, a stimulating factor was the presence of relatives abroad. A man might go first and send home for his wife, brothers, or cousins. Even if not specifically urged to go, friends and relatives would become aware of how much money was being sent back and might decide to emulate the emigrant.

More data were available on European migrants than on migrants overseas. Seventy percent of migrants were from rural areas, one-half from Epirus, Thrace, Thessaly, and Macedonia. In the 1970s there were high rates of emigration from areas characterized by illiteracy, low internal migration, an increase in the population in the 1950s, a predominance of self-employment in the primary sector, more people over 65, larger households, and high unemployment and underemployment. Migration expert Demetrios Papademetriou provided a profile of West German migrants from data for the early 1970s. Workers were blue-collar, either unskilled or semiskilled, concentrated in high-paying manufacturing jobs, especially in metallurgy; what seemed to be frequent advancement from unskilled to semiskilled status was a result of the usual reclassification after the initial contract. Most European migrants were economically motivated. A substantial number, especially those with prior work experience, had been in agriculture. Migrants to West Germany were better educated than the Greek population at large. Some 51 percent of both sexes had six years of school, and 20 percent had four years; only 24 percent, though, had prior training, usually on-the-job. Twenty percent were single.

A 1980 survey of 574 migrants that had returned from West Germany to one of three Greek cities (Athens, Thessaloniki and Serrai) found similar results. The mean age was 42; the individual had left Greece at age 28, staying a mean of 11 years. A majority—80 percent—had returned in the 1976-79 period. This sample's educational level showed 70 percent having completed primary school and 10 percent having finished secondary school. Thirty-six percent were self-employed, and 58 percent were wage or salary earners, leaving only 6 percent as employers. Of the self-employed, three-quarters were in service occupations, such as construction workers, taxi drivers, or workers in groceries or cafés. Over half pursuing self-employment achieved it. The main reasons for migration were to earn money, save for ownership of a shop or company, improve the standard of living, buy a house, or escape unemployment in Greece. Ninety percent of those surveyed returned for the following reasons: to rejoin children, for family considerations, health problems, homesickness, for the sake of the children's education. Over three-quarters were able to send remittances.

The latest available figures (1982) counted 128,700 Greek members of the work force and a total of 300,800 Greeks in West Germany. It was not clear what the migrants remaining in West Germany would do. Until January 1988 Greeks will not enjoy the privilege of free emigration given to citizens of EC member countries. It may depend on how migrants weigh the state of the Greek economy against presumed security in West Germany. The 1980 survey of returnees showed that the fear of unemployment was realistic because 11.9 percent of respondents were unemployed at the time of the interview and respondents had spent an average of 9.5 months looking for work before finding it. One expert, however, suggests that the delay in finding employment was the result of overly high job expectations and the desire to use available unemployment benefits.

## Religion

The dominant religion of Greece is the Eastern Orthodox Church of Christ; over 96 percent of the population is believed to be identified with that faith. The Orthodox church is referred to in the Constitution as the "prevailing" or "established" religion of the country and thus gains certain privileges and obligations. The president of the republic must be Orthodox, sworn in according to church rites, and state holidays and ceremonies are synchronized with religious holidays. Proselytization by other religious groups is forbidden under the Constitution, but the fundamental law neither expressly defines proselytization nor enforces this prohibition. The Holy Scriptures may not be translated without permission, and the Holy Synod must be consulted on relevant drafted legislation on the organization or administration of the church. The church is dependent on the government for financial and legal support; the state pays the clergy, subsidizes the church budget, and administers its property. The government lends support through indirect taxes for church purposes, requires religious education at the primary and secondary levels, and also subsidizes higher religious education. In return, the church is supervised by the Ministry of National Education and Religion. The government announced in 1981 its official intention to separate church and state, but in 1985 the implications were not yet clear. A 1982 law offered civil marriage as an alternative to a Greek Orthodox ceremony, and abortion restrictions were liberalized in 1978 despite church teachings.

Christianity was given legal status as a religion in the Roman Empire in A.D. 313, and by the end of the century it had been established as the official faith of the empire. Also before the end of the century, Byzantium had become the capital of the eastern half of the empire, and the previously obscure bishop of that city had become the patriarch of Constantinople. Thereafter the western and eastern halves of the empire developed linguistic, cultural, and political differences.

Because of Constantinople's new political prominence, a church council awarded precedence to the bishop of Constantinople, making him second in the Christian church hierarchy after the bishop of Rome (the pope). In the ensuing centuries

*A Greek Orthodox Church
at Mistras
Courtesy Fadia Elia Estefan*

conflict between the two developed, culminating in mutual excommunication in 1054, sparked by disputed succession to the patriarchate. The schism was underlain by a combination of political, economic, linguistic, and cultural differences. On two theological issues discord proved insurmountable. In the Western church the pope emerged as the highest authority, whereas in the Eastern church the ultimate authority was conferred on the bishops in council. Another source of discord was the wording concerning the Holy Spirit in the Nicene Creed. After attempts to reconcile differences failed, the sacking of Constantinople in 1204 by the Crusaders made the split definitive between Western church and Eastern church.

In Greece the concept of motherland is closely associated with religion; thus, the day the Greeks refused to capitulate to Benito Mussolini in 1940 is classified in a catechism book as a religious holiday. As under the Byzantine (324-1453 A.D.) and Ottoman (1453-1821) empires, the modern state has been cast as defender of the faith. To appreciate the close relationship between "being Greek" and "being Orthodox," one must look back to the position the Orthodox church held during Byzantine and Ottoman rule. Despite a theoretical separation between the patriarch of Constantinople and the Byzantine emperor, there was interference in religious affairs by the emperor, as God's vice regent and ruler of an empire serving as the paradigm for heavenly order. The form of the emperor's vestments later became the form worn by Orthodox bishops, and he censed the altar, preached, and received communion like a priest. Church and state were considered unified yet distinct. The emperor initiated councils and executed their decrees but was to leave the decisions to the bishops.

The Turkish masters during Ottoman rule did not perceive their empire as a domain of various ethnic, linguistic, and political groups. Rather, they saw the world in terms of believers (Muslims) and nonbelievers (Orthodox Christians, Armenian Christians and Jews). From the first days of Muslim domination, the patriarch of Constantinople was invested with legal authority over the sultan's Orthodox Christian subjects regardless of their residence, language, or ethnicity. Because Islam did not allow for differentiating between civil and ecclesiastical authority, the patriarch became a combination religious leader and civil magistrate responsible only to the sultan (see The Ottoman Occupation, ch. 1).

The patriarch's new position gave him and the Orthodox hierarchy more power than under the Byzantine Empire with regard to civil justice, education, and ecclesiastical taxation. Church and state became interlocked as church positions were sought for temporal reasons and church policy and affairs were influenced by temporal interests. Conflicts of interest between the civil and ecclesiastical responsibilities of the hierarchy resulted. Over the years the patriarch and the hierarchy of the church became closely identified with Ottoman rule and did little to oppose the political establishment. Whatever else it had done up until Greek independence, however, the church had maintained Greek and Byzantine traditions during the centuries of Turkish occupation through the monasteries and the liturgy. The builders of the modern Greek state made use of the bond between Orthodoxy and nationalism. According to a popular history of the Greek war of independence from the Turks, the bishop of Patrai gave official church sanction to the national rebellion in early 1821 (see The War of Independence, 1821-29, ch. 1). The patriarch of Constantinople, held responsible for the rebellion, was hanged by the Turks.

The Church of Greece has been autocephalous since a group of Greek bishops joined with the new Greek parliament in the publication of a constitutional charter of the church in

1833 making the church, as well as the state, independent of Constantinople; in 1850 the patriarch recognized the Greek church's autocephaly (see Otto I, 1831-62, ch.1). For historical reasons relating to the subsequent growth of the Greek state, the Greek Orthodox church divided into the autocephalous Church of Greece, with 78 dioceses; the semiautonomous Church of Crete, with eight dioceses; the four dioceses of the Dodecanese Islands; and the theocratic community of Mount Athos, whose autonomy is guaranteed by the Constitution.

In the mid-1980s the 78 dioceses of the Church of Greece were governed by the Holy Synod, consisting of all the diocesan bishops and convening in Athens once a year at the request of and under the chairmanship of the primate—the archbishop of Athens. The primate, like the rest of the bishops, was elected by the Holy Synod, but civil interference has not been uncommon in the electoral process. Between annual convocations of the Holy Synod, the day-to-day administration of the church was handled by a small synod consisting of 12 bishops holding rotating one-year terms of office and the primate as chairman, who served as the thirteenth member of the supreme executive body.

The eight dioceses of Crete were administered by a synod presided over by the archbishop of Crete, whose see was at Iraklion. Crete and the four dioceses of the Dodecanese Islands were under the spiritual and administrative jurisdiction of the patriarch of Constantinople rather than of the primate of Greece. Mount Athos, in Greek Macedonia, was also spiritually dependent on the patriarch, but its administrative autonomy is guaranteed by the Constitution.

Although under the Ottoman Empire the sultan designated the patriarch of Constantinople politically responsible for all the Orthodox in the empire, there was never one Orthodox figure comparable in power and authority to the pope in the West. The patriarch in Constantinople is called the ecumenical patriarch and has been involved in discussions about unity with the pope since the Second Vatican Council in the 1960s, but no close union is envisioned any time soon. He may not interfere in the affairs of the 15 autocephalous churches or the other patriarchates into which Orthodoxy is subdivided. He is an ethnic Greek but must reside in Constantinople and be a Turkish citizen. Like the ecumenical patriarch, the archbishop of Athens has the honor and respect of fellow leaders but, unlike the pope, who is deemed to be infallible, depends on conciliar consensus and popularly approved decisions on ad-

ministration and doctrine. Orthodox emphasis is on the equality of all bishops and on local communities under bishops whose
relatively small dioceses mean they have time to preach, perform pastoral duties, and visit in the communities under their
jurisdiction. Each of the autocephalous churches uses its own
liturgical language and governs its own affairs but shares with
the other Orthodox churches sacraments, doctrine, and traditions regarded as "right" belief and worship emanating from
the early church, hence the term *Orthodox*.

The Orthodox church is also differentiated in several other
ways. Immediately after Orthodox babies are baptized with a
threefold immersion, the priest confirms them so that children
may receive Holy Communion, consisting of both leavened
bread and wine, from then on. The Annointing of the Sick is
not just for the dying; rather, it is believed to provide physical
healing and forgiveness of sins (showing Orthodox unity of
body and soul). Icons, which are depictions of Christ, the an-
gels, the saints, and the Virgin Mary, are venerated. There is
no belief in expiatory suffering in purgatory. The major festivals—the Twelve Great Feasts—include eight for Christ (Pen-
tecost, Transfiguration, Exaltation of the Cross, Palm Sunday,
Ascension, Candlemas [commemoration of Christ's Presentation in the Temple], Epiphany, and Christmas) and four for the
Mother of God (Presentation in the Temple, Nativity, Annun-
ciation, and Assumption [Dormition]). Easter, as the Feast of
Feasts, stands alone and is a time of great joy. If Orthodox do
not attend church at other times, they will attend at Christmas
and Easter. The highlights of Holy Week are the decoration of
the sepulcher and the watch on Good Friday and the midnight
service on Saturday, proclaiming the resurrection through the
symbolism of total darkness suddenly broken by the light of the
priest's candle, which lights those of the congregation, and by
exclamations, "Christ is risen!" In addition to the festivals,
there are four major periods of fasting—around Lent, Christmas, Assumption, and the Fast of the Apostles. Church buildings are usually a cross-in-square with a dome and always have
a wall or screen covered with icons separating the sanctuary
from the rest of the church. Because worshipers stand, and the
only pews or benches line the walls, there is an atmosphere of
informality; people may come and go and, upon entry, may
light a candle before joining the congregation.

Unlike Roman Catholic clergy, Orthodox clergy include
married as well as celibate priests (the latter are monks). The
traditional Greek priest wears a beard and long hair, a tall

black hat, and a gown with wide sleeves. Married men can become priests, but after ordination a new marriage is not permitted. In order to become a bishop, however, a priest must be celibate. Indeed, given the preponderance of priests with only primary or middle-level education and a minimum of religious training, a celibate priest with a university education in theology (many of whom come from urban backgrounds and are concentrated in Athens and Thessaloniki) could expect to become bishop after serving as a preacher, an urban parish priest, or a bishop's assistant. A small-town priest in an urban or semiurban diocese has generally completed secondary school and studied theology at a higher seminary, while in larger towns and cities priests and bishops have generally received degrees in theology from the universities of Athens or Thessaloniki.

For centuries the village priest has been the preserver of Greek culture and religious traditions, and as such he has been generally respected by villagers. There are more priests in the cities, but ratios to parishioners are smaller in rural areas. An analysis of ordinations between 1950 and 1969 showed that poor dioceses in the mountains and on the islands provided a greater share of peasant priests because of the economic opportunity offered by the priesthood; when age and educational requirements were less stringent, the number of ordinations increased. The common image drawn from such an analysis was a married villager who entered the priesthood late in life. Rural married priests often continued a trade or agriculture and hence were integrated well with parishioners not just on the grounds of having a wife and children. In the 1980s, a priests's social prestige was relatively low, so parents did not encourage children to enter the clergy; most of those who graduated in university faculties of theology did not become priests but became the more prestigious and better paid secondary school teachers of religion. A priest's functions were pastoral and administrative rather than intellectual, which also detracted from the priesthood's appeal; most theologians were laymen, and it was the bishop or preacher who gave sermons.

Monasticism has always been an important element of Orthodoxy, being seen as an alternative form of martyrdom once religious persecution stopped. Unlike Roman Catholic monks, who frequently teach and do missionary or social work, Orthodox monks (who are not necessarily priests) are solely devoted to the practice of asceticism. They have been divided into those living as hermits, those living in a community under common rule, and those living in loosely linked settlements under a spiritual director. Mount Athos has been the site of colonies of monks since A.D. 959 and continues as a spiritual "island" with its 20 monasteries of Greek, Russian, Serbian, and Bulgarian monks.

A trend in the 1960s and early 1970s has been reversed; numbers of monks on Mount Athos have increased. Until 1972 numbers of monks in Greek monasteries and in monasteries on Mount Athos were gradually declining, leading to pessimistic prognoses for the future. Men's monasteries in Greece were declining in numbers in 1983 except for the enrollment at two monasteries in Athens and a few other houses. However, over the last 60 years women's convents have been expanding, often taking over buildings deserted by men and attracting some women with university degrees as well as villagers lacking higher education. By 1974 statistics from Mount Athos showed that the depleted ranks of elderly monks were being supplemented by more, younger, and better educated monks; Mount Athos provided a haven from tourism and secularization and benefitted from departures from the religious brotherhoods to Mount Athos and from attraction exerted by particular abbots.

Religious brotherhoods, important during the 1910-60 period (and especially the 1960s) but on the decline in the 1980s, were founded on private initiative to revitalize popular religious attitudes. Although small in membership, they had great influence. The most important one, called Zoi (Life), had appealed to many in the urban middle classes through its 12 associations (including separate ones for teachers, parents, students, and professionals), publications (one magazine having a circulation of 120,000 in the 1960s), and activities (catechism classes, youth camps, student hostels, radiobroadcasts, regular preaching, and Bible study groups). Zoi was privately governed and semimonastic, that is, members took vows but wore no special garb. Zoi included both laymen and monks and emphasized frequent confession and communion, modification of church services to attract more participation, and moral personal behavior. In the 1980s Zoi no longer had an appeal for the young because of its puritanical, authoritarian, and pietistic aspects and had also lost support both because of its success at stimulating the Orthodox church to set up similar programs and because of its alleged links with the colonels and with a former archbishop installed by the military regime (see The "Revolution of 21 April," ch. 1).

The role of the church in the city has been contrasted with

its role in the villages. In Greek villages, time is marked by the religious calendar, and during major holidays, such as Easter, Greeks tend to feel the competition and mistrust between families temporarily overshadowed by the feeling of religious solidarity. The local church serves as a community focus; for example, projects to rebuild or renovate the local church provide a rare occasion for all to work toward a common community goal. Church affairs seem accessible in the village because the priest is well known to all, and villagers can keep an eye on the administration of church affairs by their lay committee. One of the few observers to make a contrast between urban and religious life, journalist Mario Rinvolucri noted that in urban areas a parish is larger and more impersonal, services are less well attended in relation to the size of the parish, gossip is a less important control of morality, and church affairs are run by a committee of upper strata laymen. Rites of passage or festivals such as Easter are often celebrated in the home village rather than in the city.

It is difficult to compare absolute church attendance in both rural and urban areas. A rough overall estimate for the 1970s would be that 20 to 26 percent of Orthodox Greeks attended services each Sunday. Weekly churchgoing is not an obligation as in the Roman Catholic Church and is seen as more appropriate for women and children than for men, and attendance is more frequent for the older than for the young adult; those who attend may do so as representative of his or her household. A 1980 poll found as many as 60 percent claiming to attend services for the major feasts or occasions such as weddings.

In the city, people may engage less in public or weekly religious practices, but both rural and urban homes may have a corner with icons, a special lamp, and holy oil and holy water. Like villagers, urban individuals may have personal relationships with saints whom they ask for intercession in a crisis. Even if urban dwellers are more likely to express criticisms of the church or anticlerical remarks, they do not necessarily claim to be atheists. Even many members of the Communist Party of Greece in the 1970s considered themselves to be Orthodox Christians, attending church during festivals. It is harder to assess numbers at pilgrimages and death rituals at cemeteries than at church; it is equally difficult to assess to what extent greater religious participation among the generation with grown children is a function of age rather than of increasing lack of interest of the young. Similarly, involvement

117

in the parish for men may mean serving on the main parish committee, while for women such involvement may include Scripture reading, charity, cleaning, or baking bread.

Orthodox liturgy provides the forms for the rituals marking birth, marriage, and death. A Greek receives religious, regional, and national identity at baptism when given a name in the presence of the priest, godparent(s), and parent(s) (the mother traditionally did not attend if it occurred within the 40 days after birth when she was considered "unclean"). The baptism is usually followed by the confirmation (called *chrismation* because of the special myrrh from the patriarchate of Constantinople) when the child, having received the "gift of the Spirit," officially becomes a member of the church.

Before a 1982 law instituting civil marriage and a 1983 law liberalizing divorce, civil marriage was not legal, and divorces were relatively few. The formation of the family has usually been marked by the church wedding, with special symbols—the flower or leaf crowns for the bride and groom; gold and silver rings for the groom and bride, respectively; a glass of wine for the couple; and the dance of Isaiah (when the bride and groom circle the altar three times with the marriage sponsors and the priest). The phrase *to crown* is used to mean to marry in Greek and reflects the key event of this ceremony; the crowns signify that the couple are emperor and empress on their wedding day and are undertaking self-sacrifice and a spiritual struggle.

Traditional death rituals in rural Greece may be characterized by black-clothed women, wakes, ritual laments by women, memorial services at specified intervals (the most important on the fortieth day and a year after death, the former referring to the period before Christ's ascension), and exhumation of the body and removal of the bones to an ossuary. These death rituals are considered as much a serious obligation as care of the elderly and may be seen as tied to the receipt of inheritance. Rituals that serve as rites of passage, that is, mark transitions from one stage of life to another, tend to have parallels; hence weddings and funerals may be compared, for example, when laments and wedding songs are similar or when an unmarried young man or woman is buried in a bridal outfit.

Freedom of religion is protected under the Constitution, and small religious minorities continue to exist as they have for centuries. These minorities include Jews, non-Orthodox Christians, and Muslims. In mid-1975 it was estimated that there were 3,800 Jews, although before Nazi persecution over 20 percent of Thessaloniki was Jewish and there were almost 76,000 Jews in all of Greece. There have been Jews in Greece since before the time of Christ, and they were once responsible for the development of trade and schools in Thessaloniki when it was known throughout Europe and the Middle East as a business and cultural center. In addition to Greek, the 3,800 Jews spoke a modified form of Spanish known as Ladino, which incorporated many Hebrew elements.

Although technically Orthodox, as a result of the substitution of the new, or Gregorian, calendar for the unrevised Julian calendar in the Greek Orthodox church and the patriarchate in Constantinople in 1924, a group called the Old Calendarists continued to follow the unrevised Julian calendar and thereby split off from the rest of the church. While encompassing perhaps 800 parish groups and a million followers in the 1930s or 1940s, in 1983 they included 500,000 people, 200 parishes, some monasteries, and about 30 bishops. Among non-Orthodox minorities, the Jehovah's Witnesses stood out in 1984 because of the imprisonment of about 200 conscientious objectors who refused to participate in compulsory military service.

In mid-1975 Sunni Muslims were 1.5 percent of the population, that is, 132,000, being mostly Turkish speakers located in Thrace near the Turkish border; almost all Muslims are Turkish speaking, only 17 percent of them being Bulgarian-speaking Pomaks. Under the Treaty of Lausanne, which formally ended the Greco-Turkish war in 1923, ethnic Greeks and ethnic Turks within the corresponding states' boundaries were exchanged. About 400,000 Turkish-speaking Muslims living in Greece emigrated to Turkey, and about 1.3 million Greek Orthodox moved from Asia Minor to Greece between 1912 and 1924. By special arrangement, ethnic Greeks living in Istanbul and Turkish speakers in Greek Thrace were exempted from compulsory exchanges. In 1981 about 110,000 members of the Turkish-speaking Muslim minority still lived in Greek Thrace in the northeastern corner of Greece, bordering Bulgaria and Turkey; only a few thousand other Turkish-speaking Muslims lived outside Thrace, mainly on the Dodecanese Islands. The Dodecanese Muslims differed only in religion from their Greek neighbors, as opposed to the more culturally distinct Turkish-speaking Muslims communities in Thrace.

In Thrace there were many villages with Turkish-speaking Muslims in the three provinces—Xanthi, Rodhopi, and Evros. According to the Greek government, in the early 1980s government funds maintained 205 mosques and 90 smaller religious buildings. Two Muslims were members of parliament. There were 261 special Turkish-language grade schools with 12,760 students, two Turkish-language high schools with 645 students, and two seminaries. A great majority of Turkish-speaking Muslims were tobacco cultivators.

According to the journal *Arabia* (cited in a Joint Publications Research Service article) and the United States Department of State's *Country Reports on Human Rights Practices for 1984*, this Muslim minority has alleged discriminatory practice on several counts—an allegation denied by the Greek government. Their ownership of land is said to have declined from 84 percent of land in 300 villages in 1923 to 40 percent in the 1980s, and they claimed that the Greek government placed restrictions on travel, purchase and sale of property, facilities for secondary and university education, and choice of textbooks and teachers. They complained of unjust closings of primary schools in several villages, evictions, confiscation of land belonging to individuals and religious foundations, conversion or deterioration of mosques, and imprisonment of agriculturists in two villages for cultivation of land to which they had title.

## Language

Greece is linguistically homogenous. Since 1951 the Greek census has recorded neither mother tongue nor religious affiliation. In the mid-1970s observers estimated that only 2 to 3 percent of inhabitants did not speak Greek as their first language. This minority spoke Turkish, Macedo-Slav, Vlach (a Romanian dialect), Albanian, or Pomak (a Bulgarian dialect). The language of the majority, Greek, is a direct descendant of the Indo-European language spoken by civilizations occupying the Greek mainland, the Aegean Islands, and nearby Asia Minor many centuries before Christ.

Greek villagers use the term *Vlach* to refer to shepherds, thus confusing an occupation with an ethnic group. The ethnic Vlachs, also called Koutsovlachs and Aromani, have lived in the Balkan Peninsula for centuries; those in Greece traditionally were shepherds, though they now may also depend on agriculture, forestry, or city jobs. Frequently mistaken for Vlachs were Sarakatsani, also transhumant shepherds and concentrated in Epirus. They are Greek Orthodox, like most Vlachs, but speak only Greek as opposed to Greek and a dialect of

Romanian. Sarakatsani culture and social institutions differ from those of the Vlachs, and relations have often been strained because of competition over winter grazing land. In the early 1970s there may have been as many as 100,000 Vlachs, and in 1974 some 80,000 Sarakatsani; more recent official figures were not available in 1985.

The 1951 census reported a little over 40,000 Slav speakers living mainly in Macedonia and close to 19,000 Pomaks living in Thrace (Bulgarian-speaking Muslims exempted from population exchanges in the 1920s). It also reported 22,000 Greek Orthodox identifying themselves as Albanian speakers in the provinces of Attica and Voiotia, in the northeastern Peloponnesus, and in nearby Aegean islands; by the mid-1970s most of those of Albanian descent identified themselves as Greek and did not strive to maintain Albanian cultural traditions.

At various points in its history, Greek has suffered from what is called the literary fallacy, that is, a tension between the evolving spoken language and a preference for a literary model from the classical period. As a consequence Greeks have switched between forms of Greek depending on the circumstances of use. This was true still in the 1980s when three forms of Greek—*koine*, demotic, and *katharevousa* ( as well as mixtures of the last two)—were being used in the country.

*Koine* (literally, common), was the language of the common people during the Hellenistic period and was used in the New Testament, Septuagint, and the writings of the early church fathers. Also an important international language, it was the language of Greek literature for 10 centuries, and the early church used it to appeal to potential converts, adopting it as the church's official language in A.D. 330. The Greek Orthodox church has continued to use it in the liturgy (see table 4).

Demotic was historically the language of the common people as Greek continued to evolve from *koine* and today is the form of Greek used in informal situations by all Greeks. It assumed its morphological and syntactic form by the seventh century A.D. Its evolution, especially during the Byzantine period (sixth to fifteenth centuries), can be traced only with difficulty because it was essentially a spoken, not a written, form. Demotic was employed only in popular literature, as opposed to a form modeled on ancient Attic Greek that was used for formal speaking and writing. Demotic was not considered appropriate or adequate for use in serious literature or in explaining abstract or scientific ideas. By the fourteenth century, elements of the spoken language were being used in poetry, but even up to the eighteenth and nineteenth centuries serious literature and translations from Western languages were not written in demotic (except in Crete and Cyprus).

In the nineteenth century a movement developed—parallel to that supporting *katharevousa*—to promote demotic. Yannis Psiharis (1854-1929), a scholar with a great interest in the speech of the common people and an expanded definition of "Hellenic," wrote the first serious book in demotic in 1888, *My Journey*, a novel that was to become a model of style in the new demotic literary movement. Even though learned works continued to be written in *katharevousa* in the 1970s, poetry and novels were written in demotic by such twentieth-century authors as Nikos Kazantzakis, Constantine Cavafy, and George Seferis. In 1976 the government of Constantine Karamanlis adopted a form of demotic called common or standard modern Greek (Neohelliniki). It is a compromise, being neither the purist demotic of literature nor the less rigorous version of *katharevousa* formerly used for scientific and technological material; standard modern Greek combines demotic structure with *katharevousa* vocabulary and phrases.

Literally meaning "pure," *katharevousa* was the language of officialdom and education as recently as the rule of the colonels (1967-74). It was an artificial language, invented by Adamantios Korais (1748-1833) in an attempt to improve written and spoken Greek by arbitrary corrections drawing on classical and Hellenistic Greek. It became the official state language by successive laws in 1834 and 1836 because of support from youth influenced by Korais, from the bourgeoisie, and from the intelligentsia. Although Korais wanted to combine elements of demotic (the people's language) with classical elements, after official adoption *katharevousa* became more and more unintelligible to the uneducated, as well as more imprecise.

Language became a political issue in the early nineteenth century as Greeks began addressing the issue of national identity. The issue at hand was what particular form of Greek was most germane to the establishment of a modern, independent Greek state. But there was no consensus on what the most desirable choice should be. The situation was complicated because some Greeks sought to identify with Attic Greek used in classical times, while others favored the form of *koine* used as official Byzantine Greek that was synonymous with the status quo of the church and the Phanariot elite (see The Ottoman

Occupation, ch. 1). Still others wanted a modified form of demotic because they equated "nation" with the majority of the people. Ancient Greek, or the Greek used by the church, could not be adopted officially without modification because of the need for a nationally comprehensible language in light of regional variations, unfamiliarity of the uneducated with any form but demotic, intrusions of foreign words (often associated with foreign domination), and lack of a strong demotic literary tradition.

After the 1976 law was promulgated, the most obvious change was the switch from *katharevousa* to standard modern Greek for secondary and university education. (Demotic had been used in lower elementary grades more or less continuously since 1917.) Some parts of the government lagged more than others in effective implementation of linguistic change— the armed forces, the courts and lawyers, the church (although sermons and pastoral work were in demotic), certain segments of the bureaucracy, and some areas of higher education. Before the colonels' reinstatement of *katharevousa* in 1967, a newspaper might have had official notices and weather reports in *katharevousa*, editorials and poems in demotic, and news in a mixture of the two. By 1985 most newspapers (with the exception of those of the right wing) were published in demotic.

In general, changeover was not automatic for those people accustomed to a lifetime of use of *katharevousa* in certain academic, intellectual, and formal contexts; nor could *katharevousa*, at least in its written form, be dispensed with entirely yet, since older laws, church communications, and materials such as government publications, speeches, forms and notices, and social science books remained in the old form. Thus, *katharevousa* still had to be studied in school, although it was no longer the language of instruction. It should also be noted that by the 1980s common modern Greek was replacing not only *katharevousa* but also many dialects in the course of only one generation, owing to universal education, military service, better transporation, and rural to urban migration; dialects tended to be preserved in northern Greece, on larger islands such as Crete, on smaller Aegean islands, and in villages.

## Education

In Greece in 1985 nine years of education, through age

123

15, were free and compulsory. Secondary and higher education was also free. All teaching was conducted in common standard Greek, and all state schools were coeducational. Education was centralized under the Ministry of National Education and Religion.

Education is highly valued and eagerly pursued in Greece. People of all social classes are proud of the country's tradition and reputation for being the birthplace of classical thought. The strong urbanization trend of the 1960s and 1970s and the overall modernization of Greece have caused much discontent with the rural way of life, and education is seen as a way out. A not uncommon reason given by rural migrants to the city for their move is the desire to send their children to good schools. Most Greek villagers have high educational aspirations for their children, in particular their sons. To be a learned person is valued in itself, but more commonly villagers view secondary schooling and university degrees as vehicles for upward social mobility. Although villagers may overestimate the professional advantages of a university degree, underestimating the importance of family influence, such a degree has been essential in providing the skill in writing and understanding *katharevousa*, required until 1976-77 for civil service or business employment.

Over the history of the Greek state, the Greek educational system has been stable, resisting change even to the point of being rigid, because of the use of *katharevousa*, insufficient funding, centralization, and the role of the Orthodox church. Major reforms (introducing demotic Greek, critical thought, and vocational education) were attempted at several points— 1913, 1929, 1959, 1964, and 1976-77. In the 1980s, nevertheless, Greek education expert Alexis Dimaras commented that Greek education needed better planning and a modernized infrastructure to keep up with the rest of Western Europe. He believed that too much emphasis was placed on traditional academic subjects, such as ancient Greek, and acceptance of provided material instead of instilling an analytic outlook and offering individualized teaching; the educational system did not teach the skills needed by the work force. In the 1970s there had been some reforms in this direction by adding stress on mathematics and physical sciences at the primary and secondary levels and by attempting to channel students to fill the need for mid-level technical graduates. Government under the Panhellenic Socialist Movement (Panhellinion Socialistiko Kinima—PASOK) had tried to meet educational needs by increasing funding; in 1981, the last year under New Democracy, the Ministry of National Education and Religion received 8.4 percent of current expenditures, although under PASOK the projected 1985 budget specified 12.3 percent.

In the 1980s the system of primary and secondary education was centralized under the Ministry of National Education and Religion so that curricula, schedules, methods, and texts were uniform; the work of school inspectors and supervisors was to ensure this uniformity. The ministry also controlled appointment and promotion of teachers. The ministry received assistance in policy, curricula, and in-service training from the Center for Educational Studies and In-service Training (Kentro Ekpaideftikon Melton kai Epimorfoseos—KEME). Less than 10 percent of students were in private schools, and many of these schools catered to foreign residents or wealthy students. All were required to follow official curricula unless given special dispensation; to receive diplomas, graduating students had to pass a special examination. There was no need for a separate religious school system because religious instruction was compulsory for Greek Orthodox pupils. Although one observer characterized the private schools as better than the public ones, another reported that a higher percentage of private students failed to gain entrance to the *lycea* (sing; *lyceum*; grades 10 to 12).

Preschool was free but not compulsory for ages three and one-half to five and one-half years and mainly available in urban areas. In the school year 1978-79, about 45 percent of this age-group attended preschool. There was little formal instruction. Primary school started at age five and one-half, continuing until 11 and one-half. In March 1981 schools switched from a six-day to a five-day week, although the total number of hours was not reduced. There were 899,546 primary school students in 1979-80, usually in schools with one to 15 teachers and 15 to 450 students. Most commonly, there was a separate teacher for each grade and an average one-to-29 teacher-student ratio (although classes were likely to be larger in Athens). The teachers were rewarded with relatively poor pay and low prestige. Students graduating from primary school received a certificate called *apolyterion* (the same name given to certificates from secondary and middle technical-vocational schools).

As a result of reforms in the 1970s there were two cycles of secondary education, the first offered at the *gymnasium* (pl., *gymnasia*) and the second at the *lyceum*. The former covered seventh through ninth grades and taught mostly traditional subjects, such as geography, literature, and history, to which courses on industrial arts and career awareness were added in the 1970s. Because attendance at the *gymnasium* was compulsory, there were no entrance examinations. In contrast, the *lyceum*, which included grades 10 to 12, was selective and did require entrance examinations on composition, literature in translation, algebra and geometry, and history or physics. *Lycea* were of two kinds—general and technical-vocational. About 82 percent of candidates passed in June 1978; in the early 1980s about 20 percent of those who passed went to technical-vocational *lycea*, and the rest (who were said to include better students) went to general schools, which were in greater demand. A total of 411,305 students were at *gymnasia* and 207,383 at *lycea* in 1979-80. Private schools represented 5 percent of the total students at *gymnasia* and 8 percent of those at *lycea* in 1978-79. There were a total of 1,092 public day *gymnasia* plus 30 public evening *gymnasia* and 170 private *gymnasia*, of which 25 were night schools; there were 714 daytime and 30 nighttime *lycea* versus 177 private *lycea*, of which 28 were night schools. In 1981 secondary schools adopted a five-day week.

Technical-vocational education was reorganized in 1977 so that three options existed: middle private and public schools; *lycea*; and Centers for Higher Technical and Vocational Education (Kentra Anoteras Technikis ke Epangelmatikis Ekpaedeuseos—KATEE) for further education. The *lyceum* could prepare a student for higher education or for work; it might offer mechanical and electrical engineering, chemical and metallurgical engineering, business administration, social services, agriculture, or building and architectural design. In 1981-82 about 70,000 students attended technical-vocational *lycea*. Reforms were designed to provide technical-vocational schools equal prestige with general schools through shared entrance examinations and faculty credentials; faculty credentials varied according to the kind of subject and the kind of schools, whether university, KATEE, or technical-vocational teacher training school.

Depending on the subject the general *lyceum* student aspired to take at the university, in the last two years he or she would pick, in addition to a common core, classical option A (ancient Greek, Latin and history) or scientific option B (mathematics, physics, and chemistry), the latter the only preuniversity option offered at technical-vocational schools. Option A, for example, could lead to theology, philosophy, law, or political science and option B to engineering, medicine, and physics.

In 1980 the Panhellenic examinations were instituted at the end of eleventh and twelfth grades as a replacement for the national examinations formerly held for university entrance; only 40 percent of the technical-vocational students took them as opposed to all the general *lyceum* students. The Ministry of National Education and Religion administered the essay form test simultaneously all over Greece; the test covered modern Greek and subjects of option A or B. Forty percent passed in 1980, but only about one in five being examined in the 1980s was admitted to higher education.

Public recognition of this competition (and also that to enter *lycea*) encouraged enrollment at private "cramming schools" called *frontisteria*. In 1977 about 83 percent of university students had attended such a supplementary school beginning either in the second or third year of *lyceum* or after finishing it. In an attempt to reduce the importance of the admission examination, the ministry divided the test over the second and third years of *lyceum* and included marks in these two years as a basis for admissions. These measure, however, resulted in extending the pressure period and encouraging teaching oriented toward the examinations. Those who failed were left with the possibilities of seeking employment, going abroad to study, attending a private college (one of which had a market for its English-language-educated graduates in business and industry), or attempting again.

There has been strong demand and competition for higher education. It has not been equally accessible to all despite the 1964 university reforms, which removed tuition costs and opened two new universities. University or equivalent training was attended by 4 percent of Greeks aged 20 to 24 in 1960 but had increased to 17 percent in the early 1980s. Forty-six percent of university applicants were accepted in 1964 as opposed to 17 percent in 1977; although slots were increased by one-third, applicants increased by over three-fold, ratios of applicants to places varying depending on the discipline (medicine, for example, having a 10.8-to-one ratio as opposed to 2.7-to-one for philosophy). As a result, many Greeks studied abroad (27 percent of all students at home and abroad)—over 35,000 in 1978-79, including 15,000 in Italy and smaller but substantial groups in Britain, France, West Germany, and the United States. A government language examination for those planning to study abroad permitted those who passed to receive a two-year military deferment and the right to take money out of Greece. Greek universities in fact depended on foreign universities to train future professors at the graduate level and conduct scientific research.

In the early 1980s Greek institutions of higher education were self-governing but under the Ministry of National Education and Religion. They were supervised and funded by the state and regulated largely by legislative decrees. Institutions of higher education were divided into *anotati* and *anotera*. The former, university-level institutions, necessarily public (the government prohibits private ones), offered courses lasting at least four years. Members of the faculty were elected and they were free to administer budgets and decide admissions criteria. The latter, also called intermediate level, offered courses lasting three years or less. Teachers were selected by the ministry, and the *anotera* had less control over their budgets. The KATEE and teacher training institutes (primary, preschool, home economics, and physical education) were typical *anotera*; in 1981-82 there were 14 KATEE centers with 22,272 students, offering courses such as business administration, engineering technology, and health occupations, as well as on-the-job training. Good students might transfer to the university after graduation. Admission was not automatic to the KATEE—the ratio of applicants to places in 1978-79 was 7.6 to one.

The School of Fine Arts was founded in 1834, the National Technical University of Athens (commonly called the Polytechnic) in 1836, the University of Athens in 1837, the University of Salonika in 1925, and the Panteios School of Political Science in Athens in 1930. The universities in the two major cities dominated until the 1960s and 1970s when universities were added in Patrai, Ioannina, Thrace, and Crete; additional universities are to be created in Thessaly and in the Aegean and Ionian islands.

In 1981-82 the University of Athens had 35,535 students and the University of Salonika 22, 064 out of a total of 89,957 university students in Greece. The most recent figures available (1977-78) for fields of study of university students divided them into 52 percent studying social sciences, 37 percent studying sciences and mathematics, and 11 percent studying humanities. Medicine was the longest course of study, lasting six years as opposed to five years for agriculture and forestry, dentistry, veterinary medicine, and engineering (and four years for the rest). *Lyceum* and *gymnasium* teachers were required to hold a university degree in their respective fields. In 1978 attempted reforms were difficult to implement, but until then the traditional Greek university structure had been organized around chairs administered by professors of one or more associated subjects; chairs were grouped together to form a division, and divisions were combined to form a school administered by the faculty. The division awarded the undergraduate degree, called *ptychion*. Graduate education was inadequate; in some schools postgraduate courses of one or two years requiring qualifying examinations existed, but only doctoral tutorials, not courses, existed as of 1982. Universities were highly politicized.

Adult education was reorganized in 1976-77. Afterward, the national ministry concentrated on policy, coordination, and guidance, while provincial and local authorities were responsible for programs and courses of study at adult education centers and night schools. In addition to enrichment and professional development, one focus of provincial-level programs was to combat illiteracy. According to the 1981 census, 20.4 percent of the Greek population—almost 2 million—were illiterate. Over three-quarters of illiterates were women. Some 6.7 percent of those aged 15 to 64 never attended school, and 20 percent of this age-group was illiterate. Some of such illiteracy was attributed to the inadequate education provided by one- or two-teacher schools in rural areas. According to the 1971 census (later figures were not available), among the population over 10 years of age, 33 percent had not completed primary school, 50 percent had finished only primary, 11 percent had finished only secondary, and 3 percent had completed higher education.

The mass media provided information and news. In the 1980s about 85 percent of Greek households had a television, and about 97 percent owned a radio. The government owned and operated the two national television networks and the four radio networks. The content of broadcasts was influenced by the party in power, and the opposition has complained of the unfair advantage received by the ruling party, although opposition views do receive an airing. Opponents and critics of the government are free to express their opinions in the press, but libel laws are strict. Modern Greece has generally enjoyed freedom of the press, except between 1967 and 1974 under the junta when reporters were jailed and publications confiscated. Only a few Athens daily newspapers broke even financially, so that survival often depended on direct or indirect government support through loans or advertising; the Socialist government has, however, proposed termination of such support (see table 5, Appendix A).

## Social Security

Greece had a complicated system of social security. There were many different social security organizations and a multiplicity of benefits and provisions, attributable to poor planning, clout of certain employee groups, the high number of self-employed, and scanty actuarial input during establishment of the system. There were in 1984 almost 650 carriers for old-age, survivor, and disability pensions and health benefits, and there were a variety of programs—primary, auxiliary (for those insured only by a primary carrier), private supplementary, and lump-sum payments. The first social security law was passed in 1914 and the latest in 1981. The system comes under the jurisdiction of the ministries of social security (work injury, sickness, and medical benefits, as well as pensions) and of labor (unemployment and family allowance).

Despite variation according to carrier and industry and work category, the system is primarily financed through employer and employee contributions (through payroll deductions), with the employer paying a greater share; depending on the carrier there may also be a government subsidy. In the 1980s the basis for membership in programs was occupational group and industry; the three biggest systems, which covered 85 percent of non-civil service insured, were the Social Insurance Institute (Idryma Kinonikon Asfaliseon—IKA), the Agricultural Insurance Organization (Organismos Georgikon Asfaliseon—OGA), and the Tradesmen and Craftsmen's Fund for the Self-employed (Tameio Eborikon Biomihanikon Epihiriseon—TEBE). The IKA was the most extensive, and since 1951 coverage has been mandatory for all individuals employed by commerce or industry if not members of the OGA, TEBE, civil service, or equivalent occupational programs. IKA programs were comprehensive—including old-age, disability, maternity, funeral, sickness, medical, and worker's compensation benefits, leaving only unemployment, military service, and family allowances to the Manpower Employment Organization (Organismos Apasholiseos Ergatikou Dynamikou—OAED). In 1981 Greece spent 16.6 percent of gross national product (GNP—see Glossary) on social security; the total included 38 percent paid by the employers, 36 percent by employees, 21 percent by government, and 5 percent by investments.

Since 1974 there have been attempts to upgrade the system, extend coverage, and aim toward uniformity and equity between insurance funds and between the sexes. Change was needed because of the growing numbers of retirees, the example set by the benefits programs of foreign and multinational corporations in Greece, the new government emphasis on noncash benefits in the face of inflation, and repatriation of migrants accustomed to the more sophisticated Western systems. Actual changes were related to extension of pensions and medical care to all elderly (including the innovation of pensions for female farmers); an extensions of the IKA to 100,000 previously excluded; and the Employee Auxiliary Insurance Fund (Tameio Epikourikif Asfaliseos Misphoton—TEAM) program to extend supplementary insurance to those not receiving it (including miners and municipal workers).

## Health

In Greece in 1982 the principal causes of death were stroke, cardiovascular disease, and cancer of the gastrointestinal system. The major infectious diseases in 1981 were influenza, pulmonary tuberculosis, viral and infectious hepatitis, intestinal infections, and chicken pox. Malaria was under control, but there were 244 cases of typhoid in 1981. Infant mortality and life expectancy were comparable to other EC countries (see Population, this ch.).

To treat the sick, there were 688 hospitals (of which 482 were private) with 59,914 beds in 1981. In 1982, however, an observer described hospitals as crowded and poorly equipped. According to World Health Orgnization norms in the 1980s, there should have been 70,000 hospital beds in Greece. Another source pinpointed the more crucial question of location, not quantity; there were excess beds in Athens, and a shortage existed in the provinces. People from outside Athens were forced to go there for care. In general, the best facilities were university affiliated and philanthropic, and because of public perceptions of care in public facilities as inadequate, a relatively large share of GNP has been spent on private care.

There was an oversupply of physicians, although their distribution was not equitable and there were insufficient numbers of general practitioners; the former problem persisted, but steps were being taken to alleviate it, such as the requirement introduced in 1968 that all physicians had to practice one year in a rural area. In 1981 there were 24,724 physicians, that is, 24.5 per 10,000 inhabitants (a ratio higher than in Sweden and West Germany), but over one-half were in the Athens area. Physicians were said to be poorly paid by hospitals (and thus forced to moonlight) and were offered inadequate postgraduate training. There were 7,727 dentists in 1981, again over one-half in Athens. Nurses were in short supply in the 1980s, as were other trained health professionals. The latest available figure for nurses was one nurse per 853 people in 1979.

Upon election, the Socialist government announced its intention of instituting a national health service. By the end of 1983 the legal framework was in place to improve quality of care and geographical equity. Goals were decentralization, preventive care, employment of full-time government physicians, an adequate supply of nurses through new training programs, and improvement of hospitals and hospital technology. Health care was to include visits by family physicians, outpatient health centers, and general and specialized care in hospitals. Plans called for construction of 185 rural clinics, 25 hospitals (including three university hospitals), kidney transplant and open-heart surgery facilities, and 18 new nursing schools (including 11 in rural areas). The government planned to employ 6,350 physicians in the state medical corps, which would staff state hospitals, and 2,300 physicians in rural health centers. IKA facilities will eventually be incorporated into the national health system. In comparison with 1979-81, the budget allocation for health care for 1982-84 was increased by 35.6 percent (after accounting for inflation). The proportion of the total government current expenditure spent for health care in 1985 is expected to represent 6.8 percent as opposed to 5.4 percent in 1981. The proportion of gross domestic product (GDP—see Glossary) for health care is projected to be 2.5 percent for 1985.

## Social Structure and Cultural Values

### Relations Inside the Household

The family is the basic social unit in Greek society. Regardless of region, class, or location, the family does not lose its central importance. In Greece no one stands alone; the concept of the independent, unmarried, childless adult who stands apart from the family circle does not exist. For economic reasons and because of long-standing tradition, young people do not have a period of living apart from their parents as single persons, and marriage is felt to concern the families involved as well as the two individuals. Despite emigration and internal migration, the norm is to remain both emotionally and physically close to the nuclear family, whether by visits and communications, location of a home nearby, or by encouraging other family members to join the migrant.

### The Nuclear Family

The nuclear family, which consists of a husband, a wife, and unmarried children, constitutes the basic household, although on occasion a parent of one of the spouses or some other relative may join them, or in certain regions a married child or married children may live with parents until they establish their own separate households. In most areas of mainland Greece the tradition is for a groom to take his wife to live with his parents after marriage or at least to a house they provide in their village; in some areas this larger household, called an extended family, might continue until the parents' death or even after if the sons wish to retain the more efficient joint household as a means of saving labor and caring for fields or livestock. In some of the Greek islands, most notably the Cyclades and the Dodecanese, it is the custom for a married couple to live in the wife's village in a house provided by her parents, perhaps because her husband might be away from home for long periods. This custom has been extended to Greek cities, where people from many different regions may live in housing provided by the wife's family as part of the dowry and often located near the wife's kin. Husbands in these two cases are not disparaged as sons-in-law without property of their own, as they would be in the areas where a couple is supposed to live with or near the husband's family. In addition, it is not unusual for an urban household to include a relative who has come to the city to work.

The Greek nuclear family, especially the rural Greek nuclear family, has various functions. It is believed that a couple marries in order to have children and that parents need children to enjoy thoroughly their life together. The family is also the guardian of the family property. A major family goal in which all members share a common interest is the maintenance or augmentation of family property sufficient to endow each child with a share.

The nuclear family is also a religious unit; its archetype is the Holy Family—Christ, the Mother of Christ, and God the Father. The family has its own icons, and the struggle to support the family is considered God's mandate as are more obviously moral and religious concerns such as fasting, taking communion, attending services, or struggling for self-discipline in the face of temptation.

The nuclear family has been the source of labor on family fields, with family livestock, in family fishing boats, or in a family business; nuclear family members have pooled their resources for consumption. Having little differences across class and region, common characteristics of the nuclear family have proved it viable in rural and urban living, in small service and manufacturing concerns, and in agriculture.

As important as all these functions are, there are two more that are central in Greek culture. First, the Greeks do not believe in perfect altruism; therefore, the only people whose interests they believe to be their own are members of their nuclear family who share their household. Thus, the nuclear family is the group to which Greeks feel the most loyalty and the group that provides trust, mutual support, understanding, and love. Its members act as if their own family were superior and defend an individual to outsiders even if they do not approve of the defended behavior. Second, the unit upon which personal behavior most directly reflects is the nuclear family, which in turn reflects onto the family members the collective reputation and honor attributed to it.

Greek descent is traced through both the mother and the father. First names as well as surnames are inherited, and property passes from both the mother and the father to the children. Surnames of fathers or husbands were traditionally used by women, but under the 1983 family law possibilities were allowed of using the mother's name for herself and her children or of using a combination of both parents' names. Beyond the nuclear family, ties called "close relations" were acknowledged with parents, first and second cousins, grandparents, and aunts and uncles, as well as at times with more distant kin; metaphors used were "shared blood" and "origin from the same womb." Cooperation and company are sought from parents and siblings, for example, even when they reside separately, but all recognize that the first loyalty is given to family members with whom a household is shared. This priority is the reason given why brothers should not marry before their sisters have received a dowry and married. Even when more than one couple share a household, the independence of each is accepted, as shown in some cases by a separate kitchen. Although close ties to former members of a shared household are recognized, a husband may be considered to be within his rights to forbid his wife to see her relatives because of an argument.

Not all ties with all kin are necessarily activated simultaneously, and feuds—especially over inheritance—are possible. The array of kin provides, nevertheless, a ready network of favorably disposed persons for a relative in need of a favor. One way of binding kin is through inheritance. In rural Greece the child with whom an elderly parent resides and who presumably would perform appropriate death rites would receive the parental house and/or an extra portion of property. Unlike in-laws or godparents, those related by blood are not chosen; but the intensity and frequency of contact with them are left open. Proximity, cooperation, or spiritual kinship might foster closer relations.

Because marriage is a relationship between families, relations with in-laws are important. A new spouse is considered an outsider by the new in-laws. The importance of relations between in-laws, especially with the spouse's siblings or parents, varies depending on the frequency of contact. If couples live with or near the husband's family, relations with this family are emphasized rather than relations with the wife's family if residence is near them. A rural dowry, for example, in Voitia, where residence is with or near the husband's family, includes land in the wife's village, resulting in continuing contact with her kin during cultivation or disposition of the land. In areas where new couples live in the husband's village, the youngest son might stay in and inherit his parents' house; his wife would care for his parents in their old age, although relations between bride and mother-in-law are often antagonistic, at least until the birth of a son. For a woman living with her husband's kin, the initial years of marriage can be an ordeal. A woman's mother-in-law might be afraid of losing contact with her son or his affections or might alienate the daughter-in-law through deprecatory comments on her dowry. Ideally, the parents who provide housing for a daughter, for example, in the city should not interfere in marital quarrels except to counsel forbearance so as not to undermine male authority. Relations between brothers-in-law (particularly husbands of sisters) might be close—a relationship of friendship and economic collaboration in which friction between siblings paradoxically might be more evident than between the in-laws (although division of inheritance can introduce strain). In urban situations when the dowry provides a residence close to the wife's parents, her husband might become involved in the economic projects of her father and she might count on her mother or sister to help with children, cleaning, and cooking if she were working outside the home.

Greek families of all classes and rural and urban families have much in common: a sensitivity toward people, an emphasis on motherhood, the role of the grandmother in child rearing, and the part played by women as social links and organizers of rites of passage. After the rural to urban move, external appearances change more rapidly than such common features. Nonetheless, in the 1980s there were some significant differences between rural and urban families, especially as intimate urban neighborhoods became more impersonal.

In rural areas a woman's neighbors and kin might form a cohesive group of people of different ages sharing work and emotional support as well as advice and child care. In urban areas a housewife was likely to be lonely and frustrated, seeing kin less frequently and having fewer lasting bonds with neighbors, with whom she might trade services and share coffee and outings. The urban extended family was more like a network of individual contacts and shared much less than the rural family—only leisure hours in the evenings, holidays, and on weekends and discussion of financial and family problems. A marriageable daughter who was on her own at work might resent parental restrictions on her freedom. At the same time that an urban mother and married daughter might yearn for intimacy and company, they might be separated by the fact that life in Athens in the 1980s has been changing so quickly that the daughter could not draw on her mother's experience. Relations between individuals were replacing friendships between families as family members worked and studied in areas of the city other than where they lived, with people the rest of their families had never met. The emotional support traditionally sought from the nuclear family was beginning to be sought outside it by children. In the upper and middle classes, marital expectations expanded to include joint decisionmaking, increasing initiative for women, and companionship.

Children are desired by most Greek adults, and a marriage without children is pitied. Sex that produces children is sanctified by the Orthodox church. Children serve as symbols of fulfilled masculinity and femininity. Virility depends partly on the ability to sire children, especially sons. Feminine fulfillment is dependent on becoming a mother who successfully rears children. Motherhood is an important ideal for Greeks, and a mother represents all the positive aspects of home. The relationship of a mother with her children may be emotionally more important to the woman than her relationship with her husband, although she will bolster her children's relationship with him, mediating at times or comforting when necessary after punishment.

A birth is a major event, especially a first birth. All relatives take an interest and enjoy helping with a child. Through age four, children are indulged and minimally disciplined. All accomplishments are seen as increases in intelligence and strength. In the late 1970s swaddling for the first few months of an infant's life was still practiced in rural areas with no apparent negative effect. As the child grows up, although a mother continues to be a source of love and comfort, a father begins to be less indulgent and more strict. By age six, when a child must begin school, he or she is considered a responsible family member and attains a clear idea of the boundaries between family and strangers in terms of the expectation of love or hostility and is careful about revealing family secrets or the emotional self. Emphasis is placed on children's learning appropriate sex roles and proper conduct in public settings.

As children grow up, their upbringing shows inculcation of important Greek values. Children expect that their mothers will allow them some initiative but will give what is needed unquestioningly. Relatives may tease, even mildly frighten children, laugh, and then comfort them to teach them to avoid and cope with ridicule. As children grow older, in return for care until they are established as married adults, they are expected to show respect and obedience to parents and help in their old age. Obedience and respect are not to be blind, however, for parents may lie or use deceit to teach children not to accept even a parent's words unless they show superior intelligence and judgement and compatibility with the child's best interests; lying is shown to be acceptable to maintain family privacy and protect its interests. A wariness in dealing with others and a skillful, even cunning, use of intelligence are valued as being necessary to get along as adults. Mothers encourage sons to be ambitious and competitive and to be able to use deception and judgement in a way that would be useful in market dealings as an adult. Children are given much verbal stimulation, for conversation is an important skill used to fence with social opponents, entertain a group of people, stimulate a discussion of options for any task at hand, or bolster self-esteem by recounting accomplishments or attributes. A last set of values to inculcate in children is that related to honor (*time*), shame (*dropi*), and integrity. Children are to learn self-control, shame (a sensitivity to ridicule and reputation, physical modesty, and emotional concealment), and a love of honor (*philotimo*—the recognition of doing what is necessary to maintain respect of others and one's own self-esteem, especially in regard to expressions of femininity and masculinity).

### Relations Between the Sexes

Marriage is the culmination of a successful courtship and is the expected status for adults. Through marriage women can establish their own households, become mothers, and receive male protection in the social world. Through marriage men can continue the family line, although they are permitted more of a delay in marrying than women. Rather than being based on erotic love, traditional marriages were based on mutual dependence and understanding, especially after the first years. The traditional pattern for courtship did not include dating. Marriages continued to be arranged in the 1970s, at least among the urban working class and villagers, although at times negotiations began at the couple's initiative. Because the marriage involved not just two individuals, marriage arrangements and dowry negotiations were conducted on a family basis. As arranged marriages declined in number, parents retained some control over the daughter's choice through contribution of housing as part of the dowry contingent on their approval.

During courtship all eyes were focused on the young woman to see how she conducted herself. Her behavior was considered by all, including the woman herself, to be a direct reflection on her upbringing and character as well as on her individual and family honor. The woman's reputation, as well as health, age, appearance, and wealth, were taken into consideration by the potential groom's family, but the ways in which a woman proved she possessed an honorable reputation have changed; for example, until the late 1960s a woman manifested her honor by dressing in a way that showed her sense of modesty and innocence, but young women in the 1980s dressed stylishly in West European fashion, did not need a constant chaperone, and sometimes held jobs.

The behavior of all women in Greece, married or not, has been thought to put the family honor, particularly male honor, at risk. Examples of sexual offenses felt to be threatening to male honor would be seduction of a related unmarried girl, adultery committed by women of the family, or even the jilting of a sister or daughter on the basis of pregnancy or inadequate dowry; the redress expected traditionally would be the murdering of male offenders and the implicated female relatives if the latter did not commit suicide. Although characterizing such crimes as currently more typical of certain rural areas, Greek criminologist Constantine Gardikis, cited in the *New York Times* article "Crimes of Honor Still the Pattern in Rural Greece," estimated in 1980 that two-thirds of Greek murders or attempted murders could be attributed to the desire to uphold family honor and respond to public humiliation.

According to such ideas of honor, women are considered to be sexually dangerous and vulnerable. It is accepted that both mature men and women have strong sexual drives; that of women, however, can be controlled without harm, whereas men may suffer madness without a heterosexual outlet, ideally found in marriage. For a wife to be faithful is not enough. Because women can tempt men without intention, they need internal moral restraints (like the sense of shame learned as a child) as well as external restraints on behavior, such as early marriage and restrictions on dress, speech, company, and scope and location of activity. Similarly, women, as the sex whose sexuality can and should be controlled (though male sexuality is not without its own dangers), have had to take the blame for male dereliction. What is feared are not acts per se, but their discovery and public recognition and discussion. If a bride had been found pregnant but was married quickly to the man to whom she had been engaged, her family's reputation might not suffer irreparably. At the same time, family reputation might suffer permanent damage as in the case of an unmarried girl who commits no sexual transgression but is the subject of malicious but convincing gossip or whose actions are misinterpreted by observers. This Greek concept of honor, then, is related to public evaluation of behavior based on a shared cultural code (which might vary between regions or even villages).

The beliefs distinguishing male versus female sexuality fit with other differences attributed to each sex. Men and women are thought by Greeks to be very different from one another. Traditionally, men have considered women to be more child-like, that is, more emotional, more vulnerable, more lacking in self-control. They have felt women had fewer positive qualities, such as wisdom, strength, and virtue. Also, different ideals have governed each sex. If women were to model themselves on Christ's Mother, to be modest, obedient, dedicated to children, and chaste, men aspired to heroism, to bravery, and to self-assertion. The differing attributes and ideals for men and women created a complementarity and a symbiosis.

Because men and women are believed to be contrasting creatures with personality characteristics derived from sex, each sex has its own set of duties and responsibilities. There is a rather strict division of labor by sex (but not necessarily based on prestige), the labor of one sex complementing that of the other; one sex may feel incompetent or feel it shameful to do the tasks of the other sex. If men are responsible for the family's material welfare, women are responsible for its spiritual welfare, interceding with heaven. Regardless of the specific evolution of a marriage depending on geographic location and social class, a woman's first duty is to have children and care for them properly. She is also responsible for, and expected to keep busy with, the preparation of food and the order and cleanliness of the home. She is expected to contribute economically as needed, always keeping in mind that she is the symbol of her husband's and family's honor and that her behavior should be beyond reproach. Overall, her role is expressive, nurturing, and otherwise related to homemaking in the most literal sense. Ideally, a wife's activities take place in the private realm in or near the home.

Greek society has seemed to be male dominated, but Greek women have had a strong sense of their worth and importance, although they have labored hard subject to strictures on behavior. The difference between the private, female-dominated realm of the hearth and home and the public, male-dominated realm of business and officialdom has been the key to understanding much of Greek society, particularly the relations between men and women. This difference can best be seen in the more public prestige of men and the more private power of women and in the differentiation of male and female space. Men and women have been frequently segregated, for example, men predominating in such public arenas as the coffeehouse and public square and women in churches, shrines, the cemetery, and the fountain. Deference has been accorded men in public by women, and until the 1983 family law, formal familial authority had lain with the man, who was expected to represent the household to the world outside the home, defend the family's reputation, and act as host and main provider. Most public roles, except those of schoolteacher and lower civil servant, have been occupied by men. Although women thus seem powerless, both men and women may be willing to admit that a woman can be a powerful force informally— through her strenuous work for the family, her diplomatic persuasion, her potential risk to honor, and her rights to the dowry. The 1983 family law implemented equality between the sexes, replacing the husband's legal right to be family head with common decisionmaking and obligations to contribute to family needs; the husband could no longer legally administer the woman's property or forbid her to work.

Women's work outside the home was often subordinated to the roles of wife and mother, but economic participation had the potential to stimulate cultural change; more and more women were living in cities and finishing childbearing and child rearing at younger ages owing to earlier marriage (see this ch.). In the early 1980s women constituted 31 percent of the Greek labor force, but a job equality law was not passed until 1984. The numbers of women in civil service were increasing, but women were concentrated at the lowest levels. Although women have not always sought job advancement because of their primary roles as wives and mothers and their deference to men, women have suffered discrimination because of delayed examinations, low priority of consideration, and the composition of review boards. According to the latest available data (1971 census and mid-1970s), married women, especially those aged 35 to 45, have tended to be concentrated in agriculture (which accounted for 45 percent of the female labor force) as unpaid labor (in harvests and tasks designated feminine); they were needed by their families because the family enterprise was oriented toward income, not profit. There was, however, a growing reluctance on the part of women and their families to remain in manual labor, for it lowers family status. Single women, whose maximum work commitment came between ages 25 and 30, were concentrated in nonagricultural jobs, often as craftswomen or laborers. Greek women, unlike men, if not working for the family, have tended to be salaried or wage earning rather than self-employed, because by receiving lower pay they provided cheap labor, especially in export industries, companies with over 100 employees, or textiles, clothing, and footwear. Women have been more vulnerable to unemployment and more likely to lose jobs if competing with men, who, by cultural definition, are considered breadwinners. Women, especially those in the working class, have worked only as long as their salaries were needed by the family, often allowing domestic concerns to compete with business. Generally, it is preferred that married women and especially mothers of young children stop working. Those most likely to continue working after marriage were career women with higher or vocational education.

The Greek institution of the dowry reflects the importance of the pragmatic element in marriage. According to Greek law, all children must inherit equally from their parents, the girl traditionally receiving her share as a dowry. The dowry may include land, livestock, money, a house, a trousseau, and furnishings that the bride has received from her parents at the time of her marriage. Traditionally, the father and unmarried brothers have been responsible for amassing the cash and property of the dowry, whereas the mother and daughter created the trousseau together. Family honor is reflected in provision of a substantial dowry that can attract desirable marriage partners for the family's daughters. A major family goal, especially for the parents, is to provide children with the wherewithal for a good standard of living as adults even if it means a delay in the children's marriages.

Dowries have been used to promote the family's upward social mobility. They have reflected the status of the giver and of the taker. A woman with a substantial dowry has had a good chance of marrying someone from a higher social level, thus enhancing her siblings' opportunities for marriage. Lower-middle-class families may have used the dowry to find a groom with a university degree. Rural families frequently attempted to entice urban suitors through the dowry, thereby providing their daughters with a more prestigious and comfortable lifestyle, while ensuring family members urban contacts. Dowry inflation in the last few decades, however, has commercialized the dowry and demanded increasingly greater sacrifices over many years from family members, necessitating long-term savings and purchase of urban property.

The 1983 family law abolished the legal requirement for parents to provide daughters with dowries and invalidated the settlement of property vested in the wife as dowry prior to the law (returning it to the wife). Because the same law equalized the husband's and wife's responsibility to contribute to family

*A Greek village woman plowing a field*
*Courtesy Mari Clark*

*An elderly Greek
woman in traditional
black attire
Courtesy
Peter J. Kassander*

needs, the intent was to eliminate any prejudice suffered by sons or any family frictions caused by dowries as well as possible abuse by greedy prospective grooms. One effect of this law may be to eliminate the tax loophole offered by a 1972 law making dowries up to Dr 200,000 (for value of the drachma— see Glossary) tax-free (over two years' average salary at that time). The law may cause the legal transfer of property to daughters to be reclassified as gifts or as special grants for children of either sex taxable at half the rate of gifts, because members of the working and lower middle classes and rural Greeks may be reluctant to abandon the dowry until they feel assured that the marital prospects of their daughters will not suffer.

In the 1950s when young, single women started working outside their homes in factories, they acquired the opportunity to earn money for their dowries. It is still not clear to what extent the increasing numbers of better educated, working women will change the cultural notion of a woman's contribution to her marriage from a dowry to an education, a career, or a paycheck. Emphasis may switch from what a working woman's family provides to what she herself saves, or switch from the woman's cash and property to personal qualities, just as it has already changed from family reputation and qualities to cash.

Among those who have taken an interest in abolishing the dowry are numerous feminists who see it as an impediment to the equality of the sexes, poor families who would be delighted to be free of such an economic burden, and various politicians and intellectuals who wish to see Greece a modern European nation no longer tied to outdated traditions. A strong case can be made to retain the dowry, however, because it has provided the wife with independent economic resources (kept by her in case of divorce) and has allowed her a stronger voice in the economic decisions of her new family. The dowry's role in providing assets for the new couple and their unborn children and in supplying housing for many urban residents and Greek islanders may not be easily replaced. Some daughters have felt that the dowry protects them from disinheritance. Many young women, particularly in the countryside, fear the stigma of not marrying and believe a dowry is necessary to attract a husband.

### Relations Outside the Household

Relations between households are more important than

relations between individuals. Relations between Greek households, usually composed of members of one nuclear family, fall into a range of degrees of cooperation and competition. Greeks feel an ever present tension in human relations. Ethnographers agree that Greeks see life in terms of a contest or struggle in several senses: wrestling a livelihood from nature if a farmer, sailor, fisherman, or shepherd; competing for wealth or reputation; and seeking advantage and guarding against exploitation by anyone who is not a trusted relative. There is a notion of "limited good," meaning that there is only a fixed amount of the object of competition; if one family should prosper materially or enhance its reputation, it necessarily will be at someone else's expense.

The extent to which one household benefits at another's expense is determined not just through the opinion of the households competing but also through general social evaluation. A city neighborhood or a village can be compared to a stage, and friends, neighbors, and kin to a Greek chorus commenting on unfolding marriages, hospitality, or sexual infidelity. No one can remain solely in the audience, however; neutrality is impossible to maintain. No one can expect to receive support of his or her reputation unless he or she defends that of allies. Manipulation of opinion depends on gossip, which in turn depends on the breaking of confidences, amusement derived from ridicule, and malicious attempts to exploit the situation. Scope is given to curiosity and the considerable skills of conversation, both of which are used to ferret out the latest news or scandals. Before the 1950s or 1960s, when villagers used to share an ascetic lifestyle, the basis of competition was often conduct. As income increased and urban standards of living seemed attainable, material goods and external appearances became important, too. Conduct was attacked or justified on grounds of either promotion of family interests (perhaps even condoning lying, slander, or exploitation of the weakness of others) or reference to the ideal values taught by the church, depending on which was more expedient.

The degree to which this competition impedes cooperation between households seems to vary over time and space. Kin and neighbors who are friendly are likely to cooperate. The competition and mistrust of those outside the same household are undoubtedly a result of poverty in a country where landholdings are fragmented and agriculture is not bountiful. In mountain communities of shepherds or struggling farmers, competition tends to be the fiercest; in lowland villages some

145

cooperation is necessary between landowners and laborers who need to make work contracts on a personal basis. Where marriage does not depend on male receipt of inheritance, men might need patrons to bestow jobs. The viewpoint of the observer also determines the degree of cooperation perceived. To a Greek psychologist raised in Athens, where families and neighbors are less united, rural groups of kin and neighbors in Epirus seem to work together as collectives, whereas to Anglo-Saxon anthropologists accustomed to a multiplicity of voluntary organizations, cooperation in Greek villages seems weak.

Despite the value placed on family independence, no Greek household can aspire to complete social or economic autonomy because of a need for supporters, witnesses in legal disputes, guests to whom to offer hospitality, mutual aid, and favors from the influential. Alliances must be sought for exchange of services, loan of tools, help in the fields, or relaxing company in the coffeehouse. A family reputation can gain reflected glory or opprobrium from that of relatives if not from other allies. It is not prudent to alienate all nonfamily members simultaneously and is morally reprehensible to exploit those poorer (though sin could be equated with anything that hurt the family). To be able to influence public opinion means gaining social contacts outside the family. Loyalties can never be completely restricted to one household, as in those households composed of former household members, such as a married sibling. Those most likely to make friendships are coffeehouse companions, especially unmarried men having few household responsibilities to conflict with friendship. Because of latent mistrust, however, friendships are fragile. The individuals or families linked keep family interests in mind and insist on maintaining perfect reciprocity and remaining complete social equals, neither losing in exchanges nor feeling confidence misplaced; any break over ingratitude or the public shame caused by spiteful gossip can create enmity.

### Patronage

Because of a mistrust for the motives of those outside the family, Greeks believe it is necessary to disregard their distaste for dependence in order to form asymmetrical friendships with persons of power and influence who can apply pressure where necessary. Villagers in particular do not expect fair or equal treatment from officials or government representatives who seem reluctant to help them on the sole basis of their being

Greek citizens. Past experience has led them to feel that officials and other nonfamily members must be induced to perform services through personal channels; they will not do it automatically. For example, if a Greek wants a new job, a telephone installed, a place at the university, a small loan, admission to a hospital, or a passport, he or she can offer the patron loyalty and political support or a gift, such as agricultural produce. The patron then uses personal and professional connections to perform the favor and in a sense accepts the duty of protecting the client. The patron feels flattered by the recognition of his or her importance and gains some service in return. The client feels protected from an incomprehensible bureaucracy and numerous rules and regulations seemingly unrelated to his or her problems. In the political context, this relationship is often called clientelism, and the favors and support exchanged are called *rousfeti* (see Interest Groups, ch. 4). Patrons are sought among kin living in the city, local officials, fellow villagers who might have become professionals, or merchants with whom one deals. PASOK announced in its government program in 1981 that it would eliminate political favors, corruption, and unequal treatment of citizens by public functionaries; earlier attempts at these reforms, for example, in the 1950s, had met with no success.

### Ritual Kinship

An example of patronage and an alliance between potentially competitive families found in both rural and urban areas is the relationship between a family and its *koumbaros* or *koumbara*; the *koumbaros* (masc. sing.; *koumbara*, fem. sing.) is the person selected by a family to be the godparent at a baptism or the sponsor at a wedding. At times the person who is the baptismal sponsor of the child had also been the sponsor at the marriage of the parents of the child or later becomes the marriage sponsor of the child. The *koumbaros* is like a member of the family in an artificially created relationship called spiritual kinship. As in a relationship by blood, canon law restricts marriage between godchildren of the same individual and between the family of the godchild and of the godparent. It is the next most important linkage for mutual cooperation after blood or marriage and has advantages neither of them possess, such as lack of competition over inheritance and of competition with unmarried siblings. The relationship then is not just between the godparent and the child, but between two families.

147

In addition to watching over the spiritual development of the child he or she has sponsored as a Christian, the godparent might be called upon to perform certain favors related to the material welfare of the family of the child; refusal is believed to threaten the child's spiritual welfare. A *koumbaros* is usually of higher or at least equal status with those who offer the honor, and the invitation affirms the honor and influence of the *koumbaros*. Because the relationship is voluntary, families might follow a variety of strategies in choosing ties to establish; they might pick one godparent from a local family of influence, another with political or business connections, and another who, childless, might leave property to the godchild in return for care in old age and performance of death rites. The relationship is friendly yet respectful and operates to both parties' advantage, often through the exchange of gifts and services. A merchant who comes to do business on an island might want to pass from being an outsider to an insider, receiving hospitality, news, and trust, or an employer might want to count on an employee's labor at peak periods.

### Social Stratification and Social Change

Greece can be said to have interrelated rural and urban stratification systems in which education and property are highly valued. Patronage links people of different classes and urban and rural residents, as does kinship. Social mobility in the last several decades has been achieved through education or accumulation of property as a result of savings or dowry, and migration outside Greece has been one means of saving. Greeks believe that success is not primarily a result of merit, but rather the result of connections acquired through kinship and marriage or of unscrupulous business methods.

In rural areas where villages were large enough to have significant social differentiation, there were three strata in the 1980s. At the upper level were the most prosperous farmers, large storekeepers, merchants, and professionals (doctors, teachers, and government officials). The middle layer consisted of most of the farm owners, small storekeepers, and the few skilled workers who resided in the village. The bottom rung included propertyless farmers and those socially marginal for physical or psychological reasons.

The disposition of Turkish estates when the Turks fled, the land reform of the 1920s, and the Greek system of equal inheritance did not allow for concentration of large tracts of land in

*Greek mountain village of Arachova, near Delphi*
*Courtesy Peter J. Kassander*

the hands of a few owners. The division of land in each generation through inheritance prevented the growth of an elite landowning class at the same time that the emergence of a large class of landless peasants was prevented by various family strategies to offer some sons an alternative to agriculture, such as education or seasonal or overseas migration. In the 1980s the big and middle landowners who represented 20 percent of landholdings held 55 percent of land area, in sharp contrast to the poor farmers who owned 5 percent of the land area in 26 percent of the holdings. The majority group of landowners was the stratum of the lower-middle-class farmers, who represented 54 percent of the holdings, which ranged in size from four to 20 hectares. These figures for land tenure, however, give only a crude indication of standing; crops, intensity of cultivation, and location relative to urban markets could determine how profitable a piece of land could be regardless of its size, and many supplemented agriculture with other pursuits.

In the 1980s three major social divisions also existed in the urban context, although not strictly parallel with those simpler and less comprehensive divisions in the rural areas. Property was a relatively more important criterion for the upper and lower social extremes while education was relatively more important for the urban middle strata; Athenians who were not recent migrants found job prestige to be more important. Membership in the urban upper class, in some senses an elite of independent commercial entrepreneurs, consisted of the bankers, big merchants, shipowners, and industrialists; it also included a few very wealthy and successful professionals and administrators. A distinction might be made between those having money and prestige for at least several generations and newer members who had only recently acquired money and were said by the others to be less cosmopolitan. The middle class, including nonmanual occupations and the majority of those in cities, comprised two groups—one of professionals, senior officials, executives, and lesser entrepreneurs, and the other of junior civil servants, shopkeepers, clerks, small merchants, craftsmen, and skilled workers. The lower class encompassed people without property or substantial education compared with the upper classes. This lower class included what might be called the Greek working class, which emerged during the interwar period with the absorption of the Asia Minor refugees; it was relatively small compared with other European countries because of the nature of Greek industrialization (see Historical Development, ch. 3). Greek social mobility after 1950 has been such that a large percentage of powerful Greek industrialists came from modest backgrounds and accumulated what they had during their own lifetimes.

Cross-cutting ties of kinship and patronage may be partly responsible for unsystematic aspects of notions of class. Also contributing may have been processes of change, such as tourism, urbanization, emigration, and the expansion of the tertiary sector. The effect of tourism on the distribution of income is not yet clear, and one pair of observers suggested that emigration and brain drain might be responses to overly rigid class structures as well as to economic opportunities offered abroad. A family's ranking in rural stratification might affect the possibility of a member's moving to the city or class membership and status once there because of differing access to education, substantial dowry, and urban contacts. From the point of view of living standards, security, and job prestige, rural-urban mobility may be often seen as social mobility. In both rural and urban areas the petite bourgeoisie and the middle strata have been constantly recruiting new members from the salaried and wage earners, helped by and feeding postwar expansion of services and urbanization. One route was saving over a period of years, perhaps through migration outside the country, by which thrifty and better educated Greeks by middle age could become self-employed in agriculture, transportation, tourist concerns, or manufacturng. This trend has been linked to gender—analysis of 1980s data showed that in agriculture women remained unpaid farmworkers until old age, while by age 35 there was a dramatic shift of men to the self-employed category through inheritance or purchase. The emphasis on self-employment meant that social conflict was more likely to come at the nexus between market and producer than between proletariat and middle class.

In some senses the village and the city can be considered to constitute the same social world, and a dichotomy between them may seem to be arbitrary. In Greece, unlike various other European countries, a villager's move to the city and upward mobility to the status of, for example, town tailor's wife, Athenian civil servant, or teacher does not entail a break in social relations with remaining kin in the village; to the contrary, villagers feel pride and respect for urban family members and value ties with migrant kin or compatriots as a basis for patronage or a home base in case of future urban migration. Through joint dowry deliberations, planning for the education of the younger generation, and exchange of visits, the face-to-face contact encourages villagers to imitate urban kin in dress, housing, or medical care (especially because of the value of such imitation in local competition for status). In addition to face-to-face contact, gifts and communications flow back and forth through the mail, telephone calls, private postal carriers, or obliging fellow villagers and their urban kin. Migrants may return on the occasions of Easter, the village patron saint's day, weddings, funerals, and baptisms, or the saints' days of male relatives (which are celebrated instead of birthdays).

As a result, migrants have not lost their sense of membership in the village community. Just as Greeks feel loyalty to the Orthodox church and the Greek nation, so they feel a chauvinistic loyalty to their birthplace (*patrida*) as well as to their family. As with the family, regardless of their own feelings, villagers do not brook unfavorable comparison with or criticism of their village. Despite a frequent lack of cooperation at the community level, unusual circumstances—an emergency, a common danger, or a religious or community holiday like the village festival—create solidarity. Icons or shrines mark the boundaries of the village; there is a community church; and residents born and brought up in the village share a set of customs, a patron saint, a local identity, and a sense of collective village honor. Because of rural-urban migration and emigration abroad, villagers no longer spend their entire lives in their villages, so the community may be said to encompass more than the site of the village.

This continuing membership by urban migrants may be demonstrated by subscription to a monthly newspaper that provides local news, by patronage at a café frequented by compatriots (who may offer jobs as well as news and company), or by attendance at a church with a compatriot priest. Community ties may also be formalized through membership in a migrants' organization, composed of people from the same geographical area. In one migrant's organization for those from a village on an island in the Cyclades, the village itself had about 110 households, and the migrant community comprised 250 families. In 1975 there were at least 500 migrants' organizations (mostly in Athens and a few in Thessaloniki); membership included about one-fifth the population of Athens. Members might include migrants of all social classes—for example, those of the wealthier strata who in some villages formed the first wave of migration (because of the capability of parents to pay for education) or those of the poorest who knew that no future lay in working as landless laborers in the village. Typical activities of migrants' organizations involve economic and philanthropic projects for the birthplace subsidized through either private funds or lobbying the government. Contact facilitated between classes and compatriots is important, for usually there is no one neighborhood in the city where all migrants' residences are clustered.

There has been a continuing flow of migrants to the city, so as the children or grandchildren of migrants feel less a part of the home village, there are newer migrants to maintain ties. This migration means that rural areas bear the cost of educating and raising those whose productive working years will enrich the city. Village families may choose to solve the problem of insufficient land for all children by paying the cost of a secondary and university education in place of inheritance. Daughters may insist on marriage outside the village, or parents may aspire to an easier life for their girls. Either way, rural savings in the form of dowries have been invested in urban real estate or small businesses.

Less obvious than the flow of people are the informal flows of cash and gifts aside from commercial transactions between the rural and urban sectors. Migrants may continue to own village land and houses because of a desire to maintain a summer home either as an escape hatch in case of urban emergencies or as an investment (in case of future development, until the purchase of urban property, or until there is an opportunity for sale). Meanwhile, the property may generate local economic activity through sharecropping, renovation, or visits of the owners, who will patronize local shops and bars. Produce from kin or from worked land may flow to the cities, either in an effort to save money or as an affirmation of the claimed superiority of products from the birthplace. When they can, urban migrants may send home money, but not to the extent of migrants in West Germany, Australia, Canada, or the United States.

There is no doubt that moving to the city causes modifications of conduct owing to new occupations and pastimes. Nevertheless, the relationship between urban and rural values is more complex than such modifications, involving as it does the transplantation of large numbers of villagers to Athens at the same time that migrants and the mass media are offering new cultural models to rural inhabitants; the majority of Athenians were not born there. On the one hand, migrants to the city have adopted the ideal of only two or three children and have influenced friends and family in the villages to do the same. On the other hand, rural emphasis on motherhood, dowries, market skills, and the exclusive social categories of allies and enemies have carried over into urban life.

The overall effect was that by the 1980s village community life was being undermined by depopulation and outflow of savings as well as being transformed through the penetration of such urban values as conspicuous consumption; rural people had become convinced of the superiority of the urban standard of living. The breakdown of rural isolation first through experience in wartime refugee camps in the 1940s and then through better communications and visiting between city and country offered new cultural models, which were not just offered by strangers or impersonal channels but by people who had once been in the same circumstances as the villagers themselves. In fact, the move to the city has become incorporated into the cycle of a villager's life as teenagers study in secondary school and university to prepare for a nonagricultural future and as daughters' prestigious weddings may come to imply marriage to a townsman or an urbanite. The transition to life in the city is made less abrupt by prior visits and by the welcome from kin, compatriots, or friends who may offer lodging, orientation, and job contacts.

It is not easy for rural communities to benefit from processes of change without encouraging inhabitants to move to the cities or abroad. Among six villages in the mountains and plains that historian William H. McNeill studied from the postwar period up to 1976, he found only three had prospered without massive depopulation. These three point to the directions of change for those not migrating out of rural areas. The first was an agricultural community near the tourist site of ancient Corinth that had updated its crops and agricultural methods to supply the Athens market and had benefited from the tourist industry and a small box factory. The second was a community at the foot of Mount Olympus sufficiently close to the ocean and Thessaloniki to encourage industry, opportunities for tourism, and commuting for part-time farming. The third was a Thessalian community in the fertile plains where malaria had been eradicated, agriculture had been modernized (cutting the need for labor), and new roads had stimulated renovation of buildings and installation of modern comforts. As elsewhere in Greece, even prosperous farming families in these villages were perplexed by the lack of interest of educated children or sons' potential brides in an agricultural future on family lands. The other three villages, like rural communities described by anthropologists, were losing not only population but also vitality and coherence in the sense of nonurban values and social structure.

Tourism provides an economic alternative to migration to the city. Aside from its impact on national and local economies, tourism can have sociocultural effects: reshaping of social stratification and classes; redistribution of income and assets; commercialization of cultural performances; distortion of images of foreigners; undermining of relations between the sexes, community solidarity, and social obligations; exaggeration of competitive consumption; and loss of local control of the local economy.

Since 1979 over 5 million tourists have arrived annually. Although in 1985 it was not possible to generalize for all of Greece, there were data on one Greek island in the Cyclades, Mikonos, a tourist site since the 1930s. In 1984 it was estimated to have received over 488,000 tourists, most of whom arrived between April and October. Tourists included mostly foreigners arriving as part of a cruise but also migrants returning to visit, urban elite on vacation, and Greek youths interested in sun and fun.

As a result of tourism, Mikonos has avoided depopulation

and massive migration since the 1950s. An economy faltering since the mid-nineteenth century was revived by the creation of a demand for labor, transportation, real estate, products of farm and sea, handicrafts, lodging and meals, and construction. Because of this new demand and because of redefinition of what were nonproductive assets (infertile land, surplus labor, and unused buildings became valuable), all residents benefited from tourist-derived income and opportunities to diversify sources of income. Because land tenure was not concentrated, new uses for land and the new income meant social categories were blurred, making the status of each family not as apparent as in pretourism days. Tourist development was neither sudden nor disruptive to an island formerly geared to port services and seafaring as well as to agriculture. Although permissive behavior of tourists was tolerated, it was not approved, and television and Athenian models of conduct were having at least as much effect on feminine leisure behavior as tourists; male exhibition of Greek dance and male interest in foreign women were assimilated into the double standard for the behavior of the sexes, so tourism was accentuating and facilitating already existing social tendencies. Service sector opportunities did bring women out from their role as unpaid family labor to work with cottage industries, lodging, or any number of tourist-oriented businesses. Residents of Mikonos felt tourism had affected them positively by obliterating poverty and servility; for example, bribery of and short-term relations with powerful outsiders replaced long-term dependence on the local upper class as patrons. One apparent effect was that the nuclear family ceased to be a crucial unit of labor, occupational training, and inheritance.

❁　❁　❁

There are many anthropological studies of rural Greece, and anthropologists are beginning to look at urban Greeks, too. Some of the classic accounts of rural Greece are still valuable: John K. Campbell's *Honour, Family, and Patronage*; Ernestine Friedl's *Vasilika*; and Juliet du Boulay's *Portrait of a Greek Mountain Village*. A sense of regional diversity is provided in a 1976 volume, edited by Muriel Dimen and Friedl, titled *Re-

*gional Variation in Modern Greece and Cyprus: Toward a Perspective on the Ethnography of Greece.* William H. McNeill's book, *The Metamorphosis of Greece since World War II*, provides a rare, long-term look at Greek society. The three chapters on Greece by Hans Vermeulen, Susan B. Sutton, and Renée B. Hirschon in *Urban Life in Mediterranean Europe* offer the most recent published sources on Greek urban life. The articles on Greek women in the first issue of the *Journal of Modern Greek Studies*, published in 1983, provide a rich examination of women's roles in the family, church, and public life. A recent overview of Greek culture is provided by Campbell's article, "Traditional Values and Continuities in Greek Society."

The same volume with the overview by Campbell, *Greece in the 1980s*, edited by Richard Clogg, includes articles by Kallistos Ware and Alexis Dimaras describing trends in the Greek Orthodox Church and in Greek education, respectively. Older but also a good source on Greek orthodoxy is *The Orthodox Church* by Timothy Ware. Two books discussing Greek education in the 1980s are *The Educational System of Greece* by Byron G. Massialas and *Greece* by E. Eugene Oliver in the World Education series. Unfortunately there is no up-to-date source on Greek geography; a quick introduction is provided by the chapter on Greece in Aubrey Diem's *Western Europe: A Geographical Analysis*. (For further information and complete citations, see Bibliography.)

# Chapter 3. The Economy

*The Greek merchant fleet is one of the largest in the world.*

IN THE POST-WORLD WAR II period up to 1980, the Greek economy generally grew more rapidly than the economies of other European Community members. Yet in 1983 Greek per capita gross national product was US$3,560, about half the average European Communities level, while Greece remained near the bottom of most European Communities tables of socioeconomic indicators. Only certain regions, such as the Mezzogiorno in Italy and parts of Ireland and France, exhibited a similar, relatively low, level of economic development. Greece was anxious to rectify this situation. The task was immense not only because of the country's largely mountainous or island terrain and its poor transportation network but also because the various economic sectors displayed serious structural weaknesses rooted in tradition, as well as short-sighted economic policies.

Greece began the transformation from a largely agricultural economy to one based primarily on services and industry only in the early 1950s. Industrialization did not proceed satisfactorily, however, because the country lacked a domestic entrepreneurial class willing to invest in industry. Successive governments, therefore, encouraged foreign investment in basic industry and instituted a multitude of regulations and incentives designed to promote private initiative. In time, state intervention and control gradually pervaded economic life, creating a massive, centralized, and inefficient bureaucracy. This trend was most pervasive in the banking and tax systems, as well as in the machinery for investment approval. Yet there were no mechanisms for coordinated development planning; policy signals often conflicted, or they favored certain sectors and enterprises to such an extent that they created economic distortions. In the private sector, economic activity became increasingly concentrated geographically around Athens and financially through the dominance of a few dozen industrialist families.

Outside of a small and isolated modern industrial sector, a plethora of family units characterized by low productivity and limited financial, managerial, and technical know-how predominated in both industry and agriculture. Thus, the economy became increasingly reliant on tourism, the public sector, and other services for employment and growth, while agriculture continued to play a much larger role than it played in the European Communities as a whole. Lack of a dynamic, indigenous industry meant that as Greece developed, it relied on a range of imports from consumer to capital goods; this pattern contributed to the worsening of the traditional trade gap. Dependence on imported oil to meet growing energy demand and on invisibles—shipping, tourism, and emigrant remittances—as an offsetting source of foreign exchange receipts accentuated the economy's vulnerability to exogenous economic developments.

Following the second worldwide energy crisis in 1979, the Greek economy stagnated. Economic problems, including persistently high inflation, considerable balance of payments deficits, and growing unemployment reflected recessionary world economic conditions as well as structural imbalances and the compounded impact of slow adjustment to the first oil crisis of 1973. Under these conditions Greece's first socialist government came to power in November 1981, promising far-reaching reforms for modernization and revitalization of the economy, specifically to reduce regional and socioeconomic inequalities. These reforms included the introduction of sectoral and decentralized planning; the creation of advisory committees composed of worker and community representatives for greater public oversight of corporate affairs; promotion of agricultural cooperatives, small dynamic businesses, and new technologies; state restructuring of overindebted firms; and simplification of bureaucratic procedures.

The Socialist government was forced by economic and political realities, however, to adopt a gradualist approach toward change and economic adjustment. Adjustment would entail a substantial shift of resources from domestic consumption into investment and net exports, but the government was opposed to austerity measures that would lower living standards or raise unemployment.

Therefore, although the gross national product expanded by 2.8 percent in 1984 after three years of stagnation, inflationary pressures remained high. The inflation rate—18.5 percent in 1984, compared with 24.5 percent in 1981—was falling only gradually, and prospects for reducing the public sector deficit in 1985 were not bright; the public sector borrowing requirement would likely equal about 16 percent of the gross domestic product—still an improvement over 1981. Moreover, the current account deficit remained at a high level—US$2.2 billion—despite transfers from the European Communities and more buoyant exports. The difficulties of closing this deficit were primarily responsible for the rapid increase in the country's external indebtedness.

In view of the seriousness of the country's economic problems, government policy tended to reflect pragmatic assessments rather than commitments to any specific economic philosophy. In any case, the government would be confronted with the urgency of reducing inflation as well as raising the low level of investment, which had been recognized as probably the most serious obstacle to development. In 1984 private sector investment declined for the fifth straight year, underscoring the need to enhance business confidence in the government and to establish a stable regulatory framework. Increasing both public and private investment to improve the structure of the economy and create employment will be a central policy goal for years to come.

## Historical Development

Continued political turmoil and border strife in the first years of Greek independence delayed any significant steps toward the development of a modern economy until the late 1800s (see Irredentism: Expansion and Defeat, ch. 1). Rapid industrialization did not begin, however, until the late 1950s; until that time economic growth had been largely dependent on agricultural performance. Under the leadership of Kharilaos Trikoupis, who held the prime ministership three times between 1882 and 1895, Greece's first social and industrial legislation was passed. Construction of paved roads, the country's first rail lines, and the Corinth Canal in the 1880s opened up internal transportation and stimulated domestic and foreign trade.

Because rail access to European countries was blocked by the Ottoman Empire, shipping developed rapidly in light of Greece's historical maritime orientation. It increased about fivefold during the reign of George I (1863-1913), fostering the simultaneous development of seaport towns, banking, and ancillary services. Early exports consisted mainly of agricultural products, particularly currants and, later, tobacco, followed by goods such as textiles and pottery. The little manufacturing that existed at this time depended on foreign credit and high protective tariffs. By the mid-1970s debt service on foreign loans from the colonial powers amounted to one-third of the national budget. In 1893 Greece defaulted on loans, some of which dated back to its war of independence (1821-29).

With the exception of a few large estates in Thessaly, Greek agriculture has traditionally been based on small, fragmented farms where underemployment was endemic. The inability of industry to absorb surplus rural labor stimulated a surge of emigration to the United States—more than 250,000 emigrants in the 1906-14 period alone. Even before World War I emigrants' remittances began to make a significant contribution to Greece's foreign exchange earnings.

After the accession of Eleutherios Venizelos to the prime ministership in 1910, modernization of the economy received new impetus. Health and old-age insurance programs were initiated, and a series of land-reform decrees were passed, which provided a legal framework for extensive land redistribution. With the aid of foreign capital, public works and road construction projects were initiated. Implementation of these measures was slow, interrupted first by the Balkan wars of 1912-13 and then by World War I. As in Greece's early years, the impact of external events hindered the process of economic development.

Emboldened by being on the winning side against the Turks in World War I, the Venizelos government attempted to occupy Turkish territory in Asia Minor, but Greece's defeat in 1922 resulted in a massive population transfer. Greece accepted over 1 million refugees from Asia Minor at a time when its population numbered just over 5 million inhabitants. Although serious housing and employment problems had to be borne, in the long run the additional manpower made possible considerable increases in agricultural and industrial production.

By 1936 about 150,000 refugee families were resettled, mostly in Macedonia and Thrace. Much of the land had been in pasture, but the small size of the resettlement plots dictated a more intensive land use. These plots were therefore converted to crop production by the Anatolian refugees, who were accustomed to farming cash crops, such as tobacco, raisins, and currants. The area under cultivation increased by more than 50 percent in the 1920s, and the value of agricultural production doubled. Less favorable, however, was the aggravation of the pattern of small, fragmented landholdings.

The refugee resettlement program also had an impact on industrial development. Some of the refugees who settled around Athens and Thessaloniki (Salonika) brought capital in the form of portable valuables as well as skills and handicraft knowledge, enabling them to set up small shops and factories. Silkworm breeding and carpet weaving were introduced, the textile industry expanded significantly, and the pottery and copperware crafts were further developed. Although many of these new enterprises were small, inefficient, and dependent on cheap refugee labor, they contributed significantly to the sevenfold increase in industrial production between 1921 and 1929.

Nonetheless, throughout the 1920s the standard of living remained low, and unemployment and underemployment were common in both the cities and the rural areas. Cities were becoming overcrowded, while emigration was slowed by stricter quotas and controls in the United States and in the British dependencies. The economy was heavily dependent on imports, particularly of basic foodstuffs, which were not being produced economically in Greece. Exports consisted mainly of a few cash crops vulnerable to international price fluctuations. Remittances from emigrants and seamen were the only significant foreign exchange offset to chronic trade deficits, and these payments slowed with the approach of worldwide depression. The economy was poorly equipped to bring the nation through the turbulence of the next two decades.

During the 1930s and 1940s the economy suffered from the impact of depression, dictatorship, war, foreign occupation, and civil war. When peace returned in 1950, over one-third of the population was dependent on the government and on foreign aid for resettlement or subsistence. Agriculture production was down by over two-thirds, and half the country's woodland had been burned or felled. About 75 percent of the railroad system and the commercial shipping fleet, as well as nearly the entire road network, were destroyed. Any industry that had survived World War II suffered badly during the Civil War (1946-49). Foreign aid began to flow from the United States in 1947, but much of it was initially expended by the army or diverted to direct relief rather than to reconstruction and development (see Foreign Aid and Investment, this ch.).

Recovery began in 1953 when a currency revaluation restored confidence in the drachma (for value of the drachma—see Glossary), brought some stability to inflationary prices, and boosted exports. This was followed by the restoration of roads, the railroad system, and other infrastructure facilities, which was carried out largely under the leadership of Constantine Karamanlis, who served as minister of public works in the Alexander Papagos government and then as prime minister from 1955 to 1963. There was marked economic progress during the first Karamanlis government—the longest uninterrupted tenure in modern Greek history. Karamanlis was also instrumental in bringing Greece into the European Economic Community (EEC—see Appendix B) in 1962 as an associate member. Over a long-term period this relationship fostered increased earnings from exports, shipping, tourism, and emigrant remittances.

In the postwar years development strategy focused for the first time on industrialization. The basic approach was to restrict the government role to creating the necessary infrastructure and establishing financial mechanisms for channeling private capital into import-substituting industries. Successive governments also encouraged foreign investment with favorable legislation.

During the Karamanlis era considerable industrial development took place, including construction of the country's largest shipyard at Skaramanga near Piraeus, an aluminum plant, oil refineries, and the beginning of an iron and steel industry (see Industry, this ch.). The country's development potential was not fully realized, though, for private investment in manufacturing remained inadequate. Indigenous capital favored real estate and financial investments that brought quick returns and high profits. Reluctance to make long-term investments was influenced by Greece's historical political and economic instability and strong family loyalties. Because the purpose of many businesses was to provide family members with socially prestigious positions, expansion that would dilute family control was often rejected.

Although the immediate causes of the government crisis that ended in the establishment of a military junta in 1967 were apparently political, economic grievances contributed to government instability. The benefits of economic growth had not been widely shared and were aggravated by the increasing concentration of population and economic activities in Athens. Rural areas suffered from low productivity and unemployment, while in urban areas there was considerable dissatisfaction over poor housing, low wages, rising taxes, and inadequate social services. Dissatisfaction was heightened by the affluent minority's tendency toward conspicuous consumption. Rural and urban unrest were manifested in the increasing frequency of strikes involving government workers and teachers as well as industrial, agricultural, and service employees.

In 1964 the government of George Papandreou sought to

accelerate industrial growth and to address the problems of welfare and social equity. Although many of the measures taken alleviated genuine hardships, others, such as subsidization of wheat, were inflationary and were more difficult to justify on social grounds. By mid-1965 the negative effects of Papandreou's expansionist and inflationary policies were felt. The trade deficit widened alarmingly, running down official reserves. After Papandreou was forced to resign for political reasons in July 1965, unstable political conditions militated against serious reform of the economy. When the colonels seized control, the industrial sector was extremely uncompetitive; protective measures obliged manufacturers to buy components and services from domestic suppliers at inflated prices.

The record of the junta (1967-74) in managing the economy was mixed. In spite of relative stagnation in agriculture, which grew at an annual rate of only 2.2 percent between 1968 and 1972, the economy grew at an 8.6-percent annual rate. The junta completed many of the infrastructural projects laid out by previous governments, making the economy look stronger than it had looked at any other time since the Civil War. It failed, however, to launch an effective development plan or to create the machinery for doing so.

The colonels' policies effectively tipped the balance of the economy toward services, reinforcing the country's image as "Hotel Greece." International investors were wary of sinking funds into industrial development in a politically unstable country, so the colonels promoted construction and tourism. Restrictions on lending to these two sectors, as well as to shipbuilding and repair, were greatly relaxed. An understanding was reached with the Greek shipowners, who until the late 1960s had often registered under flags of convenience (see Glossary). They were effectively granted tax-free status in return for a small levy on tonnage under the Greek flag.

In 1974 a long period of economic growth came to an end. The gross domestic product (GDP—see Glossary) declined for the first time in 25 years—by more than 2 percent. The economic problems that had been festering in the last years of the military regime were compounded by the worldwide recessionary conditions associated with the first oil shock and the inflated defense budget in the wake of the Turkish invasion of Cyprus. Although the economy by most statistical measurements was substantially healthier when the regime collapsed than when it started, it was in several respects considerably worse off. The annual deficit in the current account balance had risen from under US$300 million to over US$1.2 billion. Except for oil prospecting near Thasos in the Aegean Sea off the coast of Macedonia near Kavala and an automobile assembly plant built by Peugeot of France, few industrial projects had been undertaken.

Even in the tourist sector there was a lack of planning and disregard of banking criteria in approving projects for financing. The principal economic failure during the last year of the junta and a major contributor to its downfall was the sudden skyrocketing inflation that almost reached a 50-percent annual rate. Inflation was caused by a number of factors, including a growing shortage of commodities and soaring import costs as Greece continued to link the drachma to the United States dollar, which was devalued in 1973.

After the restoration of democratic rule in July 1974, the Karamanlis government initially followed an anti-inflationary policy. A wage explosion was inevitable, however, because the colonels had enforced strict wage restraint. The government felt it politically unwise to clamp down too much on wages, so although most Western governments were tightening their belts in response to the oil crisis, Greece tended to follow expansionary policies.

In 1975 the economy resumed its rapid growth; a boom in manufactured exports to the EEC, mainly textiles and clothing, brought the annual increase of GDP to 4 percent between 1975 and 1978, one of the highest rates among members of the Organisation for Economic Co-operation and Development (OECD—see Glossary). Unemployment was reportedly very low, but high inflation, the continuing lack of productive investment, and low productivity clouded long-term economic prospects. In mid-1978 the government moved gradually to less expansionary policies and price controls, but the economy was seriously affected by the second oil shock in 1979 and entered a phase of stagflation. The worst year was 1981, when to muster support for October elections the incumbent government pursued expansionary policies. The rate of inflation reached 24.5 percent, the public sector borrowing requirement amounted to just over 17 percent of GDP, and the current account deficit exceeded a record US$2.4 billion. The initial effect of entry into the EEC in January 1981 was largely negative (see European Economic Community, this ch.).

The economy was a major issue in the 1981 election campaign. Worker demonstrations against rising prices took place in Athens in May 1981 notwithstanding the gradual move toward inflation-linked pay increases and shorter working hours. Little progress had been made in adjusting to the oil shocks of the 1970s or in correcting the historical distortions that characterized the economy.

## Role of Government

Faced with economic challenges, the Socialist government has sought to provide an alternative to the strategies of growth and modernization advocated by previous administrations. Its overriding economic objective has been to achieve self-sustaining economic growth while promoting a more equitable distribution of income and wealth. Policy was based on the premise that the economy should function in the broader social interest rather than benefit a small, yet powerful, business elite.

On November 21, 1981, Prime Minister Andreas Papandreou made his first official policy statement to parliament, outlining a program for economic recovery and modernization of Greece's highly centralized, interventionist economic system. This would entail deep changes in governmental, industrial, and agricultural structures to promote popular participation in economic decisionmaking at all levels. To this end the government has pursued decentralization of administrative and economic functions from the central authorities to the municipalities and communities—particularly in regard to planning—as well as the "socialization" of the key sectors of the Greek economy (see Economic and Regional Planning, this ch.).

In the 1982-84 period the policies of the Panhellenic Socialist Movement (Panhellinion Socialistiko Kinima—PASOK) furthered the development of a mixed economy in Greece. At the time of the restoration of democratic rule in 1974, the government already operated all public utilities, including electric power and water, telephone and telegraph services, radio and television, and railroads. Under the New Democracy (Nea Demokratia—ND) regime of Karamanlis, the public sector grew to account for nearly half of GDP. By 1975 a number of dominant firms, including the Commercial Bank of Greece, the Aspropirgos oil refineries, Olympic Airways, and the Athens bus companies, had come under government ownership. The language of Article 106 of the Constitution supports an active public sector role. It authorizes legislation for state take-over of, or participation in, enterprises that are either monopolistic, vitally important to the development of national resources, or primarily involved in rendering services to society as a whole.

Regarding the role of the public and private sectors, PASOK's economic policy echoed to some extent that of the ND government. Both governments repeatedly expressed commitment to private enterprise and the right to a reasonable profit but vowed to take action to prevent monopolies and oligopolies. PASOK proved, however, to be more emphatic about requiring private business to operate within the framework defined by government policy and development goals. To expedite development in fields where private capital was unavailable or where there was unwillingness to assume risk or high costs of initiation, the two governments promoted state investment initiatives. Thus, both were widely perceived as extending the public sector, although private business regarded the tone of PASOK rhetoric as more hostile to its interests.

PASOK stressed a third sector—that of "social experimentation"—in which new production forms and relationships would be established. Agro-industrial cooperatives, municipal and community enterprises, overindebted firms restructured by the state, and other kinds of worker-managed enterprises were considered part of this sector. PASOK's view was that balanced, decentralized development would come from the coexistence of these three sectors; it could also be promoted through socialization.

Socialization, one of the key tenets of PASOK economic policy, did not prove far-reaching a change as suggested by its wording. In essence, socialization meant the establishment of advisory committees composed of workers' representatives, local or central authorities, members of public interest groups, and shareholders. Modeled on the West German system of worker involvement on management boards, these committees were not to interfere with daily management. Rather, their purpose was to ensure that corporate policies were in line with government economic objectives. They would also guarantee that issues affecting the community, such as pollution and employment, were taken into consideration by management. This form of worker participation was also encouraged by the EEC and required for firms that wished to incorporate as European rather than as national firms. One can therefore expect comangement gradually to become a more common practice in Greece.

Advisory committees were expected to begin operating in public sector companies by the summer of 1985. Socialization of public sector companies was supposed to replace centralized, bureaucratic management systems that were dependent on the ministries in Athens with a democratic and decentralized form of social control. The goal was to improve the efficiency of their operations through greater public oversight. The first public corporations scheduled for socialization included the Public Power Corporation (Dimosia Epicheirisi Ilektrismou—DEI), the Hellenic Telecommunications Organization, and Hellenic Railways.

In the private sector, socialization was proceeding at an even slower pace. Advisory committees were to be set up only at the sectoral level rather than at the company level. Socialization would be carried out in the key sectors of the economy—potentially the banking, insurance, mining, shipbuilding, steel, cement, fertilizer, pharmaceutical, and defense industries.

Another aspect of the Socialist economic program—the restructuring of ailing, overindebted firms by the state— proved controversial among both industrialists and PASOK members. Business critics viewed government actions as tantamount to creeping nationalization and feared unfair competition, while some party members criticized the strain the rescuing of these "problematic enterprises" would place on public finances. Liberal lending to a number of industrialists in the traditional sectors of the economy had led to the creation of a large number of insolvent firms when business conditions began to deteriorate in 1979. In this environment the government decided it had to step in to preserve employment and the nation's industrial base.

As of mid-1985, some 39 companies with a total debt of Dr167 billion and some 27,000 employees had been officially recognized as subject to state intervention. Rescue operations usually involved conversion of at least 51 percent of a company's outstanding debt into equity shares owned by the government. The most notable conversions included the Skalistiri group of companies, which manufactured products for use in the metals and cement industries, and Piraiki-Patraiki, Greece's largest textile manufacturer. In addition, Heracles General Cement Company, the largest cement company in Europe, was brought under state bank control after controversial charges of fraud and illegal export of foreign exchange were levied but later dismissed. In mid-1984 the Halyvourgiki Steel Company was fined almost Dr9 billion, roughly twice its assets, based on charges of illegal export of foreign exchange. This incident raised business suspicions that the government was deliberately weakening certain firms to justify state take-over.

Altogether, about 500 firms were being investigated in 1985, and government statements implied that about one-third of industry was in need of restructuring. The largest number of problematic firms were in the textiles sector, followed by those in the metallurgy, construction, foodstuffs, and beverages sectors. How many of these firms would come under government control was unclear. Initially, state rehabilitation of ailing firms was seen as an opportunity to promote worker participation in management, but there have been no examples of true worker management stemming from this policy. Statements by government officials in late 1984 indicated that if former owners paid in new share capital, they would be allowed to retain management of their firms but would be required to have an inspector on the board of directors to represent creditor banks. In the words of Gerassimos Arsenis, minister of national economy and finance, the government's goal was "to render both the private and public sectors competitive, and we are not dogmatic about how this will be carried out."

Under the PASOK administration business-government relations have been strained, although sharp business criticism of economic policy was not a new phenomenon in Greece. The PASOK government aroused the hostility of business from the start by its early measures, which were aimed at raising corporate taxation and instituting a redistributive income policy. Stricter and more widespread application of price controls, which were first instituted by the ND government in 1979, also upset business people. The Bank of Greece repeatedly warned that profit margins were inadequate in parts of the manufacturing sector, thereby discouraging productive investment. This was a serious charge, given that one of the chief problems for the Greek economy had been the generally low level of productive investment since the mid-1970s (see fig. 14). Although PASOK streamlined the approval process for industrial investments, the outlook for private investment activity remained poor. PASOK rhetoric and the increase in size of the public sector contributed to deteriorating business confidence.

170

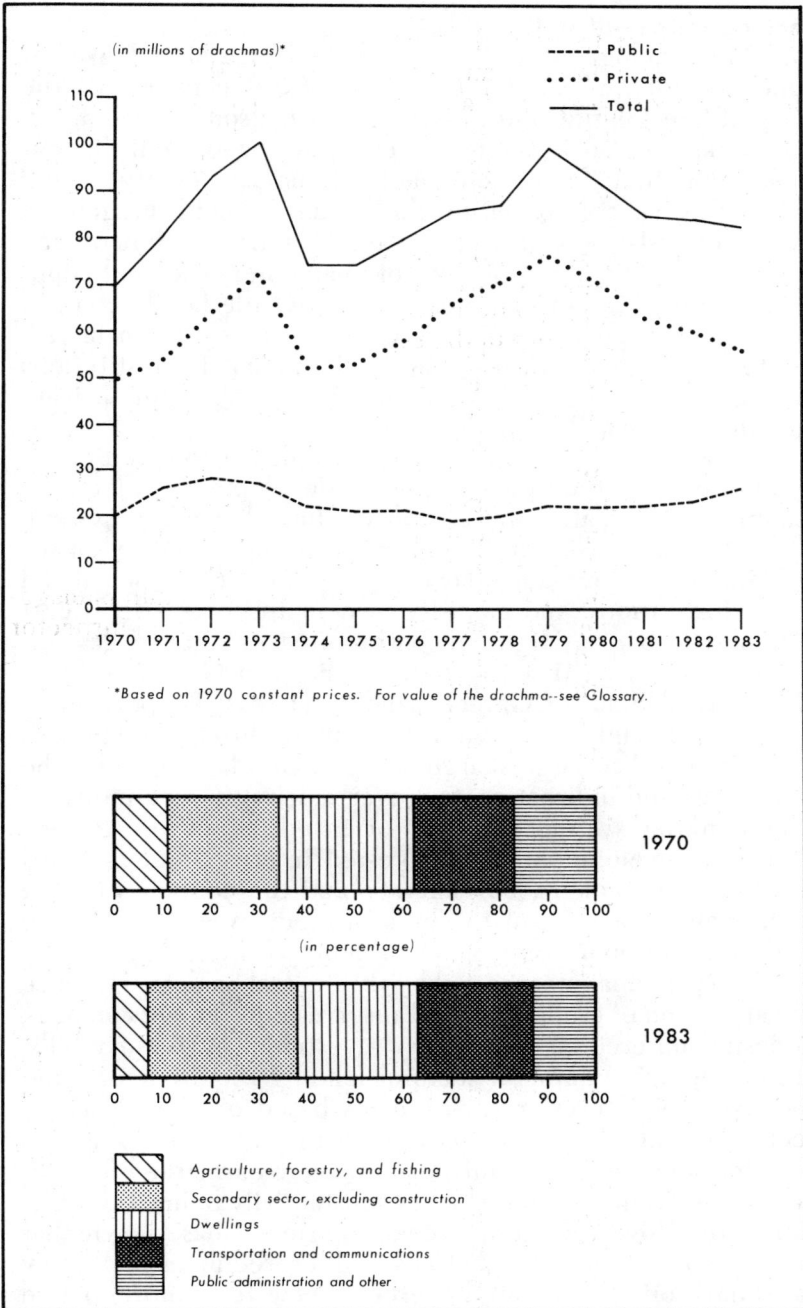

(in millions of drachmas)*

------ Public
•••• Private
——— Total

*Based on 1970 constant prices. For value of the drachma--see Glossary.

1970

(in percentage)

1983

Agriculture, forestry, and fishing
Secondary sector, excluding construction
Dwellings
Transportation and communications
Public administration and other

*Figure 14. Public and Private Fixed Asset Formation, 1970-83*

## Banking and Credit System

The banking system is characterized by a high degree of concentration and state control. In 1985 it consisted of the Bank of Greece, the country's central bank; some 35 commercial banks; five government-owned, specialized credit institutions; and three investment banks. Bond and equity capital markets were still underdeveloped despite encouragement through legislation and tax incentives. Their growth had been hampered by the predominance of small enterprises and popular reluctance to entrust one's money outside family control. Owners of surplus funds have tended to invest them in real estate or hold them as bank deposits. Thus, banking institutions have played a crucial role in mobilizing and allocating private and public financial resources.

Successive governments have relied heavily on credit policy in efforts to attain their economic development objectives, leading to the creation of a complex, inflexible banking system. The state influenced credit allocation through comprehensive banking regulations, annual credit programs for the specialized credit institutions, and majority ownership in the two largest commercial banks. High concentration strengthened government influence in that the National Bank of Greece and the Commercial Bank of Greece handled at least 75 percent of commercial banking activity. Moreover, through these two banks, which had large shareholding in Greek companies, the state exercised indirect control over much of Greek industry. The banking system was not oriented, however, toward Greece's development needs. Vested interests and personal ties between bankers, bureaucrats, and the country's largest industrialists meant that the bulk of credit was channeled to traditional, often uncompetitive or monopolistic firms.

The principal means used by the central bank to influence the allocation of credit included reserve requirements on bank deposits and credits, compulsory investment in treasury bills, credit ceilings, minimum sectoral lending requirements, and the fixing of interest rates on loans based on the economic sector or kind of expenditure to be financed. In 1983 some 56 percent of commercial bank deposits were earmarked for specific transactions at interest rates substantially below the inflation rate. However, past Greek experience has shown that interest subsidization has not ensured desired investment; low rates have often stimulated overborrowing for nonproductive purposes.

Gradual modernization of the banking system and reform

of credit policy have been among the most significant and least controversial economic measures of the PASOK government. The central aim was to simplify credit regulations, giving bankers greater responsibility for conducting their affairs on the basis of standard banking criteria. Other goals were to tighten monetary policy, increase access to finance for all sectors, create incentives for private savings accounts, and establish a more uniform cost of credit. Thus, interest rates, although still set by the authorities, were raised to more realistic levels and were unified. By 1984 only three basic rates, compared with over 100 previously, applied to 90 percent of credit extended to the private sector. Only rates for loans to agriculture and small-scale industry, sectors without many resources of their own, remained substantially negative.

In addition, specialized credit institutions were directed to intensify their efforts to attract savings from the public and to reduce their dependence on the central bank. In 1984 the Agricultural Bank of Greece, the largest such institution, was expected to finance about 75 percent of its lending operations out of private deposits. Another step in the direction of a more market-oriented credit system involved control of credit extended by the Agricultural Bank of Greece and the National Mortgage Bank. In 1983 the Bank of Greece stopped determining the allocation of credit by these two institutions. Instead, it began to concentrate on control of the overall expansion of their outstanding credit through limits on drawings from central bank funds. It also instituted a penalty rate on commercial bank overdrafts with the central bank.

### Monetary and Exchange Rate Policy

Since the mid-1970s monetary policy has been faced with the difficult task of reconciling the need to reduce inflation with the financing of substantial government deficits. Government borrowing from the public is not widespread. Fiscal needs, therefore, affect monetary policy by forcing the government to cover budget deficits through money creation regardless of prevailing economic conditions. Money growth has usually exceeded targets, especially before elections, contributing to the persistence of inflationary pressures in Greece.

As part of its reform of the banking and credit system, the PASOK government has given the Bank of Greece more autonomy in administering monetary, credit, and foreign exchange policy. Until June 1982 the Currency Committee—consisting

173

of the governor of the Bank of Greece and the ministers of national economy and finance, commerce, and agriculture— regulated the issuing of bank notes and made all major monetary and credit policy decisions.

Under a new division of powers, the government continues to shape general monetary and credit policies through the cabinet-level Council of Government and Economic Policy, while the Bank of Greece retains responsibility for policy development and implementation. However, limits have been placed on short-term government borrowing from the Bank of Greece, and lending rates have been set closer to the private market level. By preventing the government from routinely turning to the central bank to cover public sector deficits, these measures will give the Bank of Greece greater control over monetary growth. At the same time, they will improve conditions for the development of the capital market. The Bank of Greece was to begin dealing in marketable treasury bills in April 1985.

Exchange rate policy has aimed at maintaining the competitiveness of the drachma in conjunction with the maximum limitation of inflationary pressures from abroad. The Greek exchange rate system has been gradually liberalized since 1975, when the drachma was first floated. Initially the official exchange rate was set daily by the Bank of Greece in relation to a weighted basket of the currencies of Greece's main trading partners. After the establishment of an interbank market in 1979, certain commercial banks were authorized to set the daily rate within broad limits determined by the central bank. As of April 1985 Greece did not participate in the exchange rate and intervention mechanism of the European Monetary System, but the drachma had been introduced into the European currency unit (ECU). In conjunction with this move, the Bank of Greece permitted Greek residents abroad to open convertible drachma deposits in domestic banks.

Owing to high inflation in Greece, a steady depreciation of the drachma against the United States dollar and other major currencies began in 1980. A devaluation of 15.5 percent in January 1983 stimulated exports in the short run, but with the unpegging of the drachma from the United States dollar in August of the same year, inflationary pressures were reasserted through the rise of the drachma cost of imports. Inflation averaged 24.5 percent in 1981, 21 percent in 1982, 20.3 percent in 1983, and 18.5 percent in 1984. In comparison, the rate for the EEC as a whole fell from 11 percent in 1982 to 6.6 percent in September 1984.

## Fiscal Policy

Up to the early 1970s increases in public expenditure were largely self-financing. Public sector investment, especially in infrastructure, spurred economic growth, generating extra revenues. Inflationary pressures were contained, and the public sector deficit was limited to about 1.5 percent of GDP. Between 1973 and 1981 the situation changed drastically. Public expenditure rose from about 26.5 percent of GDP in the early 1970s to around 43 percent in 1981. Compromising long-term economic development, this rise was associated with a marked fall in the share of public investment against a rise in current government expenditure that was considerably greater than in other OECD countries. Much of the increase was to accommodate the pressing need to improve social services, health, education, and social security benefits, but some of it was spent in the hope of gaining electoral support. In particular, employment in government and public corporations expanded rapidly, largely exceeding manpower requirements. Overstaffing and low prices for services offered by public enterprises for political purposes have hampered effective operation; a large portion of central government deficits are attributed to public corporations.

Against the upsurge in expenditure, the country's archaic tax system could not provide adequate revenue. Among West European countries Greece had the lowest rates of income tax and possibly the highest rate of tax evasion. Because of the overwhelming personal element in the Greek economy, where individual units are simply extensions of the family, tax evasion is easily perpetrated in the service sector and in agriculture. Tax losses were estimated to be between US$1.7 and US$2.5 billion in 1981, equivalent to about 25 to 40 percent of the total public sector deficit. The deficit itself—including the deficits of public corporations and local authorities—soared to a record 17.1 percent of GDP in 1981.

In this context the PASOK government was determined to reduce the public sector deficit while increasing government investment in relation to current spending (see table 6, Appendix A). Since the spring of 1982 there has been a slight tightening of fiscal policy. On the expenditure side the government has slowed the rate of hiring, an important measure in that each year approximately 40 percent of annual budget expenditure is accounted for by the wages, salaries, and pensions of civil servants. It also eliminated or reduced a large number of subsidies. In the farm sector price support was taken over by the Economic Communities (EC) under the Common Agricultural Policy (CAP). Slower expenditure growth in selected areas was complemented by increased revenue collection. The government raised prices on publicly supplied goods and services, increased various indirect taxes, and enlarged the tax base by cracking down on evasion. In 1983 the number of violations that were uncovered more than doubled from the previous year, totaling 142,260 cases. As a result of these efforts, the public sector borrowing requirement was brought down to around 15 percent of GDP in the 1982-84 period. Even though the 1985 budget was clearly an election-year budget, it proposed to maintain the deficit at this level, but many analysts doubted that this goal could be met.

Overall, the 1985 budget that was approved by parliament was aimed at helping low- and middle-income people through significant improvements in social benefits for health, education, welfare, and agriculture, as well as through sweeping tax cuts (see Education; Social Security; Health, ch. 2). Total budget outlays were expected to increase by 27.4 percent to Dr1,784.3 billion. Allocations for health-welfare and social insurance would increase by 38.7 percent total Dr247.1 billion. Part of these funds would be used to set up a national health plan involving the establishment of health centers in the provinces. Spending for education was projected to increase by 30.1 percent to Dr169.8 billion, and for agriculture, 36 percent to Dr98.4 billion. In contrast, the defense budget, which was the largest in relation to national income of all North Atlantic Treaty Organization (NATO) countries, was expected to increase by 19.1 percent to Dr215.9 billion.

The most direct benefits for lower- and middle-income groups in the 1985 budget would come from tax cuts and an increase in farmers' pensions. To balance the loss from exemptions—estimated at Dr25 billion—there would be tax increases for professionals, merchants, artisans, and better paid wage and salary earners, and there would be a continued fight on tax evasion. Revenue should rise 29.6 percent in 1985 to total Dr1,330 billion, while revenue from direct taxes should rise by 43.8 percent. Direct taxes will provide one-third of total tax revenue, a 3-percent increase from 1984.

Changes can be expected in the tax system over the next

few years owing to harmonization with EEC standards as well as national efforts to modernize the tax system. The tax system is riddled with exemptions, and direct taxation contributes very little to total revenue. The most significant changes will be associated with the reduction of revenue caused by the abolition of tariffs on imports from the EEC, the reduction of tariffs on imports from non-EEC countries, and the introduction of a value-added tax (VAT). The VAT was originally scheduled to be implemented by 1984, but Greece was granted an extension until 1986 partly because of the huge administrative task of absorbing about 500 indirect taxes into the VAT system. Because of the limited number of production stages in Greek industry, the VAT will probably generate less revenue than the present system of turnover and excise taxes. Greece will be forced to make up the difference by a relative increase in direct taxes and/or the imposition of new taxes, i.e., property taxes or taxes on interest income and capital gains. Because indirect taxes tend to be regressive, greater emphasis on direct taxes should increase the distributive effects of the Greek tax system.

Municipal and community authorities have their own budgets, but their share of public expenditure and receipts declined continuously in the postwar period because of the increasing centralization of government economic management. In 1980 spending by provincial and local authorities was only 9 percent of total public expenditure. To support regional development and promote decentralization, the PASOK government attempted to bolster the financial base of the municipalities. It transferred control of public forests, mountain areas, lakes, and all beaches to local authorities. Local governments could thereby raise revenue by collecting local property taxes or fees for the use of wildlife, nature, and resort areas. In addition, in 1985 some 6.7 percent of the central government budget, or Dr94.7 billion, was to be transferred to provincial budgets, an increase of 40 percent compared with 1984.

PASOK's ultimate goal was to make local governments financially independent. Provincial councils were to accept greater responsibility for developing the economic potential of their jurisdictions, but by early 1985 few councils were ready to take on investment projects. Many did not possess adequate financial resources or were hesitant to launch new enterprises when the largest public corporations were deeply in debt.

**Economic and Regional Planning**

Overall responsibility for the preparation and implementation of medium- to long-term development plans lies with the Ministry of National Economy. Since 1964 technical support has been provided by the Centre of Planning and Economic Research (CPER), a public agency under the supervision of the minister of national economy. Development plans have set targets for growth in the various economic sectors, investment and employment levels, and other macroeconomic variables. They have failed, however, to ensure balanced regional growth or industrial development because of the indicative nature of Greek planning, discontinuities in leadership, and ineffective coordination of incentives and development objectives.

Against this background the PASOK government sought to make planning a more effective tool of government policy. Given the deficiencies of past planning efforts, it moved to develop a participatory planning process rather than a rigid investment plan. The plan would be rolling, subject to adjustment each year. Planning was both "democratic" and "active" in the sense that it was closely linked to administrative decentralization yet provided for initiation of projects by the central government and development banks. Provincial councils were given responsibility for designing provincial five-year plans, which were evaluated for incorporation into the national plan.

A new five-year economic development plan for 1983 to 1987 was approved by parliament in November 1983—despite opposition from the ND and the pro-Moscow Communist Party of Greece (Kommunistikon Komma Ellados—KKE). The plan was basically patterned on the government program unveiled in November 1981; its main objectives were to decrease employment and inflation; improve the quality of life and status of the underprivileged through better environmental conditions and social services; mobilize provincial resources for balanced regional development; develop research and development facilities and high technology industries; and increase the participation of individuals in local government, the cooperative movement, unions, and public enterprises. Substantial investments in health, education, and welfare were foreseen, and the government expected to receive EEC contributions of Dr200 to Dr250 billion.

Private investment was to be encouraged within the framework of the plan. For the first time in Greek planning history, a sectoral policy for industry was being prepared in 25 branches. Each industry survey was to lay down a plan designed to improve competitiveness and productivity as well as to encourage vertical integration of production. To stimulate private initiative and investment, the government would negotiate special contracts with private firms for the implementation of these sectoral development plans. The first studies, completed in late 1984, covered the steel, textiles and ready-mades, agricultural machinery, tanning and shoemaking, paper milling, and industrial mineral sectors.

The macroeconomic framework of the plan was predicated on an average 3- to 3.5-percent annual growth rate for GDP. The PASOK government hoped that the unemployment rate could be brought down to 4 to 4.5 percent from around 8 percent in 1984 and that inflation could be reduced to the OECD average by the end of the decade. To attain these goals the public sector would play a key role not only in improving the institutional and infrastructural framework but also in taking responsibility for high risk or new technology investments that private enterprise would be unwilling to undertake. The bulk of public investment would be channeled to energy, communications, transportation, and water and sewage projects. The DEI and the Hellenic Telecommunications Organization would receive the largest allocations of all public corporations under the five-year plan. Over the plan period, estimated public sector investments at 1982 values would reach over Dr1 trillion, placing a burden on public finances.

In conjunction with the objectives expressed in the five-year plan, the government passed a series of laws aimed at economic and regional development. Law 1262/82, as amended by Law 1360/83, provided incentives and a framework for the promotion of Greek and foreign investment. In line with Socialist policy, the law's primary innovation was government participation in share capital as a form of incentive. Depending on the size of the investment, greater portions of investment grants may be in the form of state equity. Other incentives included interest subsidies on loans, tax deductions, and accelerated depreciation. Incentives were granted for investment in any part of the country for projects in energy conservation, environmental protection, technological development, or employment of the handicapped. For other projects, incentives were graduated according to region and the significance of the planned investment. The total amount of investment grants ranged from 10 to 65 percent of the total project cost, substantial contributions being provided for small- and medium-sized enterprises. Despite these incentives, private investment at constant 1970 prices declined in both 1982 and 1983, continuing the downward trend manifested since 1980.

## Industry

From the early 1960s to the mid-1970s industry constituted the most rapidly expanding sector of the economy. Industrial production grew at an average annual rate of 9.4 percent between 1962 and 1975, compared with a 3.8-percent rate in the EC. By 1983 industry represented 29.2 percent of GDP, still a lower ratio than in most of industrialized Europe (see table 7, Appendix A). Food and tobacco processing, textiles, clothing, and cement have been the traditional branches of industrial expansion, while investment in metals, shipbuilding and repair, chemicals, petroleum refining, and vehicle assembly have broadened the industrial base.

Along with the increase of industrial output, there has been a corresponding increase of manufactured exports and certain imported inputs. By 1983 manufactured and processed goods accounted for 52.4 percent of exports. Their expansion was aided by the fact that since 1968 Greek industrial products have entered the EEC market duty-free (see European Economic Community, this ch.). Much of the modern industrial sector depends heavily on imported capital goods and technology as well as on imported petroleum. Depreciation of the drachma has therefore raised production costs for Greek manufactures and has contributed to reducing their competitiveness in recent years. Greece has some potential, however, for increasing domestic energy production. There is also considerable mineral and ore wealth, which Greece has begun to exploit as energy costs have permitted.

Greek industry is highly concentrated in size and geography. It is characterized by a few large industrial groups and a plethora of small family units; at least 85 percent of all manufacturing enterprises had fewer than 10 employees in 1984. Like most developing countries, Greece has tried to promote industrial development with tariffs, various trade barriers, easy credit terms, and tax concessions. Although industrial policy under successive postwar governments encouraged a number of large-scale, modern investment projects, it also helped preserve the weaknesses of the traditional industrial structure: low productivity, lack of vertical integration and quality control, and limited product specialization. Moreover, government-sponsored industrial promotion measures were pursued without coordinated planning in regard to sectors of predominant importance and their ability to compete internationally. Even on the Greek market, consumers prefer a higher standard of goods than produced by many domestic industries.

Industrial activity is concentrated in the Athens-Piraeus-Eleusis area and in Thessaloniki. Smaller concentrations exist in newer industrial areas sprouting around the port cities of Patrai, Volos, and Iraklion, as well as near the lignite deposits of Ptolemais. In the mid-1980s more than half of the country's manufacturing establishments and more than 60 percent of the labor force were located in the development axis based on the cities of Athens, Thessaloniki, Volos, and Patrai. The concentration of population and industry in the Greater Athens area has been recognized as an economic weakness, leading to large regional disparities in income and employment and a deterioration of living conditions in Athens. Athens has become the most polluted city in Western Europe, where most of the time a brown cloud of smog hangs over the area. In recent years new industry has been discouraged by the government from settling in Athens. Existing industries may modernize, expand, or merge, but they must not add to pollution levels or increase employment significantly. The PASOK government has instituted a few antipollution measures, yet more drastic actions, which could carry a high political price, appear to be called for.

## Manufacturing

The manufacturing sector grew rapidly until the mid-1970s. Its performance was especially dynamic in the decade 1963-73, when output rose at an annual average rate of 12 percent in constant prices, and employment rose by 2.3 percent per year. The share of manufacturing output in GDP reached 20 percent by the early 1970s and has stayed at about that level ever since. In recent years manufacturing has been in trouble. Output declined between 1981 and 1983, exports were down almost 20 percent in United States dollar terms, and many firms slid into bankruptcy. Those companies that relied heavily on bank financing were squeezed by the high cost of debt service. Investment has been weak, however, ever since the early 1970s, especially in the advanced technology

181

sectors, and manufacturing investment only averaged 16 percent of total investment over the 1974-81 period.

Accession to the EEC and the coming to power of a Socialist government (whose policies created uncertainty among industrialists) compounded the problem. In the first eight months of 1984 there was a slight upturn of 1.2 percent in manufacturing output, yet there was little prospect of regaining historical growth rates. Greek manufacturers, in the words of Andreas Papandreou, "lack the gigantic production volume and costly advanced technology with which to lower per-unit production costs as in the high wage countries of the industrially developed West; and at the same time lack the very low wage and salary scales paid by their competitors in the developing world." Structural change will not be easy with an economic base made up of tens of thousands of small manufacturers.

The largest component of the manufacturing sector in 1983 was the food, beverage, and tobacco products group, representing an estimated 19.2 percent of the value of manufacturing output. Manufacturing establishments in this branch were small and tended to use their production capacity on a seasonal basis, fulfilling the packing, preserving, and processing needs arising from crop harvests. Textiles, clothing, and footwear were the second largest component of manufacturing in 1983, but their share had declined from 27.5 percent in 1977 to 24 percent in 1983. The strength of the textile and clothing sectors lay in cotton goods. More than most other manufacturing branches, these sectors felt the competition from the low-wage developing countries. For the first time in its history, Piraiki-Patraiki, Greece's largest textile firm, began to report operating losses in 1981.

In the mid-1960s a number of large manufacturing complexes were established in the metallurgical and chemical industries. These were in some instances established by foreign enterprises in association with Greek business interests. It was in this manner that a large-scale aluminum industry was developed by Aluminum de Grèce, backed by French capital. This firm had the highest profits of all private firms operating in Greece in the 1979-83 period. The largest manufacturing complex in the Thessaloniki area, now under state control, was established in 1966 by the Thessaloniki Oil Refining Company, a subsidiary of the Exxon Corporation, and the Esso-Pappas Chemical Company. The complex laid the foundation for the development of a petrochemical and synthetic products industry with ancillary plants for production of petroleum deriva- tives, solvents, chlorine, detergents, plastic resins, and ammo- nia for the fertilizer industry. Six large plants—all either state or foreign owned—produced base chemicals in 1985. A larger number of manufacturers were involved in secondary produc- tion, including production of pharmaceuticals, cosmetics, in- secticides, and pesticides.

Another key branch of Greek industry that expanded in the 1960s was shipbuilding and repair, which accounted for around 6 percent of manufacturing value in 1983. Hellenic Shipyards, established in 1956 by the Niarchos group at Skaramanga, operated the largest yard in Greece. It had a capacity of over 200,000 deadweight tons a year in 1984. It also had a 300,000-ton dry dock—the largest in the Mediterra- nean—for repair purposes. The other major complexes includ- ed the Eleusis yards located west of Athens and the Neorion Syron yards on the island of Siros in the Aegean Sea. They had a combined capacity of about 210,000 deadweight tons in 1984. The Eleusis yards were taken over by the government from the Andreadis interests in 1976. Other yards operated at Pilos, Kalamai,and Khalkis. Nearly 500 small yards, mostly in the Piraeus area, built fishing craft, small cargo ships, and ferries for interisland and coastal trade. Although Greek ship- yards have in the past enjoyed considerable success in the building of vessels, a worldwide shipping slump of long dura- tion has caused them to depend more heavily on repair work. In April 1985 Hellenic Shipyards, one of Greece's largest in- dustrial employers, announced it would have to suspend oper- ations, a decision its management attributed to the shipping crisis and to persistent strikes. In response, the government was consulting with corporate and labor officials, exploring ways to avert closure. Socialist and Communist union officials were reportedly pressing for nationalization. A final agreement on the government purchase of the ailing shipyards was ex- pected by the end of July 1985.

A relatively small steel sector was associated with the ship- building and various metalworking industries. It accounted for only about 1 percent of raw EEC steel output and 1.2 percent of finished steel production. Greek mills have been expanding in the direction of scrap-melting furnances and cold-rolling mills. Since most of their investments were made in the 1970s, their technology and equipment were generally sufficiently modern to make them competitive with other EEC mills. The industry has been negatively affected, however, by the output reductions required of all members of the European Coal and Steel Community (ECSC) and a more rapid phaseout of protective tariffs than required in the transitional period of EEC membership—a concession to industrial users of steel.

### New Technologies

Following in the footsteps of other EEC countries in attempting to upgrade technological resources, the PASOK government established the Ministry of Research and Technology, which is responsible for the transfer of new technologies and development of a modern research system. Per capita expenditure on scientific and technological research has tended to be lower in Greece than in other EEC member countries. In addition to the development of alternative energy sources, the government was interested in promoting computer and information science technology, aquaculture, earthquake engineering, biotechnology, and the general technical upgrading of manufacturing production. The introduction of information technology and computers in retail trade, banking, shipping, communications, transportation, medicine, and other services should help increase the productivity of the services sector, which was lower than that of the manufacturing sector. In public administration the Ministry of Research and Technology has been charged with computerizing the various ministries in an attempt to improve their efficiency. Poor results in introducing systems have resulted not from lack of funds or specialized personnel but from bureaucracy and overstaffing. The computer market in Greece was dominated by foreign firms, for only one Greek firm, Gigatronics, had designed and manufactured its own computer system by 1984.

### Construction

Construction has been an important industrial activity in postwar Greece. In terms of dwellings under construction per 1,000 inhabitants, Greece has consistently been among the leaders of countries in the OECD group. This sector accounted for 8.4 percent of total employment in 1982, about the same level as in 1971. Construction still represented a substantial portion of GDP—7 percent in 1983, even though between 1979 and 1983 it was one of the most depressed industrial sectors. Its decline contributed to the deceleration of overall growth in the economy; in past decades construction stimulated growth because of its high labor content and low dependence on imported inputs. In the immediate future, prospects for recovery were not that favorable, with the exception of state-funded public works projects. Since 1980 housing policy and the high cost of labor and materials have dampened private building.

The construction of dwellings has played a larger role in the economy than in most countries at an equivalent stage of development. In the 1973-82 period the share of investment in housing relative to total investment averaged 30 percent. Limited property taxes and high inflation increased incentives for channeling savings into housing and real estate speculation, to the neglect of productive investments. The emphasis on house construction has also been attributed to a national predilection for ownership of real property and for investment in one's dwelling as a reservoir of wealth and a symbol of prestige. Traditionally, women's dowries included a house or apartment, while Greek emigrant workers sent funds back home to build family or retirement homes. Migration to the cities also stimulated urban building to the point of overexpansion. With the recent slowing of migration to Athens and Thessaloniki, there was a surplus of apartments but a shortage of low-income housing. Even though the government ran two mortgage banks and provided subsidized mortgage loans to civil servants, the percentage of self-financing was high. The housing policy of the PASOK government was, therefore, to reduce even further the share of self-financing for civil servants and low-income workers.

Construction, unlike other industrial activities, places a relatively small demand on imported materials. Greece has an abundance of building materials for masonry and is an important producer and exporter of cement. Greek construction companies and engineering contractors earn substantial foreign exchange abroad, principally for housing developments and infrastructural projects in North Africa and the Middle East.

### Mining and Quarrying

Although mining and quarrying represented only 1.3 percent of GDP and less than 1 percent of employment in 1983, Greece has considerable mineral wealth. Projects for more intensive and efficient exploitation of Greece's nonfuel minerals and ores have been important elements of economic planning for years, but they have proceeded slowly. The high costs of transporting low-quality ores and the volatility of international metal prices have prevented the orderly development of the mining industry. Although mining plans have stressed the development of processing facilities to replace the export of ores with exports of refined metals and metal products, some 65 percent of production was still exported raw or after first enrichment in 1984. Exports for this sector totaled US$205 million in 1983, or about 5 percent of total exports for that year.

Lignite and bauxite are Greece's most abundant mineral resources, reserves totaling 2.7 billion and 1 billion tons, respectively, in the early 1980s. There are also substantial deposits of ferronickel ores, magnesite, mixed sulfurous ores, marble, ferrochrome ores, and kaolin. Mining is in the hands of a few companies, which are to some degree vertically integrated, while quarry production is fragmented among a large number of small enterprises.

Alumina exports will increase in the future as a result of Soviet investment in a US$450 million alumina plant having a capacity of 600,000 tons. Three-quarters of output will be exported to the Soviet Union and Bulgaria over a 10-year period. The Skalistiri group of companies was also planning to increase its alumina production to more than 1 million tons. Despite cash-flow problems caused by the recession, Bauxites Parnasse Mining, the largest independent bauxite producer in the EEC, was continuing with ambitious investment plans. In 1981 it mined 1.8 million tons of bauxite, mainly around Delphi. Its goal was to increase output to 3 million tons per year to meet the demand of the new alumina plants.

The government retains a major role in the development of mineral wealth and mineral-related industries. Two public corporations, the Institute of Geological and Mining Research and the Public Petroleum Corporation (Dimosia Epicheirisi Petrelaiou—DEP) were involved in research and development in their respective fields. Another public corporation, the Hellenic Industrial and Mining Company, a banking consortium established in 1975, provided for the financing of mining and industrial projects. The Socialist government promised to allocate up to US$2 billion to the consortium between 1983 and 1987. Using these institutions and other state-controlled companies, Greece has stepped up research to identify new reserves for use by the minerals and metals industry. Greece's entry into the EEC has given impetus to efforts to upgrade local ores and thus has become a major supplier of primary industrial goods within the EEC. In the five-year plan Dr26.4 billion at 1982 values was allocated for various mining projects.

### Energy

Since the 1960s Greece has exhibited much higher growth in energy demand than have its EEC partners, a result of the rapid industrialization of the country. As in other developing economies, energy consumption has generally risen at a faster rate than has economic growth. The cost of final energy consumption in terms of GDP almost doubled between 1973 and 1981, from 6.9 percent to 12.7 percent. However, in 1984 per capita energy consumption was still less than half the EEC average, but demand for electricity was expected to increase significantly—5.5 percent annually between 1981 and 1990. Primary energy demand in 1983 was 16.8 million tons of oil equivalent, of which 64 percent was imported energy—primarily crude oil. Since the first oil price shock in 1973-74, successive administrations have stepped up efforts to reduce dependence on imported oil as the major energy source through fuller exploitation of domestic resources. It was unlikely, however, that imported petroleum could be reduced to less than half of total energy needs by 1990.

In 1983 some 63 percent of total energy demand was filled by imported and domestic oil, 25 percent by lignite, 7 percent by electricity, and 5 percent by coke and coal. Since 1981 Greece has been producing modest quantities of oil from the Prinos and South Kavala fields east of the island of Thasos in the Aegean Sea. Discovery of oil near Thasos in 1974 initially held out the prospect of self-sufficiency, but this expectation proved too optimistic. Production reached full capacity of 28,000 barrels per day in 1983, only about 13 percent of Greece's annual oil requirements. Recoverable reserves were estimated at 10 million tons, indicating a useful life of only about seven years at current production rates. Moreover, the quality of the crude oil and associated natural gas posed processing problems. The North Aegean Petroleum Company (NAPC), a consortium of three foreign companies, of which Denison Mines of Canada was the major shareholder, was responsible for all exploration and development of the Prinos field. Although the government denied rumors that it was seeking to nationalize or acquire a majority stake in the NAPC, it wanted to revise parts of the contract—already revised once in 1975—so that the state could receive a greater share of profits and maximize its control.

In 1975 the DEP was formed as the state body responsible for development of the petroleum industry at all stages, including prospecting for oil and natural gas, production, refining, storage, and distribution. The government wanted to strengthen the technical capabilities of the DEP to enable it to undertake all future exploration work. The goal was to convert the DEP into a production company in which foreign companies acted only as subcontractors. Oil experts questioned whether the DEP, with its organizational structure and stringent finances, could fulfill its mandate. The previous administration abandoned self-reliance to return to the concession route because of cost factors. This possibility had not been ruled out by the Ministry of Energy and Natural Resources. Because of the softening of oil prices, increasing attention has been given to securing imported oil on favorable terms. Exploration has continued, however, in the Ionian Sea and on land in Epirus and the northwest Peloponnesus. At the beginning of 1985 findings were meager, except for a small, exploitable reserve off the port of Katakolon, but new drilling was slated in the Gulf of Thessaloniki.

Greece usually relies on bilateral state-to-state deals for its oil supplies, which come mostly from the Soviet Union, Saudi Arabia, Libya, Iraq, Iran, Algeria, and Kuwait. In 1984 Greece signed a barter agreement with Iran for crude oil equivalent to US$200 million, the largest such deal that Greece had ever concluded. During the 1983-84 period Greece became increasingly dependent on imports of energy from the Soviet Union and East European countries. The Soviet Union was Greece's largest oil supplier in 1983, accounting for 22.5-percent of imports. Moreover, around 75 percent of coal imports and 40 percent of electricity imports were also supplied by the Soviets.

Greece had four petroleum refineries having a capacity of 21 million tons in 1984. Problems have arisen in recent years owing to overcapacity and sluggish demand for products; production only ranged between 10.2 and 12 million tons in the 1980-83 period. The Exxon Corporation's giveaway sale to the Greek government of its Thessaloniki petrochemicals group took place in this context. Greece's second largest refinery, a 5.5 million-ton capacity complex at Aspropirgos near Athens, was also state owned, being taken over from the Niarchos group in 1976. Two smaller, privately owned refineries, Motoroil at Corinth (7.5 million-ton capacity) and Petrola at Eleusis (4.5 million-ton capacity), produced primarily for export. According to EEC regulations, by the end of 1985 the freeing of marketing companies from state control and allocation was supposed to be completed, which meant that state refineries would come under competition on the domestic market. In early 1985 the Ministry of Energy and Natural Resources was seeking a five-year extension of the time limit. In the interim the Aspropirgos refinery was being modernized under a three-year, US$300 million program to install new cracking facilities to boost output of more valuable light products.

Since 1956 the generation and distribution of electrical power has been the responsibility of the DEI. The DEI's goal was to practically eliminate oil from electricity generation by 1992, replacing it primarily with lignite and hydroelectric power but also with peat and domestic oil. Public investment for this purpose was expected to total more than Dr450 billion in the 1980s, of which half would go toward development of lignite. Greece has approximately 5 billion tons of confirmed lignite reserves located primarily at Ptolemais in western Macedonia, Megalopolis in the Peloponnesus, and Drama in eastern Macedonia. About 15 percent of energy development funds were slated to go into hydroelectric power. Major hydroelectric dams existed on the Akheloos River in Central Greece and the Ladhon in the Peloponnesus, but at least 22 additional stations were planned. Total electricity production capacity was 6,084 megawatts in 1983, compared with a target of about 9,500 megawatts by 1987.

Despite ambitious development plans, projects have not proceeded on schedule. The DEI's goal was to shift the shares for electricity generation by 1992 to 82.2 percent for lignite, 15.6 percent for hydroelectric power, and 2.2 percent for petroleum. In 1984 electricity demand was 24,069 gigawatts, an increase of 5.7 percent over 1983. Lignite covered 58 percent of this demand; hydroelectric power, 12 percent; petroleum, 19.4 percent; and imported electricity, 10.6 percent. For the first time in its history, the DEI had to begin importing electrical energy in 1981. The imports, along with disruptions of power service and huge losses for the DEI, reflected delays in the implementation of energy projects, especially as concerned the coming on line of hydroelectric stations. Furthermore, although production at lignite quarries increased by

12.4 percent in 1983 and by 17 percent in 1984, exploitation was insufficient to supply all the lignite-fired plants. Delays were caused in part by the policy of increasing the domestic content of energy projects. Some small domestic contractors did not have the capacity to deliver equipment on time. DEI management came under fire from all opposition parties as well as from government sources, including the Ministry of Energy and Natural Resources, whose supervisory role was put in question. More systematic and coherent plans for energy development were required.

In the future, other energy sources might include natural gas, for Greece has discussed the construction of a pipeline to supply gas from the Soviet Union. By 1992 this pipeline, which has a capacity of 3 billion cubic meters a year, could cover about 13 percent of forecasted energy demand. The main obstacle was the lack of a distribution network in Greece. A limited network existed in Athens and was undergoing renovation in 1985. Considering the high cost of oil in relation to gas, as well as the pollution factor, DEI planners were evaluating the project's feasibility, particularly for the Athens and Thessaloniki areas. In the private sector numerous industries were conducting feasibility studies on conversion to steam coal. Coal imports could presumably displace some lignite in Greek energy plans.

Energy conservation and the use of renewables were also promoted. The previous government's practice of reviewing industrial projects in terms of energy efficiency and of maintaining high prices on gasoline and stiff taxes on automobiles was maintained. Moreover, the Ministry of Energy and Natural Resources placed emphasis on renewables, such as geothermal energy, wind, and solar energy. For the 1983-92 period, at least 19 alternative energy projects were planned. The cost of these projects was estimated at Dr1.1 billion, of which 40 percent would be funded by the EEC. Although by the year 2000 renewables will not cover more than 2 to 3 percent of Greek energy needs, they have great significance for certain remote areas as yet unsupplied with electricity because of difficult terrain. Nuclear energy is not likely to figure into the picture until sometime in the next century because of earthquake activity.

## Agriculture

Greek agriculture plays an important though declining role in the economy. It grew at an annual rate of only about 3.5 percent in the 1950-80 period, compared with 6 percent for the economy as a whole. Agriculture's share of GDP thus declined from 32 percent in 1950 to 25 percent in 1963 and 17.5 percent in 1983. The social importance of agriculture remained strong, however, because over 1 million persons— about 28.8 percent of the economically active population— were recorded in 1982 as being engaged in agricultural pursuits. Although the agricultural labor force declined considerably after 1970 and was declining by 1 to 2 percent annually in the 1980s, it remained large in comparison with the other EEC countries and in terms of agriculture's contribution to the economy. Moreover, unfavorable terrain, arid climatic conditions, insufficient irrigation, extreme fragmentation of farms, lack of capital investment, and weakness in the cooperative movement held productivity at a low level—about half the average level among Greece's EEC partners. The aged farm population and low level of technical training among Greek farmers in relation to EEC farmers also contributed to the low efficiency of the Greek agricultural sector.

Despite these constraints, progress had been made toward modernization in machinery, animal husbandry—particularly in poultry and hog operations—and cultivation techniques. With the important exceptions of red meat, dairy products, and animal feedstuffs, Greece was largely self-sufficient in farm goods. In addition, agricultural products, including processed foods, beverages, and tobacco, accounted for 33 percent of total exports in 1983. Further improvements in processing and marketing were needed, however, to enhance the international competitiveness of Greek agricultural exports.

### Land Use and Production

Long dry seasons, the natural poverty of the soil, and a mountainous topography account for the fact that only 30 percent of Greece's surface area is arable. Furthermore, about 45 percent of agricultural land is in mountainous or semimountainous regions where yields are low because of difficult farming conditions. In these areas scattered holdings—a legacy of inheritance laws, dowry practices, and land distribution schemes—make it difficult for single farmers to specialize on a commercial scale or to produce crops at competitive prices. The plains of Macedonia, Thessaly, and Thrace are the largest and most favored agricultural regions, where irrigation is widespread and a large number of medium- and large-sized farms exist. Their advantageous position is borne out by the regional distribution of income; all three areas claim a share of agricultural income disproportionately larger than their share of cultivated land.

Certain regional specializations in production existed, depending on soil and climatic conditions. About half the national output of wheat, corn, and tobacco, nearly two-thirds of peaches, and almost all apples were produced in Macedonia. Over half of all cotton was harvested in Thessaly, and the Peloponnesus was an important fruit- and vegetable-growing area, accounting for more than half of national output of citrus fruits and apricots. The islands, notably Crete, also tended to specialize in fruits and vegetables.

In terms of value, crops made up 68.8 percent and animal husbandry, 27.7 percent, of total agricultural production in 1982. The major crops were cereal gains—notably corn, soft wheat, durum wheat, and barley (see table 8, Appendix A). Corn production reached a record nearly 2 billion tons in 1984 and was expected to increase again in 1985. Other important crops were industrial crops—sugar beets, cotton, and tobacco—and alfalfa, tomatoes, potatoes, olives, and fresh fruits—primarily oranges, peaches, apples, lemons, pears, and apricots. Gradual elimination of the price differentials between Greek and EEC farm products and the abolition of countervailing duties on certain exports to the EC have stimulated production of olives, table grapes, tomatoes, peaches, apples, oranges, and cherries.

There was, however, strong competition from Italy and Spain in tomatoes as well as in other vegetables and fruits. Greece had a good market for citrus fruits in East European countries, which absorbed about 70 percent of total citrus exports in 1983. The government has encouraged the rapid expansion of fruit and vegetable production, for in view of its labor-intensive nature it is well suited to the small landholding patterns in Greece. Other crops that produced a surplus for export included tobacco (mostly Oriental varieties), raisins, and currants. Although overall crop production still fluctuated widely in the 1980s, the long-term trend was toward increasing production by improving yields per hectare.

Poultry and pork accounted for an estimated 60 percent of total meat production in 1983. Beef and veal accounted for around 16 percent of production, while sheep, goat, and rabbit composed the remainder. Where pastureland was limited, sheep and goat raising predominated so that significant quantities of milk were produced from these sources as well as from cattle. Growth in meat and dairy production has not kept pace with consumption, thus leading to a significant increase of imports. Imports were particularly marked after accession to the EEC. Greece was required to stop subsidizing sales of feed grains to farmers, a common practice since 1970. The price of the feed grains nearly doubled between January 1981 and July 1982. This made cattle raising especially costly because in many areas natural grass dries up in the summer. Production of both red and white meat was negatively affected by increased EEC competition. Domestic production decreased, and beef prices rose substantially so that consumption was lowered.

The processing, packaging, and marketing of agricultural products were becoming increasingly important as consumers became more discerning and as the distance between the places of production and sale widened. Greek agriculture faced serious deficiencies in this area, affecting costs and productivity. These problems arose from the low level of processing technology and the small scale of processing industry, as well as poor coordination between production in the field and absorption by the factories. In the meat sector, for example, the lack of a processing industry for by-products raised slaughtering costs. In 1984 plans were being prepared for the building of 14 slaughterhouses and three meat markets to create a national network of modern units. The Dr18.8 billion project would be financed by the Agricultural Bank of Greece, the Guidance Section of the EEC's Common Fund for Agricultural Policy, and the Greek government through its annual public investment program. Similar development projects were envisioned in other agricultural branches to increase the share of processed products in agricultural exports.

### Agricultural Policy and Credit

Greek agricultural policy has focused on raising and stabilizing farm incomes, increasing productivity, and promoting exports of agricultural products. The means to attain these goals have included consolidation of landholdings, promotion of irrigation and mechanization, and restructuring of crops. In addition, under the PASOK government the improvement of processing and marketing facilities within the cooperative movement was encouraged.

Since 1963 Greece has had a voluntary land consolidation program and since 1959 a second compulsory one in areas where large irrigation projects were being carried out. Overall, progress in consolidation and irrigation has been judged unsatisfactory. The planning, legal, and financial aspects of consolidation, the inherent distrust of officials among Greek farmers, and the prestige of landownership have together created complex barriers to government initiatives. As a result, by 1982 only 724,000 hectares had been consolidated. In areas where consolidation was applied, however, the average number of land plots was reduced from seven to 1.5, and the average size of each plot increased from 0.3 to 1.6 hectares. Of the 3.6 million hectares under cultivation in 1982, only 27 percent was under irrigation. At least another 45 percent of the cultivated area was suitable for reclamation; the government hoped to extend irrigation to 1.1 million hectares by the year 1987.

Except for credit extended by crop brokers, wholesalers, and private moneylenders, the state-owned Agricultural Bank of Greece is the primary agency for extending credit to farmers, cooperatives, and public agricultural agencies. The bank funneled most of its short-term credit to producers through the cooperatives. It extended a total of Dr283 billion in credit in 1983. Beyond its function as a credit institution, the bank has traditionally been the primary vehicle for carrying out the agricultural policy of the government. Its involvement in the agricultural sector encompassed infrastructural development, technical instruction, distribution of fertilizers, and development of food-processing industries. In the latter area, involvement extended to joint-venture operations with cooperatives. Its nearly 190 branches and its staff of more than 5,500 allowed the Agricultural Bank of Greece to reach over 90 percent of all farmers.

Despite the slow historical development of agricultural cooperatives, the PASOK government has promoted them as a major vehicle of change in bringing about the revitalization of the countryside. They were encouraged not only for ideological reasons but also for the expected benefits from economies of scale that result from collective action. Cooperatives were first officially established in 1915 as a means of improving the production and marketing of crops from smallholdings. Local or village cooperatives often acted in the past simply as a formal link with the provincial unions and at the national level with the Pan-Hellenic Confederation of Unions of Agricultural Cooperatives.

The power of the movement has traditionally rested at the provincial and national levels. In many cases membership in village cooperatives and contributions to share capital were too small to permit full development of the cooperatives' potential. Because the cooperative institutions and activities that had any significance lay outside the village, it was not surprising that the salaried and professional officials of provincial and other national cooperative bodies appeared to the small farmer to be little different from administrators in the government services. Private merchants who offered larger cash down payments eroded the cooperatives' position as marketing organs. These merchants created a class of local dealers and wholesalers that significantly raised distribution costs. The PASOK government's goal in strengthening the cooperatives was to induce farmers to bypass these middlemen so as to raise their income through direct marketing while reducing costs to the consumer.

In the early 1980s there were about 7,000 local agricultural cooperatives representing over 705,000 members, or over two-thirds of the farming population. Under the PASOK government, membership has likely grown. Cooperatives received special interest rates and export subsidies, making private trade uncompetitive in some commodities. Law 1262/82 concerning investment incentives for regional development and economic decentralization also encouraged the formation and expansion of agricultural cooperatives. Generous grants up to 50 percent of investment costs and subsidized loans were available to cooperatives that established agricultural, manufacturing, or other productive enterprises. Greek rural cooperatives increasingly integrated their operations vertically from production to marketing. Opposition leaders and private traders opposed the strengthening of export cooperatives for certain commodities; they accounted for 30 percent of agricultural export activities in the 1982-83 period.

### Forestry and Fishing

Forests covered nearly 2.5 million hectares, or about 19 percent of the total Greek land area in 1982. At least two-thirds of the forest area was owned by the state but was being transferred to local authorities, and the balance was owned by private interests and monasteries. Forestry contributed only about 1.3 percent to agricultural GDP in 1982 and consisted mainly of firewood production. To make up for forest damage by fire, excessive lumbering, and overgrazing, Greece pursued very conservative forest management policies between 1955 and 1980. By the mid-1970s Greek forests were generally overmature and could produce two to three times more wood than was being exploited. Certain constraints existed, however—namely, inadequate access roads, a shortage of trained manpower caused largely by poor living conditions in the mountain areas, insufficient mechanization in logging, and an underdeveloped pulp and paper industry. As a result, Greece had to import increasing quantities of wood for construction and industrial purposes. To allay these problems, successive governments sought to implement comprehensive forestry development projects, including reforestation and infrastructural development in rural villages. The World Bank (see Glossary) loaned US$25 million in 1979 for a six-year integrated development program, including infrastructural projects for mountain villages. In the long term Greece has the potential for achieving self-sufficiency in forest products.

Despite Greece's maritime character, fishing is much less important to the economy than one would expect. Fishing contributed 2.2. percent to agricultural GDP in 1982 but less than 1 percent to national employment. The sector has encountered serious problems because of pollution and overfishing in coastal waters. The total catch was 88,681 tons in 1983, compared with 97,177 tons in 1977. Because the coastal catch has decreased in recent years, high-seas fishing off Mauritania and South Africa has been increasing. The three largest ports for fish landings were Piraeus, Thessaloniki, and Kavala. Greece was a net importer of fish products but a traditional exporter of sponges, for which demand had decreased after the development of synthetics. Under the five-year plan the government's major objectives in the fishing sector were to protect the fish stock, modernize the fishing fleet, develop fish farming, and improve processing, distribution, and marketing facilities.

## Employment and Income

Greek government statistics and census information reveal significant changes in labor force characteristics since the early 1970s. Agriculture was the largest employment sector for decades, but in 1975 it was surpassed by the service sector, which, including public administration, counted for 42 percent of employment by 1982. Industry, traditionally the smallest employer, has also surpassed agriculture. In 1982 industry, including handicrafts and public works, represented 29.2 percent of employment, while agriculture represented 28.8 percent, significantly down from the 40.5 percent recorded in 1971 (see fig. 15). The drop in the farm sector was attributed not only to migration to urban areas but also to improved statistical methods. Projections for the late 1980s forecast a further decline in the agricultural work force and a rise in the industrial sector to almost one-third of the labor force.

In the 1971-81 period the economically active population increased by 10 percent to 3.5 million. Because this growth was larger than the growth rate of the working-age population, the labor force participation rate rose. Its increase to 45.6 percent in 1981 from 42.9 percent in 1974 could be attributed almost entirely to the growing number of working women, who by 1983 represented 31 percent of the labor force. The overall participation rate was, however, still below that of West European countries and the United States because of the comparatively lower involvement of young people 14 to 24 years old and women in the work force. For example, whereas the female participation rate in the United States was 50 percent of the female population of 14 years and older, in Greece the rate was only 25 percent. This rate will rise in the future if the growth rate of the active female labor force remains on par with that of recent years. By 1988 women could constitute 35 percent of the labor force.

Substantial differences existed between the occupational categories of women and men. Women were heavily represented among clerical and service workers; they also provided low-cost labor in traditional export industries, such as textiles, clothing, and footwear. The most dramatic cases of growth in the proportion of women employed has been in management and clerical work. In 1981 women represented 11 percent of employed managers and administrators and 47 percent of employed clerical workers, compared with 5.4 percent and 38.8 percent, respectively, in 1974. Clerical work will likely be the only occupational category where women occupy the majority of positions in the near future. Women represented 25 percent of the rural work force in 1981, but about 70 percent of them worked as nonpaid family members. It was not until 1984 that legislation was passed granting women equal access to job op-

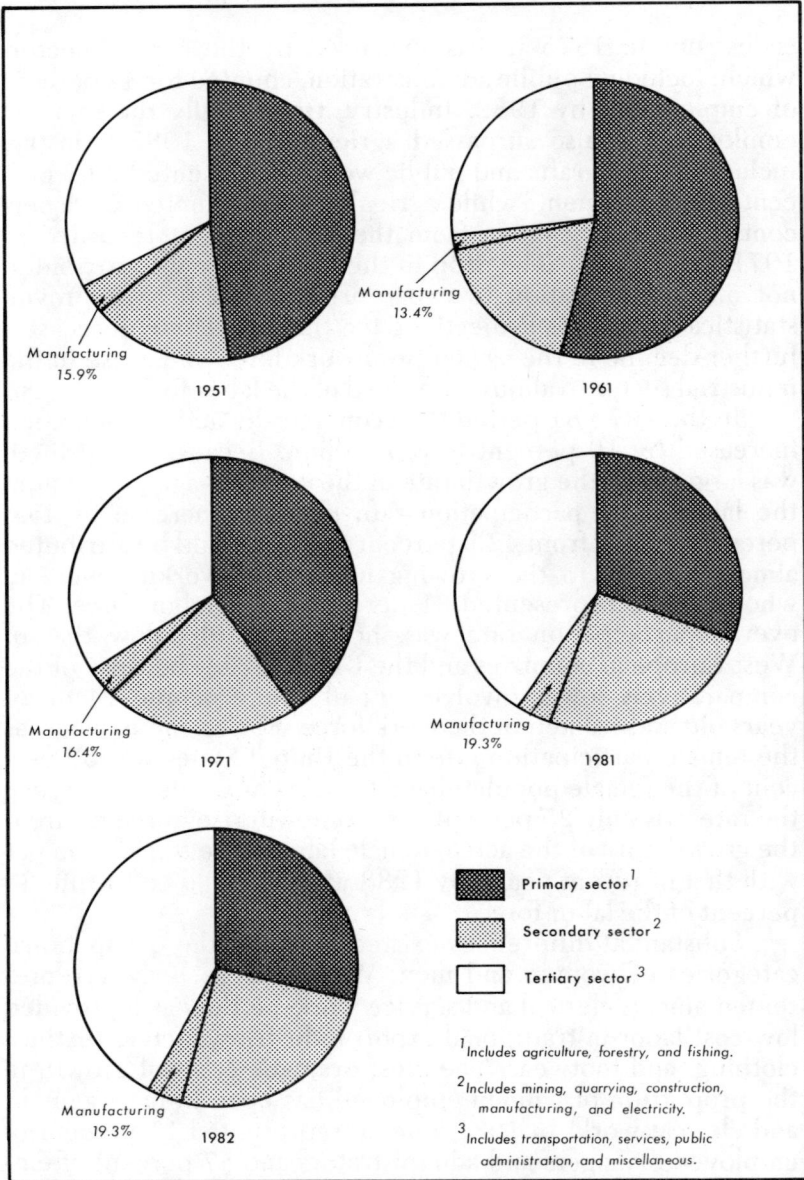

Manufacturing
15.9%
1951

Manufacturing
13.4%
1961

Manufacturing
16.4%
1971

Manufacturing
19.3%
1981

Manufacturing
19.3%
1982

Primary sector [1]

Secondary sector [2]

Tertiary sector [3]

[1] Includes agriculture, forestry, and fishing.

[2] Includes mining, quarrying, construction, manufacturing, and electricity.

[3] Includes transportation, services, public administration, and miscellaneous.

Source: Based on information from Robert LaLonde and Nick Papandreou, "The Manpower Report of K.E.P.E.: The Characteristics of the Greek Labor Market," Princeton, April 1984, Appendix B, Table B-3 and Table B-4; and United States, Embassy in Athens, *Foreign Labor Trends: Greece, 1983-84*, Washington, 1984, 2.

*Figure 15.  Economically Active Population by Sector, Selected Years 1951-82*

portunities and equal pay for equal work. This legislation only applied to the private sector, however.

Another change after 1971 was that an increasing number of Greeks were accepting wage or salary positions in preference to working for their families. The number of such workers rose to nearly 50 percent of the economically active population in 1981, against 42.3 percent in 1971. In comparison, wage and salary earners constituted about 90 percent of the employed labor force in the United States in 1981. The low level of wage and salary earners in Greece reflected the lingering predominance of traditional sectors, such as agriculture, and the large number of self-employed shopkeepers, small-scale middlemen, and nonpaid family workers. Relative to population, Greece had more retail outlets than any other EEC country and a greater absolute number than Britain, whose population was five times larger. A notable feature of the Athens landscape are the many curbside kiosks that sell a host of small necessities.

Unemployment has generally been quite low in the postwar years mainly because of extensive emigration. The labor force decreased by almost 10 percent in the 1960s, and the loss of scientists and professionals led to shortages of skilled labor. Consequently, the government has placed high priority on vocational education (see Education, ch. 2). Even with the reversal of the emigration pattern after 1973, unemployment was held at 4 percent or less until 1979, although underemployment, particularly in rural areas, was a problem. In the 1980s net immigration, coupled with economic downturn, has caused increasing unemployment. Much of this increase could be attributed to drastic contraction in construction and falling agricultural employment. Unemployment would be higher without the PASOK government's strict laws discouraging layoffs and the traditional padding of public employment rosters. Despite these measures, by 1984 unemployment had reached an estimated 8 percent overall and 10 percent in urban areas. Much of the increase could be explained by longer durations of unemployment. Those seeking employment for the first time had the most problems securing a position, and unemployment rates for workers from age 14 to 29 were extremely high— approximately 65 percent of the unemployed were in this age category. To aid in the assimilation of repatriated emigrants, training in fields that were in demand in Greece was projected in the 1983-87 economic plan. The EEC pledged to shoulder half the cost of the Dr900 million program. It had already contributed funds to programs to combat youth unemployment.

Official statistics on employment and unemployment were deficient in many respects, especially because the underground economy was large, accounting for as much as 25 percent of economic activity. The small payrolls of Greek enterprises provided a high degree of maneuverability in regard to the public authorities. A business might have more employees than it declared, thus avoiding social security taxes and payment of higher wages. The workers in turn did not pay income or social security taxes but were excluded from unemployment records when they lost their jobs. Numerous Greeks held down multiple jobs, however, but only one officially recognized position. If the official position was lost, the employee was classified "unemployed." Multiple-job holders were most common in the agricultural and service sectors of the economy. Underground activity complicated economic planning and denied the government substantial revenue. Yet the activity went on openly in Greece, for it added to the resilience of the economy. No government ever made an issue of it until the PASOK government began its campaign to reform the tax system and stem tax evasion (see Fiscal Policy, this ch.).

### Labor Unions

Greece has traditionally lacked a strong labor movement because of the predominance of small, family-owned businesses, a general preference for representation and patronage through political channels, and a restrictive government policy toward unions. Labor organization is centered on small craft or trade unions limited to a single community. These locals, of which there were about 3,000 in 1985, usually were affiliated with national federations in both given industries and geographical labor centers. These secondary unions in turn combined to form national confederations. By far the largest and most influential confederation was the General Confederation of Greek Workers (Geniki Synomospondia Ergaton Ellados— GSEE). As of 1984 it claimed approximately 650,000 members from 77 federations and 84 labor centers.

Development of the GSEE as an effective agent of workers' interests was long hampered by restrictive legislation, government control of union funding, and rigorous repression during periods of dictatorship. Moreover, conservative governments found it relatively easy to maintain a tight rein on the unions because the right wing has dominated union leadership in the postwar period, a legacy of anticommunist sentiment after the Civil War. Union leaders have tended to depend more on the goodwill of the government to remain in power than on worker support.

The PASOK government has taken greater steps than any other postwar Greek government to create an effective union movement. The centerpiece of its labor policy was the trade union reform act of 1982. The law granted protection from layoff to union officials and required employer-furnished facilities for union meetings at work sites having over 100 union members. It also prohibited lockouts, legalized sympathy strikes, and strengthened the right to strike by reducing notice to one day and eliminating the requirement for formal consultation with employers. Moreover, labor centers and federations affiliated with the GSEE were obliged to inscribe more than 100 unions, largely communist, that were excluded under previous governments. Lastly, the practice of financing unions through the Ministry of Labor was being replaced by direct collection methods administered by either the employer or the unions themselves. These steps improved conditions for unionists, but much remained to be done to establish a genuinely representative union movement. The PASOK government proved just as manipulative as other administrations in getting their supporters installed as union leaders. In addition, legislation passed in 1983 on socialization in public enterprises made it more difficult to strike in public companies by requiring a majority vote of union members.

Strike funds being practically nonexistent, labor unrest has traditionally been expressed through one-day warning strikes commonly confined to the service sector. These were seldom effective in securing worker demands. In recent years, although the warning strike has remained the principal protest vehicle, Greece has witnessed a growing number of prolonged work stoppages and repeated warning strikes not only by the more militant unions in banking, construction, and teaching but also by unions in the transport, public utility, and industrial sectors. In 1984 the worst wave of labor unrest since the PASOK government came to power arose because of dissatisfaction with the national wage settlement (see Living Standards and Income, this ch.). Whereas in 1983 there were a total of 218 strikes, there were 192 in the first three months of 1984 alone. Most employers ended up agreeing to settlements about 5 percent higher than the collective agreement, the

201

same amount labor claimed it lost in purchasing power in 1983.

## Living Standards and Income

From 1975 to 1978 Greece experienced an unprecedented period of economic prosperity. Expansionary policies promoted growth in a relatively favorable international economic climate, and average wages and salaries increased at an annual rate of 5 to 10 percent above inflation. Even when international economic conditions began to deteriorate in 1979, nominal wages continued to increase very rapidly, far exceeding increases in output or productivity. At the end of 1981 and early in 1982, the PASOK government fulfilled its campaign promise to raise substantially the earnings of the lowest income groups and to promote a more equitable income distribution. A graduated wage indexation system (ATA) was introduced to provide for automatic adjustments every four months, based on changes in the consumer price index. Although ATA officially applied only to civil servants, it set the standard for collective bargaining agreements.

In 1982 minimum wages increased as much as 50 percent while average earnings in manufacturing rose by 37.5 percent. Workers were thus largely shielded from the impact of high inflation so that family expenditures reflected a higher standard of living in 1982 compared with 1974, although Greeks still spent a comparatively high portion of their family budget on food. Personal care expenses rose by one-third, and other large increases were registered by entertainment, gasoline, appliances, and health services. Although rapid wage increases, longer holidays, and shorter working hours (standard 40-hour week) have improved the lot of the working class, they raised unit labor costs to such an extent that profit margins and industrial competitiveness were seriously eroded.

Thus in 1983 PASOK switched to a more restrictive incomes policy. This policy resulted in a cut in real wages of from 3 to 5 percent in 1983, but under union pressure the government sought to compensate for any loss of income the next year. In 1984 a new collective labor agreement for workers in the private sector was signed, the first time in several years that labor and management did not have to resort to arbitration. The agreement, which set the minimum national wage and standards for negotiations in individual industries, provided an average increase in total compensation of 3 to 4 percent above the anticipated inflation rate of 18 percent. An agreement was also reached for 1985, providing for the continued indexation of wages to inflation and an average 2-percent real increase in income. Industrialists accepted ATA use through 1985, but not its institutionalization. In both years the GSEE representatives in the United Antidictatorial Labor Movement-Socialist (ESAK-S), which was affiliated with the pro-Moscow KKE, refused to sign, charging that the agreements did not meet the basic aims of the working class. Much to the government's chagrin, a cooperative relationship with ESAK-S members in the GSEE did not protect it from strike actions.

The International Monetary Fund (IMF—see Glossary), the EEC, and the OECD advised the PASOK government to pursue a more anti-inflationary wage policy. However, viewing inflation as a structural problem rather than one caused by demand pressures, the government opted for a gradual reduction of inflation and rejected strict austerity for the working class. Moreover, to reduce migration to the cities, the government instituted numerous measures to improve the welfare of farmers and rural labor. Retirement and health benefits were expanded to include women, while social security benefits for unemployment and sickness were increased for farmers and agricultural laborers. Because wage agreements covered less than one-half of the labor force, PASOK increasingly emphasized its efforts to improve the quality of life. Water supply, sewage disposal, and environmental protection projects, improvements in health services, and the development of cultural and educational activities were viewed as corollaries to economic development.

## Transportation and Telecommunications

Because of the coastal location of most of Greece's population centers, the rugged topography of the country's interior, and its scattered islands, sea transportation has been of vital importance throughout Greek history. Greece is a world leader in international shipping, and interisland maritime links are well developed. Most of Greek industry focused around seven major ports. These include Piraeus and Eleusis, which serve the Athens area, Thessaloniki, Patrai, Volos, Igoumenitsa, and Iraklion on Crete. In total, Greece has about 175 ports. Coastal shipping has declined in recent years owing to improvements in overland transport, but passenger service has greatly increased port traffic with the development of tourism. To reduce congestion in the major ports and to further the objective of decentralizing economic activity, a number of other ports, including Kavala, Kerkira, Preveza, and Rodhos, were being developed. To promote Greece's position as a crossroads between the EEC and the Middle East, the ports of Igoumenitsa and Volos were being modernized, and a national roadway was being constructed between the two cities. The EEC will finance 80 percent of the work slated to commence in 1985.

Greece's road and rail networks were still inadequate in the 1980s (see fig. 16). The resulting high transportation costs for agricultural and other products reduced the competitiveness of Greek exports. Road transport was dominant, covering over 80 percent of intercity passenger and freight traffic. The total road network was about 37,416 kilometers long, 90 percent of which was paved in 1984. National highways covered 8,777 kilometers, and the remainder were provincial roads. Considerable work has been done to improve the road system, but in the effort to link small mountain villages with central highways, many roads were poorly constructed. New improvement works were under way in 1984-85 to alleviate geographical bottlenecks and upgrade roads for the increasing volume of commercial and private traffic. EEC aid was expected for completing and modernizing the vital north-south road link from Yugoslavia through Athens to Kalamata at the southern tip of the Peloponnesus.

Car ownership has grown very rapidly; the number of motor vehicles more than tripled between 1971 and 1981, from 465,700 to over 1.5 million. Nevertheless, per capita car ownership was the lowest in the EEC—partly because of extremely high import duties—and bus transportation was relied upon heavily. Over 45 percent of all motor vehicles were registered in the Greater Athens area, causing serious traffic problems. The planned expansion of the existing subway system could provide a partial solution, but it was plagued by repeated delays. Two major arteries were supposed to be completed by the end of 1985.

Greece was one of the last European countries to begin construction of an integrated railroad system. Work started in 1881, and in 1984 the system—2,478 kilometers of track—was not much longer than it was before World War II. Moreover, because of neglect caused by the rapid development of automobile and air transportation, much of the railroad equipment was obsolete, and operation costs were high. The state

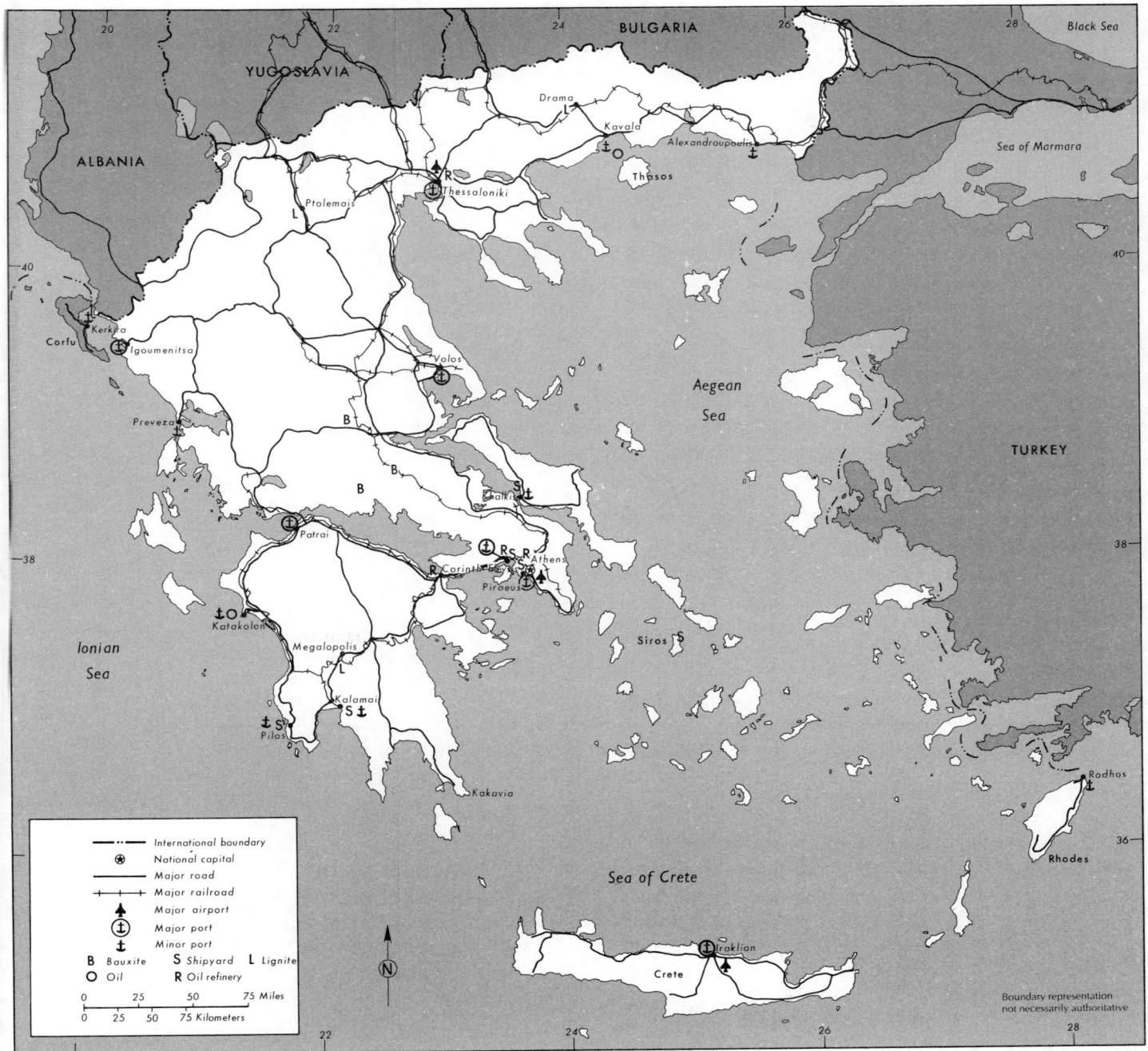

Figure 16. Transportation System and Economic Activity, 1985

took over Hellenic Railways in 1976, planning to carry out a 15-year development program. Priority has been given to double tracking and electrification of the Athens-Thessaloniki-Yugoslavia line by 1987. Greater speed and increased capacity on this line should enable the railroad to compete more effectively with road transport on long hauls. Since 1973 freight traffic has remained more or less static at about 3.5 million tons annually, while passenger traffic has declined from 15.7 million persons per year to about 10 million.

Air transportation within Greece is provided exclusively by Olympic Airways, the government-owned national air carrier that provides passenger and cargo services to some 30 airports. Although regular air service is confined to the larger islands, most of the inhabited islands have landing strips. A number of international airlines link Greece's major airports with more than 50 foreign cities. International and domestic air transport has increased considerably, but in January 1983 the government deferred until March 1986 a final decision on whether to proceed with construction of a new Athens airport at Spata. It was thought the existing airport at Hellenikon would meet requirements for another five to seven years. Arriving and departing passengers total between 7 and 8 million a year, and freight carried by air has increased steadily in recent years.

Telecommunications have been considerably improved since the early 1970s. In comparison with other countries at Greece's stage of development, the density of telephone connections was high, and facilities were relatively new. Practically all telephone communications were connected with an automatic trunk-line network, and calls could be made to about 60 countries on a direct-dial basis in 1985. The Hellenic Telecommunications Organization was planning to install additional antennae for communication via satellite and to build communications facilities for connection to the European Satellite Communications System (EURTELSAT).

## Foreign Economic Relations

The relatively strong performance of the Greek economy during the 1960s and 1970s led to the doubling of total exports of goods and services in GDP, from 10 percent in 1963 to 20 percent in 1981. In terms of United States dollars, exports grew at a 15-percent annual rate between 1974 and 1981, considerably higher than the average for other EEC countries. After peaking in 1981, exports declined in United States dollar terms by 13.2 percent in 1982 and by less than 1 percent in 1983. Exports were affected by the rapid increase of production costs in Greece, a decrease of demand on the international level, and more acute competition.

Greece's export structure has changed significantly over time (see table 9, Appendix A). A sharp rise in exports of refined petroleum products and manufactured goods, such as textiles, cement, metals and metal articles, alumina, chemicals, and pharmaceuticals, accompanied the rapid growth of exports. Petroleum products accounted for 18 percent of total exports in 1983, whereas manufactures represented 46 percent of total exports compared with 10 percent in 1963. During the same period traditional exports—food, beverages, tobacco, raw materials, minerals, and ores—declined from 90 percent of total exports to 33 percent. Moreover, in 1982 about 17 percent of manufacturing output was exported, compared with 14.3 percent of agricultural output. In the 1982-84 period, however, traditional exports have proved more resilient than manufactured exports.

Imports expanded at a 13.7-percent annual rate during the 1974-81 period and witnessed a greater decline in demand than exports had between 1982 and 1983. Nonetheless, by 1984 exports still covered only 45 percent of Greek imports (see table 10, Appendix A). As in other countries, the increase in energy prices since 1973 changed the composition of imports significantly. The share of petroleum products increased from 13 percent in 1973 to 28 percent in 1983. Manufactured consumer goods, capital goods, and intermediate goods, including raw materials, each accounted for around one-fifth of imports, the remainder being foodstuffs. Since 1979-80 the declining value of imports of nonfuel raw materials and intermediate capital goods has reflected the slowdown of Greek investment activity. Dependence on such goods is expected to decline gradually as the process of industrialization continues and as vertical integration of the economy is enhanced.

Greece's principal trading partners are the member countries of the EEC, the Federal Republic of Germany (West Germany) being the leading supplier and market (see table 11, Appendix A). Since Greece's accession to the EEC in January 1981, there has been a significant shift in the source of imported products—especially animal and other agricultural products—in favor of EEC suppliers. Thus, imports from the EEC represented 48 percent of total imports in 1983, compared with 39.7 percent in 1980. Greek exports to the EEC experienced a similar development, rising from 47.6 percent of exports to 52.5 percent.

The greatest expansion of trade in the 1974-83 period has been with the Middle Eastern and African countries, particularly Saudi Arabia, Iraq, Egypt, and Libya. Trade with countries in these regions accounted for 27.4 percent of imports in 1983 and 17.2 percent of Greek exports. Between 1982 and 1984 Greece signed trade agreements with Iran, Saudi Arabia, Algeria, and Libya to promote Greek exports and to secure oil supplies. Greek businesspeople have been skeptical about the practical results of such agreements, regarding them as little more than letters of intent. Moreover, Greek conservatives sharply criticized a US$1 billion Greek-Libyan trade accord announced in September 1984. The three-year deal gives Libya a large market for 3 million tons of its oil and US$500 million worth of Greek arms, (for which a separate arms supply accord was formalized in December 1984) in addition to pledging contracts for infrastructure projects in Libya and for repair of Libyan commercial vessels (see Greek Defense Industries, ch. 5). In 1984 Greece was also exploring the possibilities for economic cooperation with Israel, Jordan, and Syria. An agreement for developing an existing ferry link between Greece and Syria into a boat, train, and truck service for the transport of goods between continental Europe and the Middle East was expected to be negotiated by 1986 (see Transportation and Telecommunications, this ch.).

The East European countries and the Soviet Union took 7.4 percent of Greek exports and provided 5.2 percent of imports in 1983. Trade relations with these countries were more important than proportional size indicated because these countries were a significant market for Greece's surplus agricultural commodities. Moreover, Greece has become increasingly dependent on energy imports from the Soviet Union and its allies (see Energy, this ch.).

Until 1981 a considerable part of trade with Eastern Europe was governed by bilateral clearing account arrangements (see Glossary), but EEC regulations obliged Greece to discontinue them. In their place Greece signed trade agreements or protocols with all the East European countries. A 10-year Greek-Soviet accord was signed in 1983, covering cooperation in economic, industrial, scientific, and technical fields (see Mining and Quarrying, this ch.). Most of the agreements were designed to promote the export of Greek manufactures or co-operation in fields such as tourism as part of Greece's effort to reduce its large trade deficit with Eastern Europe. Although the terms of these agreements largely resembled past clearing arrangements, the EEC acquiesced to them, and Greece expanded its farm exports by similar means with Middle Eastern partners.

In 1983 trade with the United States amounted to 6.3 percent of exports and 3.7 percent of imports. Given the strength of the dollar, the United States share of the Greek market had dropped since the mid-1970s, and Japan became the fifth largest importer to Greece after West Germany, Saudi Arabia, Italy, and France. Although Greece had been seeking to expand trade ties with many countries, in 1984 it rejected offers by Turkey's prime minister, Turgut Ozal, for increased economic cooperation. Some businesspeople were, however, trying to expand trade relations.

Greek exports have generally suffered from inadequate standardization, packaging, and marketing. The first 300 out of a total of 9,429 Greek export companies accounted for 71.5 percent of exports in 1983, while 4,000 of the total accounted for only 0.4 percent, underscoring the need for greater government support of exporting. Thus, the PASOK government created a state export organization to carry out market research, provide official representation at international trade fairs, and help small- and medium-sized exporters with procedural arrangements. The new organization pushed joint export ventures, in which it participated with 50 percent of equity capital, to help small, isolated firms establish an export identity. The government also created an export trading company to handle trade for public enterprises and to administer state-to-state trading agreements. Despite opposition from private traders, a third state organization was established to import goods in short supply as well as basic items for which the state wanted to control prices.

### Other Foreign Exchange Earners

Greece runs a permanent trade deficit, which is covered in part each year by three significant foreign exchange sources: shipping earnings, tourism, and emigrant remittances. In 1983 these activities returned earnings equivalent to an estimated 10 percent of GNP and accounted for 35 percent of total foreign exchange receipts. The recessionary conditions of the

1980s, coupled with the repatriation of emigrants from 1974 onward, has meant that earnings from the three sources have declined both in absolute terms and as a percentage of imports. Whereas the surplus on invisibles covered 50 percent of imports in 1971, it had fallen to 33 percent by 1983. In early 1985 only tourism showed potential for a substantial comeback. Additional foreign exchange revenues were expected, however, as Athens continues to emerge as a financial and trade center for the eastern Mediterranean.

### Shipping

Although Greek exports and imports represent a minute fraction of world trade, Greek international shipping activities are of great significance. The merchant marine, including Greek-owned vessels under foreign flags, numbers 3,444 ships with 41.4 million registered tons in May 1984, while those ships flying the Greek flag totaled 3,082 vessels with 34.7 million registered tons. Despite the world shipping crisis of the 1980s, which caused substantial reductions in the Greek fleet, Greek shipping—counting only ships flying the Greek flag— kept its rank as the third largest in the world after Liberia and Japan. The large percentage of Greek-owned ships flying the national flag in 1984 contrasted favorably with the situation in the early 1960s when only about 20 percent did so. Their return was fostered largely by a government policy of fiscal and financial incentives as well as the improvement of infrastructural and service facilities within Greece. For such a large fleet Greece's shipbuilding and repair industries developed late but have been strongly encouraged by government incentive schemes and bilateral repair agreements with foreign countries.

With the inclusion of the Greek fleet, the EEC controlled 22.3 percent of world shipping tonnage in May 1984. Because about 90 percent of the revenue earned by Greece's merchant fleet came from carrying the cargo of foreign nations, receipts were vulnerable to sharp fluctuations. In the 1975-81 period shipping receipts more than doubled to reach US$1.8 billion (the remittances of Greek seamen were recorded among these receipts). Owing to recessionary conditions, surplus tonnage, and low freight rates, nearly one-third of the fleet was laid up in 1983, and receipts declined 28 percent between 1981 and 1983. They totaled $1.3 billion in 1983, contributing about 16.6 percent to total goods and services exports. According to preliminary figures of the Bank of Greece, foreign exchange earnings from shipping were down 16 percent in 1984, compared with the same period in 1983.

Older, more experienced Greek shipowners have generally been handling the crisis better than newcomers to the business and have been striving to renew their aging fleets. In an effort to stem shipping losses, the Socialist government has reneged on some of its promises to seamen's organizations regarding manning regulations and the engagement and pay of foreign crews. Despite high unemployment among registered Greek seamen, owners have had increasing difficulties recruiting Greek officers and crews. Thus, in 1983 the government announced new measures to improve the social welfare of seamen. However, some of these measures were unpopular with shipowners, who in 1984 showed a renewed tendency to register under foreign flags.

### Tourism

Since the mid-1970s tourism has shown the greatest potential for growth among the three major sources of nonmercantile earnings, outstripping shipping earnings and emigrant remittances in some years. Except for 1974, when political turmoil and the Cyprus crisis discouraged tourism, tourist arrivals and receipts increased steadily in the 1970s. From 1979 onward the increase in arrivals was halted, however, and annual numbers have fluctuated between 5.2 million and 5.7 million. In 1981 receipts reached a high of nearly US$1.9 billion, but like other sectors of the economy, tourism was affected negatively by the global recession, and earnings fell to US$1.2 billion in 1983. Preliminary figures for 1984 indicated the first signs of recovery, as shown by the 11.8-percent increase in tourist receipts.

Because the National Tourist Organization (NTO), a government agency, has cited 6.5 million as the optimum number of arrivals, the Socialist government has sought to put new life into the industry while seeking to avoid some of its adverse effects, such as environmental problems and overcrowding. Government policy focuses on four objectives: extending the season because 75 percent of tourists arrive between July and September; spreading tourist development to less frequented spots; attracting a wider variety of tourists; and raising the average level of expenditure per tourist. To create more stability in earnings, the NTO is shifting the emphasis away from the

*The Acropolis in Athens, fifth century B.C.*

*Traditional weavings*
*in Athens*

*Flea market in Athens*

*Photos courtesy Peter J. Kassander*

213

inexpensive tour packages and mass tourism that usually attract about two-thirds of vacationers.

Accordingly, a greater percentage of arrivals in 1984 came from non-Europeans, high-income countries such as the United States, Canada, Japan, and Australia. Western-style resort activities are being promoted along with traditional Greek culture. Golf courses and ski runs are being built by the NTO, and parliament passed a law permitting nude sunbathing. A government program has been started to restore historic houses and properties and to turn them into exclusive guest homes. Subsidies are also available for builders of small hotels and guest houses in less developed areas, while further hotel development in 93 overcrowded locations has been banned. Pragmatism in tourism policy is illustrated by the fact that, contrary to its actions in other lagging sectors, the Socialist government is divesting itself of the Xenia chain of government-owned and -operated hotels, which have been criticized for poor management. The wealth of archaeological sites, mild climate, picturesque beaches, and extensive tourist facilities will make tourism a dynamic sector of the economy for years to come.

### Emigrant Remittances

Remittances could provide a large and stable portion of foreign exchange earnings for decades because of the Greek tendency to maintain strong ties with the home country (see Emigration, ch. 2). Whether the emigrants returned in person or sent savings and gifts back to relatives, the flow of ideas and money has had a strong impact on the economy, contributing to rising economic expectations. A large portion of the foreign investment capital that has come to Greece has been sent or stimulated by expatriate Greeks and Greek nationals who have made business fortunes abroad, often but not always in international shipping.

Owing to the reversal of migration flows in 1974, as well as high unemployment in the countries where emigrants have settled, remittances have been declining since 1979. Another factor has been the depreciation of the drachma, confirmed by the growth of deposits in convertible currencies by Greeks living abroad. Remittances totaled US$935 million in 1983, compared with a high of US$1.2 billion in 1979. With as many as 3 million emigrants still overseas, remittances will continue to be a factor in offsetting the trade deficit, although their significance will decline.

**Balance of Payments and External Debt**

Greece's current account deficit has fluctuated widely between 3 percent and 8.3 percent of GDP over the 1970-84 period. These fluctuations largely reflected cyclical factors in worldwide economic conditions. Since 1980 there has been a substantial weakening in the services account—with the sole exception of net EEC transfers—largely because of the depth of the international recession. Accordingly, the deficit on current transactions widened, reaching over US$2 billion in 1980 and 1981 (see table 12, Appendix A). Notwithstanding an increase in imports from the EEC, Greece's trade deficit has shown some improvement since 1981. It was reduced from almost 18 percent of GDP to 15 percent in 1982. Largely based on merchandise trade performance and a drop in oil imports because of the drawing down of reserves, the current account deficit declined to US$1.9 billion in 1982, or 5 percent of GDP. In 1983 the deficit stabilized around this same level, but estimates from the Bank of Greece indicated that it exceeded US$2 billion in 1984.

Large deficits recorded in the current account balance, coupled with a sizable drop in autonomous capital inflows, have resulted in a rapid buildup of foreign debt. Between 1979 and 1983 medium- and long-term foreign debt held by the state, the central bank, public enterprises, and private corporations had more than doubled to about US$11.8 billion, according to data from the OECD. Consequently, debt servicing rose from about 10.5 percent of foreign currency earnings from exports and invisibles to 17 percent in 1983. Although Greece had not faced difficulties in servicing its debt, its situation was far from optimum in 1985. Foreign debt was estimated to have increased by US$1.8 billion in 1984. Thus, the consensus among official international bodies such as the IMF and the OECD was that Greece's burden of debt would get heavier before the end of the decade. If stronger austerity measures were not taken, the IMF predicted that debt service could rise to 24 percent by 1989.

From 1983 on, borrowing by the Bank of Greece has been earmarked largely for servicing the foreign debt, while public enterprises have assumed new borrowing for the state. This qualifies statements by government representatives to the effect that the Greek state would not seek further loans in international markets. The government vowed to avoid recourse to the IMF because the terms normally imposed by the IMF were viewed as antithetical to PASOK's social policies. Some analysts thought, however, that the government would have to assume a balance of payments loan from the EEC to get over the future debt service bulge.

## Foreign Aid and Investment

Foreign capital has played an important role not only in financing chronic trade deficits but also in financing postwar reconstruction and development. In the early postwar years this capital mostly took the form of United States grant aid. It was not until the early 1960s that private direct investment came into the country on a large scale. Economic aid directed toward the creation of infrastructure provided the underpinning for economic growth. Beginning with various postwar programs, such as the Marshall Plan, from 1946 to 1977 Greece received a total of approximately US$5.1 billion in economic aid. During the 1947-66 period total United States aid amounted to US$3.75 billion, about half of which was military assistance and half, economic aid. Over 90 percent of total United States aid was in grant form; the rest was in loans. Technical assistance was terminated in 1962, and major economic aid ended in 1964. Only military assistance under the auspices of NATO continued thereafter. Between 1967 and 1979 Greece was eligible for assistance from the World Bank. Over that period 17 project loans were approved, amounting to US$490.8 million.

Since the postwar reconstruction period Greece has encouraged private foreign investment through guarantees and incentives based on the Basic Investment Law Number 2687 of 1953, entitled Investment and Protection of Foreign Capital. This law protects property rights and the preservation of the status quo and permits the repatriation of capital after one year at a 10-percent-per-annum rate. In addition, profits and interest may be exported at 12 percent and 10 percent per year, respectively. Later guarantees for foreign capital were provided by Article 107 of the Constitution of 1975.

Over the 1953-77 period direct foreign investment in Greece amounted to US$876 million. By way of comparison in 1969 alone, US$2.5 billion went into the gross formation of fixed capital in the Greek economy. Although foreign investment has amounted to less than 3 percent of the gross formation of fixed capital over time, its impact on the economy has been much greater than its size suggests. It is highly visible in the small area of modern industry. Between 1953 and 1977 nearly 54 percent of foreign investments were in the mechanical engineering sector, some 15 percent in chemicals, and 7 percent in the petroleum industry. In the early 1980s, out of the 39 largest industrial firms in Greece, more than half were foreign owned. The capital intensity of these new industries accentuated the monopolistic tendencies of the Greek economy.

During the period of the military regime, the flow of foreign investment began to slow. Yet since the restoration of democracy and the first oil crisis in 1973-74, the situation has deteriorated; no significant amounts of foreign investment capital entered the country in the 1974-84 period. The foreign investment capital that has flowed into the country in the past few years has come from the Arab countries, West Germany, the United States, Finland, and Canada.

## European Economic Community

After an extended period of limited association with the European Economic Community (EEC), Greece became its tenth full member on January 1, 1981. This marked the beginning of a five-year transition period for the adjustment of the Greek economy to EEC tariffs, standards, and regulations, including the elimination of all quantifiable restrictions and customs duties on imports from other EEC countries. A seven-year adjustment was set for the free movement of labor. Although some integrative measures were implemented during the association period, overall it did not adequately prepare Greece for full membership. Shortly after accession to the EEC, it was apparent that Greece would not meet all the terms of accession on schedule. Because these terms sharpened many of the country's economic problems, the Socialist government was seeking special arrangements to meet Greece's development requirements.

In the first three years of full membership, net financial transfers from the EEC amounted to approximately Dr115 billion, and an estimated Dr83 billion was to be added in 1984. The 1985 Greek budget anticipated net receipts of Dr100 billion. Transfers from various EEC funds have increased substantially each year as Greek officials have grown more efficient in processing applications for finance to Brussels. A large part of the inflows has been directed to the farm sector as price or income support and as financing of infrastructural development. Receipts through the agricultural support machinery were estimated to be Dr215 billion during the first four years of EEC membership. Including EEC expenditures for agricultural investments, the total approached Dr300 billion. As a result, farm incomes have risen faster than incomes in urban centers. Greece also received approximately Dr87 billion in loans from the European Investment Bank over the 1981-84 period.

There were, nonetheless, some serious negative economic consequences stemming from membership. The more rapid opening of the Greek economy under membership than under association encouraged an influx of EEC goods, which contributed to a substantial worsening of Greece's traditional trade deficit, displacement of Greek goods on the market, and inflationary pressures. Given the more efficient production and distribution methods of the other EEC partners, coupled with problems of quality control in Greece, Greek goods came under heavy competitive pressure. Additional problems were associated with the effects of distance from the other EEC countries on transport costs as well as with the deficiencies in Greece's own transportation network.

In the first year of membership Greece's overall trade deficit with the EEC increased by 19 percent in terms of United States dollars and 48 percent in terms of drachmas. The agricultural trade balance with the EEC, positive before accession, was transformed into a deficit of Dr10 billion in 1981 and about Dr20 billion in 1982. The agricultural trade deficit was slashed to Dr8 billion in 1983 because of an increase in vegetable, fruit, and olive oil exports to the EEC, a decrease in cereal imports, and the stimulation of exports outside of the EEC. Preliminary figures for 1984 indicated that improvement continued on both the agricultural balance and the trade balance, and it appeared likely that the former would be back in surplus.

Based on the Greek economy's initial performance in response to the new trade regime, in March 1982 the Socialist government submitted a memorandum to the Commission of the European Communities requesting, in effect, the revision of Greece's accession agreement. Specifically, the government called for increased financial support in conjunction with Greece's own five-year development plan and a new program for the Mediterranean region as a whole. It also sought temporary exemptions from EEC regulations in order to gain time to tackle Greece's own structural economic problems and to seek the revision of basic rules in the EEC's functioning, which inadvertently favored the more developed member countries. The memorandum placed emphasis on the underdevelopment of Greece's agricultural and rural regions.

The commission was responsive to the memorandum, promising additional aid if Greece was prepared to operate within EEC rules. It nevertheless allowed application of import quotas on a range of productions in the 1982-84 period, imposition of an import regulatory tax to cover the years 1984-89, extension of the deadline for introducing the value added tax (VAT), and higher percentages of EEC financing in Greek development projects. These concessions were minimal, however, compared with the range of temporary exemptions Greece continued to fight for in 1985. Given some 200 alleged Greek infringements of EEC regulations, the number of cases facing Greece in the EC's Court of Justice mounted, although in January 1985 Greece still ranked third after France and Italy on the court docket. Growing friction between the Greek government and the EEC commission centered on violations of free competition in regard to state agricultural export and crude oil monopolies, the setting up of a state pharmaceuticals monopoly, government bias toward domestic producers in public supply contracts, and restrictions on capital repatriation and property ownership by EEC nationals. The commission's primary concern was that unilateral bending of the rules by Athens created a de facto special relationship beyond that accepted by the other partners.

The commission preferred that the primary vehicle for meeting Greek demands be the proposed Integrated Mediterranean Program (IMP) unveiled in February 1983 to aid regions in Greece, Italy, and France that could be negatively affected by enlargement. At the EEC's Dublin Summit in December 1984, Athens made it clear that it regarded the IMP as a condition for agreeing to Spanish and Portuguese accession. Concern was expressed over increased competition from Spanish agricultural products, such as olive oil, wine, tomatoes, and fruit. Support thresholds were placed on several Mediterranean products to contain the anticipated surpluses. Greece's concerns also extended to Spain's considerable capacity in the shipbuilding and textiles industries.

Northern member states, such as West Germany and Britain, rejected the level of funding desired by Greece in recognition of the stringent state of EEC finances. In March 1985, shortly after negotiations on the entry of Spain and Portugal into the EEC were successfully concluded, a compromise on the IMP was reached. Greece would receive approximately US$1.4 billion in grants over a seven-year period for infrastructural projects, regional development, and investment in the farm sector. Passage of the IMP represented an important commitment to Greek development on the part of the other EEC members. Although this amount of aid was substantially lower than Greece had hoped to receive, statements by Papandreou signaled Greece's resolve to stay in the EEC. Since the 1981 election the Socialists had been backpedalling on their campaign promise to hold a referendum on EEC withdrawal. Despite the signficant costs of integration with more advanced economies, the Socialists apparently now believe that Greece will gain in the long term from EEC membership. Development of a more competitive productive structure will be hastened, while inflows of financial, managerial, and technological assistance will aid the country in implementing necessary but difficult socioeconomic reforms.

\* \* \*

Descriptions of the Greek economy during the 1950s and 1960s can be found in John Campbell and Philip Sherrard's *Modern Greece*, Wary O. Candilis' *The Economy of Greece, 1944-66*, and Nicos P. Mouzelis' *Modern Greece: Facets of Underdevelopment*. Nicholas V. Gianaris' *Greece and Yugoslavia* also provides an analysis of the historical development of the economy, focusing on current economic conditions and the policies of the PASOK government. Perhaps the best indicator of the government's economic and social development goals for the medium term are found in the English summary of the *Economic and Social Development Plan: 1983-1987* prepared by the Centre of Planning and Economic Research (PER). The PER occasionally publishes useful research monographs in English on such topics as the Greek labor market. For current statistical information, the Bank of Greece and the National Statistical Service of Greece each produce periodical statistical bulletins. In addition, the annual surveys of the Organisation for Economic Co-operation and Development, as well as the annual report of the governor of the Bank of Greece, are comprehensive yearly assessments of economic performance. For the most up-to-date information on government and private economic activities, the London daily *Financial Times* provides excellent coverage of Greek affairs. Both are also thorough in reporting on Greek-EEC relations. (For further information and complete citations, see Bibliography.)

# Chapter 4. Government and Politics

*Eleutherios Venizelos (1864-1936), Greek statesman*

IN OCTOBER 1981 THE Panhellenic Socialist Movement led by Andreas Papandreou ended the 45-year monopoly of power by conservative groups, which included a period of military rule from 1967 to 1974. The Socialist movement accomplished the feat through a startling victory at the polls by promising the voters a wide range of reform measures aimed at the realization of "political, social, and economic democracy." The ultimate goals of democracy were stated in lofty terms such as "social liberation" and "social justice." Prime Minister Papandreou, the first Socialist head of government ever for the country, wanted to steer the nation toward more vigorous democratic dialogue, substantial decentralization in decisionmaking, more effective unionism, and a leaner and more efficient public administration. He also announced a number of new steps to be undertaken in many other governmental endeavors.

At the start of 1985 Papandreou was cautiously optimistic about the way national and international affairs were unfolding as well as about the future of his administration and of Greece. From the observers' corner, however, the political scene was too fluid, to say the least, to warrant even a tentative assessment on the accomplishments of his government. For one thing, the Socialist regime was only in its fourth year. For another, it was being challenged increasingly by the conservative opposition New Democracy party, which was determined to supplant the Socialist government in the general election slated for June 2. On that day voters will have handed down a verdict on whether the Papandreou administration deserves another four years of mandate or whether the New Democracy can better manage the affairs of state on both domestic and foreign fronts.

## The Constitutional Framework

Greece is a parliamentary republic under a president as head of state and a prime minister as head of government. Its governmental and political system is buttressed by the Constitution of 1975, the latest of many fundamental laws dating from the 1820s. The most frequent reason for changing the constitution had to do with the endemic dispute over whether Greece should be a monarchy or republic—a major source of

225

political tensions for 150 years (see The Interwar Period: From Republic to Dictatorship, ch. 1).

The Constitution, effective from June 11, 1975, was drafted in 1974 by a popularly elected legislature following the restoration of civilian rule. It provides the basis for a republican form of polity, made possible by the popular verdict favoring the abolition of the monarchy once and for all in a referendum held in December 1974. Sovereignty is to emanate from the people and to be exercised as specified by the Constitution. Governmental structure and functional responsibilities are broadly divided into three branches: executive, legislative, and judicial. These branches are to operate under the principle of checks and balances. The presidency of the republic is placed above the three branches and above partisan politics as well. The authority of the president is on the one hand so limited as to prevent a concentration of power in his hands and, on the other hand, so phrased as to enable the president to exercise some important political initiatives. In April and May 1985 the Constitution was amended to ensure that the president remained strictly a titular head of state. A full range of human rights is protected under the Constitution, which states that every person shall have the right to develop freely his or her personality and to participate in the social, economic, and political life of the country. All persons residing within the Greek territory may enjoy, "full protection of their life, honor, and freedom, irrespective of nationality, race or language and of religious or political beliefs," unless otherwise disallowed by international law. The state and all its agents are directed to ensure that individual rights and liberties are exercised fully. The state may, for its part, call on all citizens "to fulfill the duty of social and national solidarity."

Basic rights and liberties include, among others, freedom of speech, of the press, of peaceful assembly and association, and of travel; economic freedom and property ownership; privacy of correspondence and the inviolability of the home; due process of law; and the principle of no retroactive legislation. Also guaranteed are the right to petition the state for redress of grievances and the right to employment, to social security and housing, to education, and to health care.

Traditionally the Orthodox Christian church has maintained a close link with the state—a link that is neither a case of union nor one of total separation. The special status of the church is acknowledged in the Constitution, which declares, "The prevailing religion in Greece is the Eastern Orthodox

Church of Christ." Nevertheless, the freedom of religious conscience is declared inviolable, and "all known religions" are to be free, and their rites of worship are to be performed unhindered. They are also to be protected by law to an extent not prejudicial to public order or to moral principles. Oddly, though, the Constitution prohibits proselytization by religions other than the Eastern Orthodox Church of Christ, but the implications of this prohibition are unclear inasmuch as instances of religious persecution are rare.

Censorship and all other preventive measures relating to the freedom of the press are prohibited. The seizure of newspapers and other publications is permitted, however, by order of the public prosecutor in the case of an offense against "the Christian or any other known religion," of an insult against the person of the president of the republic, or of an obscene article offensive to public decency. A publication that prejudices national security matters, or advocates the violent overthrow of the constitutional order, or is directed against the territorial integrity of the state is also liable to seizure. Within 24 hours of seizure the public prosecutor must submit the case to the judicial authorities, who must act on the seizure order within the next 24 hours. Otherwise, the seizure is nullified. Three or more convictions within five years for any of the offenses listed above become grounds for either a permanent ban or a temporary suspension of printed news media or a publication. Convicted journalists may be debarred from their profession as prescribed by law.

Work is a right, and all workers, irrespective of sex, are entitled to equal remuneration for equal services performed. The freedom of unionism, including the right to strike for higher wages and better employment conditions, is constitutionally protected, but judicial functionaries and members of the security forces are prohibited from striking. Civil servants and employees of other public corporations may strike, subject to the limitations of the law.

In the early 1980s Greece had an excellent human rights record, and individuals could exercise rights and liberties generally free from state interference. The press was highly politicized and actively competed for readership, at times in a sensationalist and intensely partisan manner. Radio and television were state owned but operated with considerable independence from the government. The only disturbing note on the state of human rights in Greece was the relatively frequent incidence of terrorist killings and bombings. The Greek government has strongly condemned these acts and has taken some countermeasures.

The Constitution provides for amendment of all but the most basic articles, such as those defining Greece as a parliamentary republic, those guaranteeing fundamental rights and liberties, and those vesting legislative, executive, and judicial powers in the appropriate branches of government. To amend the Constitution, a proposal must be introduced into the legislature by at least 50 members. It must then be confirmed by a three-fifths majority vote of the total parliamentary membership on each of two ballots held at least one month apart. The next session of parliament finally enacts the bill by an absolute majority vote of the total membership. Constitutional revision is not permitted before the lapse of five years from the completion of a previous revision; this is designed to ensure the stability of constitutional order.

## The Governmental Organization

Greece is a unitary state based on a system of parliamentary representation. The powers of the state are separated into three branches to prevent their concentration in a single authority. They are highly centralized at the national level, however, and efforts were under way after 1981 to lend a degree of substance to the constitutional stipulation that "the administration of the State shall be organized on the basis of decentralization."

### President of the Republic

The president is the principal link between the executive, legislative, and judicial establishments of the state and stands above partisan strife. The president is elected for a five-year term (renewable once) by the parliament, which votes by secret ballot. A candidate to the office must be the descendant of a Greek father, a Greek citizen for five years, at least 40 years of age, and must be entitled to vote in parliamentary elections. To be elected, a two-thirds majority (200 votes) is necessary for the first and second ballots, and a three-fifths majority (180 votes) for a third-ballot election. Failure to elect on the third round results in the dissolution of parliament within 10 days and the holding of new elections. Should the presidency be vacated, the parliament meets within 10 days and elects a successor for a full term. In the event of incapacitation, the president's duties are temporarily assumed by the Speaker of parliament.

The president performs ceremonial duties, such as conferring state honors, convening the annual parliamentary session, granting pardons, and appointing the prime minister, who is the leader of the party with an absolute parliamentary majority, or, if no party enjoys such a majority, the leader of the party with a plurality. To be formally confirmed into office, the prime minister-designate must win a parliamentary vote of confidence. If not, the president—after conferring with an advisory and consultative body called the Council of the Republic—designates another person, who need not be a member of the legislature. If this person fails to secure a vote of confidence, the president, with the concurrence of the council, may dissolve parliament and call for new elections within 30 days. The president and the new parliament then start the selection and confirmation process all over again.

In addition to ceremonial functions, the president may perform certain legislative and executive powers that are expressly conferred on his office by the Constitution. In exercising these prerogatives he can perform an influential role, depending on his personality and leadership style, beyond the scope of involvement usually afforded a figurehead of state. The president sanctions laws passed by parliament within one month of a vote or may return for reconsideration any bill he opposes. If the vetoed legislation is passed again by an absolute majority of parliament's total membership, the president must assent to it within 10 days of the vote.

In extraordinary situations of an urgent and unforeseen nature, the president, on the proposal of the cabinet, may issue a decree having the force of law. Such a decree must be submitted within 40 days to parliament for ratification; it becomes invalid if not submitted to the legislature or if that body does not ratify it within three months. A presidential decree may also be issued to suspend portions of the Constitution in cases of war or national mobilization or in case of serious disturbances or a clear threat against public order and security of the state—in both cases countersigned by the prime minister. Furthermore, the president may, as of the issuance of such a decree, take all necessary legislative or administrative measures required to meet the emergency and to restore the operation of constitutional institutions as early as practicable.

Potentially the most significant constitutional prerogative

pertains to the president's power to proclaim on his own initiative referenda on "crucial national issues." He may, "in exceptional circumstances, address messages to the nation, which shall be published in the Government Gazette." The Constitution does not define what "crucial national issues" mean or what "totally exceptional circumstances" are and, in any case, the power to call a referendum has never been tested under the present Constitution. If taken literally, this power enables the president to go directly to the electorate without even consulting the prime minister. Such a consultation is required, however, in case the president decides to dissolve parliament if it is "in obvious discord with the popular feeling or if its composition does not ensure governmental stability." In these instances, the Council of the Republic must be first consulted. The council is a constitutional organ composed of "democratically elected former presidents of the republic, the prime minister, the Speaker of parliament, the leader of the parliamentary opposition, and former prime ministers who have been members of parliament or who headed governments [the cabinets] having received a vote of confidence by parliament." The president may convene the council to seek its advice on the dissolution of parliament, when selecting a prime minister after two unsuccessful ballots and, according to the Constitution, "in every other national circumstance he deems to be serious."

Unquestionably, the president's prerogatives can lead to confrontational crisis between the head of state and the prime minister, and such potentiality was cited as the reason for Papandreou's decision to amend the Constitution in 1985. Papandreou's proposed bill called for the elimination of the presidential power to exercise political initiatives; it passed the two-ballots test in April and May, but its final outcome must wait until after a new parliament is elected in June 1985.

The president represents Greece internationally and, with the concurrence of parliament, declares war and concludes agreements of peace, alliance, and participation in international organizations. He is also the head of the armed forces, but actual command is exercised by the government. Much of the presidential power is limited, however, by the constitutional provision that most presidential acts must be countersigned by the competent cabinet ministers. The president cannot be held responsible for any acts performed for the state, except for high treason or "intended violation of the Constitution." He may be impeached if charges against him are signed by at least one-third of the members of parliament and subsequently approved by at least two-thirds of the total membership. A special ad hoc court presided over by the chief justice of the Supreme Court then tries the president.

## Branches of the Government

### *Executive*

The executive establishment, or government, consists of the cabinet led by the prime minister and, as of early 1985, 19 departmental ministers and two cabinet-rank ministers to the prime minister (see fig. 17). Ministers, who need not be members of parliament, are chosen by the prime minister for formal appointment by the president. Together with the prime minister, they are collectively responsible to parliament for the formulation and implementation of the general policy of the government; each minister is also individually responsible for all acts undertaken within the competence of his office. Cabinet members are free to attend parliamentary sittings and must be heard when they request the floor. Conversely, parliament may request ministers to appear at sittings to account for policies or answer questions.

The cabinet must receive and maintain the confidence of parliament; a confidence vote must be held within 15 days from the date a new cabinet is announced. The voting focuses on what is officially called "the government program," which broadly outlines the government's proposed policies and programs. Parliament may withdraw its confidence by passing a censure motion, which must be signed by a minimum of one-sixth of that body's total membership and be adopted by an absolute majority of the total membership. Only one such motion may be introduced every six months; a censure motion signed by a simple majority of the total parliamentary membership, however, may be tabled at any time. Ministers and undersecretaries who are members of parliament may vote on confidence and censure motions. When the confidence motion is defeated and the government resigns, it is customary for a temporary, nonpartisan caretaker government to be formed to administer the new elections.

### *Legislative*

Parliament is a unicameral body of 300 deputies, who are elected through direct, universal, and secret ballot (see The

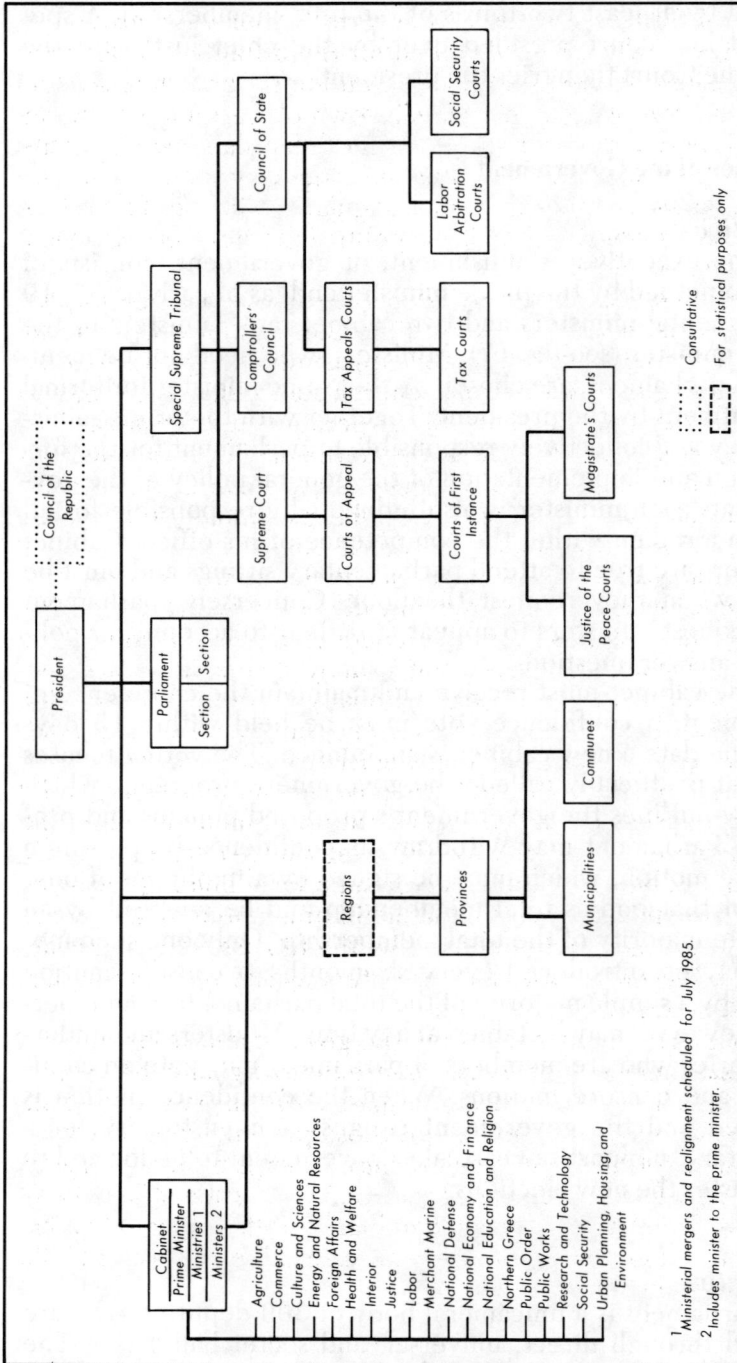

Figure 17. Governmental Organization of Greece, 1985

Cabinet
Prime Minister
Ministries 1
Ministries 2

Agriculture
Commerce
Culture and Sciences
Energy and Natural Resources
Foreign Affairs
Health and Welfare
Interior
Justice
Labor
Merchant Marine
National Defense
National Economy and Finance
National Education and Religion
Northern Greece
Public Order
Public Works
Research and Technology
Social Security
Urban Planning, Housing, and Environment

President

Council of the Republic

Parliament
Section    Section

Special Supreme Tribunal

Council of State

Comptrollers' Council

Supreme Court

Courts of Appeal

Courts of First Instance

Tax Appeals Courts

Tax Courts

Labor Arbitration Courts

Social Security Courts

Justice of the Peace Courts

Magistrate's Courts

Regions

Provinces

Municipalities    Communes

Consultative

For statistical purposes only

1 Ministerial mergers and realignment scheduled for July 1985.

2 Includes minister to the prime minister.

Electoral System, this ch.). The term is four years except in time of war, when it is extended for the duration. Parliament convenes on the first Monday in October for an annual session of at least five months. It elects its own officers and a standing committee that determines the order of legislative work. Committees that examine bills and investigatory committees are formed at the beginning of each regular session on the basis of the proportional strength of the political parties represented in the whole chamber.

Parliament generally conducts legislative business in plenary sessions, as required under the Constitution when certain subjects are deliberated. These subjects include parliamentary standing orders and elections, church-state relations, religious freedom, and individual liberties; operation of political parties; delegation of legislative authority to the president or to a cabinet minister; and authorization of the state budget. Plenary sessions may also be requested by the government to consider "a bill of major importance" for debate and passage.

When parliament is in recess, its legislative work—with the exception of subjects specifically reserved for consideration by full session—may be conducted by a section (also called department). Parliament usually divides into two sections, equal in size and proportionally representative of the strength of the political parties in the legislature. The competence of each section includes legislative subjects relating to the functions of roughly half the government ministries. A bill passed by a section has the same status as that adopted by the full assembly. Any dispute over the legislative competence of a section may be referred to the plenum for a binding decision. The Constitution stipulates that a bill or a motion of law pending before a section be debated by the full assembly of parliament and be adopted by an absolute majority of the total parliamentary membership.

Bills may be introduced by the government or by a member of parliament. In practice, more bills originate in the government than in parliament. To pass a bill in plenary session requires an absolute majority of those present or no less than one-quarter of the total membership. Passage by section needs a majority of those present; the majority must be at least two-fifths of the total sectional membership. A bill rejected by either a section or by the plenum cannot be reintroduced in the same annual session.

## Judicial

The current legal system is based on codified Roman civil law, as well as on French and German sources, all of whose evolution owe much to Greece. Greek philosophy, in general, and the tenets of rationalism and natural law, in particular, contributed significantly to the evolution of Roman Law. Furthermore, it was the eastern, or Greek, part of the Roman Empire that was instrumental in preserving Roman Law after the collapse of the empire in the west.

Since the coming to power of the Panhellenic Socialist Movement (Panhellinion Socialistiko Kinima—PASOK) administration in 1981, the judicial system has been under close official scrutiny. In mid-1982 a former Supreme Court prosecutor claimed in a published report that the judiciary was corrupt and susceptible to political pressures. In acknowledging that his government had inherited "an unacceptably downgraded legal system," Papandreou announced plans to improve the system as a whole. In mid-1985 what changes, if any, were instituted remained unclear.

Justice is administered by an independent judiciary, which is divided into the civil, criminal, and administrative courts. Judges are independent and enjoy personal immunity and are subject only to the Constitution and the law in discharging their constitutional responsibilities. Judges and other judicial personnel are appointed, promoted, and transferred formally by presidential decree, based on the prior decisions of a self-policing judicial council. Lower-level judges, including those in the courts of appeal, serve until 65 years of age and those in the higher courts until 75 years of age, unless disqualified by criminal conviction, a grave breach of discipline, disability, or professional inadequacy.

The judicial council comprises the president of the three high courts, which are the Supreme Court for civil and criminal justice, the Council of State for administrative cases, and the Comptrollers' Council for fiscal matters. Other members of the council are chosen by lot from among those judges or councillors who have served in the high courts for a minimum of two years.

The lowest courts in the civil and criminal court structure are the 360 justice of the peace courts and 48 magistrate's (or police) courts. These basic courts are responsible for minor civil and criminal cases. Above this level are the 59 courts of first instance, which handle the bulk of civil and criminal litigations. Serious cases are tried before juries. Juvenile and commercial cases may be tried also by these courts of first instance. Twelve courts of appeal hear appeals from the courts of first instance. In exceptional cases, such as those involving major crimes, the appellate courts may function as courts of original jurisdiction. The Supreme Court, comprising four civil sections and two criminal sections, hears appeals from the courts of appeal on questions of law. All court sessions are public, except when a court decides that publicity would prejudice public morality or would endanger the safety of litigants or witnesses. Felonies and political crimes are decided by mixed juries composed of judges and lay jurors.

Administrative cases are adjudicated by special courts that include labor arbitration courts and social security courts. Also included are tax courts of first instance and tax appeals courts. The supreme administrative court is the Council of State, which rules on, among other things, administrative disputes referred to it by lower bodies. The council may also annul, based on petition, executive acts by government authorities that involve abuses of office or violations of existing law. Compliance with the council's ruling in such a case is mandatory; a government official who refuses to comply is liable to prosecution through regular criminal proceedings. The Council of State may also render judgments regarding the elaboration of governmental regulatory decrees.

State finances, also under the administrative sphere of the judiciary, are overseen by the Comptrollers' Council, which is independent of the Council of State. The comptrollers audit central and local government as well as public corporation expenditures and present an annual financial report to parliament. They also rule on public pension disputes and try cases involving the liability of civil and military officials who, by alleged fraud or negligence, have caused financial loss to the state.

At the pinnacle of the judicial system is the Special Supreme Tribunal, comprising the presidents of the Supreme Court, the Council of State, and the Comptrollers' Council; four councillors of the Council of State; four members of the Supreme Court chosen by lot every two years; and, in some cases, two law professors also chosen by lot. The tribunal hears cases involving parliamentary election disputes, public referenda returns, and jurisdictional disputes between courts and government agencies, between the Council of State and other courts, and between the Comptrollers' Council and other courts. The ultimate authority for judicial review—the Special

Supreme Tribunal—also rules on the constitutional validity or meaning of laws in cases where the Council of State, the Supreme Court, or the Comptrollers' Council have rendered conflicting judgments. The ruling of the tribunal is irrevocable. Constitutional interpretation in all other cases is a matter for the legislature, not the judiciary.

## Local Government

The Constitution acknowledges the importance of local government and decentralization, but little was done to change the pattern of overcentralization until the PASOK government initiated steps toward strengthening local autonomy in 1982. Traditionally, local government was popularly viewed as the more or less exclusive preserve of the wealthy local elite; the concept of popular involvement in local affairs was remote at best and failed to take any firm root. In March 1982 the PASOK government, which had promised to foster administrative and economic independence at the local level, enacted a bill called Exercise of Government Policy and Establishment of Popular Representation in the Provinces. Under this legal framework the provincial governors as well as the municipalities and communes below the provincial level were to be delegated the authority to make decisions that had previously been made by the central government. The status of actual changes under the framework of decentralization was unclear in 1985.

The country is divided into nine regions, the boundaries of which are based on geographical, historical, and cultural factors (see fig. 17). The Greater Athens area is sometimes designated as an unofficial tenth region. Although used for statistical purposes, the regions have no administrative significance. They are subdivided into 51 provinces (also called prefectures), which serve as the basic subnational administrative units and hence the principal links between the central and local government.

The head of a province is a *governor*, who is appointed by and responsible to the central government. In addition to local administration, the governor functions as the principal central government agent and is responsible for coordinating the activities of various ministerial field offices within his or her jurisdiction. The governor is assisted by a provincial council, which is composed of the mayor of the province's capital, two representatives drawn from the municipalities and communes, representatives of mass organizations for farmers, workers, professionals and employers, selected members of public corporations, and the provincial governor. From time to time two or more provincial councils hold joint meetings with senior officials of the central government ministries for mutual consultation concerning local affairs.

The basic tier of local government consists of 264 municipalities and 5,744 communes or communities. Usually the municipality has a population exceeding 10,000 inhabitants; the commune has 5,000 to 10,000 persons. Municipal and commune units have elected councils headed by mayors and presidents, respectively; the mandate of these councils is renewed every four years (the most recent local elections took place in October 1982). The membership of these local councils varies from five to 61 deputies, depending on population.

The Mount Athos peninsula, the site of a monastic center for the Eastern Orthodox church since A.D. 959, is autonomous from the regular administrative structure. Nevertheless, the state of Greece is represented there by a governor, whose duty it is to ensure that public order and safety is maintained and that the charter of autonomy is faithfully implemented. Mount Athos is governed by the ecumenical patriarchate of the Orthodox Christian church of Greece in accordance with its centuries-old legislative, executive, and judicial practices. No female of any species, except for cats and hens, has been allowed on Mount Athos for nearly 1,000 years.

## Civil Service

Entry into the civil service is generally by competitive examination supervised by a board of civil servants, but various ministries sometimes avoid the regular recruitment channel and engage personnel by contract. In the latter case the recruitment depends on the discretion of each minister and hence is highly conducive to political favoritism. Specialists are hired through a noncompetitive procedure at higher salaries than would be possible otherwise. After several years of service, contract personnel often acquire a civil service tenure.

Civil service personnel are organized into three lettered categories. A-category personnel are university graduates who perform administrative and executive functions. B-category is for high school graduates who perform clerical duties. There are no educational requirements for C-category personnel, who are accepted without examinations or other tests of skill. Automatic promotion from a lower category to A-category occurs upon receipt of a university degree. In most cases civil service tenure is secure, subject only to major political upheavals or dismissal for misconduct or incompetence. Mobility between ministries, or even between directorates and bureaus within a ministry, is minimal, and it is not unusual for a civil servant to spend an entire career working for the same office. The lack of an adequate training program for civil servants remained a problem for the Greek system in the early 1980s.

Inefficiency and favoritism have caused the general public to criticize the civil service and to attach little prestige to it. Although rural and less educated persons might look to employment in the government service as a means of bettering their lot, the educated urbanites prefer the private sector to civil service. The relatively low salaries received for government employment do not increase its attractiveness. It is not uncommon for civil servants to have a second job to augment their pay. Upper-level administrators often practice a variation of this scheme by accepting memberships on several government committees, commissions, or boards—all of which pay honoraria—reducing the time the administrators can spend on their primary duties.

The government in 1974 recognized the problems and limitations of the civil service. Soon after his election, press reports quoted Prime Minister Constantine Karamanlis as stating that "modernization of public administration" would be one of his government's major goals. That modernization was to include a "material and moral strengthening of the human manpower of the administration" and "structural changes" that would facilitate the central government's national planning role. Generally, bureaucratic reforms are, however, more easily planned than executed. Evidently, the civil service was no better off in ensuing years. In a preelection analysis of public administration in 1981, PASOK identified favoritism, red tape, corruption, and excessive centralization as major targets for reforms. Among the specific changes proposed was the establishment of "a more open [civil service] system concerning recruitment, appointments, transfers, and promotions." As of mid-1984 changes, if any, appeared to be minimal, as there were continuing public demands for more merit-based recruitments, for greater bureaucratic responsiveness to public needs and grievances, for the establishment of a uniform salary and a uniform grading and rating system, for the reduction of civil service personnel, and for the elimination of bureaucratic "highhandedness."

## The Electoral System

Electoral processes, an integral part of the Greek political system, have played a central role in the peaceful resolution of partisan competition in recent decades—except during the period of military rule from 1967 to 1974. Elections are based on direct, universal, and secret ballot. They take place every four years for parliament—unless called sooner because of parliamentary dissolution—and for the municipal and commune councils. Voting is compulsory for all citizens aged 18 and above; nonvoting is liable to legal penalties.

The 300 members of parliament are elected from 56 constituencies, each returning from one to 32 seats, depending on its population. Candidates are elected under a proportional representation system. Under the Greek version 288 members of parliament (as in the 1981 election) are chosen directly on the basis of constituency votes; these members must belong to a particular constituency and must compete for election, whereas the remaining 12 members, who are called "national deputies," are elected at large, the whole country being treated as a single constituency. The national deputies need not belong to any constituency, or contest the election.

The electoral system is weighed heavily in favor of larger parties, making it difficult for smaller parties to form an electoral alliance or a coalition government. Ostensibly it is designed to assure stable party politics, but actually it is intended to prevent communist and other radical groups from gaining representation in parliament. Thus, under the Greek system of proportional representation a parliamentary majority can be achieved and a government formed even if a winning party fails to secure a simple majority of the popular vote. This is made possible through a method of awarding extra representation, a bonus system, so to speak, to the larger parties that obtain a minimum percentage of the national vote. This percentage, or "threshold" as it is sometimes known, ranged from 10 to 17 percent in the post-World War II years (it was 17 percent in the parliamentary elections of 1974, 1977, and 1981). In Greece this particular proportionate system is called one of "reinforced proportional representation." Political scientist Phaedo Vegleris commented in this regard that "it is not *proportionality* that the system 'reinforces,' but the representation in Parliament of the political tendencies prevailing at a given moment."

Not surprisingly the reinforced proportional representation system was opposed by small parties. In 1981 even the PASOK government announced its intention to adopt a simplified representation system to make sure that popular will could be more accurately reflected in parliament "without any distortions." It also pledged at that time to eliminate the long-standing practice of "preference votes" whereby candidates on the party list could be elected according to the preference of voters rather than party leaders. The preference vote system was long seen as undermining party discipline and enabling locally influential barons to sway constituency votes through the maintenance of patron-client networks.

In early 1985 a new electoral law was passed to bring about what the PASOK government called "a simple proportional system." The passage of this law was in line with the practice of successive governments of devising an electoral scheme in anticipation of forthcoming elections. This was the fifteenth time dating back to the 1920s that an incumbent regime modified an electoral law to ensure its own success at the polls. The 1985 law abolished the minimum 17-percent requirement to qualify for the bonus allocation of seats, making it possible for small parties such as the Communist Party of Greece-Exterior (Kommunistikon Komma Ellados—KKE-Exterior), which received 10.9 percent of the vote in 1981, to benefit from the bonus allocation. Nevertheless, although PASOK's main rival, New Democracy (Nea Demokratia—ND), accepted the new law without demur, the KKE-Exterior strongly opposed it as being no different from the reinforced proportional representation system. Indeed, many observers felt that the new law would continue to favor the parties gaining the largest shares of votes. The new law did away with the preference vote system, but whether this would strengthen party discipline and result in elections stressing issues rather than clientelism in local politics remained to be seen.

## Political Development, 1981–85

In parliamentary elections held on October 18, 1981, PASOK, led by Andreas Papandreou, won a landslide victory. With about 79 percent of the registered electorate voting,

PASOK received over 48 percent of the vote and—owing to a complicated system of "reinforced proportional representation"—over 57 percent of the seats in the legislature (172 out of 300). The only other parties to win seats in parliament were the ND (35.9 percent of the vote and 115 seats) and KKE-Exterior (10.9 percent of the vote and 13 seats). Over a dozen minor parties received a combined total of only 5.2 percent but won no seats.

PASOK's election campaign centered on the relatively poor economic performance of the incumbent ND government, headed since 1980 by George Rallis. Although some progress had been made in restoring economic equilibrium after the second oil shock in 1979, inflation was still running at about 25 percent; the public sector financial deficit amounted to about 14 percent of the gross domestic product (GDP—see Glossary); the balance of payments deficit had grown to US$2.2 billion by 1980; and the annual growth rate of the economy hovered around 1 percent. In response to widespread strikes in late 1980, the government instituted a new policy of indexing salaries to inflation and shorter working hours, but these concessions failed to mollify the workers, and new demonstrations against rising prices broke out on May 1.

PASOK's slogan was "Change" (Allaghi). The exact dimensions of the promised change were left vague but included promises of a wide-ranging program of "socialization," administrative decentralization, educational and welfare reform, a streamlining of the bureaucracy, indexing of salaries and pensions, and ending *rousfeti*, the traditional practice of trading favors between patrons and clients. The party's appeal was directed at the "broad masses of the Greek people" who had historically been subject to the "odious exploitation" of the financial oligarchy and tied in with a widely felt desire to end the conservative parties' 45-year monopoly of political power.

The ND's campaign offered few policy proposals and instead focused on Papandreou's foreign policy pronouncements. Rallis insisted that PASOK's pledge to terminate Greece's membership in the North Atlantic Treaty Organization (NATO, also called the Atlantic Alliance) would "lead this country to catastrophe" and would "create a vacuum in the Aegean which would inevitably be filled by Turkey." Similarly, PASOK's call to withdraw from the European Economic Community (EEC) would disrupt Greece's agricultural sector and destroy the economy's best hope for sustained recovery and growth. As for Papandreou's domestic program, Rallis denounced the plans for the socialization of key industries and the extension of social welfare programs as disruptive and hopelessly extravagant, given the current state of Greece's economy.

The ND's plea to the electorate "not to waste the achievements of a generation" failed to rally support. At the same time, PASOK's success is probably attributable more to a general desire for change than to any commitment to the "socialist" alternative. The recent election of a socialist to the French presidency in May 1981, with no dire consequences, doubtless also helped to dispel any residual fears of the left in Greece.

### "Socialism" in Action

The new government, sworn in on October 21, 1981, was unusual by Greek standards. Of the 21 cabinet ministers, only the prime minister, Papandreou, had previously held a government office. The average age of the cabinet was under 50, and more than half had been active in the internal or external resistance movement against the junta between 1967 and 1974. The inexperience of the government contributed to a pattern of indecision and sharp shifts in policy that characterized its first two years in office. Some observers noted that Papandreou's personality may have contributed to the volatility and unpredictability of some of the new government's actions.

The new government's program was presented to parliament on November 22, 1981. After two days of debate the government won a vote of confidence by a comfortable margin (172 to 113). Papandreou's program of social, economic, and administrative reform began to take shape almost immediately thereafter.

In general, the new government tended to moderate its policies, if not its rhetoric, as it learned first-hand the difficulties of governing. Some observers suggested that the disparity between the radical words and pragmatic action of the government was deliberate and designed to ensure support from both the radical left and the moderate center. The moderate pace of reform provoked some elements of the PASOK membership to charge the government with failing to live up to its electoral promises of radical reform. Papandreou, however, drawing on precedents in Greek history and citing the experience of Chile under Salvador Allende Gossens, warned that precipitate reform would merely provoke a reaction from the right-wing.

Moreover, he insisted that his government was forging a new path to socialism that required frequent tactical adjustments but that the ultimate targets remained unchanged.

For foreign observers the government's foreign policy initiatives have received the most attention, but within Greece Papandreou's domestic program has been considered far more important and dramatic. The stated aims of the government's programs have been to increase the degree and quality of popular participation in Greece's political and economic life, to promote social equality and economic modernization, and to pursue an "independent" foreign policy.

### Social Legislation

The new government quickly proposed a series of largely cosmetic and cost-free laws to satisfy the immediate call for change. On December 31, 1981, the voting age was lowered from 20 to 18. The next month the government announced a language reform, replacing the complex system of accents and aspirations in written Greek with a simplified single accent system. In April 1982 some 500 prisoners were released to ease prison overcrowding, and charges were dropped on all minor offenses carrying one year's imprisonment.

A major goal of the new government was to strengthen the Greek democracy and end the legacy of bitterness left over from the Civil War (see The "Terrible Decade": World War II and the Civil War, 1940-49, ch. 1). One of its initial acts was to recognize for the first time the role of the Communist-led national resistance movement during the Axis occupation (1940-44) and abolish the official observance of anniversaries commemorating the Civil War. Many of the laws from that period curtailing personal liberty were annulled. Most notably, the police would no longer keep dossiers on the political affiliations of individuals. In addition, the government encouraged the repatriation of over 30,000 exiles who had fled to Eastern Europe in 1949. A limited repatriation had been in place since 1974, resulting in the return of an estimated 20,000 exiles.

These actions, though largely symbolic, appeared to be generally popular, especially among the PASOK faithful, and apparently succeeded in clearing the air of the residue of the Civil War. By 1985 the Civil War was no longer an issue for most of the electorate, and the left, both socialist and communist, was generally recognized as politically legitimate. The conservative, right-wing elements remained resentful, however, and feared the return of the Communists.

The Socialist government also initiated a series of laws designed to eliminate many of the strictures on personal freedom and the regulation of family life. Civil marriage was officially recognized in July 1982, and in the same month adultery was dropped from the list of criminal offenses. A new family law was passed in January 1983 to supersede the Greek Civil Code of 1946, which outlined in detail the rights and responsibilities of husband and wife and under which a married woman was legally subject to her husband in all matters. The 58-page law was designed to ensure equality of the sexes as a legal right under the Constitution and in every aspect of the civil code. The husband's monopoly on decisionmaking was changed to the right to common consent. At the same time, the woman's obligations, particularly the duty to support the family financially, are now equal to the man's. Divorce by common consent or after four years of separation is recognized, and alimony and child support are to be decided on a case-by-case basis—the woman equally liable for alimony as the man. A woman's constitutional right to work is reaffirmed, and dowries are prohibited. The law also redefines the position of children within the family, establishing 18 as the legal age of majority and replacing absolute parental authority with "parental care." Finally, the landmark legislation gives equal rights to legitimate and illegitimate children, especially in matters relating to inheritance.

Discussions on changing the old law began as early as 1977 under the conservative Karamanlis government but never went beyond the talking stage. The Papandreou government, in contrast, made the law a high priority. The most vocal support for the new law came from the feminist movement, of which Margaret Papandreou, the prime minister's wife, is president. In 1985 the effects of the law remained unclear. Given the oft repeated difficulties in legislating morals, it is likely to be some years before the legal equality between the sexes stipulated in the code becomes the norm.

In its address to parliament, the new government pledged to introduce legislation to establish a decentralized national health service to provide medical care for Greek citizens regardless of economic status or geographic location. In the past, the poor found it difficult to keep up with rising medical costs, and many rural areas suffered from a severe shortage of physicians, other medical personnel, and facilities while Athens was heavily overpopulated by physicians. In October 1983 the legal framework for the national health system was passed by the legislature, and the 1985 budget included allocations for its implementation. The program has been criticized by many as too expensive for Greece's strained economy, and physicians have mounted an offensive against what they see as an attack on their right to the free practice of their profession. Disputes within the government itself over plans for the health system led to the resignation in September 1983 of a cabinet member. The exact issues involved in the dispute were not disclosed, but it was widely believed that the resigned minister, known to favor greater austerity in budgetary policy, objected to the projected cost of the national health system. In mid-1985 the progress of the program was unclear.

The social security system, which provides state-guaranteed pensions for specified categories of workers, has undergone modifications since 1977, but the pace and range of those changes have increased since late 1981. The net effect has been to extend the pension system to most of the working population and to guarantee a minimum standard of living for the aged, the sick, and the disabled. The Socialist government's commitment to equality of the sexes has been shown once again by its well-publicized extension of equal pension rights to farmers' wives. The number of workers and occupations covered by the state system has grown, and the level of minimum benefits has been increased, as have benefits to the farmers.

### Economic Policy

In his policy statement to parliament, Papandreou outlined a program for economic recovery and modernization of Greece's highly centralized, interventionist economic system. The program, which included substantial changes in government, industrial, and agricultural structures and despite the government's rhetorical flourishes, generally corresponded to trends in state policy since at least 1974.

The most important elements of Papandreou's long-range program were the introduction of sectoral and decentralized planning to enhance the moribund planning apparatus that had been in place since the 1950s; the introduction of "socialization" in the commanding sectors of the economy to make enterprises more responsive to the needs of their employees, consumers, and local and central government; management with the creation of advisory committees of workers; the promotion of new technologies and the most dynamic small businesses; the encouragement of agricultural cooperatives; state restructuring of overindebted firms; and simplification of bureaucratic procedures that have traditionally caused massive delays in business expansion and construction (see Role of Government, ch. 3).

Papandreou's government initially encountered considerable opposition from businesspeople who felt that the government had an antibusiness orientation and that they were being made the scapegoats for the worsening economic crisis. With the inflation rate rising, unemployment reaching record levels, and strike activity increasing, the government in 1981 and 1982 instituted Keynesian policies of reflation (wage increases and indexation of wages to inflation, price controls, the shortening of the workweek, and increases in social security benefits). By January 1983, however, it was clear that those policies were exacerbating an already tense situation; the government reversed its direction by imposing an austerity program, including a rigid wage freeze, and curtailing the right to strike.

The drachma (for value of the drachma—see Glossary) was devalued in June 1982 by 3.2 percent against the United States dollar and again in January 1983 by 15.5 percent in order to make Greek exports more competitive. The salutary effects of the devaluation appeared to be short-lived as rising inflation once again overtook the currency adjustments.

Although there had been some improvement in the economy, the situation remained problematic in 1985, and strike activity appeared to be on the rise. The mixed economic performance of the PASOK government was reflected in the rising unemployment and continued inflation.

**Decentralization**

In accordance with its commitment to increasing popular participation and government accountability, and pointing to the pernicious effects of rigid bureaucratic centralization on the economy, the political system, and the larger society, the PASOK government made "decentralization" a primary goal. In his statement to parliament in November 1981 Papandreou pledged to reduce the domination of the centrally appointed provincial governors and to charge them with [preparing] the ground for the completion of decentralization and their own future replacement by genuinely elected organs."

Because control of the bureaucracy will be crucial for the success of this program, the PASOK government replaced some 300 key civil servants with PASOK sympathizers. Opponents charged that the new government was engaged in a purge, reaching into positions previously nonpolitical, but Papandreou reiterated his intention to end the traditional system of patronage in the bureaucracy.

In the first stage of decentralization, the government set up councils, composed of representatives from municipal and commune councils, farmers, workers, and employers, to advise the governors and reduced their control over the local councils. It is also doubled the central government grant of funds to these councils. Although the amounts remained small, the government announced that its intention was ultimately to make local government financially independent. In the second stage of the reform, the central government has planned to set up about 10 directly elected regional councils and up to 150 provincial councils. It is expected that these councils will have extensive spending powers and will be responsible for the economic development of their jurisdictions but will have no legislative power. By early 1985 the extent to which these plans had been implemented was unclear, and no timetable had been made public for completion of the decentralization program (see Local Government, this ch.).

### Foreign Policy

The axiom that style can be just as important as substance in foreign policy holds true for Greece. Papandreou's inflammatory rhetoric on key foreign policy issues tended to shake the confidence of the West in Greece as a reliable ally despite his occasional reassurances to the contrary.

Papandreou has said in many public forums, both in Greece and outside, that he believes Greece's only hope of being taken seriously by its allies is to remain independent. When the West—or, more precisely, the United States—feels secure about Greece, it ceases, in his view, to pay attention to Greece's needs. Papandreou points to the entire period since the mid-1950s during which the conservative forces in Greece, firmly entrenched in power, slavishly followed the prescriptions of the United States, both militarily and politically. But that same period, according to the prime minister, was characterized by a continual weakening of Greece's position in the Aegean and a blatant pro-Turkish bias in United States policy.

The recent Greek fractiousness within NATO and the EEC and Papandreou's overtures to the Soviet Union and East European nations have, in his view, succeeded in convincing the United States that Greece cannot be taken for granted and that Washington must win Greece's loyalty, not assume it as a right.

The government's attitude toward NATO was part of a strategic, long-range policy of working toward the dissolution of both NATO and the Warsaw Pact. The issues at hand were the terms accepted by the Rallis government in 1980 for Greece's reintegration into NATO's military wing. The PASOK government considered these terms to be unacceptable, among other things, because they left unclear Greece's operational control of the Aegean, and pledged to "detach" Greece from them. By mid-1985 the controversy remained unsettled (see Greece and NATO, ch. 5).

Another issue that had vexed bilateral relations between the United States and Greece for many years, the status of United States bases on Greek territory, was finally settled in September 1983 with the extension of the Defense and Economic Cooperation Agreement (DECA). The successful completion of negotiations, on terms considered favorable to Greece, was considered by the PASOK government to be a major achievement (see Relations with Selected Countries, this ch.).

Papandreou's stance on Greek membership in the EEC has also moderated. PASOK's original campaign rhetoric called for complete withdrawal from the EEC, but as the election approached, the party position was changed to reflect a recognition of general public support for membership in the EEC. That support was manifested in the European Parliament elections held simultaneously with the general election in October 1981. PASOK's share of that vote was about 8 percent lower than its share in the general elections, almost all of that loss apparently captured by two parties that strongly favored membership in the community. The KKE-Interior won 5.3 percent of the vote (as compared with 1.4 in the general election), and Democratic Unity won 4.2 percent (0.7 in the general election). Three other parties won seats: the ND with 31.4 percent (4.5 percent lower than in the general election); the KKE-Exterior received 12.8 percent (almost two points higher); and the Progressive Party received a stable share of the vote with 2 percent.

At the opening meeting of the European Council of the EEC on November 26, 1981, Papandreou announced that

Greece would seek a special status within the community, citing the advantage given under the existing rules to the advanced industrialized economies of northern Europe over the less developed nations of the Mediterranean. Since 1981 Greece has managed to redress some of its problems, wringing financial concessions from the rest of the community by holding hostage the expected entry of Spain and Portugal.

Papandreou's friendly relations with the Soviet Union and other communist countries have particularly troubled Greece's allies. Greece refused to participate in the EEC's condemnation of the Polish regime's imposition of martial law in December 1981, signed an agreement to resume servicing Soviet naval supply vessels in January 1982, and in March 1984 opposed the deployment of cruise missiles in Western Europe. Relations with the Soviet Union became increasingly cordial, culminating in a February 1985 visit by Papandreou to Moscow.

**Electoral Politics**

Elections for both president and the parliament were scheduled for 1985, and partisan politics quickly took center stage. In a surprise move in March, Papandreou withdrew his support for the reelection of Karamanlis to the presidency, nominating instead Christos Sartzetakis, a centrist Supreme Court judge who first gained wide recognition for his dogged investigation of the 1961 assassination of Grigoris Lambrakis, a leftist deputy. Karamanlis, the former head of the ND, was the major postwar figure in Greek politics and was both popular and well respected for his conservative and pro-Western views. He had been seen by many Greeks and by their foreign allies as a counterweight to Papandreou's rhetorical excesses.

There was wide speculation that Papandreou's unexpected move just six days before the presidential vote was calculated to restore PASOK's sagging support on the left, which was disenchanted by the slow pace of change. Karamanlis had become the target of increasingly vehement criticism from the left wing of PASOK and the KKE-Exterior. At the same time, PASOK's support among voters in the center had somewhat deteriorated. Polls therefore suggested that the party would gain more in electoral support from the left than it would lose from the center in the upcoming election by distancing itself from Karamanlis. No definitive explanation can be given for

249

Papandreou's shift, but it seemed likely associated with preparations for the general election later in the year.

Papandreou's action was quickly applauded by the KKE-Exterior, whose support had become significant for PASOK since 1981. Even as early as the municipal elections in October 1982, PASOK's victory in 89 of 136 municipalities and communes was possible only because of a tacit alliance between PASOK and the KKE-Exterior. The more recent elections for the European Parliament in June 1984 (in which PASOK, though maintaining its position as the largest party, lost 1.5 percent of its vote compared with the European elections in 1981) gave disturbing evidence of a possible resurgence of the ND, which gained almost seven points over its 1981 showing. Thus, pressed from both the right and the far left, some PASOK strategies suggested that the government's hopes of reelection depended on active KKE-Exterior cooperation and a renewed appeal to the party's own left wing. Indeed, the government had to rely on Communist support in parliament for the new president's controversial election in March 1985—after two unsuccessful votes. Nevertheless, the choice of Sartzetakis, not a member of PASOK and generally seen as a centrist, probably indicated that the party had not given up hope for its appeal to the center, estimated to be as much as 15 percent of the electorate.

Papandreou justified his decision not to support Karamanlis for another term by saying that it would be inconsistent with his intention to amend the Constitution—adopted in 1975 under a government headed by Karamanlis—to eliminate the "excessive" powers of the president (see President of the Republic, this ch.). Although neither Karamanlis nor his predecessor, Constantine Tsatsos, had used the full powers of the office, he hoped to end the potential for the president to "frustrate the will of the democratically elected parliament" or for the emergence of a "party political president." Both the KKE-Exterior and the KKE-Interior welcomed Papandreou's proposal for constitutional reform. Constantine Mitsotakis, leader of the ND, denounced the move as dangerous to the country's political stability. That fear was echoed by many foreign observers, already shaken by Karamanlis' departure, who expressed concern that the demise of the presidency as an apolitical stabilizing force might lead to the kind of political fragmentation that had characterized the 1960s.

*Panhellenic Socialist Movement (PASOK)*
*election campaign posters, spring of 1985*

*New Democracy*
*party headquarters*
*in Delphi*

*Communist Party of Greece-*
*Exterior(KKE-Exterior)*
*election campaign poster,*
*spring of 1985*

*Photos courtesy Peter J. Kassander*

## Political Parties

Traditionally the Greek political parties were based largely on personal connection and personalities, lacked real organizations with mass membership, and tended to appeal to narrow segments of the electorate. Because of the emphasis on personal politics, Greeks invoked their own contacts—usually through a patron-client relationship—to promote their individual interests, rather than developing and pursuing common interests through mass political organizations or interest groups. Another reason for the fragility of the party system was the pervasiveness of state paternalism, which tended to hamper the evolution of strong autonomous voluntary organizations outside the ever-present bureaucratic tentacles.

In the mid-1980s party politics continued to exhibit some of the old characteristics, but at the same time there were indications, albeit tentative, that the Greek political parties might in time evolve into more mass-based, issue-oriented parties similar to those found in West European political systems. The transition from a predominantly personalist to a mass party basis was under way in Greece, spurred in part by the forces of change unleashed by urbanization and industrialization. Another principal pressure for change came from the political engineering staged by the Socialist administration, whose political machine—PASOK—was the first mainstream Greek political party to apply discipline and organizational work to the process of party politics. The PASOK government also enacted a law to provide state subsidies to the parties to minimize the undue influences that private funding can bring to bear on the operation of political parties.

### Panhellenic Socialist Movement

The rapid rise of the Panhellenic Socialist Movement (Panhellinion Socialistiko Kinima—PASOK), founded in 1974 by Andreas Papandreou, has been attributed to three factors: Papandreou's charismatic personality, a well-articulated internal structure—unique for a mainstream Greek party—and a clear ideological orientation that in many ways matched the popular sentiment for change.

PASOK came about as an attempt to create a modern, mass, populist party, rejecting the traditions of personalism and clientelism. PASOK is a cadre party, organized geographically, with the local organization, consisting of no more than

80 members who live and work in the same locality, as its basic unit. In addition, professional organizations link members of professions having affinities with each other. These two organizations elect representatives to the provincial assemblies, which are run by the provincial executive committee, whose 11 to 15 members are elected for 18-month terms. The cadres, or party functionaries, perform the key organizational and mobilizing activities and serve as the intermediaries between the national and local party levels. They have been very successful in challenging the dominance of traditional political families in many rural constituencies. In addition to the party apparatus, there are affiliates for youth and women and a number of professional and employers' organizations dedicated to particular groups or special issues. The party is also attempting to gain control of other mass organizations, such as trade unions and agricultural organizations.

According to PASOK's charter, its highest organ is the party congress, which in theory decides on the party's policy and controls the Central Committee and the Disciplinary Council. The congress consists of members of parliament, of the Central Committee, and of the Disciplinary Council as well as representatives of the local and professional organizations. Between congresses, control is exercised by the Central Committee, consisting of 80 members—20 members of parliament and 60 elected by the congress—and the party's president (from its inception through mid-1985, Andreas Papandreou). The Central Committee meets at least once every three months. It elects an Executive Bureau and a five-member economic control committee. The Executive Bureau, composed of nine members (including the party president) elected by the Central Committee, meets twice weekly as the effective ruling body of the party, controlling the decisions of the central committee and developing party policy. Although in principle the congress is the highest organ, its practical function is primarily symbolic: to provide a democratic legitimation of decisions made by the Executive Bureau. Indeed, the first party congress was held only in May 1984.

The party has made a concerted effort to instill the principle of party discipline and ideological coherence, previously unknown among the noncommunist Greek parties. Membership in the party is based on ideological affinity. The nine-member Disciplinary Council, elected by the congress, ensures the compliance of the general membership, and a separate four-member disciplinary committee oversees the parliamentary group. Discipline is strict, and a number of dissenters, including some parliamentary members, have been expelled from the party.

Papandreou's iron-fisted control of the party and its ideological and policy-related evolution have been helped in no small part by its organization. He has created a modern, fairly cohesive political party that is unique in Greek history. But precisely because of the importance of his personality to both electoral success and the internal cohesion of the party, it remains uncertain if PASOK will be able to survive after Papandreou's departure. The party remains uninstitutionalized, and many analysts have noted the inexperience of the membership, even of those in positions of authority, and the lack of a second tier of leadership that would be able to assume control of the party if necessary. However, in mid-1985 there were no indications of an imminent change in leadership. Papandreou was, by all accounts, robust, and it is possible that during a second term—if PASOK wins the June 1985 election—he may address the question of succession.

Like Eleutherios Venizelos' party 70 years before, Papandreou brought with him a generation of "new men" to reinvigorate the political system. By 1977 PASOK was clearly a mass party, claiming a membership of 27,000, which grew to more than 60,000 by 1980. It was a broad coalition of groups, including, in Papandreou's words, "farmers, workers, employees, craftsmen and artisans, the youth and all the people who are subject to odious exploitation by modern monopoly capital, local as well as foreign." The 1981 victory showed that the party had support from a cross section of the population but was particularly strong among younger voters (24 to 34 years old), the new managerial classes, and urban dwellers. Perhaps most surprising, however, was the increased vote it received from the petty bourgeois sectors and in rural areas, both traditional strongholds of conservative parties, particularly the ND.

PASOK has tried to carve out a niche for itself in the center-left of the Greek political spectrum, claiming to unify three currents in Greek politics: the wartime communist resistance, his father's Center Union party, and resistance to the military junta between 1967 and 1974. Although these historical movements span a wide range of ideological orientation—from orthodox communism to middle-of-the-road liberalism to an inchoate socialism—Papandreou has insisted that they share a commitment to national independence, popular sovereignty, and social liberation. Although PASOK has appealed to a wide audience since coming to power, reconciling the diverse views in the party has proved troublesome. The party's more conservative or moderate elements have been displeased by some of Papandreou's incendiary rhetoric, especially on foreign policy issues, and have been critical of his "anti-business" economic policies. The leftist elements, at the same time, have been critical of the slow pace of reform.

Polls taken in the early spring of 1985, prior to the general elections, seemed to indicate that the balancing act may not have been entirely successful. There were indications that some in the left wing of the party had defected to the KKE-Exterior. Even more troublesome, however, were hints that PASOK may have lost support among the unaffiliated center voters who, accounting for about 15 percent of the electorate, largely determine the outcome of elections.

### New Democracy

New Democracy (Nea Demokratia—ND) was founded in 1974 by Karamanlis. It was largely a revival of his National Radical Union (Ethniki Rizopastiti Enosis—ERE), which had dominated Greek politics from 1955 to 1963. The ND won parliamentary majorities in both 1974 and 1977, and Karamanlis remained prime minister until his election to the presidency in 1980. George Rallis, a party veteran and a moderate, succeeded him as prime minister and head of the party after a bitter and divisive internal election.

The party's showing in the 1981 general election was disastrous, the ND winning only 35.9 percent of the vote, becoming the second largest party after PASOK. After the defeat, Rallis was replaced as party leader by Evangelos Averoff-Tositsas, a right-wing conservative who had been narrowly defeated by Rallis for the position in 1980. In 1984 Averoff resigned from the party after a long illness to be replaced by Mitsotakis, a moderate conservative, formerly a member of George Papandreou's Center Union government. The defection, or "apostasy," as it is known, of Mitsotakis and a number of other senior ministers from George Papandreou's government in 1965 caused a furor at the time, and Andreas Papandreou, who has continued to vilify Mitsotakis for his "treason," has blamed the defection for the imposition of military rule in 1967. However, it is thought that Mitsotakis is the only politician who can rival Papandreou in eloquence and charisma.

The ND has tried to respond to PASOK's challenge by

establishing a more articulated structure. Formal party statutes outline a hierarchical, mass-based organization from the local to the national level, with auxiliary organizations for students and others, but these have not yet been meaningfully implemented. The party in the spring of 1985 remained true to the traditional Greek clientelistic pattern. Efforts to transform the ND into a modern, mass party were made difficult by the absence of the usual incentives for party activism—a coherent ideology, centralized party control over candidate selection, or general participation in party policymaking. Individual politicians and their private networks of clients continued to form the basis of party strength.

The party remained dominated by the older generation of politicians who had been active since the 1950s. Recruitment of younger members has been hampered by the traditional practice of "family seats," parliamentary seats that are virtually handed down generation to generation as a family legacy. This has not only stifled recruitment of new blood into the party but has also crippled the efforts to develop local organizations for mobilizing public support. Since 1977, however, the party has made a concerted effort to overcome this closed system, and the 1981 election showed some evidence of limited success.

The ND's inability to compete effectively with PASOK and the left has become painfully obvious since Karamanlis' departure in 1980. The party has suffered a consistent and significant decline. Following the traditional pattern of Greek parties, the ND has never imposed an ideological test on those who have wished to join. As a result, the party has been internally divided into centrist and extreme right-wing factions. The contest for leadership of the party in 1980 aptly summed up the dilemma. The two candidates, Rallis and Averoff, represented widely divergent streams within the party. Rallis, a well-known moderate, was elected by only a four-vote margin over his arch-conservative rival, Averoff. Following the 1981 defeat, Rallis was unceremoniously replaced by Averoff. Within a year, therefore, the ND dramatically shifted its message, leaving the electorate reeling and indicating that the party placed little premium on ideology. Since 1981 the ND has concentrated on criticizing PASOK's policies rather than on offering any positive program of its own.

The 1984 European parliamentary elections again were a disappointment. Averoff had expected a substantial gain, even predicting that the ND would resume its position as the largest party. But, despite a retraction of support for PASOK (6.5

percent below the 1981 general election), the ND gained only 2.2 percent over its 1981 showing. Mitsotakis, who owed his election to the most conservative elements of the party, was expected to go on the offensive, hardening the ND's opposition to the PASOK government, particularly in economic affairs, in an attempt to fashion a clear conservative alternative to the government's program. John C. Loulis, a noted analyst of Greek politics, is skeptical of the ND's renewal, maintaining that "New Democracy appears incapable of saying anything fresh; its utterances are characterized by vagueness and confusion . . . What the New Democracy party needs are new faces articulating new ideas . . ." He and others suggest that the party may distance itself from its past under Karamanlis and embark on a new direction toward some form of neo-liberalism—"limiting the state, freeing the economy, and encouraging initiative, responsibility and choice and greater freedom in all areas." However, Loulis notes, "it will take a completely reformed party to articulate this course convincingly."

In the three general elections between 1974 and 1981, the party consistently polled over 2 million votes, although its percentage of the vote during that period fell from a high of 54.4 percent in 1974 to 35.9 in 1981. Because of the preponderance of personal links between voters and deputies, membership rolls were an unreliable indicator of party strength among the electorate. Over 100,000 voters participated in the election of representatives to the first party congress in 1977, but just one year earlier the party had reported a membership of only 20,000. It is likely that the 1977 turnout was attributable to a special mobilization of personal supporters by sitting members of parliament.

The party has had significant support throughout the country, but the 1981 election results showed losses in almost all regions and in every socioeconomic category. The party fared poorly with voters under 35 years of age. The ND's principal constituency has been the middle class, but the PASOK government has made a concerted effort to attract support among the lower middle class (small businesspeople). The impact of that effort remained unclear in the spring of 1985. However, polls taken prior to the general election indicated a general reluctance on the part of the electorate to commit themselves to the ND.

### Communist Party of Greece

The Communist Party of Greece (Kommunistikon Komma Ellados—KKE), formerly called the Socialist Workers' Party, was founded in November 1918. From its inception it was strongly tied to Moscow and was a loyal member of the Communist International (Comintern). Most of its support came from the Anatolian refugees and linguistic and ethnic minorities. In the interwar period it participated in elections but polled only 9 percent of the vote at its height in 1935. Its vote, however, was sufficiently large to precipitate a successful coup by General John Metaxias and the imposition of a military dictatorship in 1936, after which the KKE, like all other political parties, was outlawed.

The KKE formed the backbone for the wartime resistance between 1940 and 1944, becoming for the first time a popular party, with perhaps as much as 25 to 30 percent of the population associated with one or another of its auxiliary organizations. The period of the Civil War, however, cost it most of its popular support (see The "Terrible Decade": World War II and the Civil War, 1940-49, ch. 1). It was outlawed again in 1947. Its leadership and much of its membership fled to Eastern Europe; those that remained in Greece operated through surrogate parties: the Democratic Front in 1950 followed in 1952 by the United Democratic Left (Eniea Dimokratiki Aristeras—EDA) until it was disbanded by the military junta in 1967. The KKE was legalized in 1974 by the new civilian government of Karamanlis.

In 1968 the KKE split into two separate wings. The origins of the split lay in the 1950s and early 1960s when the EDA served as the forum for communist activity within Greece. Over time a gap developed between those Communists who had remained in Greece and those, particularly the leadership, who had fled abroad, and thus the ground for later distinction between the KKE-Interior and the KKE-Exterior. Only with difficulty did the exiled leadership maintain its control over an increasingly pragmatic and flexible domestic membership. By 1968, a year after the installation of the junta, the schism was institutionalized.

The KKE-Exterior, the larger faction, retained its former character and leadership. It openly acknowledged its ties with the Soviet Union and continued to employ the principles of "democratic centralism" to ensure strict discipline and ideological orthodoxy. The breakaway group, the KKE-Interior, emphasized its national character and took the Eurocommunist parties of Western Europe as its models. It pledged to abide by the rules of democracy, eschewing revolutionary tactics in favor of electoral politics, and openly disavowed any ties with the Soviet Union. The schism was not fully formalized until the restoration of democracy and the legalization of the KKE in 1974. Since that time, the two parties have grown even further apart, developing different internal structures and constituencies.

### Communist Party of Greece-Exterior

The Communist Party of Greece-Exterior (KKE-Exterior) is organized according to the standard Soviet model; control of local party cells is centralized in the highest party organization, the Politburo, led by the secretary general. Harilaos Florakis occupied this post in mid-1985. The Politburo is elected by the Central Committee, which meets every six to eight months. The committee in turn is elected by the party congress—held every four years—which is in principle the highest authority, laying down the general policy of the party. In practice, power within the party is highly concentrated in the Politburo. In addition to the party apparatus, there are a number of associated mass organizations. Until recently the major trade union, the General Confederation of Greek Workers (Geniki Synomospondia Ergaton Ellados—GSEE), was heavily influenced by the party, but since 1982 PASOK has largely wrested control of the union away from the Communists.

The strength of the KKE-Exterior has grown slightly since the interwar period but has remained stable since the end of the Civil War. In the three elections between 1974 and 1981 the KKE-Exterior polled between 9 and 11 percent of the vote (sometimes in coalition). Its 1981 vote of 10.9 percent represented its historical high and made it the third largest party. The KKE-Exterior has engaged in tacit electoral alliances with PASOK since 1981, and its support, both in parliament and in elections, has grown more important for the PASOK government (see Electoral Politics, this ch.).

The KKE-Exterior's constituency comes primarily from the traditional left-wing voters—some sections of the working class and Greeks from refugee backgrounds. Its strength among younger and urban voters appears to be growing. Its total vote in 1981 was approximately 600,000, including between 15 and 25 percent of the vote in major urban areas such as Athens, Piraeus, and Thessaloniki (Salonika) as well as some provincial capitals. Nevertheless, the party's performance was well below its goal of 17 percent, which would have qualified it for participation in the bonus allocation of parliamentary seats.

The KKE-Exterior is in direct competition with PASOK for voters and for issues. The party's hold on the extreme left of Greek politics is probably secure, but many of its mobilizing issues have been preempted by PASOK, which has also emulated the KKE-Exterior's organization in many ways. PASOK has challenged the KKE-Exterior's dominance of the national mass organizations, such as the trade unions and agrarian organizations. There are bright spots for party recruiters, however. Rural constituencies, heretofore ignored, may provide additional members. There were indications in the spring of 1985 that disenchantment with Papandreou among left-wing PASOK supporters may be producing a desertion to the KKE-Exterior. The proportions of the movement were unclear; but leaders of PASOK appeared to be concerned, and some observers attributed Papandreou's presidential about-face in March 1985 to fear of a wholesale migration of his left wing. Nevertheless, the opportunity for significant growth of the KKE-Exterior beyond its present dimensions appears to be limited.

The KKE-Exterior occupies a difficult position in the Greek system under a PASOK government. It is at once an ally and a rival. It shares many of the programmatic goals of the government, but PASOK's successes may very well be at the KKE-Exterior's expense. Between 1981 and 1985 the KKE-Exterior generally cooperated with the government, though pressuring for more far-reaching policies, especially in the economy and in foreign policy. The party sometimes offered crucial support to Papandreou's initiatives, as in the presidential election. If PASOK were to win a clear mandate in the 1985 election and maintained its parliament majority, the KKE-Exterior's influence would likely remain stable. However, in the event of a close election resulting in a PASOK victory, the KKE-Exterior could become a critical swing vote, thus giving the party an influence disproportionate to its electoral strength.

### Communist Party of Greece-Interior

The Communist Party of Greece-Interior (KKE-Interior) has had a difficult time establishing a separate identity and attracting support; in both 1974 and 1977 it joined in electoral coalitions, first with the KKE-Exterior and then with a number of insignificant, minor parties. Only in 1981 did KKE-Interior campaign on its own and polled a dismal 1.4 percent. In contrast, the party, which strongly supported Greek membership in the EEC, succeeded in electing a representative to the European Parliament in 1981 by a vote of 5.3 percent. Its own hesitancy and tentativeness accounts for much of the party's failure to establish itself, but equally important is that the KKE-Interior—even more than the KKE-Exterior—is in direct competition with PASOK for issues and supporters, a competition that PASOK is clearly winning. The KKE-Interior has expressed an interest in coalitions with other parties, but to date it has little to offer in the way of electoral strength or programmatic innovation.

The KKE-Interior has tried to establish an internal structure distinct from the traditional Soviet-model. Its constitution is more democratic, codifying the right of members to debate party policy; minority opinions are protected and officially published, and censorship is limited. Popular participation within the party is greater than in the KKE-Exterior, with about 30 of the delegates at the national congress elected directly by the party cells, the basic unit of party organization. In addition, the party leaders must rule by consensus rather than by directives. Resort to "democratic centralism" to quash "deviations" is, however, not unknown. Nevertheless, the party encourages popular initiatives and appears to respect majority opinion when formed by democratic procedures, as in trade unions.

**Other Parties**

In the mid-1980s the future of small parties was uncertain at best, because they were overshadowed by PASOK and the ND. Very little was reported on these parties, which were concerned mainly with specific, narrow interests and were geographically limited and ideologically ambivalent. The number of small parties decreased substantially in recent years, suggesting that the party system was becoming stabilized. In the general elections of 1974 there were 46 parties competing for the vote. The number was down to around 15 in both the 1977 and the 1981 elections. In all three elections only a few of these parties won one or more seats, and only three were able to each receive more than 10 percent of the vote.

In the number of votes received in the 1981 elections, the

Progressive Party was fourth in the standing of all parties, receiving 1.7 percent of the vote but no seat. The party was founded originally in 1955 by Spyros Markezinis, who was the prime minister in October and November of 1973 under the junta. He revived the party in 1979 to promote his very conservative cause. He once accused the government of Karamanlis of adopting a semisocialist economic policy. In 1981 the party campaigned on the platform calling for a free enterprise economy and a pragmatic foreign policy geared heavily to the West.

The Party of Democratic Socialism (Komma Demokratikou Socialistikou—KODESO) was formed in 1979 by Ioannis Pesmazoglou to counter the ND. Its objectives were to bring about national reconciliation, an equitable distribution of the national income, planned economic and social progress based essentially on a free enterprise economy, a decentralized bureaucracy, full membership in the EEC, and "an independent and forceful foreign policy, free of foreign influences." In 1981 the party campaigned in alliance with a small agricultural party under the label of Democratic Unity.

The Union of the Democratic Center (Enosis Demokratikou Kendrou—EDIK) is the remnant of a liberal, centrist party formed in 1974 by George Mavros as the Center Union-New Forces. In 1974 it became the second largest party, gaining 60 seats, but was replaced by PASOK in the 1977 elections. The EDIK stood for economic democracy through a "programmed development of the economy" and reinvigoration of the trade unions, and the constitutional amendment aimed at greater "democratic development." The party's specific policies differed little from those of the ND, and the party declined steadily after 1977 through defections. In 1985 its leader was Ioannis Zigdids.

The Liberal Party was set up shortly before the 1981 elections by Nikitas Venizelos, the grandson of the great statesman of modern Greece, Eleutherios Venizelos. Its aim was to "revive the political heritage" of the Venizelos era. In the mid-1980s there was very little prospect of its survival in light of its virtually nonexistent popular appeal.

Two parties that had been active in the late 1970s but did not take part in the 1981 elections were the right-wing National Front and the left-wing EDA. Some of the National Front's leading members ran as ND candidates. The EDA, which had served as a front for the outlawed KKE in the 1950s, endorsed

PASOK candidates. In addition, Greece had several obscure political groups on the extremes of left and right.

In 1984 two new parties were formed to contest the elections to the European Parliament in June of that year. One was an extreme right-wing group calling itself the Greek National Political Society, founded by George Papadopoulos, who ruled the country with an iron fist from 1967 to 1974. Papadopoulos was serving a sentence of life imprisonment at the time, and with his civil rights legally deprived it appeared unlikely that he would have any major impact through the party, sometimes known by its Greek acronym, EPEN. The other party was the United Socialist Alliance of Greece, a liberal group formed by a former PASOK dissident, Stathis Panagoulis.

## Interest Groups

Historically, there has been a strong emphasis on individuality and a dislike of conformity in Greece. The idea of articulating individual or family interests through outsiders or voluntary organizations was antithetical to most Greeks. These characteristics contributed to a highly personalized approach to politics and interest aggregation. When one needed some political action, and particularly if one needed it quickly, institutional channels were avoided in favor of personal contacts, usually in patron-client relations. The local patron, often a wealthy landowner, would do political favors for clients in return for their services, such as working his fields. The patronage networks could extend to provincial notables and, in turn, to national elites. An individual could be a client of some, a patron to others. With the advent of suffrage, the client's vote increased his ability to barter with his patron. *Rousfeti* (the exchange of favors) replaced official procedures and became what one observer has termed the "lubricating oil of the system."

Observers have indicated that, because of increased social mobility and greater state intervention in social and economic matters after World War II, the patron-client relationship began to decline. Political scientist Keith Legg commented that "at first, client networks expanded to include a wider range of individuals with more diversified transactions, all tied through reciprocal obligations. At some point, however, these networks tended to falter. The patron-client relationship became more precarious as mutual obligations were more difficult to fulfill. The magnitude of individual demands outran possibilities for satisfaction." In any case, a growing number of articulate Greeks came to believe that *rousfeti* was responsible in part for the fragility of institutional development in Greece. In the 1970s the Karamanlis government sought to modernize and depoliticize the civil service, aware that if successful, such an effort would eliminate much of the cause of *rousfeti*. In the early 1980s the Papandreou government was also attempting in earnest to weaken the patronage networks. Indications in the mid-1980s were that the age-old pattern of patronage continued to persist in one form or another.

In the mid-1980s the politics of interest aggregation were largely in the domain of the political party system. As a result, such potential political pressure groups as students, labor unions, the church, and the military were, from many indications, quiescent—except perhaps the unionists whose grievances were translated into occasional strikes. The students were highly politicized, divided along the partisan lines of political parties. They were, however, far less vocal than they had been in the 1960s and 1970s, when they took to the streets to oppose the junta rule and to demand equal representation on university committees and improvement in the quality of higher education.

Another familiar target of student activism was the United States military presence in Greece; criticism was particularly strident among the left-wing students associated with the left-of-center political parties. Anti-American rhetoric was still heard in the mid-1980s in intermittent student demonstrations.

Labor unions, like other mass organizations, have been historically weak, reflecting the emphasis on personality within the society. Furthermore, union activities have frequently been subjected to legal restrictions by regimes that considered stable economic conditions the paramount domestic goal. Union development has also been inhabited by the large agricultural and self-employment segments of the Greek economy.

Unions do exist, however, and organized labor was, and appeared likely to remain, a political factor; in fact, under PASOK's encouragement, its influence seemed to be on the rise in the 1980s. Union militancy, supported by leftist political parties, had resulted in strikes and demonstrations in the 1970s. A strike in May 1976, the largest since the fall of the junta, was precipitated by a labor bill that the Karamanlis government successfully pushed through parliament. The bill officially protected the rights of Greek workers to organize, participate in collective bargaining, and strike. At the same time it prohibited wildcat strikes and strikes that had political motivations. The May protest involved strikes by employees in public services, airlines, banks, mass media, private schools, and hospitals.

Trade unionism received considerable official attention under the PASOK government, whose major campaign pledge included granting more independence to the unions. In the mid-1980s the trade union movement centered on the GSEE. The confederation, founded in 1918, embraced most of the 3,000 registered unions that were grouped, in turn, into 57 federations. Unions affiliated with PASOK, the ND, KKE-Exterior, and other parties were members of the confederation and maintained a sometimes tenuous cooperative relationship based on policies established for them by their respective party sponsors.

In dealing with the GSEE the PASOK administration, notwithstanding its promise of more freedom from state interference for the unions, followed the precedent established by its predecessors. In mid-1982 several PASOK-affiliated Socialist unions issued a legal challenge to the validity of the confederation's elections to the 45-member executive council, held prematurely shortly before the 1981 parliamentary elections. That union election returned a majority of ND supporters and nonpolitical labor leaders. The challenge was on trivial grounds, but its larger purpose was to prove that the union election was politically motivated to prolong the mandate of the ND-controlled executive council if the conservative party lost the parliamentary election. The challengers obtained a temporary injunction under which the existing council was disbanded, and the court appointed a provisional council; 35 of the 45 council members were PASOK supporters. The deposed council members accused the PASOK government of "fabricating" the court ruling in collusion with the PASOK unionists and the Communists. New GSEE elections in December 1983 returned 26 PASOK-affiliated unionists, 17 for the KKE-Exterior, and two for the KKE-Interior.

Despite its campaign promises to liberalize unionism, PASOK adopted—much to the dismay of the Communists and other left-wing unionists—a pragmatic compromise policy. Initially, its proposals called for legalizing most political and sympathy strikes. In the face of strong opposition from leading employers' organizations, such as the Federation of Greek Industries, the Athens Chamber of Commerce and Industry, and the Confederation of Artisans, the Socialist government modified its position. Among the modified measures was the enactment of a bill that would empower the government to refer strikes to binding arbitration—a measure viewed by militant unionists as "antilabor." In the mid-1980s, as in the past, the unionists' principal demands were for higher wages, better conditions of employment, and reduction of unemployment.

The separation of church and state is a concept that is alien to Greece, because there is a very close relationship between Orthodox Christianity and the Greek national identity. Historically, the Orthodox church hierarchy has been a conservative political force, generally supporting the monarchy and opposing communism. Its organization and administration, if not its religious tenets, have been subject to state influence. Thus the church has not escaped politicization and has frequently experienced internal factionalism. With this situation in mind, the PASOK government announced its intention to bring about administrative separation between church and state, meaning the church's reliance on the Ministry of National Education and Religion, the principal agent of the state over religious matters.

In mid-1985 evidence was sketchy concerning the political potentials of the Orthodox church, although priests appeared to exercise varying degrees of influence in spiritual matters in their parishes, particularly rural ones. On balance, though, the church's capacity to bring pressure to bear on the political process seemed to be on the decline. A case in point was its failure, despite its public opposition, to prevent the PASOK-sponsored family law from being enacted in 1983. That law permitted, among other things, civil marriage and divorce.

To foreign observers, among the least known aspects of Greek politics in the mid-1980s was the political orientation of the military officer corps. The military has traditionally been politicized and as factionalized as the rest of society. It has frequently intervened in politics, usually to install the political party of its choice in power and more rarely, as in 1967, to seize power for itself. The junta rule was a disaster in both domestic and foreign policy. Many observers believe that the military was so discredited after the junta regime and the Cypriot coup debacle that ended it that it would only intervene again in politics in a catastrophe, such as an imminent Communist takeover or a Turkish invasion. In the mid-1980s the military remained under civilian control, but its potential for direct political intervention remained an unknown variable.

## Foreign Relations

### Background

Historically, Greece's strategic location in the Mediterranean and Balkan regions caused many foreign powers to meddle in and at times control both the domestic and the external affairs of the country. More often than not, the policies and actions of foreign powers concerned their competing interests in the region; the impact on Greece per se was at best a secondary consideration. Foreign influence was deplored by Greece yet accepted grudgingly to ensure the country's independence and well-being.

In the years after World War II the United States emerged as Greece's principal patron, a special relationship that Britain had relinguished earlier. Foreign involvement became synonymous with American involvement, Greece having become heavily dependent on the United States for military and economic aid. Such dependence evoked mixed reactions; it was generally popular with right-wing Greek leaders but was harshly attacked by Communist and other left-wing groups. By the early 1960s a growing number of moderate and centrist Greeks had come to voice the need for more independence in foreign affairs, but without undermining their nation's close relationships with its Western allies—the United States in particular.

Greek assertiveness was especially heightened in the years after the 1974 Turkish military intervention in its relations with the United States because of alleged United States complicity in a chain of events dating from the junta's rule in 1967. The Greek government wanted to renegotiate a military bases agreement with the United States and to reassess its ties with NATO. Both NATO and the United States has come under heavy criticism for their alleged favoritism toward Turkey. Nevertheless, Greece's basic pro-Western foreign policy posture was never brought into question by its allies. On balance the Karamanlis government's foreign policy did not deviate significantly from Greece's pre-1974 posture, except where Turkey was concerned. Relations with arch-rival Turkey grew more acrimonious because of unresolved disputes over Cyprus and the Aegean Sea. It was only after the accession to power of

PASOK in 1981 that foreign observers began to detect rhetorical shifts in Greece's foreign policy orientation.

## Relations with Selected Countries

### Turkey

In 1985 Greece's most serious international problems pertained to relations with Turkey. Disputes between the two countries over Cyprus and the Aegean region have persisted since the early 1970s. The dispute involving the minorities, however, dated back to the aftermath of the Greco-Turkish war (1921-22).

The Treaty of Lausanne formally ended the Greco-Turkish war in 1923 (see The War with Turkey, 1921-22, ch. 1). Under its provisions, large minority groups of each state's nationals living within the other country's boundaries were exchanged. The exchange, however, did not affect two significant groups: Greeks living in the Istanbul area and Turks living in Greek Thrace. Each community numbered approximately 100,000 in 1923. The treatment of the two groups has been an issue ever since.

A partial solution to the establishment of minority rights was achieved in 1968, when Greece and Turkey agreed by treaty to allow the groups to be educated in their own languages. The press in both countries, however, continued to publish inflammatory articles on the issue, and the groups were the objects of periodic hostility from the surrounding populations of their adopted countries.

Turkey has sought to repatriate members of its Greek community. Nevertheless, in the mid-1980s Greeks continued to be a major non-Muslim minority in Turkey. In 1965 some 48,000 inhabitants of Turkey claimed Greek as their mother tongue, but more recent estimates put the number of Greeks at fewer than 25,000. Greece, however has not attempted to repatriate its Turkish minority. In 1985 unofficial estimates placed the size of the Muslim minority in Greece at approximately 115,000. Some Greeks were reportedly worried that the size of the Turkish-Muslim community might serve as an expedient for future Turkish territorial claims in Thrace, but there was no indication that Turkey was considering such action. The Turkish minority in Thrace appeared to be generally tolerated by the surrounding Greek population.

In the mid-1980s Cyprus remained a contentious issue

between Greece and Turkey, the two guarantors, along with Britain, of Cypriot independence under the 1960 treaties. Since the island republic was partitioned de facto, in 1974, for Greece the Cyprus problem has become "a vital national issue"—a critical litmus test of Turkish intentions and policies vis-à-vis Greece. Both Greece and Turkey have taken similar positions, declaring that they have the legal right, as well as the obligation, to render active support to the Cypriots, who are divided ethnically into a Greek Cypriot majority and a Turkish Cypriot minority.

Since 1974 intercommunal talks have taken place intermittently under the auspices of the United Nations (UN) secretaries general, augmented by the numerous efforts by foreign powers, such as Britain and the United States. The UN General Assembly and Security Council have produced no fewer than 35 resolutions in their unsuccessful efforts to pave the way for a permanent settlement of the Cyprus problem.

There were fundamental differences on the framework of a future Cypriot state and on the manner in which the independence of Cyprus should be guaranteed by outside powers. Essentially, the Greek Cypriots wanted—especially after 1974—a strong central government under a single constitution and substantial autonomy for the bicommunal regions. This unitary government was to have a bicameral legislature in which the Greek Cypriot majority would hold 80 percent of the seats as against 20 percent for the Turkish Cypriot minority, reflecting the approximate ethnic ratio of the island. In the upper chamber both communities were to be represented equally, while cabinet membership was to be divided according to a seven-to-three ratio.

Fearing that such a division of power would likely be prejudicial to their own interests, the Turkish Cypriots demanded a biregional federation; each region would have its own constitution and an equal voice in decisionmaking on major intercommunal issues. They also insisted on the continued stationing of Turkish troops on the northern region of the island until a satisfactory settlement concerning international guarantees could be worked out. To protect their minority status, they also demanded veto powers over majority decisions.

Intransigence on one or both sides—each side accusing the other of failing to negotiate in good faith—hardened the split on the status of the island republic. In November 1983 the Turkish Cypriots unilaterally declared the establishment of an independent "Turkish Republic of Northern Cyprus" in the northern region where Turkey maintained 18,000 troops and which represented about 37 percent of the island; actually, this Turkish republic replaced the "Turkish Federated State of Cyprus" that had been set up in 1975 to consolidate the Turkish Cypriot rule following the Turkish invasion in the previous year. Greece was quick to condemn the "pseudo-state" as a stalking horse for Turkey's aggressive expansionism, alleging that the Turkish Cypriot community was unable to express its free will given the "absolute control" the Turkish occupation troops had over that community. The Greek government declared that there could be no solution to the Cyprus problem without the withdrawal of these troops.

UN-mediated intercommunal talks were held again in January 1985 between Greek Cypriot president Spyros Kyprianou and Turkish Cypriot leader Rauf Denktash. This summit meeting, arranged by UN Secretary General Javier Pérez de Cuéllar, was the first in six years. The four-day meeting—following "the handshake of the century," as Denktash put it—collapsed, however. Nonetheless, the fact that the meeting took place at all warranted guarded hope for a future settlement because the two Cypriot leaders had come prepared for some mutual concessions. Reportedly, an outline of these concessions had been worked out by November 1984 through the good offices of Secretary General Pérez.

The two sides were reported to have agreed in principle on the framework for a federal—not unitary—republic, under a Greek Cypriot president and a Turkish Cypriot vice president, in which the two ethnic communities would exercise considerable self-governing powers. In the lower legislative chamber the two ethnic communities would be proportionally represented in a seven-to-three ratio, while the upper house representation would be divided equally. Moreover, the Turkish Cypriot zone was to be reduced to 29 percent. On the critical question of international guarantors, however, the two sides were far apart, just as they were on the timetable for a phased withdrawal of foreign troops—18,000 Turkish troops and 2,000 Greek troops. The Turkish Cypriots favored the same three guarantors set up under the 1960 treaties, insisting that Turkey, which had saved the Turkish Cypriot community "from destruction in 1974," should be one of the guarantors. But the Greek Cypriots wanted a new arrangement for international guarantors, including the UN Secretary Council and some unnamed nonaligned countries or other countries. The problem was that although Turkey reportedly agreed to pull out its troops from Cyprus, it would do so only if the question of international guarantors was satisfactorily resolved. Meanwhile, in mid-1985 there was growing speculation among observers about the possibility of an internationally guaranteed demilitarized Cyprus.

The Greek-Turkish disputes involve several issues. Included are the demarcation of the continental shelf for the purpose of establishing underwater mineral rights, extension of territorial sovereignty, airspace and air traffic control authority, the militarization of the Greek islands near the Turkish coast, and the creation of and deployment of the Turkish Aegean Army in western Turkey (see Greek-Turkish Aegean Disputes, ch. 5).

Greek oil exploration in the Aegean began in 1970 and resulted in small natural gas and oil strikes off the western coast of Thasos in 1974. In 1973, however, Turkey also granted oil concessions in several Aegean Sea areas. Some of the areas were regarded by Greece to be within the limits of the Greek continental shelf, entitling Greece to economic, if not full sovereign rights, over the area. The dispute centered on the seabed of several of Greece's eastern islands near the Turkish mainland.

The Greek claim was based on the 1958 Geneva Convention on the Continental Shelf, which it ratified in 1972. The convention provides that, in general, adjacent islands produce the same seabed rights on the island's continental shelf as does a state's mainland coastal area. In short, islands extend a state's continental shelf past the landmass to which they politically belong.

Turkey rejected the Greek claim on two grounds. First, Turkey argued that the islands in the Aegean create a "special circumstance" under Article 6 (1) of the Geneva convention in that a boundary of the continental shelf drawn between Turkey and the Greek islands closest to the Turkish coast would have the effect of almost completely depriving Turkey of an Aegean continental shelf. Second, Turkey asserted that the islands actually rest on Turkey's Anatolian continental shelf and should not be entitled to continental shelves of their own, although they are entitled to territorial waters.

Further, the Turkish government has denied that the islands were entitled to anything in excess of six nautical miles of territorial sea. The Turks have warned that an extension of the territorial limit of 12 nautical miles (to which Greece is entitled as a signatory of the Law of the Sea Convention) would have the effect of turning the Aegean into a "Greek lake" and would be viewed by Turkey as a hostile act.

The position of the Greek government has been that matters relating to the continental shelf were subject to legal resolution and in August 1976 brought the question before the UN Security Council and the International Court of Justice (ICJ). The council adopted Security Council Resolution 395, urging the Greeks and the Turks to resolve their differences by negotiation, a recommendation reiterated by the ICJ. In mid-1985 these differences remained unresolved, and negotiations had yet to be scheduled.

The specific defensive and offensive measures engaged in by both countries were a reflection of the overall relationship between Greece and Turkey. In late 1984 the PASOK government issued a revised statement on its defense posture. Turkey was now officially regarded as the principal threat to Greek security; this perceived threat has been used to justify the increased emphasis on military spending in the 1980s (see Manpower and Defense Expenditures, ch. 5).

### United States

In the mid-1980s Greece and the United States continued their mutually beneficial relations, even though these relations were clouded by occasional rhetorical jabbings from Athens. Although the Papandreou administration expressed the view that there were no fundamental problems to the restoration of what had been highly cordial ties between Athens and Washington in earlier years, such a view was not shared by many Americans, who regarded Papandreou's stance toward Washington as something of a deviation from full-fledged partnership in alliance.

In the years after World War II the United States played a major role in Greece. Its reorganization of and assistance to the Greek armed forces was generally credited with thwarting a communist seizure of power during the Civil War, and its economic aid under the Truman Doctrine proved the major factor in Greece's postwar economic reconstruction. Nevertheless, some Greeks expressed the opinion that the United States had an ulterior motive—meaning that the aid was directed less toward Greece as such than against the Soviet Union. In the 1960s and 1970s, as Turkey became a major issue in Greco-American relations, other Greeks maintained that United States policy toward Greece was only one aspect of a broader strategic policy aimed at the stabilization of the Eastern Mediterranean—the southern flank of NATO. Greek attitudes toward the United States grew more critical.

The first serious strains in Greco-American relations surfaced in the wake of the 1967 colonels' coup. Many Greeks believed that a more forceful United States reaction against the military takeover could have thwarted the junta rule. The United States publicly pressed the colonels to move more swiftly toward the restoration of the democracy, as they had often promised, and even halted its delivery of heavy weapons to Greece from May 1967 to September 1970. It refrained, however, from taking any drastic action in the area of mutual security, continuing its delivering of light weapons to the country and advising other Western allies not to impose sanctions on the military regime. Greece's strategic location and the security interests shared by Greece and its other Atlantic Alliance partners were important considerations in the United States policy calculations. Washington's prudence, however, unwittingly deepened the Greek suspicion of United States complicity in the junta rule.

A second major source of strain was the Cyprus crisis of 1974, whose impact on Greco-American relations was still reverberating in the mid-1980s. The crisis was triggered initially by a Greek junta-backed coup against the constitutional authorities on the island. Turkey responded by sending troops to Cyprus, occupying more than one-third of the island. Most Greeks felt at the time that stronger United States pressure would have deterred the invasion, forced a troop withdrawal, or at least ensured better treatment for Greek Cypriots caught in the Turkish occupied zone. Under pressure from Congress, the United States soon stopped supplying arms to Turkey.

The return of democracy in July 1974 was heartily welcomed by the United States, but the politics of the post-junta government showed a new wrinkle insofar as relations with NATO and the United States were concerned. In August Greece withdrew from the military wing of NATO to dramatize its displeasure with NATO's alleged failure to restrain Turkey from invading Cyrpus. In February 1975 Karamanlis was quoted as saying that Greece was "no longer under American protection" and that it "no longer depended financially or militarily on the United States." Shortly thereafter his government began talks on the United States bases in Greece in a publicly proclaimed effort to recover full sovereignty over the bases.

In April 1976 the two countries initialed an agreement in principle, laying the basis for a more concrete future accord on mutual defense cooperation. This was done, however, only after Greece was satisfied that a defense cooperation pact that the United States had signed with Turkey in the preceding month would not adversely affect the balance of power between Greece and Turkey. Moreover, Greece had to be reassured that the terms of the defense cooperation pact then under negotiation between Athens and Washington were equivalent to those of a pact between Turkey and the United States. At that time the Greek and United States negotiators reached an informal understanding that a seven-to-10 ratio would be applied in the United States provision of aid to Greece and Turkey, respectively.

The tentative pact of 1976 contained, inter alia, the stipulation that all United States installations would be in principle under Greek commanders and that they would be operated only in a manner endorsed by the Greek government. Another stipulation banned the storage of nuclear weapons at these bases as well as the use of these facilities for purposes other than defensive. In July 1977 a new Defense and Economic Cooperation Agreement (DECA) was initialed by the two countries but was not formally signed because of an apparent misunderstanding on Greece's rights in the Aegean Sea under the 1923 Treaty of Lausanne.

Meanwhile, many Greeks continued to harbor suspicions about the United States' favoring Turkey over Greece in the area of defense. They argued that United States efforts to upgrade Turkey's military posture were misguided because such undertakings would increase Turkey's threat to Greece's security. Nonetheless, Greco-American relations remained generally cordial under the Karamanlis administration. In 1980 the two countries signed an umbrella agreement for cooperation in the economic, scientific, technological, educational, and cultural fields.

The "new foreign policy" that the PASOK government set in motion included opposition "in principle to all military blocs and condemnation of United States support of "dictatorial militarist and oppressive regimes like those of Turkey and Latin America." In an apparent gesture of evenhandedness, it also "condemned the Soviet intervention in Afghanistan." Papandreou also called for the removal of United States bases from

Greece and Greek withdrawal from NATO, but not before all military alliances were eventually phased out. Another feature of policy was Greece's tougher stance on relations with Turkey.

Nevertheless, the Papandreou administration proved pragmatic. Official renegotiations on the future of the United States bases—started in January 1981 and suspended five months later by the previous government—were resumed in October 1982, and a new DECA covering the operation of these bases was signed on September 8, 1983. During the negotiations Papandreou had expressed the view that the United States bases did not serve Greece's defense interests and that "Greece should receive substantial contributions to the defense of the country" if the United States bases were to be allowed on Greek sovereign territory.

The agreement provides for the continued presence of four United States bases through 1988, to be followed by a 17-month period for the dismantling of these facilities. It may be terminated by either party through a written notice five months before expiration. The pact is to "continue in force until modified or terminated by agreement." The accord also calls for United States assistance in the modernization and maintenance of Greek defense capabilities in such a way as to preserve the military balance between Greece and Turkey under the seven-to-10 ratio of United States aid to these recipients. In this regard the PASOK government has unilaterally taken the position that Greece has the right to terminate the DECA if in its judgment the United States reneges on the balance of power principle in favor of Turkey. Under the pact Greece and the United States, in acknowledging the linkage between defense posture and development, pledged their "maximum efforts" for cooperation in the economic, industrial, scientific, and technological fields.

The 1983 DECA gives Greece the right to restrict United States military activities in Greece to "defensive purposes" only and thus precludes the possibility of any United States actions that may adversely affect Greece's national interests. It also recognizes that Greece has "the inherent right" under international law to take "all appropriate restrictive measures required to safeguard its vital national security interests in an emergency." Greece is required, however, to consult with the United States immediately upon implementation of such measures, yet this process of consultation is not to derogate from the Greek exercise of its inherent sovereign right. Another

DECA provision abolished extraterritoriality for United States military and civilian personnel and their dependents in Greece, as in other NATO countries where the United States maintains military presence. The 1983 accord was hailed by Papandreou as "historic" in the achievement of Greek national independence as well as in the establishment of the principle that "Greece is an equal member of the international community."

In February 1984 the PASOK government warned that it would possibly suspend the DECA unless the United States aid bills for Greece and Turkey were amended to accord with the seven-to-10 ratio. About the same time, the government also renounced the civil aviation agreement of 1946, asserting that the agreement was unequal and "colonial in character" (a new agreement was signed in April 1985). Another broadside came in the following month when the Socialist regime repeated its earlier assertion that the four United States bases had not served Greece's defense interests.

The Papandreou administration was unremitting in its contentious and gratuitous public criticisms against the United States, even as it was proclaiming that it had been pursuing "a policy of moderation" toward Washington. In May 1984 Papandreou singled out the United States as "the metropolis of imperialism," casting it in an unfavorable light against the Soviet Union. Also in the same month the Greek leader denounced the stockpiles of United States nuclear warheads in Greece as a "true threat to the welfare of the Greek people." In October 1984 he alleged publicly, without offering concrete evidence, that the South Korean airliner shot down by the Soviets in September 1983 had been "on a spy mission" for the United States—a year after the fact. These inflammatory remarks were aggravating the already strained Greco-American relations and in fact did much to obscure the many positive aspects of economic and commercial relations existing between the two countries.

As of mid-1985 the PASOK administration was hopeful that its "moderation" vis-à-vis the United States would help improve its relations with Washington—without, however, Greece's being subjected again to its "former dependent status." Such an improvement was believed to hinge on United States recognition of Greece's "national interests and its identity as an independent country with a democratically elected government." The PASOK regime stressed that Greece had "interests that do not necessarily coincide with the U.S. government's and [had] its own voice on major or international issues." It was equally insistent that Greece's "reliability as an ally" should not be called into question whenever Greece expressed "some differences of opinion within an alliance of democratic states." Furthermore, the Socialist government continued to affirm the post-1974 foreign policy axiom that its relations with the United States would depend on two main criteria: whether the United States would effectively restrain Turkey's "aggressiveness" in Cyprus and in the Aegean and, equally significant, whether it would honor the seven-to-10 ratio in both quantitative and qualititative terms.

For its part the United States reiterated its policy of seeking the best possible relationship with Greece, confident that the sometime ruffled Greco-American ties could be restored to their former cordiality through patience and reconciliation. In underlining the importance of civility and trust in the conduct of relations between the two allies, a senior United States Department of State official commented in February 1985: "We ask only for a reciprocal approach on the part of the Greek government. Good relations are a two-way street. We ask that our differences be handled constructively and privately, not openly and contentiously. We do not and cannot ask that all our differences be magically resolved, only that they be deal with in a fashion befitting long-time friends and allies."

### Western Europe and Regionalism

Greek relations with Western Europe in the mid-1980s generally cordial, just as they had been throughout most of the postwar years, the major exception being the junta period (see The "Revolution of 21 April," ch. 1). Relations were carried out at both the bilateral and the multilateral levels, although greater emphasis appeared to be placed on the latter. Greece had joined NATO in 1952 and became the EEC's first associate member in 1961, acceding to full membership in 1981. Despite campaign rhetoric to pull Greece out of NATO and the EEC, the PASOK government preserved Greece's commitment to the West, resolving to remain a member of both organizations. The PASOK government proved, however, more assertive than its conservative predecessors in pressing for Greek interests within these collective bodies, at times straining relations with other members.

In 1985 overriding security and economic interests required that Greece's foreign policy continue to be essentially

Western-oriented, despite the PASOK government's seemingly anti-Western posturing. First, although since the Cyprus crisis of 1974 relations between Greece and its NATO partners had been strained, successive governments had concluded that Greece could more effectively defend itself against Turkey by remaining in the Alliance (see Greece and NATO, ch. 5). In addition to military aid from the United States, Greece depended heavily on assistance from Britain, France, and the Federal Republic of Germany (West Germany)—assistance channeled through NATO. Second, for at least 15 years the EEC had accounted for around 50 percent of Greek exports and imports. This made the EEC Greece's most important trade zone, a crucial linkage that was reinforced by EEC membership (see Foreign Economic Relations, ch. 3).

Within the EEC, the PASOK government tended to emphasize functional cooperation on the economic rather than on the political plane because on numerous occasions it found itself isolated in opposition to EEC foreign policy initiatives. Speeches given by Papandreou during the second half of 1983, when Greece held the rotating presidency of the European Council (also called Council of Ministers), were characterized by calls for greater European cooperation in regard to industrial policy and strategies for coping with the negative effects of the overvalued dollar, high United States interest rates, and foreign competition in general. Greece also pushed for a larger EEC budget and more substantial redistribution of resources as a show of solidarity, given the growing economic disparities within the EEC. This caused some friction with other member countries, particularly Britain and West Germany, both of which supported greater financial stringency (see European Economic Community, ch. 3).

In regard to the long-range development of the EEC toward political integration, Greece, along with Britain and Denmark, in early 1985 opposed the calling of an intergovernmental conference to redraft the 1958 Treaty of Rome that founded the EEC. Although these three countries—the newest members of the EEC—declared themselves in favor of more majority voting in the Council of Ministers, they opposed proposals for the removal of the right of veto over decisions affecting "vital national interests."

Beyond supporting European self-reliance in the economic sphere, the PASOK government called for a more independent role for Western Europe in foreign policy formulation vis-à-vis the United States and the Soviet Union. However, on foreign policy issues that did not directly affect Greece's regional security interests, the PASOK government tended to adopt a more neutralist attitude—viewed by many non-Greek observers as pro-Soviet—than the other West European countries in NATO. Differences mainly arose on East-West issues because, unlike its European allies, Greece viewed Turkey rather than the Soviet Union as its primary national security threat.

A prime example of diverging foreign policy interests concerned the deployment of intermediate-range nuclear missiles in Western Europe. Greece requested a six-month postponement of the NATO deployment in August 1984 when the first Pershing II missiles arrived. Claiming that the new missiles upset the strategic balance on the continent, Papandreou, along with Romanian president Nicolae Ceausescu, sent a joint letter to President Ronald Reagan and Soviet leader Yuri Andropov pleading for a halt to NATO deployment, remaining silent, however, on the presence of Soviet SS-20 missiles in Eastern Europe. In an earlier incident, Greece refused to participate in either the EC's condemnation of the Polish regime's imposition of martial law in December 1981 or in accompanying economic sanctions.

### Soviet Union and Other Communist Countries

Greek-Soviet relations, cool during the junta years, were improving in the 1980s, continuing a trend discernible since the late 1970s under the Karamanlis administration. In 1978 the two countries signed an accord on trade and economic cooperation and began exploring prospects for the Soviet construction of an alumina plant in Greece and of a natural gas pipeline to bring Soviet gas to Greece. In October 1979 Karamanlis paid a state visit to Moscow and jointly signed with his Soviet counterpart a plan for expanding economic and political cooperation.

A month before the Moscow visit the two countries had signed a servicing contract for repair work on Soviet merchant and naval "auxiliary" vessels at Greek shipyards. This arrangement gave Russian access to Greek facilities for the first time in 140 years and, not surprisingly, became a focus of considerable concern to Greece's NATO allies. In early 1981 the contract was suspended under NATO pressure, but the PASOK government decided to resume the repair work under a new pact negotiated in January 1982. The Greek government described the pact as "a renewal of the one commenced under the previous right-wing administrations." In the following month another agreement was reached for the Greek purchase of Soviet oil in exchange for the Soviet import of Greek agricultural products. In 1983 the two countries concluded a pact for a 10-year program of economic, industrial, and scientific-technical cooperation. This accord was to cover the fields of energy, machine building, ferrous and nonferrous metallurgy, gas, chemical industry, and agriculture. In 1984 the years of negotiations culminated in the signing of an agreement for a joint financing and construction of an alumina plant, whose product was to be absorbed mainly by the Soviet Union and to a lesser degree by Bulgaria.

There was no question that in the eyes of some Western observers PASOK's "independent and multidimensional" foreign policy had the appearance of a pro-Soviet bias. Whether this policy was in fact skewed toward Moscow by design was difficult to ascertain definitively. Whatever the case, the Papandreou administration was more restrained in its criticism of Soviet intervention in Afghanistan than was the Karamanlis administration. It refused to condemn the declaration of martial law in Poland, whose leader, Wojciech Jaruzelski, was praised by the Greek leader as "a patriot." Parallel to the Soviet position, the Socialist government opposed the deployment of Pershing II and cruise missiles in Western Europe. In May 1984 Papandreou stirred a storm of criticism in the West by depicting the Soviet Union as "a force against imperialism and capitalism" in what many observers thought was an insidious comparison with the United States, which was alleged to be "the metropolis of imperialism." He also argued that the Soviet struggle for détente was "genuine."

Papandreou's pronouncements did not go unchallenged at home. The principal opposition leader, Evangelos Averoff-Tositsas, accused him of adopting a pro-Soviet policy in an attempt to forestall strikes incited by the pro-Soviet KKE-Exterior. Averoff contended that the Socialist leader came out hand in hand with Moscow, "even on issues jeopardizing [Greece's] security."

Publicly, Papandreou sought to reassure his critics that his statements were meant to be neither pro-Soviet nor anti-American, adding that Greece belonged to neither power bloc. He argued that the current tensions between Greece and the United States were the result of a friendly squabble, occasioned by the Greek effort to rid itself of "a policy of one-sided alignment with one specific bloc." Within days of such a statement in January 1985, Papandreou left for Moscow on an official visit.

After two days of meetings the two governments agreed to resume talks on a US $1.5 billion gas line to be built via Bulgaria to ship Soviet gas to Greece and concluded a five-year (1985-90) maritime cooperation agreement calling for an increase in the chartering of Greek ships and for more repair work to be done on Soviet vessels at Greek facilities. The two government leaders also discussed possible Soviet assistance in building a subway for Athens, Greek help in building hotels in the Soviet Union, cooperation in the field of highway transportation, and Soviet interest in the use of the Volos ferry as well as in the construction of a stainless steel plant in Greece.

Papandreou and his Soviet counterpart also issued a joint statement supporting the creation of nuclear-free zones in the Balkans and elsewhere, opposing the militarization of space, and calling for an international conference on Cyprus. On the Greek dispute with Turkey over Cyprus and the Aegean, the Soviet side took a cautious line, avoiding any explicit and full support for either Greece or Turkey. The joint statement also contained a provision for mutual political consultations; henceforth the two countries were to consult each other periodically on bilateral or international issues of compelling interest.

Greek relations with East European countries were generally good in the 1980s, as they had been since the mid-1970s, when the post-junta government wanted to improve relations, especially with its Balkan neighbors. Greece desired stability in an area that had long suffered from conflicting territorial claims and other political turmoil. It also hoped to win support for Greece's Cyprus policy from these neighbors.

Greece initiated an inter-Balkan conference on cooperation, held in Athens from January 26 to February 5, 1976. The conference was attended by representatives from Greece, Yugoslavia, Romania, Bulgaria, and Turkey. Albania refused to take part because of its conflicts with Turkey. Observers noted that Greece and Romania seemed to be the most enthusiastic about inter-Balkan regionalism, envisioning some form of eventual political cooperation. Turkey and Bulgaria were more hesitant. Turkey's position was that the settlement of bilateral differences had to precede regional cooperation. Political scientist Richard Clogg has noted that "signficantly enough the most intractable of these bilateral differences . . divide countries *within* [emphasis Clogg's] the same broad ideological groupings," the primary examples being the rival Macedonian territorial claims between Yugoslavia and Bulgaria and the Aegean Sea disputes between Greece and Turkey.

The 1976 inter-Balkan conferences resulted primarily in an agreement to hold future meetings on the development of economic and technical cooperation. In December 1976 the Greek government announced that preparations for a second inter-Balkan conferences were underway. The second conference was held in Ankara in 1979, but the result was disappointing. Although prospects for economic cooperation were discussed, the only tangible result of this forum was an accord on cooperation for more efficient postal services.

The concept of Balkan cooperation drew renewed attention after PASOK assumed power. In 1982 Papandreou began promoting the idea of "denuclearizing" Greece and the Balkan region—an idea similar to an old Romanian plan for a "denuclearized Balkan zone." In November of that year Greece and Romania agreed to convene a conference of Balkan leaders within 18 months to address the issue. An inter-Balkan conference convened twice in 1984—in Athens in January and in Belgrade in June. The denuclearization issue was discussed by the leaders of six nations (Argentina, Greece, India, Mexico, Sweden, and Tranzania) in New Delhi in January 1985. While in New Delhi Papandreou was reported to have stated that the United States would be asked to remove its nuclear weapons from Greece, irrespective of the fate of Greek initiatives to create nuclear-free zones in the Balkans and elsewhere.

On the bilateral front a noteworthy development was an improving relationship between Greece and Albania, although in 1985 the two countries were still technically at war under a Greek royal decree issued in 1940. Traditionally, Greek-Albanian relations were complicated over the issue of the Greek minority in Albania, where the Greek-speaking minority was estimated to range from 250,000 to 400,000 accounting for a sizable proportion of the Albanian population. After 1978, when Albania began friendly overtures to Greece, cooperation in trade expanded steadily. In December 1984 an official Greek delegation visited Albania—the first since 1945—to sign several agreements covering road transportation, education, telecommunications, scientific cooperation, and postal services. In January 1985 the border between the two countries at Kakavia was reopened for the first time in 45 years; this event was greeted by both as heralding "a new era" in their relations.

*Middle East*

Greek governments have pursued a policy of friendship with the Arab states. Their relationship is based on both historical and contemporary factors. Greece shares with the Arabs a common history of subjugation to the Ottoman Turks, and a large proportion of Christian Arabs are of the Greek Orthodox faith. Many Arab states have had large and prosperous Greek communities within their boundaries. The largest such community was in Egypt. In the 1950s, however, the Egyptian government forced most resident foreign businessmen, including Greeks, to leave the country. The move was part of an attempt to broaden the Egyptian middle class by reducing the number of foreign entrepreneurs.

Since 1967, as the politics of the Middle East grew more complex, Greece has called for Israel's evacuation of all occupied Arab land and supported the Palestinian struggle for an independent homeland. It has at the same time supported Israel's right to exist within safe and internationally guaranteed borders; this was consistent with Greece's de facto recognition since 1948 of Israel's right to statehood. In the wake of the oil crisis and the Turkish invasion of Cyprus—both in 1974—Greek policy toward the region appeared to slant toward the Arabs. Doubtless this was dictated by two considerations: to gain Arab support for Greece's Cyprus policies and to secure stable oil supplies from the Arab oil producers.

The PASOK administration has followed a policy of befriending both Arabs and Israelis. In October 1981, within days of assuming power—and three days after the Soviets disclosed a plan to grant the Palestine Liberation Organization (PLO) diplomatic status—Papandreou let it be known that his government would soon recognize the PLO. This news was hailed by the PLO spokesperson in Athens as "a stunning victory for the Palestinian people and their legitimate representative, the PLO," adding that the recognition "will surely help consolidate the political and economic ties between Greece and the Arab nation." In December, after conferring with the visiting PLO leader Yasir Arafat, Papandreou announced that the PLO office in Athens would be upgraded to the status of a "diplomatic mission"—the same status Greece had granted the resident Israeli mission in Athens. Almost coinciding with the Arafat arrival in Athens, Greece's state-controlled Hellenic Radio Television station added an Arabic news program to its foreign-language broadcasts in English, French, and German.

Meanwhile, although the PASOK support of the PLO was

unwavering, as manifest in its increasing contacts with such hard-line Arab states as Algeria, Iraq, Syria, and Libya, the Socialist regime was pursuing quietly a policy of greater accommodation with Israel. Against the background of apparent Greek unhappiness over the lack of more forceful Arab support for the Greek position on Cyprus, an Israeli tourism delegation showed up in Athens in September 1984, and two months later a high-level Greek agricultural delegation returned the visit—the first in nearly four decades. If Papandreou's Middle East policy was designed to be evenhanded and pragmatic, it was baffling to some, including his own former cabinet member, Asimakis Fotilas, who was quoted by Mushtak Parker in the January 1985 issue of *Arabia* as saying that the PASOK policy was "paradoxical and irrational." The signs of improvement in Greek-Israeli relations were apparently more symbolic than substantive, however.

* * *

Among the recent works on Greek politics recommended for further reading are Roy C. Macridis' *Greek Politics at a Crossroads: What Kind of Socialism?*, which examines the nature of socialism in action under Andreas Papandreou's leadership; *Greece in the 1980s*, edited by Richard Clogg, which highlights the principal themes of Greek social and cultural life as well as major domestic and foreign policy developments; and Howard R. Penniman's *Greece at the Polls: The National Elections of 1974 and 1977*, a collection of articles on electoral politics offering an informative background against which to assess the signficance of Socialist victories in the elections of 1981 and 1985. The following articles prove useful in gaining insight into the current Greek political setting: "On the Way to Self-Reliance? PASOK's Government Policy in Greece" by Heinz-Jürgen Axt and "The Stability Quotient of Greece's Post-1974 Democratic Institutions" by Theodore A. Couloumbis and Prodromos M. Yannas—both in the *Journal of Modern Greek Studies*; Clogg's "PASOK in Power: Rendezvous with History or with Reality" in *World Today*; "The Greek Party System: A Case of 'Limited but Polarized Pluralism'?" by George T. Mavrogordatos, "Political Parties in Post-Junta

Greece: A Case of 'Bureaucratic Clientelism'?" by Christos Lyrintzis, "Transition to, and Consolidation of, Democratic Politics in Greece, 1974-1983: A Tentative Assessment" by P. Nikifrŏs Diamandouros, and Kevin Featherstone's "The Greek Socialists in Power"—all in *West European Politics*; and Nicos P. Mouzelis' "On the Greek Elections" in *New Left Review*.

Political clientelism, rooted in the age-old tradition of exchanging favors and essential to the understanding of Greek political patterns, is explored in the articles "On the Problem of Political Clientelism in Greece in the Nineteenth Century" by Constantine Tsoucalas, in the *Journal of the Hellenic Diaspora*; "Class and Clientelistic Politics: The Case of Greece" by Mouzelis, in the *Sociological Review*; and "Political Clientelism in Athens, Greece: A Three-Paradigm Approach to Political Clientelism" by George A. Kourvetaris and Betty A. Dobratz, in *East European Quarterly*.

Aspects of Greek foreign policy are well presented in John C. Loulis' "Papandreou's Foreign Policy," in *Foreign Affairs*; and in "Dateline Athens: Greece for the Greeks" by F. Stephen Larrabee and "Greece: A New Danger" by Panyote Elias Dimitras—both in *Foreign Policy*. Also valuable are the articles by Couloumbis, Clogg, and John O. Iatrides, appearing in *Greece in the 1980s*. (For further information and complete citations, see Bibliography.)

# Chapter 5. National Security

*Ancient Greek warrior*

IN 1985 GREECE MAINTAINED regular armed forces at a strength of 178,000 officers and enlisted personnel, three-quarters of whom served in the army. Conscripts accounted for 137,000 of the total. These figures represented the government's desire to be prepared militarily for any possible conflict with Turkey, which has been characterized by the government of Andreas Papandreou as the principal external threat to Greek security. The armed forces also had at their disposal approximately 282,000 trained reservists and were further strengthened by the 123,000-member Territorial Army, which included the 100,000-member National Guard. In addition, the 25,000 officers and men of the Gendarmerie also possessed some paramilitary capability. The mission of the armed forces is defined in Greek law as providing national security against threats by external powers.

Greece has been a member of the North Atlantic Treaty Organization (NATO) since 1952, but in mid-1985 it continued to question the nature of its role within the military wing of the alliance because of continued disputes with Turkey. The status of United States air and naval installations in Greece was also in question, given the Greek interpretation that basing agreements were to expire in 1988.

The organization of Greece's defense structure has evolved steadily since World War II. Prior to the removal of Greek forces from the NATO integrated command in 1975, changes occurred largely to accommodate the weapons systems, logistics, communications, force levels, and tactics required by affiliation with NATO. Civilian control of national security was reasserted by the Constitution of 1975. The president of the republic is commander in chief of the armed forces, but actual supervision and control is exercised by the prime minister through the minister of national defense. The chiefs of staff of the individual services are separately and directly responsible to the minister of national defense for command of the three service branches.

The armed forces derive a rich heritage from the exploits of Greek military heroes—ancient, medieval, and modern—and are conscious of their traditions. The officer corps views itself as the embodiment of the nation's highest ideals and assiduously projects that image to the public. Greece has a history of military intervention in civilian politics. In the nineteenth and early twentieth centuries the military was regarded as a generally progressive political force. Beginning with the dictatorship of John Metaxas in 1936, however, military influence became increasingly authoritarian. During the 1967-74 military dictatorship, however, the military uniform became a symbol of oppression instead of devotion to patriotic ideals. Post-junta civilian governments have removed those officers from service who had been associated with the junta but have not permitted blame for the dictatorship to fall on the armed services as a whole.

Disputes with Turkey over airspace, seabed, and other issues have centered Greek defense policies on a perceived threat from a traditional rival in the Eastern Mediterranean. This commonly shared Greek perception has exacerbated anti-NATO sentiment within Greece but has also fostered a steady defense buildup, in equipment as well as personnel, since 1974. Greece has also begun to develop a self-sustaining defense industry.

## The Armed Forces in National Life

### Officer Corps

The corps of 15,000 professional military officers has had a distinct corporate identity. Officers have enjoyed a unique status in Greek society, where they have formed what amounts to be a separate caste with its own special code of ethics. Their preoccupations have been primarily professional rather than political and include career advancement, improved pay and benefits, procurement of modern equipment, a voice in the decisionmaking process of national security policies, and recognition of their position in society.

The officer corps has pictured itself as embodying the national ideals of Greece and has consequently equated the goals of the armed forces with those of the nation. During periods when military influence on government was strongest, an image was created and displayed prominently to identify the armed forces—particularly the officer corps—with the nation's sense of purpose and history. It was commonplace for officers to suggest that they represented the mainstream of Greek values and the views of the majority of Greeks more clearly than did the elected politicians and the bureaucrats. In the past officers spoke—often in chauvinistic terms—of the military's "sacred mission," and military cadets were referred

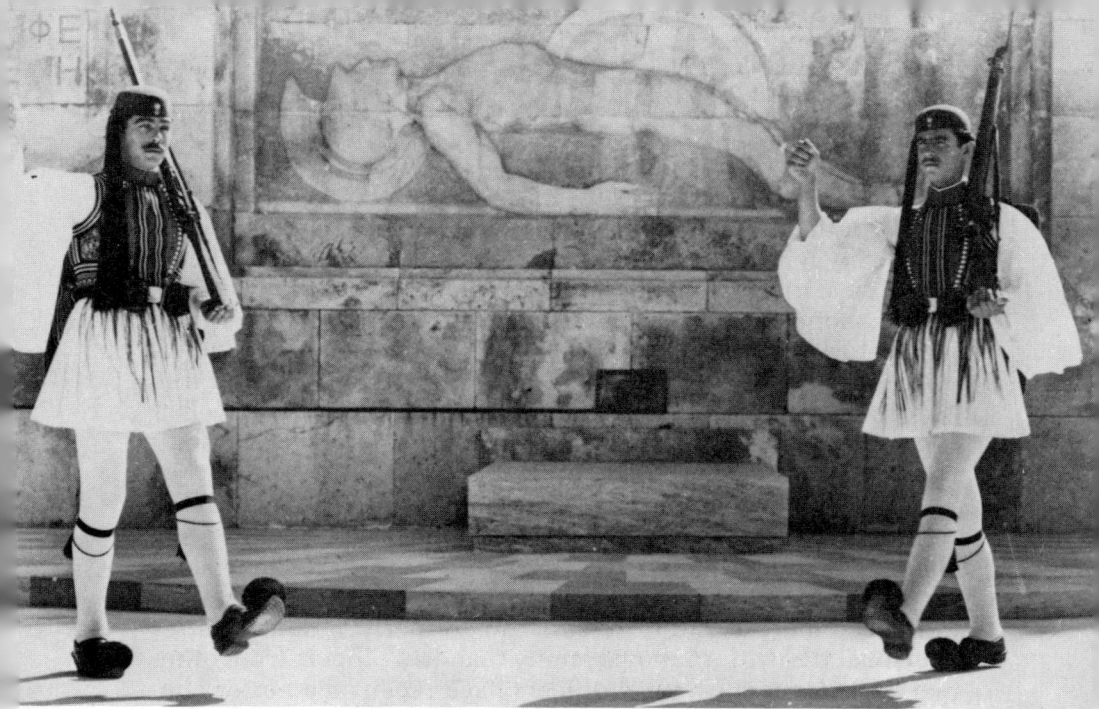

*Members of the Evzone (Honor Guard) at
the Tomb of the Unknown Soldier
Courtesy Greek National Tourist Organization*

to as *evelpis*, "the best hope of the nation." The self-perception of the military as an indispensable instrument of progress and modernization stemmed in part from the variety of social programs and economic development projects in which the armed forces have been employed since 1945.

The families of many officers suffered from communist atrocities during the Civil War, and the postwar political attitude of the military has been stridently anticommunist. Officers also have tended to be philosophical populists, viewing the more cosmopolitan higher socioeconomic strata of Greek society critically and with a degree of suspicion. As a group, the officer corps has also displayed a stronger religious orientation than is common among other professional groups.

Members of the officer corps often questioned the right of civil authorities to intervene in strictly national security matters, which the military has interpreted as being part of its professional responsibility. The military has particularly resented those occasions when the civil government seemed to be lenient toward groups the officers considered a threat to national security.

In the mid-1980s recruits for the officer corps—especially those in the army and air force—continued to be drawn from relatively humble socioeconomic segments of society. Officers in those services usually have been the sons of minor functionaries, shopkeepers, priests, schoolteachers, and farmers from small towns or rural areas in the Peloponnesus and Central Greece. They were, and continue to be, attracted by the free education offered to cadets in the service academies as well as by the opportunity for a career that assured them social mobility and status.

The navy, by contrast, was more representative of the affluent sectors of society. Traditionally, naval officers have been accorded a higher social standing than have their army and air force colleagues. Many were known to have had links with commercial interests and had formerly retained closer personal ties with the royal family than had officers from other services. Generally, naval officers have received a better education and have been considered more liberal politically than the others. Perhaps one-quarter of them—a far higher proportion than found in the army or air force—have come from families having a tradition of naval or other military service, a far higher proportion than found in the army or air force.

The frequently cited generalizations about the character of the officer corps appear to be substantiated by a 1971 survey of candidates for admission to the service academies' classes of 1975. This survey also underlines the striking disparity between the socioeconomic and regional backgrounds of naval officers and those of the army and air force. Although more than half of the country's population lived in urban areas, candidates for army and air force commissions were overwhelmingly from the countryside and small towns. The Peloponnesus and Central Greece, excluding Athens, supplied 40 percent of the candidates, although these regions had only 20 percent of the general population. With the exception of Macedonia (22 percent), no other region contributed officer candidates in proportion to its population. Few army or air force candidates were from Greater Athens. By contrast, 68 percent of the candidates for the naval academy were from Athens. Furthermore, a majority of the army (67 percent) and air force (71 percent) candidates were from a lower socioeconomic class. A majority of the naval candidates, however, were described as being either middle class (31 percent) or upper class (26 percent). Aside from those applying to the navy, few candidates had parents with university educations or professional occupations. These percentages remained constant in the mid-1980s, although efforts have been made to recruit more urban candidates into the army and air force.

From this and other studies, observers have concluded that sociological analogies with West European military organizations and professional models are bound to be misleading when applied to parallel Greek institutions and standards. Nor, from the standpoint of the military's role in politics, has civil control over the military establishment advanced at a pace similar to that of the West European democratic states. Generally the Greek military tends to reflect a historical development that has more in common with other Balkan and Eastern Mediterranean states than it does with its West European allies.

Surveys of officer candidates have also shown that socioeconomic considerations and careerism were generally more important reasons for entering professional military service than, for example, service to the nation. Family tradition was a relatively important factor only among the naval candidates (16 percent), who also cited socioeconomic advantages by a much higher percentage (32 percent), as compared with 26 percent in the army and only 15 percent in the air force. The navy rated service to the nation lowest (13 percent as compared with 21 percent in the army and 32 percent in the air force).

The service academies furnish the armed forces with most of their regular officers. The military academy in Athens commissions about 200 army officers each year; the air academy, about 90; and the naval cadet school, 40. The admissions process for all service academies is very competitive, an average of 10 applicants apply for each annual opening. In addition to physical, athletic, and academic requirements, each applicant must be an unmarried Greek Orthodox male and have a record of good conduct. Until recently a security background investigation was also required to preclude the admission of applicants from left-wing or communist backgrounds, but this requirement was relaxed in 1984 by the government of Andreas Papandreou. Each academy offers a well-rounded, four-year course of study that includes an academic program as well as professional training.

The law provides that each year a number of enlisted personnel equal to 10 percent of the graduates of the service academies be commissioned as well. This is seen as an incentive to the career enlisted men, many of whom take academic and professional courses in order to qualify for promotion.

## Political Role of the Military

In recent Greek history the military services, particularly as represented by the officer corps, have been involved directly in the country's political life. Five times after 1922—in the 1922-24, 1925-26, 1935-41, 1951-55, and 1967-74 periods—the heads of government were active or retired military officers. At almost all times men with military backgrounds have held senior government positions. Within the context of factionalized parties and unstable governments before World War II, the military played a major role in governmental stability and preservation. During periods when Greece had a king, the military was regarded as the preserve of the monarch. Struggle for control of the armed forces was at the heart of the dispute in the mid-1960s between King Constantine II and Prime Minister George Papandreou, eventuating in the 1967 coup d'état (see The Military Dictatorship, 1967-74, ch.1). At all times it has been considered important for senior civil officials to influence key military assignments in order to ensure proper policy alignments. In the view of the military, its role continues to be one of maintaining its effectiveness in protecting the nation's security and in fostering political stability.

Crisis and chaos have been familiar parts of the Greek national experience. As a result of weak political institutions, political intervention by the military to "save the nation" occurred rather frequently. The officer corps has not been a praetorian guard, however, and it has been more common for politicians to manipulate the military than it has been for the armed forces to seize control of the nation's political apparatus.

The armed forces have had a monopoly on the use of physical force in Greece. The military has been the best organized, most disciplined, and most cohesive institution in Greece. These factors have enabled the military to act as the ultimate arbiter in times of political deadlock or indecision.

Scholars have identified five main reasons for the military intervention in twentieth-century Greek politics: conflicts between republican and monarchist factions within the army; a humiliating defeat suffered by the army and blamed on the politicians—as during the 1922-24 period; a perceived leadership vacuum created by sustained political crises; an ostensible attachment of the army to principles of social justice and modernization; and perceptions by the military of a real or imagined communist threat. These factors were translated into intermittent coups and countercoups.

Military coups were integral to the evolution of Greek politics toward parliamentary rule in the nineteenth century. For example, the first coup occurred in 1843 and was carried out to compel Otto I to accept constitutional rule and to end absolute government. A subsequent coup in 1862 forced his abdication. In both instances the military acted in coordination with civilian politicians, and in neither case was there any question about military ascension to power.

After the disastrous defeat by the Turks in 1897, the armed forces took on the role of an extraparliamentary pressure group. When the parliamentary leaders proved unresponsive to their demands, the Military League, a group of junior officers inspired by the example of the Young Turks, brought Eleutherios Venizelos to power, giving impetus to a program of political and social reform. The conflict between the antiroyalist Venizelos and King Constantine I divided the officer corps and polarized factions within the military. The establishment of a provisional government in Thessaloniki (Salonika) by Venizelos in 1917 confronted officers with the choice between support for Venizelos and loyalty to the king. A succession of purges of officers on either side—pro-Venizelos republicans and pro-royalists—created discord and bitterness in the nation and in the armed forces during the interwar period. Coups were used repeatedly during the 1920s and early 1930s to pressure politicians as well as to protect or renew careers made or broken by the purges, culminating in the return of the monarchy in 1935 and the subsequent dictatorship of General Metaxas (see The Metaxas Dictatorship, 1936-40, ch. 1).

With few exceptions, most members of the officer corps—whether republican or royalist—supported the national government against the communist guerrillas during the Civil War (1946-49). The anticommunist and, more generally, antileftist political outlook of most middle- and senior–ranking officers still serving in the armed forces was formed during the Civil War.

Clientelism has been a factor in military as well as in political and commercial life (see Interest Groups, ch. 4). Professional advancement has been linked often to the success of the political faction to which an officer has had ties—promotions, transfers, and assignments often being influenced by political connections within the Ministry of National Defense. Regardless of the complexion of a given regime, political leaders have cultivated their clientelism within the military and, although officers may have resented the implications of the system, they have not hesitated to use the exchange of favors (*rousfeti*) as a means of career advancement.

Despite its effort to influence defense policy and, in some instances, acting with relative independence of civilian control in matters of national security, the military had been reluctant before 1967 to assume responsibility for the actual operation of the government. The conventional pattern of the Greek coup has been to replace one civilian government with another, more often than not dictating policy behind the scenes. Occasionally, a general officer stepped out of his professional role to become the head of a government.

On April 21, 1967, a junta of 20 active-duty officers, primarily colonels and lieutenant colonels, executed a bloodless coup, ousting the constitutional parliamentary government. The coup followed the guidelines of the Prometheus Plan, a contingency military plan in the event of internal, communist subversion in Greece. Relations between military and civilian authorities had been strained since the Center Union (CU), a liberal and centrist party, had won a parliamentary majority in 1964 (see Postwar Democracy: A Fragile Stability, ch. 1). Many officers were apparently convinced that the CU posed a threat to the integrity of the armed forces and endangered national security. Some also perceived an imminent threat of subversion by the left-wing elements of the union, as personified by Andreas Papandreou, son of the prime minister. The coup was an army operation but quickly attracted air force support. The royalist-controlled navy acceded to it with reluctance. Senior officers and traditionalist elements in the armed forces were uncomfortable with the colonels but failed to rally against them. Most lower-ranking officers apparently backed the junta for professional rather than ideological considerations.

In the classic pattern, the junta appointed Constantine Kollias, a civilian who had been president of the Supreme Court, head of government. However, Kollias sided with Constantine II in an attempted countercoup in December 1967 (backed by some navy and air force units), and Colonel George Papadopoulos, leader of the junta, then assumed the office of prime minister. The military junta retained control of the government and restricted political activity in the country.

In 1973 the crew of a warship mutinied in opposition to the regime and took asylum in Italy, but the junta retained the support of most of the officer corps. When the junta was overthrown in 1974, it was also at the instigation of the armed forces (initially the navy) and was done more for professional than for political reasons—that the regime had impaired the fighting efficiency of the armed forces.

The puritanical values of Greek military regimes and the stumbling means by which military leaders sought to impose them on an unwilling Greek population have been remarkably similar throughout the twentieth century, from General Theodore Pangalos in 1926 through General Metaxas in 1936-40 to the Papadopoulos junta in 1967-74. The leaders were devoted adherents of the idea of "Hellenic-Christian civilization" in which Greeks were portrayed as the noble abstractions of the mythological past. Each regime was determined to return Greece to its noble past through an enforced regimen of barracks discipline. The inability to achieve this, however, gave way to frustration within the army, where the dominant virtues of order, duty, and patriotism continued to foster ambitions that in reality were totally hopeless.

Pangalos, like his successors, began his regime by censoring the press, exiling his opponents, and demanding efficiency from the civil service, but soon his regime could do little more than forbid women to wear skirts more than 14 inches above the ground. Metaxas followed much the same course, with the added attractions of social welfare measures for the rural population, public works, and the creation of a massive security police apparatus. In 1967 the Papadopoulos regime pursued the same course (even requiring compulsory haircuts for hirsute tourists at the Greek border), hectoring and cajoling the population to be worthy of their Greek heritage in tones almost identical to that of Metaxas. One observer has referred to the philosophy of the junta as "a giant act of historical ventriloquism."

Since 1974 civilian governments have sought military support for their policies while simultaneously working to prevent future military takeovers. Under the Constitution the president of the republic is commander in chief of the armed forces, and overall command is exercised by the minister of national defense, who supervises the operation of the three branches of service. The heads of each service alternate as chief of the national defense staff, which is directly subordinate to the minister. This centralized command structure was instituted in

1977 specifically to limit opportunities for military coups. When Andreas Papandreou became prime minister in 1981, he also assumed the position of minister of national defense in order to allay the military's distrust of him and of the goals of the Panhellenic Socialist Movement (Panhellinion Socialistiko Kinima—PASOK) for Greece.

The post-junta parliamentary governments have been reluctant, however, to force the officer corps to endorse the principle of civilian control, and some observers have questioned to what extent the military has become acclimated to the concept of civilian control. Papandreou and his predecessors have been careful to shield the professional officer corps from criticism and have not allowed blame for the junta to reflect on the armed forces as a whole. All post-junta governments have put increased emphasis on military preparedness and have been sensitive to the professional demands of the officer corps. Although little information was available concerning the morale and disposition of the officer corps in the mid-1980s, there has been no visible indication that the Greek armed forces are not up to their task of protecting the homeland from external threats.

### Manpower and Defense Expenditures

All Greek citizens capable of bearing arms are bound by the Constitution to contribute to the defense of their country. At the end of 1985 the active armed forces numbered 178,000 men, about 77 percent of whom were conscripts serving minimum tours of 24 months of active duty. Most conscript tours had been extended involuntarily to 32 months. The active-duty military represented 8 percent of the potential labor force and approximately 10 percent of the 1.8 million men of military age (17 to 26 years old) considered fit for duty—proportions well above the average for other European NATO members. Universal conscription maintained the armed forces at their prescribed strengths and provided a constantly renewed source of trained reserves.

In addition to the standing force, approximately 282,000 men who had completed their national service were considered trained reservists and were liable for recall. Observers agreed, however, that to activate even a minority of this reserve force for more than just a few days would have a negative effect on the national economy. Another 123,000 men were members of the Territorial Army (which included the National

Guard), and 25,000 were members of the paramilitary Gendarmerie.

Young men become eligible for military duty at age 17 and may enlist voluntarily until the age of 21. The Ministry of National Defense offers occasional bonuses, such as cash payments or preferential consideration for postservice employment, for voluntary enlistment. If they have not volunteered, they are considered for conscription after reaching age 21. Approximately 75,000 men reach military age each year. Women are not subject to conscription but may enlist voluntarily in the armed forces. In 1984 approximately 1,800 women were serving in the Greek armed forces.

When an individual becomes eligible for induction, his case is reviewed by the local draft board, which is empowered to grant deferments to students, those who are the sole support of their families, and other special cases. Each able-bodied man must serve in some category, however, either in the National Guard or, after the expiration of the educational deferment, in the regular armed forces.

The board also screens and rates all conscripts to determine if the individual is suitable to be an officer, a noncommissioned officer, or a technician. It also determines if the conscript should be sent to an infantry company after basic training or if some remedial education may be necessary. Few of those categorized as officer material are immediately commissioned, however; in the army they are designated as "candidate reserve officers," and apparently most platoon leaders hold this rank. They can be commissioned as second lieutenants at any time, as frequently happens shortly before their release from active service. If the person were commissioned while on active duty, possibilities for promotion would be extremely limited. During the several years of reserve duty, however, promotion policies are less stringent, and an individual can be, and usually is, promoted at regular intervals.

The conscription system operates effectively and is an accepted part of Greek life, particularly in rural areas where military duty may provide the conscript with an opportunity not only to leave home but also to experience training opportunities not otherwise available in rural Greece. Men from the rugged mountain districts of northern Greece generally expect to be assigned to army duty, while those who come from coastal areas and the islands and are familiar with the sea and ships are more likely to be assigned to the navy.

The Papandreou government submitted a record defense

budget in 1984 containing a 63-percent increase over the previous year. The armed forces were slated to absorb the equivalent of US$2.3 billion, approximately 25 percent of the total 1984 budget. Additional funds were allocated to support the domestic arms industry. Within the NATO context, Greece had the highest percentage of defense spending as a percentage of gross domestic product (GDP—see Glossary).

Since 1971 defense expenditures have risen steadily; the increase has been especially pronounced since 1974, the year that saw the Turkish intervention on Cyprus, a buildup of tension in the Aegean, and the return to civilian control of the government. Since 1974 defense spending has increased by more than 117 percent. Additional funds have been authorized for weapons procurement and modernization of equipment. The military buildup was justified at first by the need for comprehensive modernization of military equipment and more recently as a vital instrument of national policy in carrying out a dignified and peaceful dialogue with Turkey. As Turkey came to be perceived as more bellicose, the increased defense spending was seen as politically imperative if Greece were to present an effective deterrent to the Turkish threat. In mid-1985 Turkey retained a significant quantitative advantage over Greece in terms of men and major weapons. Turkey had about 600,000 men under arms, about 2,800 medium tanks, and 17 fighter and ground-attack (FGA) squadrons, compared with Greece's 178,000 men, about 1,000 medium tanks, eight FGA squadrons, and six interceptor squadrons. Some observers commented that Greece possessed a qualitative advantage in some technical areas but that through 1984 it fell behind Turkey somewhat in the rate of growth of military expenditure.

**Armed Forces Organization**
In mid-1985 the three services—army, air force, and navy—are integrated under the Ministry of National Defense, which is responsible to the prime minister for its actions. Until August 1977 the defense minister's immediate subordinate was the armed forces commander, under whom were the separate service commanders as well as the Gendarmerie. This structure had been introduced by the military junta in 1968 but was reorganized in 1977 in order to reduce the danger of military takeovers. The most senior serving officer was the chief of the Hellenic National Defense General Staff, a post in which officers of the three services alternated annually. The

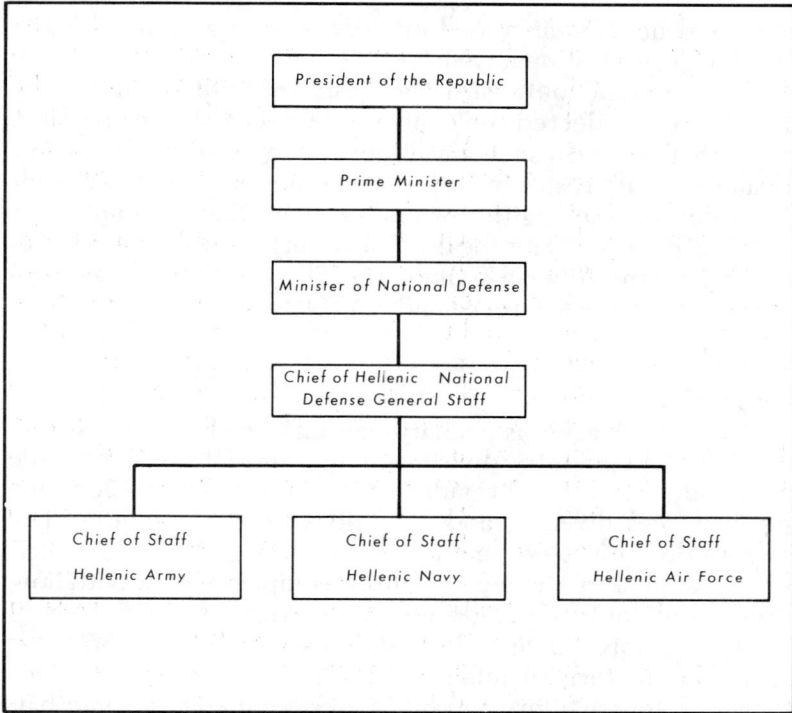

*Figure 18.    Organization of Defense Establishment, 1985*

chiefs of the army, air force, and navy general staffs were responsible separately and directly to the Ministry of National Defense. The former structure of semiautonomous high commands has been abolished (see fig. 18).

### Deployment

Two of the four Greek army corps were located on the northern frontiers with Bulgaria and Turkey in 1985. The third and fourth, which covered the rest of the country, have also provided the troops for the recently remilitarized islands along the Turkish coast. Total numbers deployed in these islands were not known, but there have been reports of over 10,000 on Rhodes alone. There were also 1,300 Greek troops, including 350 commandos, in Cyprus and several hundred officers and noncommissioned officers serving as cadre for the Greek-Cypriot National Guard.

The general southward and eastward shift of the Greek armed forces reflected the concern in Greece about a possible war with Turkey. In such a war, according to observers, major advances would result in major losses of men and material for both sides in which neither would be assured of accomplishing anything decisive. The focal point of any conflict would presumably be the Aegean Islands, the Thracian border, and opposing air bases (see Greece and NATO, this ch.).

### Army

The Greek army is primarily an infantry force, consisting in 1985 of 11 infantry divisions, one armored division, three independent armored brigades, one mechanized division, one special forces division, and 13 field artillery battalions. The infantry divisions were organized on a triangular pattern, i.e., three platoons to a company, three companies to a battalion, three battalions to a brigade, and three brigades to a division.

The armored division had six tank battalions of 55 tanks each, four motorized infantry battalions and reconnaissance battalions, four artillery battalions, plus a combat engineer battalion, communications battalion, army air corps company, and logistical support subunit. The independent armored brigade consisted of two tank battalions, one motorized infantry battalion, one artillery battalion, and other arms in proportion to these. The special forces division consisted of one parachute and one marine brigade, plus one commando and one marine battalion.

There was also a marine infantry brigade, seven antiaircraft artillery battalions, and two surface-to-surface missile battalions. Two surface-to-air missile battalions with improved Hawk missiles and 14 army aviation companies completed the army organization.

Greek infantry divisions closely resemble the motorized infantry formations of other NATO countries. There is a headquarters company, three infantry regiments of three battalions each, antitank armored personnel carriers (APC), and Army Air Corps companies. The strength of a Greek infantry division can range up to 14,300 men; 62 tanks; 80 APCs; 1,800 vehicles; six airplanes; four helicopters; 76 howitzers of 203.2mm, 155mm, and 105mm; 114 mortars; fifty 106mm recoilless rifles; and up to 450 antitank weapons. Overall, in 1985 the

Greek army had a strength of 135,000 men, including 99,500 conscripts.

The National Guard was organized in battalions parallel to those of the regular army and participated in maneuvers with regular and reserve units. It could be mobilized on short notice, and in addition to such general duties as guarding bridges, depots, and related installations, its members were trained to conduct counterinsurgency operations behind the battle lines in areas overrun by invaders. Regular army officers were assigned to command National Guard units.

The Greek soldier is tough and resourceful and is undemanding of his logistical support. The army has a favorable ratio of actual combat troops to those in support units. There is a limited but regular call-up of reservists for training in the handling of new weapons systems. Defense planning calls for the rapid mobilization of more than 250,000 reservists to fill the ranks of units maintained at cadre strength.

*Navy*

In 1985 the Greek navy numbered about 19,500 men, including 12,000 conscripts, of whom approximately 7,500 were assigned to sea duty, Approximately 24,000 trained reservists can be mobilized on short notice. The main navy bases are located at Piraeus, Thessaloniki, Volos, Mitilini, Souda Bay on Crete, Salamis, and Rodhos.

Naval units included 14 destroyers of World War II vintage transferred from the United States Navy. These vessels have been modernized, and three of the destroyers (2,400-ton Gearing class) had helicopter-landing facilities. They were deployed for antisubmarine warfare (ASW), and their weaponry included antisubmarine missiles. Sixteen French-designed missile patrol boats of the La Combattante-class in service in 1984 were armed with Exocet and/or Penguin surface-to-surface missiles (SSM). Each boat carries four missiles, has a range of 1,280 kilometers, and cruises at speeds of up to 32 knots. Additional boats of this class are being built in Greek shipyards. The Greek fleet also included 10 submarines, 11 coastal patrol boats, 11 torpedo boats, two coastal minelayers, 14 coastal minesweepers, and a number of assorted landing ships and craft.

The navy has two basic missions: operations against surface vessels and operations against submarines. Vessels were acquired because of size and other characteristics, such as speed, small draft, and maneuverability—all of which make them suitable for operation in the confined waters of the Aegean.

### Air Force

The 23,500 officers and men of the Hellenic Air Force were organized into three commands: Tactical Air Command for combat operations, Air Matériel Command for Transport and Supply, and Air Training Command. In early 1985 an estimated 30,000 trained reservists could be mobilized as required.

The Tactical Air Command had seven combat wings containing eight fighter and ground-attack (FGA) squadrons, six interceptor squadrons, and two FGA reconnaissance squadrons. The Tactical Air Command also had one transport wing of three squadrons, one medium-range squadron, nine base flights, and three helicopter squadrons. Four additional squadrons were assigned to the Air Training Command.

In early 1985 the air force inventory included 36 Mirage F-1s, 53 F-4Es, 66 F-5A/Bs, 53 F/TF-104Gs, and 52 A-7Hs. In addition, 14 F-104Gs were on order. A squadron of eight HU-16B helicopters provided marine reconnaissance and could also be used on ASW missions. In late 1984 the Papandreou government decided to purchase at least 80 new fighter aircraft—40 Mirage 2000s and 40F-16s—to modernize the FGA squadrons.

Major air bases were located at Hellenikon near Athens, Larisa, Nea Ankhialos, Tanagra, Iraklion, Souda Bay, Araxos, Andravidha, and Elevsis. An additional air base has been established on Lemnos to provide air support for the northern Aegean region. Ground air defense of installations was assigned to one air force surface-to-air missile (SAM) wing equipped with Nike Ajax SAMs.

### Recruitment, Training, and Reserves

In 1985 less than one-third of the armed forces' strength—about 52,000 men—were long-service regulars, almost all of them officers, noncommissioned officers, and specialist grades. The remainder of the armed forces was made up of conscripts performing their compulsory military service. Military liability continues from age 21 to age 50, trained conscripts passing into the first reserve for 19 years and into the second for 10 years.

Recruit contingents were being called up every three months. Since the rapid post-1974 expansion of the army, the number of young men entering the appropriate age-group each year has not been adequate to meet requirements, owing to a static birth rate of some time. Accordingly, in 1977 the government of Constantine Karamanlis attempted to open careers in the armed forces to women. (Prior to this, women had been restricted to the nursing corps.) An attempt was also made to make women between the ages of 20 and 32 eligible for compulsory military service for 14 months. Married women, unwed mothers, nuns, and orphans would be exempted automatically. It was hoped that up to 12,000 women would enter the service annually to serve in noncombat positions and thus release men for combat duties, but this policy has had limited success. In 1985 there were approximately 1,800 women serving in the Greek armed forces.

### Uniforms and Insignia

The strong British influence in uniforms that had been characteristic of Greek army dress before and immediately after World War II remained, but gradual alterations in appointments, colors, and individual equipment during the 1960s and 1970s reflected a strong American influence. Officers and senior noncommissioned officers wore olive-green, single-breasted, open-collar blouses without a belt. Olive-green, peaked caps with gold straps, black shoes and gloves, black tie, and fawn shirt completed the uniform. Light khaki summer tunics were single-breasted and had open collars. The jacket, which had four patch pockets, could be worn either with tie and shirt or, more commonly in warm weather, without, sleeves being rolled above the elbows.

Officers' dress uniforms were dark blue, except for those of army officers, which were dark green. A white dress uniform was also used in the summer. Trim and accessories for the dress uniforms could be changed to satisfy different categories for formal occassions.

Battle dress for the most part consisted of United States-style field uniforms. Branches of the army could be distinguished by the color of the beret, which was worn with service as well as with battle dress. The Army Air Corps was issued red berets; commandos and airborne, green; armored troops, black; and infantry and artillery, khaki.

When on parade or standing guard, the Evzone (Honor Guard) wear the colorful traditional costume of the mountain warriors who fought the Turks in the war of independence (1821-29). Probably Albanian in origin, the Evzone dress uniform includes tassled cap and shoes, white stockings, and the *fustanella*, a shirtwaist with pleated skirt of white fustian. Guards are distinguished by their elaborately embroidered tunics.

The navy's winter service uniform is navy blue and, in summer, white. Eight-buttoned, doubled-breasted blouses, blue caps, and white shirts, which are worn by commissioned and petty officers, are of British cut, as are summer blouses that are buttoned to the collar. Short-sleeved shirts, worn open-collared without blouses, are standard daytime wear in warm weather. Uniforms for sailors are also patterned on British styles.

The air force has adopted uniform and insignia modeled after that of the United States Air Force. The uniform, including cap, for all ranks is light blue, and includes a grey-blue shirt and black tie. Battle jackets (Eisenhower-style) and overseas caps are worn frequently on duty by enlisted personnel (see Fig. 19; Fig. 20).

### Decorations and Flags

The highest combat decoration worn by active-duty military personnel in 1985 was the Cross of Valor. It includes three classes—gold, silver, and bronze—and was awarded for acts of gallantry performed during World War II, the Civil War, and the Korean War. The Medal of Military Merit, obsolete for some years, was awarded for outstanding performance in the command and organization of military units. The War Cross, bestowed in three classes for heroism in World War II, is a plain bronze cross similar in shape to the French Croix de Guerre. The Navy Cross is worn by naval personnel who distinguished themselves in World War II. The Maritime War Cross is awarded to those who have saved lives at sea or who have rendered outstanding service to the merchant navy.

Air force decorations include the Cross of Valor in Flight, the Distinguished Flying Cross and Medal, and the Air Force Medal. An unusual award, the Order of Naval Commandos was created in 1948 to be awarded to personnel who participated

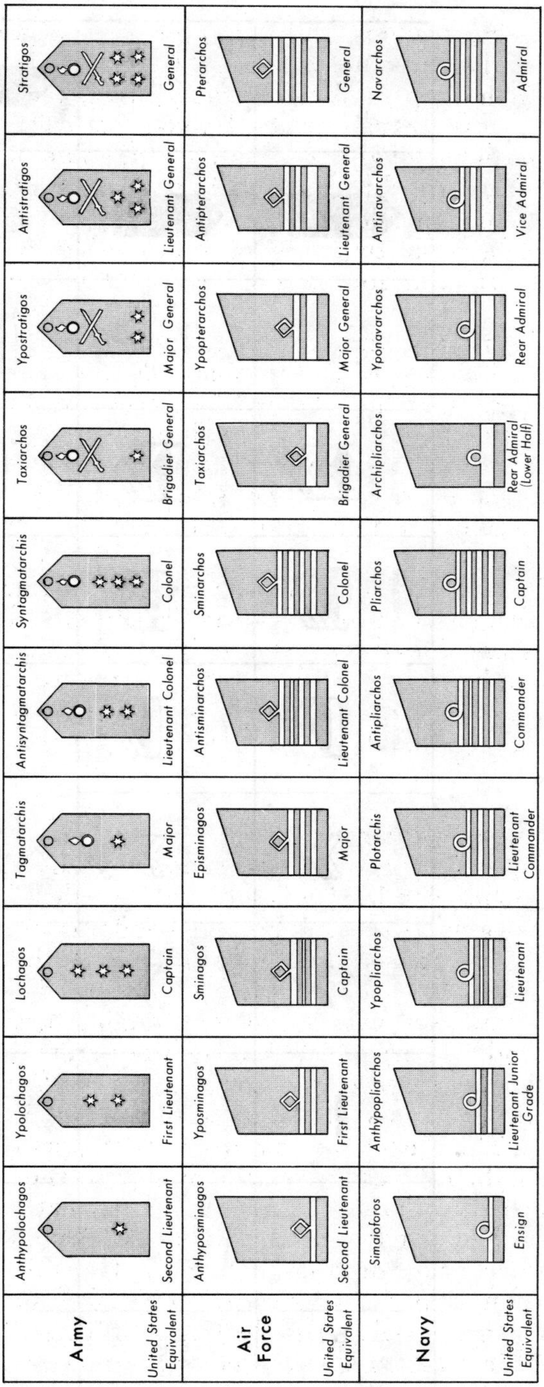

| Army | Anthypolochagos | Ypolochagos | Lochagos | Tagmatarchis | Antisyntagmatarchis | Syntagmatarchis | Taxiarchos | Ypostratigos | Antistratigos | Stratigos |
|---|---|---|---|---|---|---|---|---|---|---|
| United States Equivalent | Second Lieutenant | First Lieutenant | Captain | Major | Lieutenant Colonel | Colonel | Brigadier General | Major General | Lieutenant General | General |
| Air Force | Anthyposminagos | Yposminagos | Sminagos | Episminagos | Antisminarchos | Sminarchos | Taxiarchos | Ypopterarchos | Antipterarchos | Pterarchos |
| United States Equivalent | Second Lieutenant | First Lieutenant | Captain | Major | Lieutenant Colonel | Colonel | Brigadier General | Major General | Lieutenant General | General |
| Navy | Simaioforos | Anthypopliarchos | Ypopliarchos | Plotarchis | Antipliarchos | Pliarchos | Archipliarchos | Yponavarchos | Antinavarchos | Navarchos |
| United States Equivalent | Ensign | Lieutenant Junior Grade | Lieutenant | Lieutenant Commander | Commander | Captain | Rear Admiral (Lower Half) | Rear Admiral | Vice Admiral | Admiral |

*Figure 19.   Officer Rank Insignia and United States Equivalents, 1985*

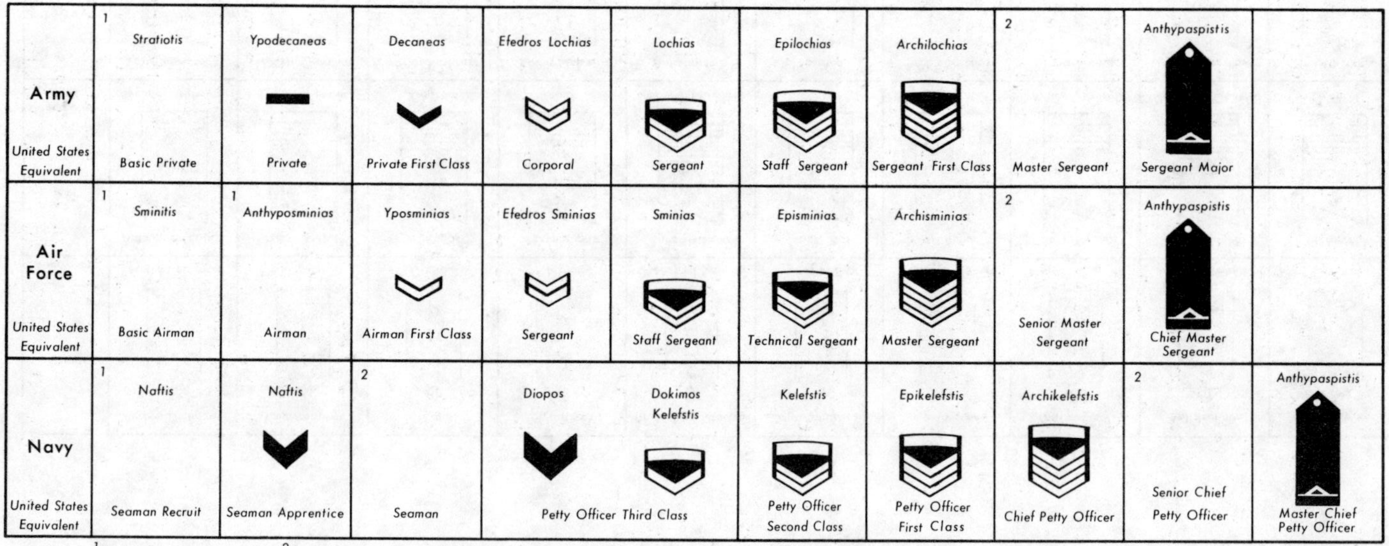

| | | | | | | | | | |
|---|---|---|---|---|---|---|---|---|---|
| **Army** | Stratiotis | Ypodecaneos | Decaneos | Efedros Lochias | Lochias | Epilochias | Archilochias | 2 | Anthypaspistis |
| United States Equivalent | Basic Private | Private | Private First Class | Corporal | Sergeant | Staff Sergeant | Sergeant First Class | Master Sergeant | Sergeant Major |
| **Air Force** | Sminitis | Anthyposminias | Yposminias | Efedros Sminias | Sminias | Episminias | Archisminias | 2 | Anthypaspistis |
| United States Equivalent | Basic Airman | Airman | Airman First Class | Sergeant | Staff Sergeant | Technical Sergeant | Master Sergeant | Senior Master Sergeant | Chief Master Sergeant |
| **Navy** | Naftis | Naftis | 2 | Diopos | Dokimos Keleftis | Keleftis | Epikeleftis | Archikeleftis | 2 | Anthypaspistis |
| United States Equivalent | Seaman Recruit | Seaman Apprentice | Seaman | Petty Officer Third Class | Petty Officer Second Class | Petty Officer First Class | Chief Petty Officer | Senior Chief Petty Officer | Master Chief Petty Officer |

1 No insignia is worn.   2 There is no rank equivalent.

*Figure 20. Enlisted Rank Insignia and United States Equivalents, 1985*

in operations to recover naval vessels whose crews had mutinied in April 1944 at Alexandria, Egypt. The Police Cross and
Police Valor Medal were presented in recognition of service
against communist guerrilla forces after the liberation of
Greece in 1944.

Some royal orders that had lapsed after the 1967 coup and
the subsequent exile of Constantine have been reinstated as
decorations since the reestablishment of democratic rule.
Among them is the prestigious Order of the Phoenix, awarded
in five classes to civilian and military personnel for conspicuous
service to the state. Although the order was first established
only in 1938, the phoenix—a bird rising from the ashes—is a
traditional symbol of Greek freedom and was used as a national
symbol by John Kapodistrias, the first president of modern
Greece. The phoenix was also prominently displayed by the
1967-74 junta as a symbol of their revolutionary movement.

Greece has two national flags. One, a broad white cross on
a dark blue field, is displayed only inside Greece and at embassies abroad. The other, more familiar to foreigners, has nine
horizontal stripes—five blue and four white—with a blue canton bearing a white cross. It is displayed at seaports and outside Greek territory and also serves as the naval ensign and
merchant flag. Standards and flags of the various army branches are also square and blue and bear a white cross, but the cloth
is edged with gold fringe. Each flag is emblazoned with the
embroidered image of the branch or unit's patron saint. Pike
staffs are striped with a blue and white spiral. The army garri-
son flag and the air force ensign are similar to the national
territorial flag but have distinguishing service insignia. The
insignia on the air force ensign is blue-white-blue. Service flag
staffs are surmounted by upright gilt crosses.

### Missions of the Armed Forces

The Greek armed forces have two primary roles: the long-
standing missions of defending the country against the possibility of Soviet attack and of assisting in the maintenance of Western control over the Eastern Mediterranean in time of conflict,
both of which have been allotted to Greece as a member of
NATO. These missions have been supplemented by the
higher-priority role of establishing, since the mid-1970s, at
least a balance of power with Turkey and of preparing to defend against the perceived threat from Turkey.

Defense against the Soviet threat means essentially defense of the border with Bulgaria. There has been no perceived military threat from officially nonaligned Yugoslavia since the end of the Civil War in 1949. Diplomatic relations with Albania were established in 1971, and though there has been no effervescence of cordiality between Greece and Albania as a result of ideological difference and lingering border disputes, there has never been any notable anxiety among Greeks about military confrontation. Neither Yugoslavia nor Albania is a member of the Soviet-dominated Warsaw Pact, and both states are probably more concerned about the threat of Soviet invasion than about Greece itself.

The Bulgarian threat, on the other hand, has been taken seriously in the past. Although Soviet troops have not been stationed in Bulgaria in recent years, the Bulgarian armed forces of about 150,000 possessed in 1984 almost twice the number of tanks and armored vehicles as those of Greece. The geography of northeastern Greece is also difficult to defend, for it is a strip of land several hundred kilometers long between Bulgaria and the Aegean Sea and averages only 48 to 80 kilometers in width. The likely direction of a Bulgarian attack in a general European war would be toward the east and the strategically vital Istanbul and the Bosporus, but few Greeks would doubt that a significant proportion of Bulgarian forces would be reserved for an attack into the region of western Thrace. The region has been thoroughly Hellenized since its incorporation into Greece at the end of the second Balkan war in 1913, but Bulgarian resentment at having been denied spoils at the end of the first Balkan war in 1912 and of its long-sought coastal access to the Aegean has been a constant if somewhat muted theme of Bulgarian irredentism ever since (see The Balkan Wars, ch. 1).

The other role of the Greek armed forces—defense against Turkey—has been growing in significance since the first Cyprus crises in the mid-1950s; however, after 1974 it became the first priority of the armed forces. The possibility of conflict with Turkey over Cyprus or over the perceived longer-term Turkish expansionism aimed at the Greek islands and perhaps at the mainland itself caused a dramatic rise in Greek defense budgets and armed forces manpower since 1974. As a result, Greek ties with NATO took on a new meaning if only because the alliance could not be of much assistance in the event of war between two of its members.

**Greece and NATO**

Relations between Greece and NATO since the mid-1970s have been troubled. A major source of the difficulties has been the bitterness engendered in Greece by the successful military intervention by Turkey in the Cyprus crisis of 1974. Because of the anger that resulted when NATO members did nothing to prevent or end the Turkish military action in Cyprus, Karamanlis directed the withdrawal of Greek armed forces from the NATO integrated military structure on August 14, 1974. Greece remained in the political wing of the alliance but did not participate in the NATO Defense Planning Committee (DPC) or assign troops to NATO commands.

Eventually, Greece worked out a special relationship with NATO whereby its forces would remain under national command and control but would be deployed in support of NATO in specific situations. The major obstacle to full military reintegration into NATO remained the question of command and control over defense of the Aegean airspace. Before Greece withdrew in 1974, airspace defense in the Aegean was the responsibility of the commander of the Sixth Allied Tactical Air Force (SIXATAF)—a United States general-grade officer based at Izmir, Turkey. He had three subordinates: one Greek and two Turks. The Greece officer had operational control of the airspace from the Greek western coast to the Athens-Istanbul Flight Information Region (FIR) demarcation line, which roughly follows the outer edge of the Turkish territorial sea. Consequently, before the summer of 1974 Greece was responsible for controlling air defense over most of the Aegean. Turkey never agreed fully to the 1964 NATO decision that had established the NATO air defense line coincident with the Athens-Istanbul FIR, but that was where matters stood at the time of the Cyprus crisis in 1974.

In July 1978 the position of commander of SIXATAF was given to a Turkish general. This action further complicated Greek reintegration problems because the Greeks were unwilling to accept control by a Turkish commander over Greek national forces—especially in light of the heightened state of tension between the two countries. Various formulas were advanced by NATO's supreme allied commanders from the late 1970s onward to resolve the Aegean command and control issue. These efforts failed as either the Greek or the Turkish side found fault with a key element of the proposals. Finally, on October 22, 1980, Greece returned to NATO's integrated military command structure under a proposal avanced by

311

NATO supreme allied commander General Bernard Rogers. This arrangement left the question of NATO command and control for the Aegean to be resolved between Greece and Turkey at a later date. At the same time, Greece rejoined the military wing of NATO.

The long-standing disputes were not mitigated by Greek reentry into the NATO military structure. Indeed, the rise to power of Papandreou and PASOK brought with it an increase in the contentiousness. This was attributed in part to the foreign policy rhetoric of Papandreou that Turkey posed a greater threat to Greece than did the Warsaw Pact and the Soviet Union. This "threat from Turkey" perspective became the mainstay of official national defense policy of Greece.

During the December 1981 DPC meeting, Papandreou called for a NATO security guarantee of Greece's eastern borders with Turkey. This led to a bitter dispute between Greece and Turkey at the conference, and for the first time in NATO history no communiqué was issued after the meeting. The United States and other NATO nations contended that such a guarantee was unwarranted and, within the alliance context, would be interpreted as an affront to Turkey.

In late September 1983 the continuing dispute over Aegean airspace and security issues with Turkey led Greece to withdraw from participation in NATO military exercises in the Aegean. The principal concern stated by Greece to justify its nonparticipation was the failure to include the island of Lemnos in the exercises. Turkey had objected in the past to the inclusion of the island because of a Greek-Turkish dispute over Greek rights to militarize the island (see Greek-Turkish Aegean Disputes, this ch.). Historically, NATO had avoided exercises involving Lemnos so as not to be drawn into the bilateral dispute. But in 1983 the initial plan was to use the island in the exercises. When Greece responded by characterizing the decision as a diplomatic victory over Turkey, NATO canceled the planned Lemnos exercise after a strong protest from Turkey.

Papandreou had also taken the position that the existing United States bases in Greece did not serve NATO interests but only those of the United States (see Greek-United States Defense Relationship, this ch.). The current bilateral Defense and Economic Cooperation Agreement (DECA) between Greece and the United States, signed on September 8, 1983, is notable for its lack of specific reference to NATO in its preamble of purpose. Nearly all mutual security agreements among NATO nations make direct reference to the fact that they are implementing the purposes of the NATO treaty, but the DECA does not.

The independent stance within NATO of Greece under Papandreou has also been shown by his strong opposition to the deployment of United States Pershing II and cruise missiles as part of NATO's Intermediate Nuclear Force (INF) modernization program. Papandreou argued that deployment would further exacerbate the nuclear arms race and called for increased negotiation between the United States and the Soviet Union before deployment. He continued to press this argument even after initial deployment had begun.

The relationship between Greece and NATO continued to evolve in the mid-1980s. Papandreou's independent stance within NATO meetings appealed to nationalist sentiment within Greece but annoyed other members of the alliance who felt that NATO was not the proper forum for airing bilateral grievances between members. NATO membership, however, provided a major international audience for Greek foreign policy views as well as a means for restraining Turkish influence within the alliance. Membership also served to check what Greek officials have felt to be a bias toward Turkey in the alliance. Were Greece to leave the NATO alliance, Turkish influence would likely be expanded, and Greece would also forfeit signficant amounts of alliance-generated military assistance.

### Greek-Turkish Aegean Disputes

Disputes between Greece and Turkey in the Aegean over a complex web of issues have served to complicate both countries' relationships not only with each other but also with NATO and the United States. They have created a volatile climate in which a minor incident could touch off a confrontation between Greeks and Turks. Talks between Greece and Turkey aimed at resolving outstanding bilateral disputes had been held since 1976 at both the technical and the ministerial levels, but little substantive progress had been made. The PASOK party program maintained that Greece should not negotiate with Turkey on the Aegean disputes. After the election of the Papandreou government in 1981, the Aegean talks were suspended by Greece, which also stated that Greece might extend its territorial waters from six to 12 nautical miles in accordance with recommendations of the Law of the Sea Convention.

The main questions in the Aegean disputes include the

extent of territorial waters in the Aegean Sea, the mining of the continental shelf, regulation of Aegean airspace, and the Greek requests for a NATO security guarantee. The Turks maintain that the Aegean is a semi-enclosed sea having peculiar features and hence is difficult to lend itself to a 12-nautical-mile territorial delimitation. The Turkish contention is that, if the limit were extended to 12 nautical miles—from the current six nautical miles—the Aegean, dotted with Greek islands and islets (many within sight of mainland Turkey), would no longer be an international body of water but a Greek lake. The extension of the six-nautical-mile limit to 12 would be regarded by Turkey as a casus belli in that it would directly violate Turkish rights of access to, and free passage through, international and Turkish waters—an implicit violation of rights guaranteed by the Montreaux Convention. The Papandreou government, although having stated its prerogative to extend the territorial water limit in accordance with the Law of the Sea deliberations, had in mid-1985 not yet chosen to implement this option. (The Law of the Sea Convention has accepted a 12-nautical-mile limit as a maximum, but not mandatory, breadth for international waters.)

Greece and Turkey also have fundamental differences over the delineation of the continental shelf of the western Aegean Sea. At stake are potential hydrocarbon (oil) resources and, more important, sovereignty over the seabed that Greeks fear might be expanded someday to affect the islands as well. The Greeks have stated that, under the 1958 Geneva Convention on the Continental Shelf, islands have a claim to their continental shelf. The Greeks then drew a line equidistant between the easternmost fringe of their Aegean Islands and the Turkish coast and claimed the shelf up to that line. According to this interpretation, virtually the entire continental shelf under the Aegean is Greek.

The Turks rejected the Greeks' claim; Turkey was not a signatory of the 1958 Geneva convention. It was pointed out that preliminary drafts of the Law of the Sea gave greater priority to coastal states rather than to islands in delimitation of the continental shelf. Using this approach, the Turks asserted that the demarcation line should be in the middle of the Aegean, halfway between the Greek and the Turkish mainlands.

The Greeks view the proposed Turkish demarcation line as a direct threat to the sovereignty of about 500 Greek islands. They believe that a continental shelf demarcation line to the west of those islands would provide Turkey with a justification for establishment of an economic zone and then a security zone around the islands. The Greek "political continuum" with these islands, as well as internal lines of communication, would then be threatened, making the islands into enclaves and eventually infringing on Greek sovereignty. The fact that in the nineteenth century Greek-inhabited islands to the east of a similar line were in Turkish hands affects this perception. The 1974 invasion of Cyprus, combined with the creation of the Turkish Aegean Army in 1975, accentuated anxiety in Greece. Virtually every segment of Greek society shares these concerns to a degree that is striking in its vehemence, making compromise difficult and accommodation nearly impossible.

In 1976 the United Nations Security Council's Resolution 395 recommended that negotiations be conducted between Greece and Turkey on the continental shelf issue. In the same year Greece and Turkey agreed at Bern, Switzerland, to resolve differences on the question through bilateral negotiations. In mid-1985, however, these differences remain unresolved, and further negotiations have not been scheduled.

The dispute between Greece and Turkey regarding Aegean airspace centers on the Turkish refusal to accept the Greek claim of sovereignty over airspace in the Aegean in excess of the six-nautical-mile territorial limit. Furthermore, Turkey does not accept the assertion that Greek national law applies in all parts of the Athens-Istanbul FIR. Control of an FIR creates an international responsibility for the safety of air traffic within it. On the basis of the 1944 Chicago Convention exempting State operated aircraft from FIR jurisdiction, Turkey and the United States have not accepted the Greek regulation that all foreign aircraft must file flight plans with the Greeks when operating in that portion of the FIR that is in international airspace. In 1982, for example, Greece protested to NATO over a series of unauthorized Turkish aircraft incursions into Greek-defined airspace during a Turkish-NATO military exercise.

The situation in the Aegean also became aggravated as a result of the mutual military buildups on the easternmost Greek islands and in southwestern Turkey. This chain of events was set off by the Turkish military intervention of 1974 in Cyprus—preceded by an attempted coup, generally believed to have been instigated by Athens, against Cypriot president Archbishop Makarios. What the Turks saw as a rescue mission for the Turkish minority in Cyprus the Greeks saw as a potential threat to the demilitarized Greek islands. As a result,

Greece began to remilitarize the islands in possible contravention of the 1923 Treaty of Lausanne and the 1947 Treaty of Paris, both of which appear to require a demilitarized Aegean.

Since 1974 Greece has built defensive fortifications and moved tanks, artillery, and 20,000 to 30,000 combat personnel onto the islands of Lesbos, Chios, Samos, and Ikaria. It has also constructed a major air force installation on the island of Lemnos. The Turks responded in 1975 by creating an Aegean army in western Anatolia and by staffing it with about 35,000 combat personnel equipped with an amphibious capability.

As a result of these developments, Greece has requested repeatedly from NATO and the United States a security guarantee of its eastern borders against Turkey. Turkey, however, regards this request as inconsistent with the principles of the NATO alliance and as a guise for imposition of fait accompli regarding Greece's Aegean Sea claims. It has stated repeatedly that it has no claims on Greek territory, whether in the Aegean Islands or in Thrace. Turkey, however, has been concerned about the militarization of the islands close to its own coast, which it has maintained is a violation of the treaties of Lausanne and Paris. The Turkish government has also refuted the Greek claim that the Turkish Aegean Army represented a threat to Greece.

### Military Assistance

The Greek armed forces were built up progressively after World War II with British and United States aid. United States military aid and economic assistance during the Civil War period, for example, amounted to 25 percent of the national income of Greece, or US$818 million, of which US$473 million was in economic assistance and US$345 million was in military aid.

Since 1947 Greece has received direct military grants from the United States, exclusive of other credits, totaling almost US$3 billion. Aircraft, armor, artillery, and small arms used by the Greek armed forces were furnished almost exclusively by the United States. Destroyers transferred from the United States Navy under the mutual assistance pact in the early 1950s were still the backbone of the Greek navy in the mid-1980s.

The United States withheld the delivery of military equipment, including heavy weapons, after the 1967 coup. It was believed at the time that the United States moral reprimand

and a squeeze on military suppliers would force an alteration in the regime. When France expressed an interest in cooperating with Greece regardless of the complexion of the regime, however, the junta placed orders for a variety of French equipment denied it by the United States. After a public debate on the question, Norway filled an order for three motor torpedo boats contracted before the coup. Britain negotiated weapons sales after the coup, and the Federal Republic of Germany (West Germany) also agreed to build four submarines for Greece. The United States resumed deliveries of heavy weapons in October 1968 after the plebiscite on a new constitution, which in Washington was understood to signal an eventual return to democratic rule in Greece.

Because of the political tension between Greece and Turkey, maintenance of a stable military balance in the Aegean region has been an important factor in the provision of United States aid for the region. Section 620C(b) of the 1961 Foreign Assistance Act (the basis for economic and military assistance by the United States) stipulates that United States assistance to Greece and Turkey "shall be designed to ensure that the present balance of military strength among countries of this region . . . is to preserved." In general, the United States has dealt with this requirement by maintaining a seven-to-10 ratio in its military assistance to Greece and Turkey. In the mid-1980s Greek officials continued to stress the point that the spending ratio should be maintained. The United States, however, has officially denied any fixed ratio concept for military assistance between any countries. Nevertheless, in 1984 the United States gave Greece US$501.4 million in military assistance—roughly 70 percent of the US$718.3 million given to Turkey.

Since 1964 Greece has also received military aid from West Germany; this aid is, according to West German sources, defense matériel free of charge but has not included training and advisory aid. The aid has been provided through the NATO framework of mutual assistance to alliance members. Although there have been no fixed rules for the amounts given, Greece and Turkey (also a recipient) have received German aid on a five-to-three ratio. Since 1964 West Germany has concluded eight separate defense assistance agreements with Greece, amounting to Dr477 million (for value of the drachma—see Glossary). An additional agreement for Dr70 million was under negotiation in late 1984. Under the current defense assistance agreements with Bonn, Greece has received Milan antitank missile simulators, components for military radios, batteries for submarines, and repair shop equipment for the Greek air force and the defense industry, as well as used F-104G aircraft, M-48 tanks, and a variety of trucks. West German defense aid has also included maintenance installations for all three armed services, production facilities for ammunition and small-caliber weapons, and support for procurement of 110 Leopard main battle tanks.

### Greek-United States Defense Relationship

United States military facilities in Greece first operated under the terms of the 1953 defense cooperation agreement. This initial agreement provided for the establishment of United States military and related technical installations on Greek soil. The major military installations used by the United States include Souda Bay Air Base and Iraklion Air Station in Crete, Hellenikon Air Base near Athens, Nea Makri Naval Communications Station near Athens, and a number of communications sites throughout the country. Functions at these stations have been useful to Greece, NATO, and the United States.

The Greek bases provide, among other things, direct operational support for the United States Sixth Fleet in the Eastern Mediterranean, important communications links, and reconnaissance information. The bases have also provided easier surveillance of Soviet activities in the Eastern Mediterranean and support for the United States Air Force Europe and Military Airlift Command (MAC) flights, as well as ammunition and supply storage sites. The installations have been operated mainly in conjunction with, and under the nominal control of, Greek commanders.

Homeporting of the United States Sixth Fleet was introduced in 1973. A controversial issue in the United States as well as in Greece, homeporting was scheduled to proceed in two phases. The first phase, implemented in 1973 and 1974, provided for the stationing of a United States destroyer escort squadron at Elevsis, near Athens. About 6,500 navy personnel and some 3,500 dependents entered Greece during this phase. The second phase, which was not completed, called for an anchorage near Megara for an aircraft carrier and its support ships. The use of the Elevsis base by the American navy was also terminated in 1975 by a bilateral agreement.

The United States developed a close political-military relationship with Greece after World War II. In the past decade, however, Greek relations with Washington have been strained. One source of this strain has been the belief among many Greeks that the United States implicitly supported the 1967 coup and that it tacitly supported the junta during its years in power. Still another source of strain has been the belief that the United States has had a bias toward Turkey in the area of defense cooperation and, as a result, has not seriously pressured Turkey on issues related to Cyprus and the Aegean disputes, (see Greek-Turkish Aegean Disputes, this ch.; The "Revolution of 21 April," ch. 1).

The suspicions about the United States, held among many Greeks, were effectively exploited by Andreas Papandreou and PASOK in the 1981 general election. During the campaign Papandreou called for the removal of the United States military bases from Greece and for Greek withdrawal from NATO (see Greece and NATO, this ch.). After his election as prime minister, however, Papandreou moderated this position.

A new five-year Defense and Economic Cooperation Agreement (DECA) was formally signed by Greece and the United States on September 8, 1983, and was ratified by the Greek parliament on November 8, 1983. United States ratification was not necessary because the DECA was regarded as an executive agreement.

By this time the question of United States bases had become a significant political question in Greece. Under the terms of the 1983 DECA, the United States was permitted by Greece to "maintain and operate military and supporting facilities" within Greece and to engage in activities at those facilities "for defense purposes" in accordance with the agreement. According to the Greeks, the intent of the 1983 agreement was to "restructure" defense and economic cooperation between the two countries, based on bilateral multilateral agreements.

Important differences remain between the two countries on some provisions of the agreement. The 1983 DECA stated that the duplicate Greek and English texts of the agreement were "equally authentic." This is standard language for bilateral agreements. In the 1983 DECA, however, the English and Greek texts clearly diverged in the use of language relating to the duration of the agreement. In the English text the agreement "is terminable" after five years, whereas in the Greek text the agreement "terminates" after five years (in 1988). The English wording could permit continuation of the existing agreement after five years, unlike the Greek text (see Foreign Relations, ch. 4). Papandreou has stated repeatedly that his

319

government regarded the 1983 DECA as a timetable for removing the United States bases in 1988. United States officials have discounted his statements as intended for domestic Greek consumption.

### Greek Defense Industries

To lessen dependency on foreign military suppliers and to develop an industrial base for local military needs, Greece officially established an arms industry organization in December 1976. Since that time it has become a regional military supplier of small arms and an exporter of tanks and other armored vehicles. The defense industry has been divided into separate branches for aerospace and small arms production.

Hellenic Aerospace Industry was established in late 1976 as a government-owned firm to provide a domestic industrial base for aircraft maintenance, repair, and overhaul facilities. In early 1985 this company had support and overhaul contracts with the United States, Egypt, and the United Arab Emirates, as well as support and coproduction agreements with international companies, such as Airbus Industries and Dassault-Breguet. These arrangements covered services, including the manufacture and installation of aviation components, extensive maintenance, overhaul of equipment, and technical support and training. The Greek aerospace industry was also expected to have a large role in the production of the F-16 and Mirage 2000 aircraft purchased in late 1984 by the Greek air force.

The growth of international demand for regional defense industries and increased competition for defense business have been beneficial to the developing aerospace industry in Greece. The terms of contracts for the supply of aircraft and equipment to Greece, military and civilian, have stipulated that offset agreements were expected. The suppliers were required to use Greek industry either to supply component parts for the aircraft or to provide other services. Examples of manufacturing opportunities to Hellenic Aerospace Industry under offset programs included production of doorframes for the Airbus 300, parts for the Dassault-Breguet Mirage F-1, components for the Snecma F-1 engines, and fuselage sections for Agusta A109 helicopters.

Hellenic Arms Industry (Elleniki Biomichania Oplon—EBO) has been established as a state-owned corporation for the manufacture of small- to large-caliber guns, small arms, explosives, propellants, and fully integrated weapons systems. Established in 1977 with the task of manufacturing light infantry weapons for the Greek armed forces, EBO has grown not only in size but also in the diversity of its products. The company has developed the capability to produce a broad range of weapons not only for domestic consumption but also for export. Greek weapons production by 1985 had expanded beyond its original purpose of domestic production of systems to support national defense and was making a positive impact on the national economy through its earnings in hard currencies. In December 1984, for example, an agreement with Libya, the details of which remained speculative, called for the Libyan purchase of nearly US$500 million of military equipment by 1988.

EBO consisted of two factories—one in Aiyion and the other in Lavrion. The Aiyion plant employed more than 800 people and produced GA3 and GA4 assault rifles; the MP5 submachine gun; MG3, HK11, and HK21 machine guns; the Rheinmetall 20mm cannon; the Mauser 30mm model F cannon; 81mm mortars; and other small arms equipment. The Lavrion plant employed over 400 in the production of ammunition and explosives.

EBO has also developed weapons systems for domestic use; the ARTEMIS-30, a small antiaircraft system, was developed for use by the Greek army in the Aegean. This system appears to have also found an international market. Under terms of the economic agreement with Libya, Greece agreed to sell equipment that was Greek designed and Greek made. Observers concluded that the Libyan purchase would include the ARTEMIS-30.

Although Greece had yet to become, in 1985, a net exporter of arms, the economic impact of the developing defense industry has been significant. In 1983 sales amounted to over US$120 million, an increase of US$7 million over 1982, or 3.6 percent of Greece's total exports. The growth of the defense-related companies and their performance after 1977 meant that Greece had become a strong regional arms producer.

## Public Order

In recent Greek history, threats to public order have been perceived as being more political in origin than economic or social. Until 1974 the definition of political dissension and the severity of treatment of political offenders varied according to the attitudes of the successive post-World War II governments. The threat of communism was a common theme that was exploited by the junta as an excuse for political repression. The junta declared a state of siege under which individual rights and the right of assembly were suspended, and martial law was declared. Hundreds of persons suspected or accused of communist sympathies were exiled to prison islands in the Aegean Sea. They included opponents of the junta from all political backgrounds, especially from the left wing.

Portions of the 1968 constitution pertaining to civil and political liberties were not put into effect. Crimes alleged to be political in nature were tried by courts-martial or by extraordinary courts established in each local jurisdiction. In 1969 Prime Minister Papadopoulos transferred responsibility for the supervision of public order and security to military authorities. Definitions of criminal activity were broad, and punishments by courts-martial were severe, especially those meted out for expression of political opposition. Police control over the exercise of economic and social activities was maintained through the identity cards that each citizen was obliged to carry. In some cases opponents of the regime were deprived of citizenship.

The Karamanlis regime, which replaced the junta in 1974, restored civil liberties, curbed the police, and stripped the military of its internal security functions. The Constitution of 1975, which formally reestablished democratic government in Greece, guarantees equality before the law and confirms the inviolability of fundamental individual rights—among them freedom of expression and peaceful assembly. According to its provisions, many of which were framed to prevent the abuses of the law, no citizen may be arrested, subjected to search, prosecuted, or imprisoned except through due process of law.

Greece has a low crime rate. Elements lending stability to the society are frequently cited as being the basic ethnic and religious homogeneity of the population, shared values, and close-knit family groups that instill in their members a sense of social discipline and order, to say nothing of the acceptance of authority. Generally, Greeks feel bound to assist kin and are supportive of close friends during periods of social stress or insecurity. An extroverted people, they make use of verbal outlets to release tensions that in other more restrained societies might lead to acts of violence. In some areas persons are deterred from breaking the law because arrest and punishment would dishonor their families. In most instances an individual accepts authority within the family or community more readily than from the police.

The police do not have a popular image in Greece. In the past they were feared rather than respected or trusted. They were treated with circumspection by the public as the sometimes oppressive agent of government authority. An undercurrent of brutality, intimidation, and petty tyranny was evident in police activities at every level of command under a succession of governments. Old habits of brutality were accentuated during the junta years, when the police were given a free rein in dealing with opponents of the regime.

Public animosity toward the police establishment was intense after the fall of the junta in 1974, and for the first time in years it could be expressed openly. There was growing concern that legitimate police activities might be impaired. The Karamanlis government dealt promptly with the problem not only to satisfy the public demand for reforms within the police establishment but also to salvage the police as an effective law enforcement agency. A number of policemen were brought to trial for torturing suspects and for other human rights violations. Others were held responsible for the deaths of demonstrators during the student strike at the National Technical University of Athens (commonly could the Polytechnic) in November 1973. Many officers were also dismissed from service. Public attitudes toward the police have moderated since these reforms. In 1984 the Papandreou government merged the command structure of the Gendarmerie and the City Police, reportedly to facilitate the decentralization of control of routine police activities from the national bureaucracy to the jurisdiction of local officials.

### Security Establishment

Civil police functions are performed by the Gendarmerie and the City Police. The latter has jurisdiction over three cities—Athens, Piraeus, and Patrai—and the island of Corfu. The Gendarmerie is responsible for maintaining law and order throughout the rest of the country. Both are national police forces, and the supervision of all police activities is centralized in the Ministry of Public Works. There are no local police departments.

The police are paramilitary in character. Both the Gendarmerie and the City Police carry sidearms and clubs while on regular duty. Police also receive regular training in the use of heavier weapons, which are kept in police arsenals. Special riot units are equipped with Swiss-built UR-416 armored personnel carriers. In 1984 the Gendarmerie and the City Police had a total force of about 25,000.

The Gendarmerie and the City Police also furnish personnel for the Tourist Police, which operate in Athens and in other areas frequented by foreign tourists. In addition to protecting and assisting tourists, they patrol railroad depots and airports, ensure public compliance with safety regulations, and serve occasionally as guides. Personnel are selected for the Tourist Police on the basis of appearance, demeanor, and education and are considered to be an elite force. Members of this branch must have a working knowledge of a foreign language, usually English.

Other branches that perform police duties of a restricted nature include the Customs Guards, who combat smuggling and collect duties at border crossings and ports of entry; the Forest Police, who patrol and conserve woodland areas; and the Agrarian Police, who enforce market regulations and protect farm property and livestock. The Harbor Corps patrols waterfront areas and also acts as a coast guard. Only a small number of women are members of the police forces; they serve in an auxilliary capacity, usually limited to clerical support and assignments involving the care or handling of women and children.

### Gendarmerie

The Gendarmerie was organized in 1833 on the model of the French police. Recruits were veterans of the war of independence and were skilled in guerrilla tactics. Their original mission was to suppress banditry in the mountainous countryside and to disarm irregular troops remaining outside the control of the government. The exploits of the first commandant, French philhellene and onetime Napoleonic officer François Gragier, became part of Greek folklore.

The modern Gendarmerie exercises a much broader range of powers than do police forces in the United States. It can, for example, enlist citizens for help in case of fire or natural disasters. It has a civil defense function and also performs duties that in some countries are carried out by the military police. Other duties include enforcement of public health and sanitation regulations and prevention of the spread of contagious

*Greek police car*
*Courtesy Peter J. Kassander*

diseases. The Gendarmerie also provides security in courts of law, guards prisons, and serves as a highway patrol.

As a paramilitary force, the Gendarmerie has seen considerable combat duty and is particularly proud of its military record. It played an active military role throughout World War II—both in Greece, where some Gendarmes joined resistance groups, and with Greek forces overseas. Gendarmes distinguished themselves in Italy in the battle for Rimini in 1944. In the same year the Gendarmerie assisted British and regular Greek army units in putting down the leftist uprising in Athens. During the Civil War the Gendarmerie also participated in combat operations against communist guerrillas. The national security role of the Gendarmerie has been limited since 1950.

Police stations throughout the country are directed from general division headquarters, which are commanded by officers of brigadier rank in Athens and Thessaloniki. The Athens headquarters shares jurisdiction in the capital with the City Police.

**City Police**

The City Police was established in 1920 to deal with urban

325

law enforcement problems peculiar to the metropolitan Athens-Piraeus area and the city of Patrai and Corfu. The City Police was organized by its first superintendent, Frederick Holliday of Scotland Yard, who patterned the new force on the same lines as the London Metropolitan Police.

The statutory duties of the City Police are to maintain law and order, preserve the social system, and protect the life, liberty, honor, and property of citizens within its jurisdiction. In essence, the responsibilities of the urban police force are identical to those of the Gendarmerie, a fact that was recognized by the unification of the command structures in 1984. Usual police duties include criminal investigation, law enforcement, and traffic control. A special unit deals with counterfeiting and white-collar crime. In Athens the City Police maintains a riot squad, organized and equipped for swift reaction. Officers on the squad are given permanent assignments and receive advanced training in riot-control tactics.

### Special Security Groups

A new police unit, the Special Security Groups, was formed in 1976, absorbing many duties formerly assigned to the Gendarmerie. These duties included criminal investigation, surveillance, intelligence gathering, and responsibility for the security of public officials. The Special Security Groups also took over certain internal security functions from the military police and intelligence agencies that had expanded their jurisdiction into civilian areas during the junta years.

The unit was created by the Ministry of Public Order in response to the 1975 assassination of a member of the United States Embassy in Athens. This and other acts of politically inspired terrorism in Greece convinced authorities of the need for a separate police force trained specifically for direct and immediate handling of emergencies such as homicide, abduction, air piracy, holding of hostages, armed robbery, and assault on public officials and foreign diplomats. Special security personnel guarded public officials, embassies, public buildings, and areas that might become targets for terrorist actions. Their duties also involved the observation of extremist groups. The Special Security Groups were organized into attack teams with special weapons and tactics (SWAT) capability to deal with crimes in progress. Members of the unit were picked from the Gendarmerie and the City Police and were required to be qualified marksmen.

## Training and Conditions of Service

Both the Gendarmerie and the City Police operate police academies for the education and basic training of police officer candidates. The academies provide a three-year university-level program that includes courses in law, criminology, sociology, psychology, economics, and other academic subjects. Course work also includes law enforcement methods, paramilitary tactics, and physical education. Candidates must have a secondary-school diploma to qualify for admission. Upon graduation they are commissioned as second lieutenants. Many officers receive advanced training abroad. Noncommissioned officers with good service records can qualify for promotion to officer rank through examination and a two-year course at the police academy. Some are occasionally commissioned for an act of valor or performance of hazardous duty.

Police recruits receive six months of basic training. They are also required to meet physical standards and to pass written examinations and must have no previous criminal record. Recruits under the age of 21 can satisfy their military service obligation by serving in the Gendarmerie. City Police recruits, however, must have completed their military service before joining the police. The police are considered part of the civil service.

## Incidence of Crime

In 1985 the only crime statistics available were those published by the Greek government, which recorded the number of persons sentenced for indictable offenses; however, the rate of crime in Greece is low by any standard. The most common offenses in the early 1980s were simple assaults, crimes against property, and infractions of commercial and motor vehicle regulations. Despite the relative poverty found in some parts of rural Greece, crimes against property are generally confined to the larger cities. Violent crimes, such as murder, rape, and armed robbery, are sufficiently rare to merit headline treatment in the newspapers.

Gun-control regulations are strictly enforced. Possession of firearms, except those licensed for hunting, is forbidden to private citizens. Prison sentences ranging from five to 20 years are imposed for selling, procuring, or transporting weapons and ammunition considered by authorities to be military in nature. Severe penalties are also prescribed for the sale or illegal possession of narcotics.

Many actions regarded as assaults upon family honor are considered private matters. Redress or, in some instances, revenge is handled by the involved parties without recourse to the courts of law. Authorities are accustomed to exercising discretion when dealing with so-called crimes of honor, which not uncommonly involve attempts of a father or brother to protect the reputation of a daughter or sister.

Offenders convicted of misdemeanors are customarily fined. Of those offenders sentenced to prison, more than 80 percent receive terms of less than three months; about 10 percent receive terms of three months to one year. Less than 20 percent of those convicted of crimes were under the age of 25. Women accounted for about 10 percent of convicted offenders.

According to Greek law, a juvenile is a person between seven and 17 years of age. Although the number of juvenile cases adjudicated in the mid-1950s rose sharply as a result of dislocation caused by the Civil War, the figure declined steadily thereafter and appeared to level off in the late 1960s. In 1985 the crime rate among Greek juveniles was insignificant in comparison with that in a similar age-group in most of Western Europe and the United States. Credit for this was attributed to the importance attached to the prevention of juvenile delinquency by the Greek Orthodox church and government agencies as well as to the abiding strength of the Greek family as the basic social institution. Most offenses committed by juveniles consisted of petty theft or property damage by young males or prostitution by young females.

### Criminal Justice

The criminal code is based on the Bavarian codes, the body of law introduced to Greece by King Otto I. It was a system based on Roman Law and the Napoleonic Code. The criminal code has been revised frequently and modernized in accordance with legal requirements and historical developments peculiar to Greece.

The Constitution provides for an independent judiciary. Judicial powers are vested in the courts of law. The creation of extraordinary courts, such as those that functioned during the junta, is expressly prohibited. The court system is divided into administrative, civil, and criminal sections. Judges are formally appointed for life by the president of the republic (see Branches of the Government, ch. 4).

The criminal code defines three grades of crime: felonies, misdemeanors, and petty offenses. The lowest criminal court is the magistrate's court—a police court operating in each province and presided over by a single magistrate who may impose short jail terms and small fines for minor petty offenses. Above these magistrate's courts are the courts of first instance, the primary civil and criminal trial courts. Most litigation begins and ends in these courts. Misdemeanor and felony cases are heard first in the courts of first instance but are subject to review by the nine courts of appeal and, if necessary, by the Supreme Court. Sentences at the lower court level may be appealed by either the defendant or the prosecutor.

The Constitution forbids unusual punishment, including unreasonably long prison terms. Imprisonment for felonies ranges from five to 20 years; sentences for petty offenses and misdemeanors range from 10 days to five years. Confinement in a reformatory may also be imposed for a period of from five to 20 years; confinement in an institution for the treatment of the mentally deranged may be indefinite. Convicted felons are usually fined and given terms of imprisonment. Confiscation of property, however, is not permitted.

Greece retains the option of capital punishment for some categories of serious crime, but the sentence has not been imposed since 1977. Death sentences may not be passed down for political crimes.

Police officers may arrest persons caught in the act of committing a crime; under some circumstances a citizen's arrest is also recognized as valid. With these exceptions, no one may be arrested or imprisoned without a judicial warrant. Suspects must be arraigned before an examining magistrate within 24 hours of arrest. Within three to five days of arraignment, magistrates are required either to release the suspects or to issue a warrant for imprisonment pending trial. The maximum detention permissible before trial is nine months or, if cause is demonstrated by the prosecutor, 18 months. Administrative measures to restrict the movement of citizens are prohibited unless accompanied by a court ruling.

After an arrest, police may conduct preliminary investigations under the supervision of the public prosecutor. Thereafter the police turn over the suspect and pertinent documents of the case to court authorities. The court then requests a regular investigation by a judge or sets a date for trial. As a rule, the state possesses the exclusive right to prosecute criminal suspects, exercising its jurisdiction through public prosecutors attached to the courts. An injured party may initiate prosecution, however, when the competent public prosecutor refuses to act and may also seek redress for loss or injury sustained in connection with a criminal prosecution.

At the outset of an investigation the public prosecutor must explain the legal rights of the accused, obtain a signed statement that the explanation has been made, and give the accused a complete and clear description of the offense with which the accused has been charged. The accused may elect to present a defense or may decline to reply, but if a written defense is submitted, he or she is subject to questioning to clarify the substance of the statement. During the investigation the accused has the right to legal counsel but under normal circumstances may not confront witnesses during the investigation. If the investigator deems that subsequent appearances by the witness in the courtroom will not be possible, however, the accused must be present or represented by counsel during the testimony of the witness.

The accused is protected by law from the use of a confession obtained by torture or other illegal means and must be informed of the contents of all documents bearing on the investigation before they are transmitted to the public prosecutor. He or she may also examine copies of these documents. The accused then has up to 48 hours to decide on a plea and has the right to post bail pending trial, except in the case of serious crimes. Criminal and political offenses are tried by panels composed of judges and lay jurors in so-called mixed courts that combine the functions of judge and jury in common-law courts. The accused is present during the trial and may compel the appearance in court of defense witnesses. The court must appoint legal counsel if the accused lacks a lawyer. Criminal trials are open to the adult public.

Under criminal law, the burden of proof rests with the prosecution. Although the criminal code specifies rules for the presentation of evidence, judicial panels are given considerable latitude in arriving at their verdict. Panelists are instructed to listen to the "voice of conscience" in weighing testimony and in examining evidence.

When imposing sentence, the presiding judge is restricted by law, which places limitations on the amount of the fine or the length of imprisonment that may be imposed at each level of the judicial system, as well as the applicable penalty for each kind of offense. Magistrates in juvenile courts are permitted considerable discretion in sentencing youthful offenders. Punishment for juvenile delinquency may range from a reprimand to probation to committal to a training school or correctional institution. Parents may also be held liable for the behavior of their children when it is considered appropriate by the authorities.

## Penal System

A central penitentiary and several correctional farms form the nucleus of the Greek prison system. District prisons are located near each court for suspects nearing trial and for convicts serving short-term sentences. Other penal facilities include open prisons and minimum-security institutions, reformatories, training schools for juvenile offenders, prison hospitals, and sanatoriums. Conditions within the prisons and detention facilities are regarded as satisfactory. Adequate health care and diet are provided to the prisoners. No distinction is made according to social class, race, sex, religion, or kind of conviction in the treatment of prisoners. Cases requiring medical treatment receive special attention. Prisoners may also be visited by family members three times per week.

The penal system emphasizes the rehabilitation of prisoners through education, vocational training, and productive labor. Assistance in securing employment is provided upon release from prison. The law requires that prisoners be employed in an occupation similar to the one they had before their incarceration but prohibits the hiring out of prison labor to private contractors. The government is the principal customer for agricultural and other goods produced by prisoners. The limited sale of prison-made products to the general public is arranged by the authorities.

Particular attention is paid to the rehabilitation of juvenile offenders. Training schools offer both academic and vocational education. Special features of these schools are the program of home furloughs on religious holidays and the opportunity for youths to attend recreational camps during the summer months. Professional probation officers are attached to all juvenile courts.

## Political Violence

In the 1970s and early 1980s Greece was not plagued by the widespread political violence that had characterized terrorist activities in much of Western Europe. Unlike the left-wing, Marxist-Leninist-oriented terrorism in West Germany, France, and Italy, political violence in Greece was generally the last resort of disillusioned extremist groups from the far right and the extreme left. Incidents were rare and claimed few lives, although government property bore the brunt of arson-related activities.

However, in the mid-1980s there were a number of unsolved, politically motivated assassinations in Athens and a bomb attack on a facility frequented by off-duty United States military personnel in Greece. The "November 17 Revolutionary Organization" (which took its name from the November 17, 1973, student riots), the group responsible for the killing of a senior United States embassy official in 1975, also claimed responsibility for the 1983 assassination of a United States Navy captain and his Greek driver, as well as the 1984 attempted assassination of a United States Army sergeant and the February 1985 killing of Greek conservative publisher Nikos Momferatos.

In 1984 seven additional murders were attributed to Arab and other foreign terrorist groups. The Papandreou government strongly condemned terrorist activity as an attempt to destabilize Greek democracy. But in mid-1985 the unified security forces were not able to halt the growing incidence of political violence in Greece.

*   *   *

Most of the generally available discussions of Greek security deal primarily with the issues of contention with Turkey. As a general introduction to the regional context, Andrew Wilson's *The Aegean Disputes* covers all the areas of contention. A useful discussion of general Greek security affairs, as well as the historical context of the role of the armed forces in Greek life, may be found in *Greek Security: Issues and Politics* by Thanos M. Veremis. Theodore A. Couloumbis' *The United States, Greece, and Turkey* is also a useful analysis of the NATO context of Greek-Turkish issues.

Reliable references to Greece's military holdings, procurement patterns, and force levels may be found in the International Institute for Strategic Studies' annual publication, *The*

*Military Balance.* Current references may also be found in periodicals such as *International Defense Review, Jane's Defence Weekly,* and *NATO's Sixteen Nations.* (For further information and complete citations, see Bibliography.)

# Appendix A

## Table 1.  Metric Conversion Coefficients

| When you know | Multiply by | To find |
|---|---|---|
| Millimeters ..................... | 0.04 | inches |
| Centimeters ..................... | 0.39 | inches |
| Meters.......................... | 3.3 | feet |
| Kilometers ...................... | 0.62 | miles |
| | | |
| Hectares (10,000 m²) ............... | 2.47 | acres |
| Square kilometers ................. | 0.39 | square miles |
| | | |
| Cubic meters .................... | 35.3 | cubic feet |
| Liters ......................... | 0.26 | gallons |
| | | |
| Kilograms ...................... | 2.2 | pounds |
| Metric tons...................... | 0.98 | long tons |
| ..................... | 1.1 | short tons |
| ..................... | 2,204 | pounds |
| | | |
| Degrees Celsius .................. | 9 | degrees Fahrenheit |
| (Centigrade) | divide by 5 and add 32 | |

Table 2. *Population by Region and Province, 1981 Census[1]*

| Region<br>Province | Population |
|---|---:|
| **Aegean Islands** | |
| Dhodhekanisos | 145,071 |
| Khios | 49,865 |
| Kikladhes | 88,458 |
| Lesvos | 104,620 |
| Samos | 40,519 |
| Total Aegean Islands | 428,533 |
| **Central Greece** | |
| Aitolia and Akarnania | 219,764 |
| Attica (less Greater Athens) | 342,093 |
| Greater Athens | 3,027,331 |
| Evritania | 26,182 |
| Evvoia | 188,410 |
| Fokis | 44,222 |
| Fthiotis | 161,995 |
| Voiotia | 117,175 |
| Total Central Greece | 4,127,172 |
| **Crete** | |
| Iraklion | 243,622 |
| Khania | 125,856 |
| Lasithi | 70,053 |
| Rethimni | 62,634 |
| Total Crete | 502,165 |
| **Epirus** | |
| Arta | 80,044 |
| Ioannina | 147,304 |
| Preveza | 55,915 |
| Thesprotia | 41,278 |
| Total Epirus | 324,541 |
| **Ionian Islands** | |
| Kefallinia | 31,297 |
| Kerkira | 99,477 |
| Levkas | 21,863 |
| Zakinthos | 30,014 |
| Total Ionian Islands | 182,651 |
| **Macedonia** | |
| Drama | 94,772 |
| Florina | 52,430 |
| Grevena | 36,421 |
| Imathia | 133,750 |

## Table 2.—*Continued.*

| Region<br>Province | Population |
|---|---|
| Kastoria | 53,169 |
| Kavala | 135,218 |
| Khalkidhiki | 79,036 |
| Kilkis | 81,562 |
| Kozani | 147,051 |
| Mount Athos[2] | 1,472 |
| Pella | 132,386 |
| Pieria | 106,859 |
| Serrai | 196,247 |
| Thessaloniki | 871,580 |
| Total Macedonia | 2,121,953 |
| **Peloponnesus** | |
| Akhaia | 275,193 |
| Argolis | 93,020 |
| Arkadhia | 107,932 |
| Ilia | 160,305 |
| Korinthia | 123,042 |
| Lakonia | 93,218 |
| Messinia | 159,818 |
| Total Peloponnesus | 1,012,528 |
| **Thessaly** | |
| Kardhitsa | 124,930 |
| Larisa | 254,295 |
| Magnisia | 182,222 |
| Trikala | 134,207 |
| Total Thessaly | 695,654 |
| **Thrace** | |
| Evros | 148,486 |
| Rodhopi | 107,957 |
| Xanthi | 88,777 |
| Total Thrace | 345,220 |
| TOTAL | 9,740,417 |

[1] All persons present at time of census, whether or not permanent residents.
[2] Autonomous administration.
Source: Based on information from Greece, National Statistical Service, *Statistical Yearbook of Greece, 1982*, Athens, 1983, 17-18.

### Table 3.   *Major Metropolitan Areas, 1981 Census*

| Metropolitan Area | Population | Metropolitan Area | Population |
|---|---|---|---|
| Greater Athens . . . . . | 3,027,331 | Greater Kalamai . . . . | 43,235 |
| Greater Thessaloniki | 706,180 | Greater Katerini . . . . | 39,895 |
| Greater Patrai . . . . . . | 154,596 | Greater Khios . . . . . | 29,742 |
| Greater Iraklion . . . . | 110,958 | Greater Aiyion . . . . . | 25,723 |
| Greater Volos . . . . . . | 107,407 | Greater Ermoupolis | 16,595 |
| Greater Khania . . . . . | 61,976 | Greater Sparta . . . . . | 14,388 |
| Greater Agrinion . . . . | 45,087 | | |

Source: Based on information from Greece, National Statistical Service, *Statistical Yearbook of Greece, 1982*, Athens, 1983, 24-26.

## Table 4. *Evolution of Greek Language*

---

Period
    Description

*First half of second millennium B.C.*
    Greek speakers arrive in southern Balkan Peninsula

*Second half of second millennium B.C.*
    Greek first written, but syllabary lost after Mycenaean downfall around 1100 B.C.

*Late eighth century B.C.*
    Phoenician alphabet adopted and modified

*Sixth century B.C.*
    Establishment of Greek literary tradition

*Up to mid-fourth century B.C.*
    Mutually intelligible dialects from each city-state and several literary variants used depending on genre

*404 B.C.*
    Dominance of Athens until this date makes Attic lingua franca and literary language

*323 B.C.*
    Death of Alexander the Great ends spread of Attic by means of Macedonian empire

*Third century B.C. to fourth century A.D.*
    Common language (*koine*) for Greeks develops for international use in trade, politics, and administration

*A.D. 330*
    Christian church adopts educated form of *koine* as official language

*Late first century B.C. to third century A.D.*
    Schools try to revive Attic Greek

*Sixth century A.D. to fifteenth century*
    Byzantine period; difficult to document evolving spoken form differing from written form of texts

*Seventh century*
    Demotic assumes modern morphological and syntactic form

*Seventh to ninth centuries*
    During struggles against Arabs no use of Attic literary model

*Ninth to fifteenth centuries*
    Revivals of use of Attic model

*1261-1453*
    "Declassicized" texts simplify literary form for uneducated

*Early fourteenth century*
    Vernacular literature approximates spoken form (poetry)

*Late sixteenth to early seventeenth centuries*
    Cretan vernacular used in drama and poetry

*Late eighteenth century*
    Language becomes politicized in Greek communities in Ottoman Greece, Danubian principalities, and Western Europe with Enlightenment influence

*1748-1833*
    Adamantios Korais, originator of *katharevousa*

*1834, 1836*
    *Katharevousa* adopted as official state language in Greece

*Table 4.—Continued.*

| Period |
|---|
| Description |
| 1854-1929 |
| Yannis Psiharis, champion of demotic |
| 1885-1957 |
| Nikos Kazantzakis, writer important in the demotic literary movement |
| 1888 |
| Psiharis publishes *My Journey*, which serves as example for demotic literary movement |
| 1901 |
| Riots in Athens over demotic New Testament translation; government falls |
| 1917 |
| Use of demotic in lower grades of elementary school |
| 1967-74 |
| Junta attempts to reinstate *katharevousa* in the schools at all levels |
| 1970s-1980s |
| Loss of regional dialects in many parts of Greece |
| 1976 |
| Demotic of Athens becomes official language called common or standard Greek (Neohelliniki) |

Table 5.   *Circulation of Leading Newspapers, December 1984*

| Newspaper | Circulation | Orientation° |
|---|---|---|
| **Afternoon press** | | |
| *Ethnos* . . . . . . . . . . . . . . . . . . . . | 120,735 | Government |
| *Ta Nea* . . . . . . . . . . . . . . . . . . . . | 90,395 | -do- |
| *Apogevmatini* . . . . . . . . . . . . . . . | 74,963 | Opposition |
| *Avriani* . . . . . . . . . . . . . . . | 59,059 | Government-Independent |
| *Eleftherotypia* . . . . . . . . . . . . . . . | 56,346 | Government |
| *Vradini* . . . . . . . . . . . . . . . . . . | 38,266 | Opposition |
| *Eleftheros Typos* . . . . . . . . . . . . . | 30,188 | Independent |
| *Messimvrini* . . . . . . . . . . . . . | 23,426 | Opposition |
| *Estia* . . . . . . . . . . . . . . . . . . | 6,900 | Extreme right |
| *Eleftheri Ora* . . . . . . . . . . . . . . . | 3,790 | Junta |
| Total afternoon press . . . . . . . . | 504,068 | |
| **Morning press** | | |
| *Rizospastis* . . . . . . . . . . . . . . . . . | 27,060 | Communist |
| *Akropolis* . . . . . . . . . . . . . . . . . . | 20,676 | Opposition |
| *Kathimerini* . . . . . . . . . . . . . . | 19,049 | Independent |
| *To Vima* . . . . . . . . . . . . . . . . . . | 16,490 | Government |
| *Athens News* . . . . . . . . . . . . . . . | 7,150 | Independent |
| *Avghi* . . . . . . . . . . . . . . . . . . . | 4,577 | Eurocommunist |
| Total morning press . . . . . . . . . | 95,002 | |
| TOTAL . . . . . . . . . . . . . . . . . . . . | 599,070 | |

°A majority of government newspapers are liberal, and a majority of opposition newspapers are conservative.
Source: Based on information from *Athens News*, Athens, December 21, 1984, 7.

## Table 6. Central Government Budget, 1980-85
### (in millions of drachmas)[1]

| | 1980 | 1981 | 1982 | 1983[2] | 1984[2] | 1985[3] |
|---|---|---|---|---|---|---|
| **Expenditure** | | | | | | |
| Ordinary budget | | | | | | |
| Personnel outlays | 158.4 | 198.4 | 264.6 | 323.1 | 442.8 | 552.1 |
| Servicing of public debt | 45.5 | 56.1 | 64.5 | 101.2 | 172.0 | 251.0 |
| Subsidies, transfers, and grants[4] | 65.2 | 110.8 | 146.3 | 209.0 | 272.8 | 321.0 |
| Payments to EC[5] | 0.0 | 9.2 | 18.6 | 25.0 | 27.7 | 36.8 |
| Other | 103.1 | 148.5 | 175.4 | 225.1 | 267.7 | 348.2 |
| Total ordinary budget | 372.2 | 523.0 | 669.4 | 883.4 | 1,183.0 | 1,509.1 |
| Investment budget | 64.3 | 97.1 | 117.8 | 169.2 | 217.4 | 275.0 |
| Total expenditure | 436.5 | 620.1 | 787.2 | 1,052.6 | 1,400.4 | 1,784.1 |
| **Revenue** | | | | | | |
| Direct taxes | 104.4 | 123.7 | 175.0 | 200.9 | 263.2 | 378.4 |
| Indirect taxes | 220.8 | 265.3 | 374.5 | 477.9 | 592.3 | 746.6 |
| Receipts from EC | 0.0 | 1.4 | 3.0 | 3.6 | 7.3 | 10.0 |
| Investment budget revenues[6] | 0.9 | 7.0 | 5.8 | 8.1 | 12.1 | 20.6 |
| Other | 33.0 | 32.2 | 36.7 | 51.0 | 151.6 | 174.4 |
| Total revenue | 359.1 | 429.6 | 595.0 | 741.5 | 1,026.5 | 1,330.0 |

*Table 6.—Continued.*

| | 1980 | 1981 | 1982 | 1983[2] | 1984[2] | 1985[3] |
|---|---|---|---|---|---|---|
| **Financing** | | | | | | |
| Domestic borrowing | 50.7 | 145.1 | 141.4 | 229.4 | n.a. | n.a. |
| Foreign loans | 26.0 | 42.9 | 47.6 | 77.9 | n.a. | n.a. |
| NATO contribution[7] | 0.6 | 2.4 | 3.1 | 3.7 | n.a. | n.a. |
| Transfers from abroad | 0.1 | 0.1 | 0.1 | 0.1 | n.a. | n.a. |
| Total financing | 77.4 | 190.5 | 192.2 | 311.1 | n.a. | n.a. |

n.a.—not available.
[1]For value of the drachma—see Glossary.
[2]Provisional data.
[3]Official forecast.
[4]Includes export subsidies and war pensions. As of 1983 it also included operational deficits in the Consumer Goods Account, the Special Accounts for Agricultural Products and Supplies, and the Special Account of Guarantees of Agricultural Products.
[5]EC—European Communities.
[6]From 1981 on it included grants from the Regional Development Fund of the European Economic Community.
[7]NATO—North Atlantic Treaty Organization.
Source: Based on information from Bank of Greece, *Monthly Statistical Bulletin,* Athens, 49, No. 7, July 1984, 55; and Joint Publications Research Service, "1985 Budget Presented to Chamber of Deputies," *I Kathimerini,* Athens, November 29, 1984.

Table 7. *Gross National Product by Sector, Selected Years, 1970-83*
(in billions of drachmas at 1970 constant prices)*

| Sector | 1970 | 1980 | 1981 | 1982 | 1983 | Percentage 1970 | Percentage 1983 |
|---|---|---|---|---|---|---|---|
| **Gross domestic product** | | | | | | | |
| Agriculture, forestry, and fishing | 46.9 | 60.5 | 59.5 | 61.4 | 57.7 | 17.8 | 13.8 |
| Mining and quarrying | 3.5 | 6.2 | 5.7 | 5.7 | 5.6 | 1.3 | 1.3 |
| Manufacturing | 49.3 | 89.1 | 88.1 | 84.4 | 84.0 | 18.7 | 20.0 |
| Construction | 23.0 | 26.4 | 24.2 | 22.3 | 23.3 | 8.8 | 5.5 |
| Electricity, gas, and water | 5.2 | 13.7 | 14.1 | 14.6 | 15.3 | 2.0 | 3.7 |
| Transportation and communications | 19.8 | 39.9 | 41.3 | 41.2 | 42.0 | 7.5 | 10.0 |
| Public administration and defense | 22.4 | 36.7 | 38.1 | 39.1 } | 58.7 | 13.0 | 14.0 |
| Health and educational services | 11.8 | 17.5 | 17.8 | 18.3 } | | | |
| Other services | 75.7 | 127.5 | 127.7 | 129.4 | 130.9 | 28.8 | 31.1 |
| Gross domestic product | 257.6 | 417.5 | 416.5 | 416.4 | 417.5 | 97.9 | 99.4 |
| Net income payments from the rest of the world | 5.5 | 10.4 | 8.6 | 6.4 | 2.5 | 2.1 | 0.6 |
| GROSS NATIONAL PRODUCT | 263.1 | 427.9 | 425.1 | 422.8 | 420.0 | 100.0 | 100.0 |

*For value of the drachma—see Glossary.

Source: Based on information from Greece, National Statistical Service, *Statistical Yearbook of Greece, 1975*, Athens, 1975, 430; and Bank of Greece, *Monthly Statistical Bulletin*, Athens, 49, No. 7, July 1984, 83.

Table 8.  *Production of Selected Agricultural Products,*
*Selected Years, 1975-84*
(in thousands of tons)

| Product | 1975 | 1980 | 1981 | 1982 | 1983 | 1984 |
|---|---|---|---|---|---|---|
| **Grains** | | | | | | |
| Wheat (soft) . . . . . . . . . . . . . . | 2,120 | 2,274 | 2,119 | 2,236 | 1,477 | 1,734 |
| Barley . . . . . . . . . . . . . . . . . | 916 | 949 | 768 | 852 | 572 | 831 |
| Corn . . . . . . . . . . . . . . . . . . | 489 | 1,233 | 1,336 | 1,449 | 1,653 | 1,992 |
| | | | | | | |
| **Industrial crops** | | | | | | |
| Tobacco . . . . . . . . . . . . . . . | 119 | 116 | 123 | 132 | 110 | 137 |
| Cotton . . . . . . . . . . . . . . . | 365 | 356 | 365 | 316 | 403 | 436 |
| Sugar beets . . . . . . . . . . . . | 2,666 | 1,440 | 2,600 | 2,548 | 2,500 | 1,700 |
| | | | | | | |
| **Other crops** | | | | | | |
| Tomatoes . . . . . . . . . . . . . . | 1,635 | 1,684 | 1,885 | 1,872 | 1,893 | 2,249 |
| Raisins and currants . . . . . . . . | 177 | 121 | 159 | 146 | 180 | 155 |
| Oranges and lemons . . . . . . . . | 762 | 688 | 940 | 917 | 879 | 976 |
| Peaches . . . . . . . . . . . . . . . . | 329 | 398 | 472 | 475 | 484 | 520 |
| Olive oil . . . . . . . . . . . . . . . | 200 | 330 | 230 | 324 | 220 | 185 |
| | | | | | | |
| **Livestock** | | | | | | |
| Mutton, lamb, and goat . . . . . . | 115 | 120 | 119 | 121 | 121 | 122 |
| Beef . . . . . . . . . . . . . . . . . . | 127 | 100 | 94 | 90 | 84 | 85 |
| Pork . . . . . . . . . . . . . . . . . . | 103 | 144 | 154 | 154 | 154 | 149 |
| Poultry . . . . . . . . . . . . . . . . | 117 | 144 | 146 | 156 | 153 | 152 |
| Milk . . . . . . . . . . . . . . . . . . | 1,670 | 1,699 | 1,721 | 1,700 | 1,687 | 1,688 |
| Eggs . . . . . . . . . . . . . . . . . | 61 | 120 | 126 | 125 | 126 | 123 |

Source: Based on information from United States, Embassy in Athens, Agricultural Attaché, *Agricultural Situation Report: Greece*, Washington, March 1985, 19-20; United States, Embassy in Athens, Agricultural Attaché, *Agricultural Situation Report: Greece*, Washington, February 1983, 32; and United States, Department of Agriculture, Economic Research Service, *Selected Agricultural Statistics on Greece, 1965-77*, Washington, January 1982, entire issue.

Table 9. *Exports by Commodity, Selected Years, 1960-83*
(in millions of United States dollars)

| Commodity | 1980 | 1981 | 1982 | 1983 | 1960 | 1970 | 1983 |
|---|---|---|---|---|---|---|---|
| | | | | | | Percentage | |
| Food and beverages | | | | | | | |
| Fresh fruit and fruit products | 364 | 413 | 350 | 311 | --- | --- | --- |
| Olives and olive oil | 96 | 86 | 119 | 172 | --- | --- | --- |
| Other | 467 | 406 | 333 | 346 | --- | --- | --- |
| Total food and beverages | 927 | 905 | 802 | 829 | 27.6 | 28.6 | 20.2 |
| Tobacco | 194 | 229 | 223 | 183 | 34.8 | 16.6 | 4.4 |
| Raw materials and semifinished products | 126 | 129 | 111 | 138 | 20.2 | 9.3 | 3.4 |
| Minerals and ores | 280 | 291 | 236 | 205 | 8.6 | 7.5 | 5.0 |
| Petroleum products | 248 | 783 | 648 | 725 | 0.0 | 0.5 | 17.7 |

*Table 9.—Continued.*

| Commodity | 1980 | 1981 | 1982 | 1983 | Percentage | | |
| --- | --- | --- | --- | --- | --- | --- | --- |
| | | | | | 1960 | 1970 | 1983 |
| Manufactures | | | | | | | |
| Textiles | 785 | 749 | 707 | 699 | --- | --- | --- |
| Cement | 249 | 274 | 265 | 210 | --- | --- | --- |
| Metals and metal articles | 265 | 276 | 222 | 197 | --- | --- | --- |
| Aluminum and alumina | 164 | 187 | 130 | 138 | --- | --- | --- |
| Chemicals and pharmaceuticals | 137 | 161 | 124 | 128 | --- | --- | --- |
| Other | 650 | 727 | 563 | 533 | --- | --- | --- |
| Total manufactures | 2,250 | 2,374 | 2,011 | 1,905 | 3.7 | 36.6 | 46.4 |
| Other | 69 | 60 | 110 | 120 | 5.1 | 0.9 | 2.9 |
| TOTAL | 4,094 | 4,771 | 4,141 | 4,105 | 100.0 | 100.0 | 100.0 |

---means included in total figure for respective category.

Source: Based on information from Bank of Greece, *Monthly Statistical Bulletin*, Athens, 49, No. 7, July 1984, 66-67; and Commercial Bank of Greece, "Development of the Greek Economy since Association with the EEC," *Economic Bulletin*, Athens, No. 106, October-December 1980, 15.

Table 10. *Imports by Commodity, Selected Years, 1960-83*
(in millions of United States dollars)

| Commodity | 1980 | 1981 | 1982 | 1983 | 1960 | 1970 | 1983 |
|---|---|---|---|---|---|---|---|
| | | | | | | Percentage | |
| **Food and beverages** | | | | | | | |
| Meat and live animals | 396 | 427 | 510 | 470 | --- | --- | --- |
| Dairy products | 163 | 214 | 231 | 237 | --- | --- | --- |
| Other | 649 | 647 | 581 | 481 | --- | --- | --- |
| Total food and beverages | 1,208 | 1,288 | 1,322 | 1,188 | 18.8 | 13.1 | 12.5 |
| **Raw materials** | 1,959 | 1,623 | 1,380 | 1,396 | 26.5 | 21.6 | 14.7 |
| **Petroleum products** | 2,982 | 3,686 | 2,778 | 2,648 | 9.6 | 6.9 | 27.9 |
| **Capital goods** | | | | | | | |
| Machinery | 1,654 | 1,548 | 1,399 | 1,261 | --- | --- | --- |
| Transport equipment | 630 | 544 | 512 | 505 | --- | --- | --- |
| Electrical equipment | 161 | 147 | 154 | 138 | --- | --- | --- |
| Total capital goods | 2,445 | 2,239 | 2,065 | 1,904 | 15.7 | 30.0 | 20.1 |

*Table 10.—Continued.*

| Commodity | 1980 | 1981 | 1982 | 1983 | Percentage | | |
|---|---|---|---|---|---|---|---|
| | | | | | 1960 | 1970 | 1983 |
| **Manufactured consumer goods** | | | | | | | |
| Intermediate[1] .............. | 301 | 302 | 282 | 291 | -- | -- | -- |
| Basic[2] ................... | 851 | 923 | 829 | 769 | -- | -- | -- |
| Nonbasic[3] ................ | 1,100 | 1,357 | 1,371 | 1,260 | | | |
| Total manufactured consumer goods ... | 2,252 | 2,582 | 2,482 | 2,320 | 29.3 | 27.6 | 24.4 |
| Freight ................... | 57 | 50 | 41 | 35 | 0.1 | 0.8 | 0.4 |
| TOTAL ............. | 10,903 | 11,468 | 10,068 | 9,491 | 100.0 | 100.0 | 100.0 |

---means included in total figure for respective category.

[1]Includes threads, yarns, metals, plastics, and synthetic materials.

[2]Includes motor vehicle articles, paper products, metal manufactures, medical and pharmaceutical products, scientific instruments, paints, and dyes.

[3]Includes most consumer goods, such as textiles, electrical appliances, passenger vehicles, and household and personal articles.

Source: Based on information from Bank of Greece, *Monthly Statistical Bulletin*, Athens, 49, No. 7, July 1984, 68-71; and Commercial Bank of Greece, "Development of the Greek Economy Since Association with the EEC," *Economic Bulletin*, Athens, No. 106, October-December 1980, 16.

Table 11.   *Geographical Distribution of Trade, Selected Years, 1970-83*
(in percentage)

| Area | Imports | | | | Exports | | | |
|---|---|---|---|---|---|---|---|---|
| | 1970 | 1980 | 1981 | 1983 | 1970 | 1980 | 1981 | 1983 |
| EEC[1] | | | | | | | | |
| West Germany | 18.5 | 13.9 | 19.6 | 17.3 | 20.2 | 17.9 | 18.2 | 20.1 |
| Italy | 8.4 | 8.2 | 9.7 | 8.9 | 10.0 | 9.7 | 7.1 | 13.5 |
| Other | 22.9 | 17.6 | 20.7 | 21.8 | 21.9 | 20.0 | 18.0 | 18.9 |
| Total EEC | 49.8 | 39.7 | 50.0 | 48.0 | 52.1 | 47.6 | 43.3 | 52.5 |
| EFTA[2] | 8.4 | 6.1 | 5.2 | 4.9 | 4.4 | 2.3 | 2.3 | 2.6 |
| Eastern Europe | | | | | | | | |
| Soviet Union | 1.9 | 1.4 | 3.7 | 2.6 | 5.4 | 1.8 | 1.7 | 3.2 |
| Other | 3.3 | 4.5 | 3.0 | 2.6 | 11.2 | 8.9 | 6.6 | 4.2 |
| Total Eastern Europe | 5.2 | 5.9 | 6.7 | 5.2 | 16.6 | 10.7 | 8.3 | 7.4 |
| Other Europe | 3.9 | 2.5 | 1.5 | 1.8 | 8.2 | 2.9 | 2.7 | 2.5 |
| Asia and Middle East | | | | | | | | |
| Saudi Arabia | 0.4 | 7.4 | 5.5 | 12.3 | 0.3 | 5.5 | 5.6 | 7.3 |
| Japan | 12.7 | 11.1 | 4.8 | 6.7 | 1.3 | 0.4 | 0.6 | 0.6 |
| Other | 4.1 | 3.9 | 4.6 | 8.4 | 4.4 | 13.0 | 14.3 | 9.3 |
| Total Asia and Middle East | 17.2 | 22.4 | 14.9 | 27.4 | 6.0 | 18.9 | 20.5 | 17.2 |

*Table 11.—Continued.*

| Area | Imports | | | | Exports | | | |
|---|---|---|---|---|---|---|---|---|
| | 1970 | 1980 | 1981 | 1983 | 1970 | 1980 | 1981 | 1983 |
| Western Hemisphere | | | | | | | | |
| United States | 5.9 | 4.6 | 5.1 | 3.7 | 7.5 | 5.7 | 8.7 | 6.3 |
| Other | 4.4 | 3.2 | 2.2 | 1.8 | 1.0 | 0.8 | 0.9 | 0.5 |
| Total Western Hemisphere | 10.3 | 7.8 | 7.3 | 5.5 | 8.5 | 6.5 | 9.6 | 6.8 |
| Africa | 3.5 | 14.9 | 13.8 | 6.6 | 3.3 | 10.5 | 12.7 | 10.4 |
| Oceania and other | 1.7 | 0.7 | 0.6 | 0.6 | 0.9 | 0.6 | 0.6 | 0.6 |
| TOTAL | 100.0 | 100.0 | 100.0 | 100.0 | 100.0 | 100.0 | 100.0 | 100.0 |

[1]European Economic Community. Britain, Denmark, and Ireland are included in the EEC category, although they did not become members until 1973.

[2]European Free Trade Association. Members include Austria, Finland, Iceland, Norway, Portugal, Sweden, and Switzerland.

Table 12. *Balance of Payments: Settlements Basis, 1979-83*
(in millions of United States dollars)

| | 1979 | 1980 | 1981 | 1982 | 1983 |
|---|---|---|---|---|---|
| Imports, c.i.f.[1] . . . . . . . . . . | 10,110 | 10,903 | 11,468 | 10,068 | 9,491 |
| Exports, f.o.b.[2] . . . . . . . . . | 3,932 | 4,094 | 4,771 | 4,141 | 4,105 |
| Trade balance . . . . . . . . | −6,178 | −6,809 | −6,697 | −5,927 | −5,386 |
| Services and transfers | | | | | |
| Receipts | | | | | |
| Tourism . . . . . . . . . . | 1,662 | 1,733 | 1,881 | 1,527 | 1,176 |
| Shipping . . . . . . . . . . | 1,519 | 1,816 | 1,826 | 1,656 | 1,309 |
| Emigrant remittances . . | 1,168 | 1,083 | 1,080 | 1,043 | 935 |
| EEC subsidies[3] . . . . . . | 0 | 0 | 148 | 550 | 834 |
| Other . . . . . . . . . . . . | 1,314 | 1,527 | 1,547 | 1,322 | 1,275 |
| Total receipts . . . . . . | 5,663 | 6,159 | 6,482 | 6,098 | 5,529 |
| Less payments . . . . . . . | −1,367 | −1,566 | −2,206 | −2,056 | −2,019 |
| Total services and transfers . . . . . . | 4,296 | 4,593 | 4,276 | 4,042 | 3,510 |
| Current account balance . . . | −1,882 | −2,216 | −2,421 | −1,885 | −1,876 |
| Long-term capital (net) | | | | | |
| Private | | | | | |
| Entrepreneurial[4] . . . . . | 329 | 444 | 317 | 208 | 181 |
| Real estate . . . . . . . . | 592 | 599 | 488 | 399 | 423 |
| Other . . . . . . . . . . . . | 111 | 65 | 13 | −46 | 13 |
| Total private . . . . . . . | 1,032 | 1,108 | 818 | 561 | 617 |
| Public . . . . . . . . . . . . . | 118 | 166 | 340 | 323 | 958 |
| Total long-term capital (net) . . . . . . . . . . . . | 1,150 | 1,274 | 1,158 | 884 | 1,575 |
| Basic balance . . . . . . . . | −732 | −942 | −1,263 | −1,001 | −301 |
| Short-term suppliers' credits . . . . . . . . . . . | 116 | 262 | 5 | −59 | 17 |
| Banks and financial institutions . . . . . . . . . | 148 | 159 | 363 | 147 | 299 |
| Errors and omissions . . . . . . | 495 | 41 | 364 | −40 | −357 |
| Balance on official settlements . . . . . . . . . | 27 | −480 | −531 | −953 | −342 |

[1]Cost, insurance, and freight.
[2]Free on board.
[3]EEC—European Economic Community.
[4]Not possible to break down this inflow into direct investment and working capital.
Source: Based on information from Bank of Greece, *Monthly Statistical Bulletin*,
    Athens, 49, No. 7, July 1984, 62-73; and Organisation for Economic Co-
    operation and Development, *Greece, 1983-84*, Paris, November 1983, 20.

Table 13.  *Parliamentary Election Results, 1974-85*

| Party | 1974 | | 1977 | | 1981 | | 1985[1] | |
|---|---|---|---|---|---|---|---|---|
| | Percentage of Votes | Number of Seats | Percentage of Votes | Number of Seats | Percentage of Votes | Number of Seats | Percentage of Votes | Number of Seats |
| Panhellenic Socialist Movement | 13.6 | 12 | 25.3 | 93 | 48.1 | 172 | 45.8 | 161 |
| New Democracy | 54.4 | 220 | 41.7 | 172 | 35.9 | 115 | 40.9 | 126 |
| Communist Party of Greece-Exterior[2] | n.a. | 5 | 9.4 | 11 | 10.9 | 13 | 9.9 | 12 |
| Communist Party of Greece-Interior[2] | n.a. | 2 | n.a. | 0 | 1.4 | 0 | 1.8 | 1 |
| United Democratic Left[2] | n.a. | 1 | n.a. | --- | --- | --- | --- | --- |
| United Left[2] | 9.5[3] | 8[3] | --- | --- | --- | --- | --- | --- |
| Coalition of the Left[4] | --- | --- | 2.7 | 2 | ° | ° | ? | ? |
| National Front[5] | 1.1 | 0 | 6.8 | 5 | 0.4 | 0 | ? | ? |
| Union of the Democratic Center[6] | 20.4 | 60 | 12.0 | 15 | ? | ? | ? | ? |
| New Liberals[7] | ? | ? | 1.1 | 2 | | | | |

## Table 13.—Continued.

| Party | 1974 Percentage of Votes | 1974 Number of Seats | 1977 Percentage of Votes | 1977 Number of Seats | 1981 Percentage of Votes | 1981 Number of Seats | 1985[1] Percentage of Votes | 1985[1] Number of Seats |
|---|---|---|---|---|---|---|---|---|
| Party of Democratic Socialism | -- | -- | -- | -- | 0.7 | 0 | ? | ? |
| Progressive Party | -- | -- | -- | -- | 1.7 | 0 | ? | ? |
| Liberal Party | -- | -- | -- | -- | 0.4 | 0 | 0.2 | 0 |
| National Political Union[8] | -- | -- | -- | -- | -- | -- | 0.6 | 0 |
| Militant Socialist Party[8] | -- | -- | -- | -- | -- | -- | 0.2 | 0 |
| Independents and Others | 1.0 | 0 | 0.8 | 0 | 0.6 | 0 | 0.6 | 0 |
| TOTAL | 100.0 | 300 | 100.5[9] | 300 | 100.1[9] | 300 | 100.0 | 300 |

n.a.—Breakdown not available.
--—Did not exist.
°—Did not contest.
?—Not clear whether this party existed and contested under different name.

[1]Elections contested by 16 parties and independents; only four of the parties won one or more seats. Information on the parties not represented in parliament not readily available as of mid-June 1985.

[2]Contested under "United Left," an electoral alliance.

[3]Figure includes figures for Communist Party of Greece–Exterior, Communist Party of Greece–Interior, and United Democratic Left.

[4]Contested under "Coalition of the Left," an electoral alliance including the Communist Party of Greece–Interior and four other minor left-wing groups.

[5]Extreme right-wing successor to National Democratic Union (1974).

[6]Called the Center Union–New Forces in the mid-1970s.

[7]Information not available on this party.

[8]Information on this party before 1980 not available.

[9]Figures do not add to total because of rounding.

# Appendix B

## The European Communities

The complex and ever changing institutions that make up the European Communities (EC—also commonly called the European Community) form more than a framework for free trade and economic cooperation. The signatories to the treaties governing the community have agreed in principle to integrate their economies and ultimately to form a political union. Frequent strong opposition from both the public and concerned politicians does not detract from the founders' intentions, born in the aftermath of World War II, to create a peaceful union of formerly hostile states.

The EC is actually a merger of three separate communities. The first, the European Coal and Steel Community (ECSC), was established by a treaty signed in Paris on April 18, 1951. After several false starts to expand the community, the original members agreed to form the European Economic Community (EEC, or Common Market) and the European Atomic Energy Community (EURATOM) by treaties signed in Rome on March 25, 1957. The EEC and EURATOM modeled their governing institutions on those of the ECSC. Another treaty, signed in Brussels on April 8, 1965, planned the merger of the institutions governing all three communities, which was achieved about two years later.

The governing bodies of the EC act under guidelines from any of the community treaties as necessary. The provisions of the EEC treaty are the broadest of the three treaties: the elimination of all barriers to trade and to the movement of persons, services, and capital; the development of common policies on trade, agriculture, and transportation; the regulation of fair business practices; the harmonization of economic policies and laws; the creation of social development funds and investment banks; and the allocation of special assistance to an association of former colonies and dependencies affiliated with the member states. Those of the ECSC and EURATOM treaties are similar but limited to their respective industries.

Belgium, France, Italy, Luxembourg, the Netherlands,

and the Federal Republic of Germany (West Germany) are original members of the community. Britain, Denmark, and Ireland joined on January 1, 1973; Greece became a member on January 1, 1981. Portugal and Spain applied for membership in 1977, and after years of tortuous negotiations regarding their accession, treaties were signed in June 1985 to allow their entry on January 1, 1986.

The leading institutions of the EC are the Council of Ministers of the European Communities and the Commission of the European Communities, which are both headquartered in Brussels (see fig. A, this Appendix). The council tends to represent the interests of the individual member states; the commission represents those of the EC as a body. In theory, the fields of competence for each organization are separate; in practice, they overlap and blur. Generally, the council makes all the major decisions, acting on advice from the commission, which proposes and implements policy.

The council makes decisions by qualified majority or unanimous vote. For a qualified majority the votes are weighted roughly by population: Britain, France, Italy, and West Germany receive 10 votes each; Belgium, Greece, and the Netherlands, five each; Denmark and Ireland, three each; and Luxembourg, two. Unless the council acts on a proposal from the commission, it must have the approval of no fewer than six members for a qualified majority. An agreement reached in 1966 known as the Luxembourg Compromise requires unanimity, however, when any one country declares a decision to be of vital importance. Although the agreement is not part of an EC treaty document, it has been breached only rarely, as, for example, in May 1982, when Britain tried to veto a vote on agricultural policy to gain leverage in other budgetary negotiations. Unanimity is preferred for all major decisions. Several initiatives have been taken to make qualified majority voting the norm for all council actions. Each member appoints a permanent representative to the council to act as ambassador. The actual representative at meetings varies, however, but is usually a cabinet minister familiar with the issues under discussion. The presidency of the council rotates every six months. The council is assisted by a secretariat, which had some 1,800 staff members in 1984.

The commission has two representatives each from Britain, Italy, and West Germany and one representative from each of the other member states. They are appointed for four-year terms. In 1984 some 12,600 permanent and 650 tempo-

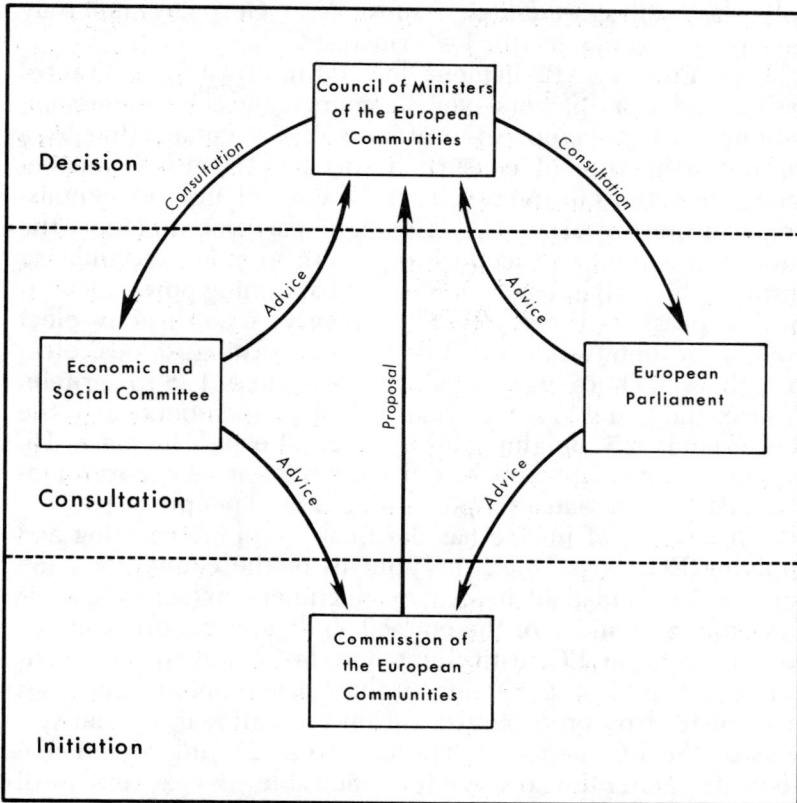

Source: Based on information from Emile Noël, *Working Together: The Institutions of the European Community*, Luxembourg, 1985, 6.

*Figure A.   The European Communities' Decisionmaking Process, 1985*

rary staff members, organized into 20 specialized directorates-general, aided the commission in performing its duties.

   Since 1974 it has become customary for the heads of state or government of the members of the EC to meet three times a year in a summit conference called the European Council. Although there is no mention of this organization in any EC treaty document, some legal experts believe it to be the supreme manifestation of the Council of Ministers of the European Communities. The European Council has become an important forum for developing common approaches to foreign policy as well as economic issues. West Germany and Italy have proposed that its role be formalized.

The European Parliament, located in Strasbourg, France, has only advisory powers over the council and the commission, although it may remove the officers of the commission by a three-fourths vote of censure. It does not legislate but responds to actions or queries from the council and the commission and must approve the budget. If parliament rejects the budget, a complex procedure of month-to-month accounting ensues, which gives parliament some bargaining power. Parliament represents the European citizenry, who directly elect their representatives every five years according to local electoral laws. (There was an election in June 1984.) Britain, France, Italy, and West Germany elect 81 members each; the Netherlands, 25; Belgium and Greece, 24 each; Denmark, 16; Ireland, 15; and Luxembourg, 6, for a total of 434 representatives. Parliament had a support staff of 2,950 people in 1984.

The Court of Justice has the final say in interpreting and applying EC "laws," i.e., the policies of the council and the commission, and may judge any document or action except nonbinding opinions of the council. Individuals, corporations, governments, or EC institutions may bring suit to the court. The court may also render preliminary opinions on cases brought to it by other courts within the national judicial systems of the EC members. The court has 11 judges and five advocates-general who serve for renewable six-year terms. All members of the court must be chosen by unanimous decision of the council. In 1984 the court had 480 support staff members.

The Court of Auditors controls and monitors all budgetary revenues and expenditures of the EC. The court consists of 10 members selected by the council for six-year terms. In 1984 the court had a staff of 300 people.

From time to time, proposals from the council or the commission are discussed with the Economic and Social Committee, which is made up of about 150 representatives from employers' groups, trade unions, and other interest groups. Other important EC institutions include the European Investment Bank, agricultural advisory committees set up for individual commodities and markets, the European Social Fund, the European Agricultural Fund, and various other funds.

The plethora of organizations dealing with agricultural problems demonstrates the central importance of this sector to the EC. Most of the EC budget is geared toward applying the

Common Agricultural Policy (CAP), which has stirred considerable debate in the 1980s. The CAP was initially successful in supporting the prices of farm products but by the early 1980s had become a drain on the EC budget. Britain, whose agricultural work force numbers less than one-third of the EC average, has been especially vigorous in demanding a reduction in both its budgetary contribution and CAP subsidies.

Another set of issues facing the EC concerned institutional reform. In June 1984 an ad hoc committee on institutional affairs was created to consider, among other proposals, the strengthening of the commission's powers, the more frequent use of the qualified majority in the council, and the expansion of parliament's responsibilities. Parliament has drafted the Treaty of European Union, which would broaden cooperation between the EC states and require the council to share its legislative powers with parliament. In 1985 it was trying to raise support for the treaty in the national parliaments of the member states. It was doubtful whether these efforts could persuade the council to relinquish any of its powers.

# The North Atlantic Treaty Organization

The North Atlantic Treaty Organization (NATO; also called the Atlantic Alliance) is a defensive alliance formed in 1949 to maintain Western military preparedness and to deter conflict with the Soviet Union and the member states of the Warsaw Pact. NATO is an association of Western nations joined together to preserve their security through mutual guarantees and collective self-defense, as recognized by Article 51 of the United Nations Charter. It is an intergovernmental, not a supranational, organization in which member states retain their full sovereignty and independence. The member states of NATO are Belgium, Britain, Canada, Denmark, France, the Federal Republic of Germany (West Germany), Greece, Iceland, Italy, Luxembourg, the Netherlands, Norway, Portugal, Spain, Turkey, and the United States.

The political task of NATO is to provide for periodic consultation on common political problems and also to give direction to the military aspects of the alliance. The military task of NATO in peacetime is to establish joint defense plans and necessary infrastructures and to sponsor joint training exercises among its members. In peacetime, national forces receive orders from their own national authorities; in war, all forces committed to NATO would be under the direction of the unified NATO command structure.

The aim of the alliance is to guarantee the security of its members and to foster stable international relations. It seeks to achieve these objectives through a policy based on principles of defense and détente. The alliance maintains a strong defense in order to ensure credible deterrence. At the same time, NATO seeks to establish a constructive East-West relationship through dialogue and mutually advantageous cooperation. This includes efforts to achieve significant, equitable, and verifiable nuclear arms reductions.

Alliance decisions reflect the collective perceptions of the member states and are reached through consultation and consensus. The major forum for consultation within the alliance is

the North Atlantic Council (NAC), which is composed of ministerial representatives of the 16 member nations. The NAC
meets twice each year, and the members are represented by
their ministers of foreign affairs. The NAC occasionally meets
at the head of state level as well (see fig. A, this Appendix).

The Defense Planning Committee (DPC) is composed of
representatives of the member countries that actively participate in NATO's integrated military structure and deals specifically with defense matters. At the ministerial level member
nations are represented by their ministers of defense. (France
withdrew from military participation in the alliance in 1966;
Iceland has no military forces.) The secretary general of NATO
presides over meetings of the DPC and the NAC.

Nuclear matters are discussed by the Nuclear Planning
Group (NPG). The NPG meets twice each year at the level of
ministers of defense and as required at the permanent representative level.

The permanent representatives of member countries (am-
bassadors) are supported by delegations at NATO headquarters in Everre, a suburb of Brussels. NATO military headquarters are located near Mons in southwest Belgium.

The Military Committee is the highest military authority
of the alliance and is composed of the chiefs of staff of all
member nations but France and Iceland. The chiefs of staff
meet at least twice each year. To allow the Military Committee
to function continuously, each member also has a permanent
military representative. The Military Committee is responsible
for recommendations to the NAC and the DPC on actions
necessary for the common defense of the NATO area and for
supplying guidance on military matters to the major NATO
commanders.

The strategic area covered by the alliance is divided
among three commands: Allied Command Europe (ACE), Allied Command Atlantic (ACLANT), and Allied Command
Channel (ACCHAN). The commanders of these commands
are, respectively, Supreme Allied Commander Europe
(SACEUR), Supreme Allied Commander Atlantic (SACLANT),
and Commander in Chief Channel (CINCHAN). ACE covers
the area extending from the North Cape to the Mediterranean
Sea and from the Atlantic Ocean to the eastern border of Turkey, excluding Britain and Portugal; the defense of this area
falls under several NATO commands. ACLANT covers approximately 31 million square kilometers of the Atlantic Ocean.
This area extends from the North Pole to the Tropic of Cancer

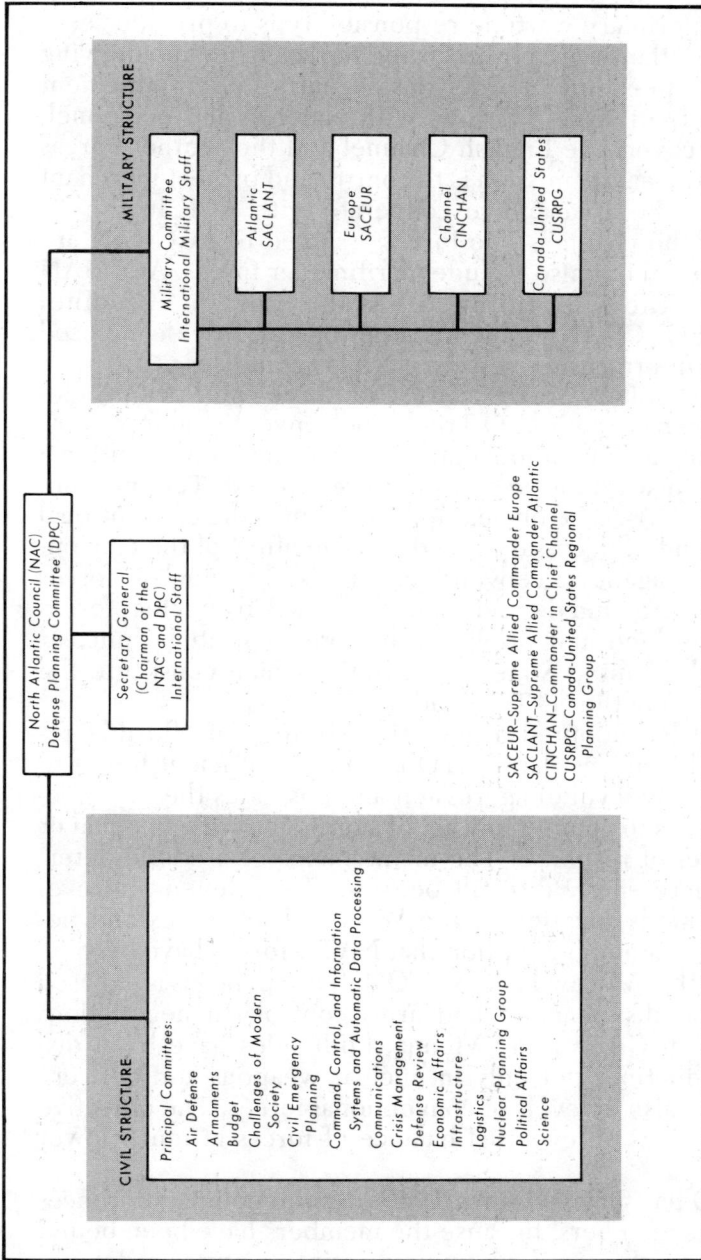

MILITARY STRUCTURE

Military Committee
International Military Staff

Atlantic
SACLANT

Europe
SACEUR

Channel
CINCHAN

Canada-United States
CUSRPG

North Atlantic Council (NAC)
Defense Planning Committee (DPC)

Secretary General
(Chairman of the
NAC and DPC)
International Staff

CIVIL STRUCTURE

Principal Committees:

Air Defense
Armaments
Budget
Challenges of Modern
  Society
Civil Emergency
  Planning
Command, Control, and Information
Systems and Automatic Data Processing
Communications
Crisis Management
Defense Review
Economic Affairs
Infrastructure
Logistics
Nuclear Planning Group
Political Affairs
Science

SACEUR—Supreme Allied Commander Europe
SACLANT—Supreme Allied Commander Atlantic
CINCHAN—Commander in Chief Channel
CUSRPG—Canada-United States Regional
  Planning Group

Source: Based on information from NATO Information Service, *NATO Handbook,* Brussels, 1983, 30-56; and NATO Information Service, *The North Atlantic Treaty Organisation: Facts and Figures,* Brussels, 1981, 89-112.

*Figure A.   Civil and Military Structure of North Atlantic Treaty Organization, 1984*

and from the waters of North America to the coasts of Europe and Africa, except for the English Channel and Britain. ACLANT's primary wartime responsibility is to provide security for the Atlantic area by guarding the sea lanes and denying their use to an enemy in order to safeguard the reinforcement and resupply of NATO Europe with matériel and personnel. ACCHAN covers the English Channel and the southern areas of the North Sea. Its mission is to control and protect merchant shipping in the area and to cooperate with ACE in the air defense of the channel. The forces assigned to ACCHAN are primarily naval but also include maritime air forces. ACCHAN includes the Standing Naval Force Channel (STANAVFORCHAN), which is a permanent force composed of mine countermeasure vessels of NATO countries.

NATO military forces consist of three interlocking elements, known as the NATO Triad. The conventional forces are able to resist a conventional attack and sustain a conventional defense in forward battle areas until reinforced. The intermediate- and short-range nuclear forces enhance the conventional deterrent and, if necessary, the defensive effort of the conventional forces against a conventional attack. The nuclear forces would also deter and defend against an attack by nuclear forces of the same kind and provide a linkage to strategic nuclear forces of the United States and Britain, which constitute the third element of the NATO Triad.

NATO has adopted a defensive strategy of "flexible response." This means that NATO maintains sufficient forces to respond to any level of aggression and possesses the full spectrum of forces to counter any act of aggression with an equal or higher level of response. The maintenance of credible deterrence is increasingly difficult because of continued improvement and modernization of the Warsaw Pact forces and because of a common perception that NATO forces have become inferior to the Warsaw Pact. NATO defense policy is also based on eventual disarmament and arms control. In negotiations conducted in Geneva and Vienna, both sides have been discussing reductions not only in nuclear weapons and delivery systems but also in levels of conventional forces. The objective of these talks is an eventual balance of forces at much lower levels.

NATO has survived since 1949, despite policy differences between its members, because the members have been bound by common values and a common desire to unite in defense against a possible military attack by Warsaw Pact forces. Recognizing the political and economic constraints facing West European governments, they have nevertheless made progress in areas considered to be contentious in the early 1980s: sharing the NATO burden (maintaining equivalent levels of financial support), coordinating sanctions against the Soviet Union, and making common policies on problems outside the NATO area.

At least four previous controversies have presented greater cause for alarm than the issues facing the alliance in the 1980s: arguments over the European Defense Community (1950-54), American anger over the Suez invasion of 1956, French withdrawal from NATO military activities in 1966, and European concern about American involvement in Vietnam from 1965 to 1975. In addition, the alliance has been torn by debates over the Multilateral Force and Greek-Turkish conflicts over Cyprus.

Difficulties in the mid-1980s reflected the different attitudes the allies had toward Soviet behavior, problems outside the area, international economic difficulties, and defense doctrine and responsibilities. NATO has faced internal tensions created by the antinuclear movement, continued Greek-Turkish disputes, and a perceived growth in Eurocommunism. Many of these controversies have been magnified because of Western Europe's growing self-confidence and willingness to express openly doubts about American policies.

NATO's formal mandate does not encompass the defense of its members' vital interests if they lie outside the treaty area. Historically, the United States has resisted bringing the colonial and post-colonial commitments of Western Europe under the NATO umbrella. This long-held view has been modified as a result of the extraordinary impact of increased Western dependency on Persian Gulf oil, the revolution in Iran, and the Soviet invasion of Afghanistan. Despite their economic dependency, West Europeans have been less emotionally affected by these events than the United States and have resisted extending the NATO security area to include the Persian Gulf. Most policymakers agreed in the mid-1980s that a formal extension of NATO's area of coverage is unrealistic.

The economic problems confronting NATO members also exacerbate problems within the alliance. Divergent macroeconomic policies are a primary source of tension between the allies. High United States interest rates have been blamed by West Europeans for attracting short-term capital to the United States, driving up the dollar's exchange rate relative to the West European currencies and pulling up interest rates in Western Europe. West European governments, especially that of West Germany, have pointed out that the more expensive United States dollar increases the cost of buying United States military equipment as well as importing oil. Higher interest rates also increase government budget deficits in Western Europe and make it harder for those states to meet defense-spending commitments.

# Bibliography

## Chapter 1

Alivizatos, Nicos C. "The Greek Army in the Late Forties: Towards an Institutional Autonomy," *Journal of the Hellenic Diaspora*, 5, No. 3, Fall 1978, 37–45.

Anderson, Lynn R. "Analyses of Student Demonstrators Involved in the Overthrow of the Greek Military Dictatorship," *Journal of Applied Social Psychology*, 8, No. 3, 1978, 215–29.

Baerentzen, Lars. "Anglo-German Negotiations During the German Retreat from Greece in 1944," *Scandinavian Studies in Modern Greek* [Copenhagen], 4, 1980, 23–64.

_____. "The Demonstration in Syntagma Square on Sunday the 3rd of December, 1944," *Scandinavian Studies in Modern Greek* [Copenhagen], 2, 1978, 3–52.

_____. *The Liberation of Greece, 1944: National and International Aspects.* (Staff paper, series 3.) Gainesville: Center for Greek Studies, University of Florida, 1983.

Brown, James. "Military Intervention and the Politics of Greece." Pages 217–41 in Steffen W. Schmidt and Gerald A. Dorfman (eds.), *Soldiers in Politics.* Los Altos: Geron-X, 1974.

_____. "Modernity Confronted: The Ghost of Pericles in Post-War Greece," *Polity*, 8, No. 2, Winter 1975, 311–16.

_____. "Politicians and Bayonets: The Greek Political Scene," *Armed Forces and Society*, 5, No. 3, Spring 1979.

Burks, R.V. "Hellenic Time of Troubles," *Problems of Communism*, 33, No. 6, November-December 1984, 45–58.

Campbell, John, and Philip Sherrard. *Modern Greece.* New York: Praeger, 1968.

Campbell, John C. "Communist Strategies in the Mediterranean," *Problems of Communism*, 28, No. 3, May-June 1979, 1–17.

Catsiapis, Jean. *La Grèce: Dixième membre des Communautés européennes.* (Notes et Études Documentaires, Nos. 4593–4594.) Paris: La Documentation Française, 1980.

Clogg, Richard. "Greece: The End of Consensus Politics?" *World Today* [London], 34, No. 5, May 1978, 184–91.

_____. "The Ideology of the 'Revolution of 21 April 1967.'" Pages 36–38 in Richard Clogg and George Yannopoulos (eds.), *Greece under Military Rule*. New York: Basic Books, 1972.

————. *A Short History of Modern Greece*. Cambridge: Cambridge University Press, 1979.

Clogg, Richard (ed.). *Greece in the 1980s*. New York: St. Martin's Press, 1983.

Clogg, Richard, and George Yannopoulos (eds.). *Greece under Military Rule*. New York: Basic Books, 1972.

Couloumbis, Theodore A., John A. Petropulos, and Harry J. Psomiades. *Foreign Interference in Greek Politics: An Historical Perspective*. New York: Pella, 1976.

Couloumbis, Theodore A., and Prodromos M. Yannas. "The Stability Quotient of Greece's Post-1974 Democratic Institutions," *Journal of Modern Greek Studies*, 1, No. 2, October 1983.

Danforth, Loring M. "The Ideological Context of the Search for Continuities in Greek Culture," *Journal of Modern Greek Studies*, 2, No. 1, May 1984, 53–85.

Danopoulos, Constantine P. "Military Professionalism and Regime Legitimacy in Greece, 1967-1974," *Political Science Quarterly*, 98, No. 3, Fall 1983, 485–506.

Diamandouros, P. Nikiforos. "Greek Political Culture in Transition: Historical Origins, Evolution, Current Trends." Pages 43–69 in Richard Clogg (ed.), *Greece in the 1980s*. New York: St. Martin's Press, 1983.

————. "Transition to, and Consolidation of, Democratic Politics in Greece, 1974-1983: A Tentative Assessment," *West European Politics* [London], 7, No. 2, April 1984, 50–71.

Fleischer, Hagen. "The 'Anomalies' in the Greek Middle East Forces, 1941-1944," *Journal of the Hellenic Diaspora*, 5, No. 3, Fall 1978, 5–36.

Gage, Nicholas. *Eleni*. New York: Ballantine Books, 1983.

————. "The Paradoxical Papandreou," *New York Times Magazine*, March 21, 1982, 42.

Gianaris, Nicholas V. *Greece and Yugoslavia: An Economic Comparison*. New York: Praeger, 1984.

Goldbloom, Maurice. "United States Policy in Post-War Greece." Pages 228–54 in Richard Clogg and George Yannopoulos (eds.), *Greece under Military Rule*. New York: Basic Books, 1972.

"Greece: A Survey," *Euromoney*, No. 1, April 1983 (supplement).

Holden, David. *Greece Without Columns: The Making of the Modern Greeks*. Philadelphia: Lippincott, 1972.

Iatrides, John O. (ed.). *Greece in the 1940s: A Nation in Crisis.* Hanover, New Hampshire: University Press of New England, 1981.

Joseph, Joseph S. "The Birth and Death of a Biethnic State: The Case of Cyprus." (Paper presented at 26th Annual Meeting of International Studies Association, March 5-9, 1985.) Washington: March 1985.

Kapetanyannis, Basil. "The Making of Greek Eurocommunism," *Political Quarterly* [London], 50, No. 4, October-December 1979, 445–60.

Karavites, Peter. "Greek Politicians and the Palace, 1961-67," (Pt. 2), *Southeastern Europe/L'Europe du Sud-Est*, 7, 1980, 171–90.

Keefe, Eugene K., et al. *Greece: A Country Study.* (DA Pam 550–87.) Washington: GPO for Foreign Area Studies, The American University, 1983.

Kitsikis, Dimitri. "Greek Communists and the Karamanlis Government," *Problems of Communism*, 26, No. 1, January-February 1977, 42–56.

Koliopoulos, John S. "Shepherds, Brigands, and Irregulars in Nineteenth Century Greece," *Journal of the Hellenic Diaspora*, 8, No. 4, Winter 1981, 41–53.

Kousoulas, D. George. "The Greek Communists Tried Three Times—and Failed." Pages 293–309 in Thomas T. Hammond (ed.), *The Anatomy of Communist Takeovers.* New Haven: Yale University Press, 1975.

_____. *Modern Greece: Profile of a Nation.* New York: Scribner's, 1974.

_____. "The Origins of the Greek Military Coup, April 1967," *Orbis*, 13, No. 1, Spring 1969, 332–58.

Langer, William L. *An Encyclopedia of World History.* Boston: Houghton Mifflin, 1968.

Leon, George B. "The Greek Labor Movement and the Bourgeois State, 1910-1920," *Journal of the Hellenic Diaspora*, 4, No. 4, Winter 1978, 5–28.

Linardatos, Spyros. "The 1958 Elections: A Reassessment," *Journal of the Hellenic Diaspora*, 5, No. 2, Summer 1978, 59–80.

Lyrintzis, Chriotos. "Political Parties in Post-Junta Greece: A Case of 'Bureaucratic Clientelism'?" *West European Politics* [London], 7, No. 2, April 1984, 99–118.

McNeill, William H. *The Metamorphosis of Greece since World War II.* Chicago: University of Chicago Press, 1978.

Mavrogordatos, George T. "The Emerging Party System."

Pages 70–94 in Richard Clogg (ed.), *Greece in the 1980s.* New York: St. Martin's Press, 1983.

———. "The Greek Party System: A Case of 'Limited but Polarised Pluralism'?" *West European Politics* [London], 7, No. 4, October 1984, 156–69.

———. *Stillborn Republic: Social Coalitions and Party Strategies in Greece, 1922-1936.* Berkeley and Los Angeles: University of California Press, 1983.

Mee, Charles L., Jr. *The Marshall Plan.* New York: Simon and Schuster, 1984.

Mouzelis, Nicos P. "Class and Clientelistic Politics: The Case of Greece," *Sociological Review* [Staffordshire, England], 26, No. 3, August 1978, 471–97.

———. *Modern Greece: Facets of Underdevelopment.* New York: Holmes and Meier, 1978.

Mouzelis, Nikos, and Michael Attalides. "Greece." Pages 162–97 in Margaret Scotford Archer and Salvador Giner (eds.), *Contemporary Europe: Class, Status, and Power.* London: Weidenfeld and Nicolson, 1971.

Papacosma, S. Victor. "The Historical Context." Pages 30–42 in Richard Clogg (ed.), *Greece in the 1980s.* New York: St. Martin's Press, 1983.

———. *The Military in Greek Politics: The 1909 Coup d'État.* Kent: Kent State University Press, 1977.

Penniman, Howard R. (ed.). *Greece at the Polls: The National Elections of 1974 and 1977.* Washington: American Enterprise Institute for Public Policy Research, 1981.

Poulantzas, Nicos. *The Crisis of the Dictatorships: Portugal, Spain, Greece.* London: New Left Books, 1976.

Rusinow, Dennison I. *The Cyprus Deadlock: Forever or Another Day?* (American Universities Field Staff. Fieldstaff Reports. Europe, No. 11.) Hanover, New Hampshire: AUFS, 1981.

Sarafis, Marion (ed.). *Greece: From Resistance to Civil War.* Nottingham, England: Spokesman, 1980.

Stavrianos, Leften S. *The Balkans since 1453.* New York: Holt, Rinehart and Winston, 1965.

Stavrou, Nikolaos A. *Allied Politics and Military Interventions: The Political Role of the Greek Military.* Athens: Papazissis, 1976.

Stevens, J.M., C.M. Woodhouse, and D.J. Wallace. *British Reports on Greece, 1943-1944.* (Ed., Lars Baerentzen.) Copenhagen: Museum Tusculanum Press, 1983.

Tsoucalas, Constantine. "On the Problem of Political Clientelism in Greece in the Nineteenth Century," *Journal of the Hellenic Diaspora*, 5, Nos. 1–2, Spring-Summer 1978, 5–15.

Veremis, Thanos M. "Greek Security: Issues and Politics." (Adelphi Papers, No. 179.) London: International Institute for Strategic Studies, 1982.

———. "Security Considerations and Civil-Military Relations in Post-War Greece." Pages 173–83 in Richard Clogg (ed.), *Greece in the 1980s*. New York: St. Martin's Press, 1983.

———. "Some Observations on the Greek Military in the Inter-War Period, 1918-1935." *Armed Forces and Society*, 4, No. 3, May 1978, 527–41.

Vlachos, Helen. "The Colonels and the Press." Pages 59–74 in Richard Clogg and George Yannopoulos (eds.), *Greece under Military Rule*. New York: Basic Books, 1972.

Woodhouse, C.M. "Greece and Europe." Pages 1–8 in Richard Clogg (ed.), *Greece in the 1980s*. New York: St. Martin's Press, 1983.

———. "The 'Revolution' in Its Historical Context." Pages 1–16 in Richard Clogg and George Yannopoulos (eds.), *Greece under Military Rule*. New York: Basic Books, 1972.

Xydis, Stephen G. "Coups and Countercoups in Greece, 1967-1973 (with postscript)," *Political Science Quarterly*, 89, No. 3, Fall 1974, 507–38.

Yannopoulos, George. "The State of the Opposition Forces since the Military Coup." Pages 163–90 in Richard Clogg and George Yannopoulos (eds.), *Greece under Military Rule*. New York: Basic Books, 1972.

Zaharopoulos, George. "Politics and the Army in Post-War Greece." Pages 17–35 in Richard Clogg and George Yannopoulos (eds.), *Greece under Military Rule*. New York: Basic Books, 1972.

Zotos, Stephanos. *Greece: The Struggle for Freedom*. New York: Crowell, 1967.

## Chapter 2

Amnesty International. *Amnesty International Report, 1984*. London: 1984.

Aschenbrenner, Stanley E. "Folk Model vs. Actual Practice:

The Distribution of Spiritual Kin in a Greek Village," *Anthropological Quarterly*, 48, No. 2, April 1975, 65–86.

Barrett, David A. (ed.). *World Christian Encyclopedia*. Oxford: Oxford University Press, 1982.

Beckinsale, Monica, and Robert Beckinsale. *Southern Europe: A Systematic Geographical Study*. New York: Holmes and Meier, 1975.

Bien, Peter. *Kazantzakis and the Linguistic Revolution in Greek Literature*. Princeton: Princeton University, 1972.

Boucouvalas, Marcie. "Adult Education in Modern Greece," *Convergence* [Toronto], 15, No. 3, 1982, 28–36.

Browning, Robert. "Greek Diglossia Yesterday and Today," *International Journal of the Sociology of Language* [Amsterdam], No. 35, 1982.

_____. *Medieval and Modern Greek*. (2d ed.) Cambridge: Cambridge University Press, 1983.

Campbell, John, and Philip Sherrard. *Modern Greece*. New York: Praeger, 1968.

Campbell, John K. *Honour, Family, and Patronage*. Oxford: Clarendon Press, 1964.

_____. "Traditional Values and Continuities in Greek Society." Pages 184–207 in Richard Clogg (ed.), *Greece in the 1980s*. New York: St. Martin's Press, 1983.

Catsiapis, Jean. *La Grèce: Dixième membre des Communautés européennes*. (Notes et Études Documentaires, Nos. 4593–4594.) Paris: La Documentation Française, 1980.

Clogg, Richard (ed.). *Greece in the 1980s*. New York: St. Martin's Press, 1983.

Coronakis, Basil A. (ed.). *Briefing Documents: Greece*. Athens: Coronakis Press, April 1983.

"'Crimes of Honor' Still the Pattern in Rural Greece," *New York Times*, Sect. 1, February 10, 1980, 22.

Danforth, Loring M. *The Death Rituals of Rural Greece*. Princeton: Princeton University Press, 1982.

Dawidowicz, Lucy S. *The War Against the Jews*. New York: Bantam, 1975.

Diamessis, S.E. "The Introduction of the 'New Greek Language,'" *Multilingua 1–3* [Amsterdam], April 1982, 167–68.

Diem, Aubrey. *Western Europe: A Geographical Analysis*. New York: John Wiley and Sons, 1979.

Dimaris, Alexis. "Europe and the 1980s: A Double Challenge for Greek Education." Pages 231–44 in Richard Clogg (ed.), *Greece in the 1980s*. New York: St. Martin's Press, 1983.

Dimen, Muriel, and Ernestine Friedl (eds.). *Regional Variation in Modern Greece and Cyprus: Toward a Perspective on the Ethnography of Greece*. New York: New York Academy of Sciences, 1976.

Doumanis, Mariella. *Mothering in Greece: From Collectivism to Individualism*. London: Academic Press, 1983.

Dubisch, Jill. "The City as Resource: Migration from a Greek Island Village," *Urban Anthropology*, 6, No. 1, Spring 1977, 65–81.

——. "Greek Women: Sacred or Profane," *Journal of Modern Greek Studies*, 1, No. 1, May 1983, 185–201.

du Boulay, Juliet. "The Meaning of Dowry: Changing Values in Rural Greece," *Journal of Modern Greek Studies*, 1, No. 1, May 1983, 243–70.

——. *Portrait of a Greek Mountain Village*. Oxford: Clarendon Press, 1974.

Economist Intelligence Unit. *Quarterly Economic Review of Greece: Annual Supplement, 1984* [London], 1984.

*Eurohealth Handbook*. White Plains, New York: First, 1982.

European Parliament. Secretariat Directorate General for Research and Documentation. *Greece's Accession to the European Community*. (Research and Documentation Papers, Economic Series, No. 4.) Brussels: August 1982.

Eurostat. *Eurostat Basic Statistics of the Community*. (20th ed.) Luxembourg: Office for Official Publications for the Community, 1983.

Fakiolas, Ross. "Return Migration to Greece and Its Structural and Socio-Political Effects." Pages 37–43 in Daniel Kubat (ed.), *The Politics of Return: International Return Migration in Europe*. Rome: Centro Studi Emigrazione, 1983.

Friedl, Ernestine. "The Position of Women: Appearance and Reality," *Anthropological Quarterly*, 40, 1967, 97–108.

——. "The Role of Kinship in the Transmission of National Culture to Rural Villages in Mainland Greece," *American Anthropologist*, 61, No. 1, February 1959, 30–37.

——. *Vasilika*. New York: Holt, Rinehart and Winston, 1962.

Gage, Nicholas. *Portrait of Greece*. New York: American Heritage Press, 1971.

Goussidis, Alexandre. "Analyse statistique et sociographique des ordinations dans l'Église de Grèce entre 1950 et

1969," *Social Compass* [Louvain, Belgium], 22, No. 1, 1975, 107–47.

Greece. National Statistical Service. *Monthly Statistical Bulletin* [Athens], 29, No. 4, April 1984.

_____. *Statistical Yearbook of Greece, 1981.* Athens: 1982.

_____. *Statistical Yearbook of Greece, 1982.* Athens: 1983.

Hellenic Industrial Development Bank (ETBA). *Investment Guide in Greece.* Athens: 1983.

Herzfeld, Michael. "Honour and Shame: Problems in the Comparative Analysis of Moral Systems," *Man* [London], 15, June 1980, 339–51.

Hirschon, Renée B. "Open Body/Closed Space: The Transformation of Female Sexuality." Pages 66–68 in Shirley Ardener (ed.), *Defining Females: The Nature of Women in Society.* New York: John Wiley and Sons, 1978.

_____. "Under One Roof: Marriage, Dowry and Family Relations in Piraeus." Pages 299–323 in Michael Kenny and David I. Kertzer (eds.), *Urban Life in Mediterranean Europe.* Urbana: University of Illinois Press, 1983.

_____. "Women, the Aged, and Religious Activity: Oppositions and Complementarity in an Urban Locality," *Journal of Modern Greek Studies,* 1, No. 1, May 1983, 113–29.

Jioultsis, Basil. "Religious Brotherhoods: A Sociological View," *Social Compass* [Louvain, Belgium], 22, No. 1, 1975, 67–83.

Joint Publications Research Service—JPRS (Washington). *West Europe Report.* "Alleged Mistreatment of Western Thrace Muslims," *Arabia: The Islamic World in Review,* East Burnham, Bucks, England, July 1984. (JPRS 84-102, August 21, 1984).

Kenna, Margaret E. "Houses, Fields, and Graves: Property and Ritual Obligation on a Greek Island," *Ethnology,* 15, No. 1, January 1976, 21–34.

_____. "The Idiom of Family." Pages 347–61 in J.C. Peristiany (ed.), *Mediterranean Family Structures.* Cambridge: Cambridge University Press, 1976.

_____. "Institutional and Transformational Migration and the Politics of Community," *Archives européennes de sociologie* [Cambridge], 24, No. 2, 1983, 263–87.

Kolodny, Emile. "Neokaisaria (Pierie)," *Greek Review of Social Research* [Athens], 1981, 18–31 (special issue).

Kourvetaris, George A., and Betty A. Dobratz. "Objective and Subjective Class Identification among Athenians in

Greece," *Sociology and Social Research*, 66, No. 4, July 1982, 484–500.

Koutsopoulos, C.J., and B.A. Vassilopoulos. "Employee Benefits in Greece: Recent Developments and Current Status," *Benefits International* [London], 13, No. 7, January 1984, 2–7.

Lambiri-Dimaki, Jane. "Dowry in Modern Greece: An Institution at the Crossroads Between Persistence and Decline." Pages 73–83 in Constantina Safilios-Rothschild (ed.), *Toward a Sociology of Women*. Lexington, Massachusetts: Xerox College, 1972.

Lianos, Theodore P. "Greece." Pages 209–17 in Daniel Kubat (ed.), *Politics of Migration Policies*. New York: Center for Migration Studies, 1979.

McNeill, William H. *The Metamorphosis of Greece since World War II*. Chicago: University of Chicago Press, 1978.

Mantzaridis, Georges. "New Statistical Data Concerning the Monks of Mount Athos," *Social Compass* [Louvain, Belgium], 22, No. 1, 1975, 97–106.

Massialas, Byron G. *The Educational System of Greece*. (Education Around the World series.) Washington: GPO, 1981.

Milleounis, E.C. "Greek Secondary Education: Current Attempts at Reform," *Compare* [Oxford], 9, No. 2, 1979, 147–55.

Mouzelis, Nikos, and Michael Attalides. "Greece." Pages 162–97 in Margaret Scotford Archer and Salvador Giner (eds.), *Contemporary Europe: Class, Status, and Power*. London: Weidenfeld and Nicolson, 1971.

Oliver, E. Eugene. *Greece: A Study of the Educational System of Greece and a Guide to the Academic Placement of Students in Educational Institutions in the United States*. (World Education series.) Washington: American Association of Collegiate Registrars and Admissions Officers, 1982.

Organisation for Economic Co-operation and Development. Directorate for Social Affairs, Manpower, and Education. *SOPEMI*. Paris: 1982.

Papademetriou, Demetrios. "Greece." Pages 187–200 in Ronald E. Krane (ed.), *International Labor Migration in Europe*. New York: Praeger, 1979.

Papademetriou, Theresa. *Marriage and Marital Property under the New Greek Family Law*. Washington: Library of Congress Law Library, 1985.

Petras, James. "Research Note: Class Formation and Politics in

Greece," *Journal of Political and Military Sociology*, 11, No. 2, Fall 1983, 241–50.

Population Reference Bureau. *1984 World Population Data Sheet*. Washington: 1984.

Rinvolucri, Mario. *Anatomy of a Church*. New York: Fordham University Press, 1966.

Sanders, Irwin T. *Rainbow in the Rock: The People of Rural Greece*. Cambridge: Harvard University Press, 1962.

Siampos, George C. "The Greek Migration in the Twentieth Century." Pages 234–55 in George Siampos (ed.), *Recent Population Changes Calling for Policy Action*. Athens: National Statistical Service of Greece and European Centre for Population Studies, 1980.

_____. "The Influence of Current Demographic Change on Social Structure in Greece." Pages 113–23 in Milos Macura (ed.), *The Effect of Current Demographic Change in Europe on Social Structure*. Belgrade: Ekonomski Institut, 1979.

_____. "The Trend of Urbanization in Greece." Pages 164–72 in *Essays on Greek Migration*. (Migration Series, No. 1.) Athens: Social Sciences Centre, 1967.

Sideris, Aloe. "Some Information about Private Education in Greece," *Journal of the Hellenic Diaspora*, 8, Nos. 1–2, Spring-Summer 1981, 55–61.

Sotiropoulos, Dimitri. "Diglossia and the National Language Question in Modern Greece," *Linguistics* [Amsterdam], No. 197, September 24, 1977, 5–31.

_____. "The Social Roots of Modern Greek Diglossia," *Language Problems and Language Planning*, 6, No. 1, Spring 1982, 1–28.

Spinellis, C.D., Vasso Vassiliou, and George Vassiliou. "Milieu Development and Male-Female Roles in Contemporary Greece." Pages 308–17 in Georgene H. Seward and Robert C. Williamson (eds.), *Sex Roles in a Changing Society*. New York: Random House, 1978.

Stott, Margaret A. "Economic Transition and the Family in Mykonos," *Greek Review of Social Research* [Athens], No. 17, July-September 1973, 122–33.

_____. "Tourism in Mykonos: Some Social and Cultural Responses," *Mediterranean Studies* [Valletta, Malta], 1, No. 2, 1979, 70–90.

Sutton, Susan B. *Migrant Regional Associations: An Athenian Example and Its Implications*. (Ph.D. dissertation, University of North Carolina at Chapel Hill, 1978.) Chapel Hill: Ann Arbor Microfilms, 79–10199.

————. "Rural-Urban Migration in Greece." Pages 225–49 in Michael Kenny and David I. Kertzer (eds.), *Urban Life in Mediterranean Europe*. Urbana: University of Illinois Press, 1983.

Symeonidou-Alatopoulou, Charis. "Fertility in Greece: Some Explanatory Factors." Pages 65–72 in George Siampos (ed.), *Recent Population Changes Calling for Policy Action*. Athens: National Statistical Service of Greece and European Centre for Population Studies, 1980.

Unger, Klaus. "Greek Emigration to and Return from West Germany," *Ekistics* [Athens], 48, No. 290, September-October 1981, 369–74.

————. "Occupational Profile of Returnees in Three Greek Cities." Pages 93–99 in Daniel Kubat (ed.), *The Politics of Return*. Rome: Centro Studi Emigrazione, 1983.

United States. Central Intelligence Agency. *World Factbook, 1984*. Washington: 1984.

United States. Department of Education. *The Educational System of Greece*. (Education Around the World series, No. E-80-14012.) Washington: GPO, 1981.

United States. Department of State. *Country Reports on Human Rights Practices for 1984*. (Report submitted to United States Congress, 99th, 1st Session, Senate, Committee on Foreign Relations, and House of Representatives, Committee on Foreign Affairs.) Washington: GPO, February 1985.

Valaoras, Vasilios G. "A Reconstruction of the Demographic History of Modern Greece," *Milbank Memorial Fund Quarterly*, 38, No. 1, January 1960, 115–39.

Vermeulen, Hans. "Urban Research in Greece." Pages 109–32 in Michael Kenny and David I. Kertzer (eds.), *Urban Life in Mediterranean Europe*. Urbana: University of Illinois Press, 1983.

Ware, Kallistos. "The Church: A Time of Transition." Pages 208–29 in Richard Clogg (ed.), *Greece in the 1980s*. New York: St. Martin's Press, 1983.

Ware, Timothy. *The Orthodox Church*. Baltimore: Penguin Books, 1963.

Wasser, Henry. "A Survey of Recent Trends in Greek Higher Education," *Journal of the Hellenic Diaspora*, 6, No. 1, Spring 1979, 85–95.

World Bank. *World Development Report, 1984*. New York: Oxford University Press, 1984.

World Health Organization. *Health Services in Europe*, 2. Copenhagen: 1981.

_____. *World Health Statistics Annual*, 83. Geneva: 1983.

Zarras, John. "Greece." Pages 161–80 in Erdman Palmore (ed.), *International Handbook on Aging: Contemporary Developments and Research*. Westport, Connecticut: Greenwood Press, 1980.


(Various issues of the following publications were also used in the preparation of this chapter: *Athens News* [Athens], October 1983-May 1985; Foreign Broadcast Information Service, *Daily Report: Western Europe*, January 1982-May 1985; and *New York Times*, January 1983-May 1985.)

**Chapter 3**

Athens News Agency. "Prime Minister Andreas Papandreou's Address to the PASOK Congress Organizing Committee at the Park Hotel on February 8, 1984, Part II." (Feature Stories series, No. 134.) Athens: February 10, 1984.

Axt, Heinz-Jürgen. "On the Way to Self Reliance? PASOK's Government Policy in Greece," *Journal of Modern Greek Studies*, 2, No. 2, October 1984, 189–208.

Bank of Greece. *Monthly Statistical Bulletin* [Athens], 49, No. 4, April 1984.

_____. *Monthly Statistical Bulletin* [Athens], 49, No. 7, July 1984.

_____. *Report of Governor G. Arsenis for the Year 1982*. Athens: 1983.

_____. *Summary of the Annual Report of Governor D. Chalikias for the Year 1983*. Athens: 1983.

Burakow, Nicholas. "Romania and Greece: Socialism vs. Capitalism," *World Development* [London], 9, Nos. 9–10, 1981, 907–28.

Campbell, John, and Philip Sherrard. *Modern Greece*. New York: Praeger, 1968.

Candilis, Wary O. *The Economy of Greece, 1944–66*. New York: Praeger, 1971.

Carson, J. Graham. "Greece: New Policies, a New Confidence," *Institutional Investor*, 1983, 1–16.

Catsiapis, Jean. *La Grèce: Dixième membre des Communautés*

*européennes*. (Notes et Études Documentaires, Nos. 4593–4594.) Paris: La Documentation Française, 1980.

Centre of Planning and Economic Research. *Economic and Social Development Plan: 1983-1987 Summary*. Athens: 1984.

————. *The Greek Economy Today*. Athens: January 1984.

Commercial Bank of Greece. "Development of the Greek Economy since Association with the EEC," *Economic Bulletin* [Athens], No. 106, October-December 1980, 8–17.

————. "Economic Policy in 1983," *Economic Bulletin* [Athens], October 1982-March 1983, 10–21.

Coronakis, Basil A. (ed.). *Briefing Documents: Greece*. Athens: Coronakis Press, April 1983.

Croll, Donald O. "Emphasis on State Enterprises," *Petroleum Economist* [London], 50, No. 12, December 1983, 466–68.

Demopoulos, George D. "Financial Markets and Institutions in Greece," *European Economy*, March 1983, 145–55.

Dryllerakis, John C. "Incentives for Regional and Sectoral Development in Greece," *Mezzogiorno d'Europa* [Naples], 3, No. 1, January-March 1983, 7–31.

Economist Intelligence Unit. *Quarterly Economic Review of Greece* [London], No. 3, 1984.

————. *Quarterly Economic Review of Greece* [London], No. 4, 1984.

————. *Quarterly Economic Review of Greece: Annual Supplement, 1984* [London], 1984.

Efstratoglou-Todoulou, Sophia. "Greece: The Agricultural Sector—The Impact of the Common Agricultural Policy." Pages 85–104 in *The Enlargement of the European Community: Case Studies of Greece, Portugal, and Spain*. London: Macmillan, 1983.

European Parliament. Secretariat Directorate General for Research and Documentation. *Greece's Accession to the European Community* (Research and Documentation Papers, Economic Series, No. 4.) Brussels: August 1982.

Faith, Nicholas. "Greece: A Survey Supplement," *Euromoney* [London], April 1983, 1–32.

"Fresh Moves to Deal with Ailing Companies," *Hellenews* [Athens], 27, No. 1423, November 22, 1984, 4.

Gianaris, Nicholas V. *Greece and Yugoslavia: An Economic Comparison*. New York: Praeger, 1984.

Giannaros, Demetrios S. "Estimation of Structural Changes in the Trade Sector Resulting from the Integration with the EEC: The Case of Greece," *Journal of Economic Development* [Seoul], 9, No. 2, December 1984, 145–70.

Greece. General Secretariat for Press and Information. *Greek Government Programme Presented by the Prime Minister, Andreas G. Papandreou*. Athens: 1981.

Greece. Ministry of Agriculture. *Greek Agriculture: Data and Facts*. Athens: 1982.

Greece. National Statistical Service. *Statistical Yearbook of Greece, 1975*. Athens: 1976.

_____. *Statistical Yearbook of Greece, 1982*. Athens: 1983.

"Greece," *Financial Times* [London], June 7, 1978, 14–19 (Survey).

"Greece," *Financial Times* [London], July 22, 1981, 1–5 (Survey).

"Greece," *Financial Times* [London], December 22, 1982, 1–4 (Survey).

Halikias, Demetrios J. *Money and Credit in a Developing Economy: The Greek Case*. New York: New York University Press, 1978.

Hellenic Industrial Development Bank (EBTA). *Investment Guide in Greece*. Athens: 1983.

Holden, David. *Greece Without Columns: The Making of the Modern Greeks*. Philadelphia: Lippincott, 1972.

International Monetary Fund. *Exchange Arrangements and Exchange Restrictions: Annual Report, 1984*. Washington: 1984.

Joint Publications Research Service—JPRS (Washington). The following items are from the JPRS series:

*West Europe Report*.

"Abundant Macedonian Lignite, Other Reserves," *Makedonia Epiloges*, Athens, June 1984. (JPRS 84–097, August 8, 1984, 88–91).

"Attempt to Diversify Energy Sources Continues," *To Vima*, Athens, August 5, 1984. (JPRS 84–115, September 19, 1984, 100–106).

"DEI to Reject 'Foreign Interests' from Operations Field," *Elevtherotypia*, Athens, September 6, 1984. (JPRS 84–123, October 15, 1984, 112–15).

"Growing Energy Dependence on USSR Noted," *I Kathimerini*, Athens, September 9–10, 1984. (JPRS 84–123, October 15, 1985, 105–108).

"1985 Budget Presented to Chamber of Deputies," *I Kathimerini*, Athens, November 29, 1984. (JPRS 85–008, January 24, 1985, 114–30).

"Review of 'Labyrinthine' Foreign Debt," *O Oiko-*

*nomikos Takhydromos,* Athens, June 21, 1984. (JPRS 84–108, August 31, 1984, 116–20).

Kalamotousakis, George. "Restructuring the Greek Monetary and Credit System," *Banker* [London], 131, January 1981, 93–99.

Katsioupis, Paulos. *Struktur des Bankwesens in Griechenland.* Frankfurt am Main: Knapp, 1984.

Kefalas, Anthony P. "The Benefits of the EC," *Greece's Weekly* [Athens], No. 30, April 7, 1984, 4–5.

_____. "Lopsided as She Goes," *1983 Greece's Weekly—B and F Yearbook* [Athens], January 1984, 2–10.

LaLonde, Robert, and Nick Papandreou. "The Manpower Report of K.E.P.E.: The Characteristics of the Greek Labor Market." Princeton: Centre for Planning and Economic Research, Princeton University, April 1984.

Lambert, Miles J. "Greek Entry into the EC Launches a Decade of Growth and Changing Focus," *Foreign Agriculture,* 19, No. 1, January 1981, 12–14.

Macridis, Roy C. *Greek Politics at a Crossroads: What Kind of Socialism?* Stanford: Hoover Institution Press, 1984.

Mitsos, Achilles G.J. "Greece: The Industrial Sector." Pages 105–27 in *The Enlargement of the European Community: Case Studies of Greece, Portugal, and Spain.* London: Macmillan, 1983.

Mouzelis, Nicos P. *Modern Greece: Facets of Underdevelopment.* New York: Holmes and Meier, 1978.

Murolo, Antonio. "The Greek Economy: The Role of the Transnationals and the EEC," *Mezzogiorno d'Europe* [Naples], 2, No. 2, April-June 1982, 197–220.

Noël, Emile. *Working Together: The Institutions of the European Community.* Luxembourg: 1985.

Organisation for Economic Co-operation and Development. *Greece, 1981–82.* Paris: May 1982.

_____. *Greece, 1983–84.* Paris: November 1983.

Panayotatos, Elisabeth N. "A Critique of Regional Planning in Greece," *Habitat International* [London], 8, No. 1, 1984, 35–44.

Papandreou, Andreas. *A Strategy for Greek Development.* Athens: Contos Press, 1962.

Pepelasis, Admantios. "Greece: The Agricultural Sector—The Implications of the Accession." Pages 70–84 in *The Enlargement of the European Community: Case Studies of Greece, Portugal, and Spain.* London: Macmillan, 1983.

Samouilidis, J.E., and C.S. Mitropoulos. "Energy and Economic Growth in Industrializing Countries: The Case of Greece," *Energy Economics* [London], 6, No. 3, July 1984, 191–200.

Siotis, Jean. "Greece: Characteristics and Motives for Entry." Pages 57–69 in José Luis Sampedro and Juan Antonio Payno (eds.), *The Enlargement of the European Community: Case Studies of Greece, Portugal, and Spain.* London: Macmillan, 1983.

Solomon, Steven. "Greece's Classical Debt Dilemma," *Institutional Investor, International Edition,* August 1984, 67–70.

"Squeeze Them More," *Greece's Weekly* [Athens], No. 28, March 24, 1984, 20–25.

"Survey: Greece," *Economist* [London], 284, No. 7244, July 3, 1982, 1–18.

Taggiasco, Ronald. "Greece Concocts a New Cure to Try on Its Ailing Economy," *Business Week,* April 16, 1984, 68.

United States. Department of Agriculture. Economic Research Service. *Selected Agricultural Statistics on Greece, 1965–77.* (Statistical Bulletin series, No. 675.) Washington: January 1982.

United States. Department of Commerce. Office of Country Marketing. *Marketing in Greece.* (Overseas Business Reports, OBR 83–01.) Washington: GPO, February 1983.

United States. Department of Labor. Bureau of International Labor Affairs. *Country Labor Profile: Greece.* Washington: 1980.

United States. Embassy in Athens. *Foreign Economic Trends and Their Implications for the United States.* (International Marketing Information series, No. FET 84–10.) Washington: International Trade Administration, Department of Commerce, March 1984.

———. *Foreign Labor Trends: Greece, 1983–84.* (Foreign Labor Trends series, No. FLT 84–49.) Washington: United States Department of Labor, Bureau of International Labor Affairs, 1984.

United States. Embassy in Athens. Agricultural Attaché. *Agricultural Situation Report: Greece.* (Agricultural Situation Report series, No. GR–3005.) Washington: GPO, February 1983.

———. *Agricultural Situation Report: Greece.* (Agricultural Situation Report series, No. GR–4008.) Washington: GPO, February 1984.

———. *Agricultural Situation Report: Greece.* (Agricultural

Situation Report series, No. GR–5010.) Washington: GPO, March 1985.

Xenakis, Yannis. "Les politiques économiques du début des années quatre-vingt en Grèce, aperçu critique," *Reflets et perspectives de la vie économique*, 23, No. 3, June 1984, 207–30.

(Various issues of the following publications were also used in the preparation of this chapter: *Athens News* [Athens], November 1984-February 1985; *Blueline* [Athens], June 1984-February 1985; *Economist* [London], January 1982-April 1985; *Financial Times* [London], June 1978-April 1985; *Greece's Weekly* [Athens], January 1984-January 1985; *Greece: The Week in Review*, November 1984-April 1985; Joint Publications Research Service, *West Europe Report*, January 1982-March 1985; *New York Times*, January 1982-April 1985; *Wall Street Journal*, January 1982-March 1985; and *Washington Post*, January 1982-April 1985.)

**Chapter 4**

Anastasi, Paul. "Greek President Rebuffed by Left on 2d Term, Quits," *New York Times*, March 11, 1985, A1.

Athens News Agency. "Agreement of Defense and Economic Cooperation Between the Government of the Hellenic Republic and the Government of the United States of America." (Feature Stories series, No. 94.) Athens: September 10, 1983.

———. "Premier Reviews First 21 Months." (Feature Stories series, No. 4654.) Athens: August 1, 1983.

Axt, Heinz-Jürgen. "On the Way to Self Reliance? PASOK's Government Policy in Greece," *Journal of Modern Greek Studies*, 2, No. 2, October 1984, 189–208.

Banks, Arthur S., and William Overstreet. *Political Handbook of the World: 1982–1983*. New York: McGraw-Hill, 1983.

Berlin, Michael. "Perez de Cuellar Sets Summit on Cyprus, Reports Progress," *Washington Post*, December 13, 1984, A21.

Boll, Michael M. "Greek Foreign Policy in the 1980s: Decade for Decision," *Parameters*, 10, No. 4, December 1980, 72–81.

Bruce, Leigh H. "Cyprus: A Last Chance," *Foreign Policy*, No. 58, Spring 1985, 134–50.

_____. "Father of Modern Greek Democracy Plays Coy Politics," *Christian Science Monitor*, December 24, 1984, 7.

_____. "Greek Approval of U.S. Bases Pulls Athens More Firmly into NATO Fold," *Christian Science Monitor*, July 18, 1983, 3.

_____. "U.S.-Style Campaigns No Longer Greek to These Politicians," *Christian Science Monitor*, February 27, 1985, 1.

Christian, Shirley. "Hero, Justice, President: Christos Sartzetakis," *New York Times*, March 30, 1985, A3.

Clogg, Richard. "Greece: The Year of the Green Sun," *World Today* [London], 37, No. 11, November 1981, 401–404.

_____. "PASOK in Power: Rendezvous with History or with Reality," *World Today* [London], 39, No. 11, November 1983, 436–42.

_____. *A Short History of Modern Greece*. Cambridge: Cambridge University Press, 1979.

_____. "Troubled Alliance: Greece and Turkey." Pages 123–49 in Richard Clogg (ed.), *Greece in the 1980s*. New York: St. Martin's Press, 1983.

Clogg, Richard (ed.). *Greece in the 1980s*. New York: St. Martin's Press, 1983.

Clogg, Richard, and George Yannopoulos (eds.). *Greece under Military Rule*. New York: Basic Books, 1972.

"Continuation of New Democracy Program Statement," Foreign Broadcast Information Service, *Daily Report: Western Europe*, 7, No. 148 (FBIS-WEU-81-148), August 3, 1981, S1–S7.

"Continuation of New Democracy Program Statement," Foreign Broadcast Information Service, *Daily Report: Western Europe*, 7, No. 149 (FBIS-WEU-81-149), August 4, 1981, S1–S8.

"Continuation of New Democracy Program Statement," Foreign Broadcast Information Service, *Daily Report: Western Europe*, 7, No. 150 (FBIS-WEU-81-150), August 5, 1981, S2–S9.

"Continuation of New Democracy Program Statement," Foreign Broadcast Information Service, *Daily Report: Western Europe*, 7, No. 151 (FBIS-WEU-81-151), August 6, 1981, S1–S10.

"Continuation of New Democracy Program Statement," Foreign Broadcast Information Service, *Daily Report: Western*

*Europe*, 7, No. 152 (FBIS-WEU-81-152), August 7, 1981, S2–S8.

Coronakis, Basil A. (ed.). *Briefing Documents: Greece*. Athens: Coronakis Press, April 1983.

Couloumbis, Theodore A. "Defining Greek Foreign Policy Objectives." Pages 160–84 in Howard R. Penniman (ed.), *Greece at the Polls: The National Elections of 1974 and 1977*. Washington: American Enterprise Institute for Public Policy Research, 1981.

_____. "The Structures of Greek Foreign Policy." Pages 95–122 in Richard Clogg (ed.), *Greece in the 1980s*. New York: St. Martin's Press, 1983.

Couloumbis, Theodore A., and John O. Iatrides. *Greek-American Relations: A Critical Review*. New York: Pella, 1980.

Couloumbis, Theodore A., and Prodromos M. Yannas. "The Stability Quotient of Greece's Post-1974 Democratic Institutions," *Journal of Modern Greek Studies*, 1, No. 2, October 1983.

"Cyprus Question in Need of a Bold New Start," *Manchester Guardian Weekly* [London], February 3, 1985, 9.

Delury, George E. (ed.). *World Encyclopedia of Political Systems and Parties*, 1. New York: Facts on File, 1983.

Diamandouros, P. Nikiforos. "Greek Political Culture in Transition: Historical Origins, Evolution, Current Trends." Pages 43–69 in Richard Clogg (ed.), *Greece in the 1980s*. New York: St. Martin's Press, 1983.

_____. "Transition to, and Consolidation of, Democratic Politics in Greece, 1974-1983: A Tentative Assessment," *West European Politics* [London], 7, No. 2, April 1984, 50–71.

Dimitras, Panayote Elias. "Greece," *Electoral Studies* [Guilford, Surrey, England], 3, No. 3, December 1984, 285–89.

_____. "Greece: A New Danger," *Foreign Policy*, No. 58, Spring 1985, 134–50.

Elephantis, Angelos. "PASOK and the Elections of 1977: The Rise of the Populist Movement." Pages 105–29 in Howard R. Penniman (ed.), *Greece at the Polls: The National Elections of 1974 and 1977*. Washington: American Enterprise Institute for Public Policy Research, 1981.

Eliou, Chris. "View from Athens," *NATO's Sixteen Nations* [Brussels], 29, No. 5, September-October 1984, 97.

Evriviades, Marios. "The New Era in Greece," *Current History*, 80, No. 466, May 1981, 218–19.

Featherstone, Kevin. "Elections and Parties in Greece," *Gov-*

*ernment and Opposition* [London], 17, No. 2, Spring 1982, 180–94.

––––––. "The Greek Socialists in Power," *West European Politics* [London], 6, No. 3, July 1983, 237–50.

Greece. General Secretariat for Press and Information. *General Elections, 18th October, 1981 for the Greek Parliament, for the European Parliament.* Athens: 1981.

––––––. *Greek Government Programme Presented by the Prime Minister, Andreas G. Papandreou.* Athens: 1981.

––––––. *Multidimensional Greek Foreign Policy.* (Interview of Prime Minister Andreas G. Papandreou over ABC and BBCI.) Athens: 1982.

Greece. House of Parliament. *Constitution of Greece Voted by the Fifth Revisionary Parliament of the Hellenes on the 9th of June 1975 and Entered into Force on the 11th of June 1975.* Athens: 1975.

*Greece: A Portrait.* Athens: Research and Publicity Center, KEDE, 1979.

"Greece Approves New Defense Realignment," *Athens News* [Athens], January 9, 1985, 4.

"Greece out of All N.A.T.O. Maneuvers: Lemnos Island Dispute at Root of Row with Alliance," *Athens News* [Athens], February 8, 1985, 1.

"Greece: The Conjurer Tries Again," *Economist* [London], January 19, 1985, 45–46.

"Greek Parties Polish Their Image for a Run-up to the Polls," *Financial Times* [London], May 2, 1985, 3.

Haass, Richard N. *The United States and Greece.* (Current Policy series, No. 661.) Washington: Department of State, March 1985.

Holden, David. *Greece Without Columns: The Making of the Modern Greeks.* Philadelphia: Lippincott, 1972.

Hope, Kerin. "Socialists End Bitter Divisions," *Europe*, No. 240, November-December 1983, 34–36.

Iatrides, John O. "Greece and the United States: The Strained Partnership." Pages 150–72 in Richard Clogg (ed.), *Greece in the 1980s.* New York: St. Martin's Press, 1983.

Ierodiaconou, Andriana. "Election Arithmetic Prompts Papandreou to Move on Constitution," *Financial Times* [London], March 14, 1985, 2.

––––––. "Greece Says Its Army Will Regard Turkey as Posing Chief Threat," *Washington Post*, December 18, 1984, A21.

Ioakimidis, P.C. "Greece: From Military Dictatorship to Socialism." Pages 33–60 in Allan Williams (ed.), *Southern*

*Europe Transformed: Political and Economic Change in Greece, Italy, Portugal, and Spain.* London: Harper and Row, 1984.

"Is It All Greek to the Greeks?" *Economist* [London], April 6, 1985, 35–36.

Joint Publications Research Service—JPRS (Washington). The following items are from the JPRS series:

*West Europe Report.*

   "Comments on Recent Events in Trade Union Movement," *To Vima*, Athens, August 21, 1984. (JPRS 84–120, October 5, 1984, 47–51).

   "The Greeks' Distress," *West Europe Report: Diario de Noticias*, Lisbon, February 17, 1985. (JPRS, March 19, 1985, 38–39).

   "KKE (Int.) Leader Drakopoulos Interviewed on Socialism in Greece," *O Oikonomikos Takhydromos*, March 29, 1979. (JPRS 073431, No. 1414, May 10, 1979, 39–46).

   "Poll Results on Youth Attitudes," *ENA*, Athens, November 29, 1984. (JPRS 85–005, January 14, 1985, 23–28).

   "Poll Shows Centrist Voters Hold Balance of Power," *I Kathimerini*, Athens, August 12–13, 1984. (JPRS 84–111, September 7, 1984, 4).

   "Poll Shows Economy Tops Greek Concerns," *ENA*, Athens, October 27, 1983. (JPRS 84–009, January 24, 1984, 10–11).

   "Poll Shows Popular Stance on Politics, Economics," *To Vima*, Athens, October 28, 1984. (JPRS 84–153, December 19, 1984, 48–56).

Kamm, Henry. "Athens Fears Rise in Arms for Turks," *New York Times*, January 18, 1985, A3.

_____. "Greek Cypriots Fight Over Peace Agreement," *New York Times*, February 24, 1985, A9.

_____. "Papandreou Links Sour U.S. Ties to Turkish Issue," *New York Times*, February 14, 1985, A17.

_____. "Papandreou: The Politics of Anti-Americanism," *New York Times Magazine*, April 7, 1985, 16–27.

Kapetanyannis, Basil. "The Making of Greek Eurocommunism," *Political Quarterly* [London], 50, No. 4, October-December 1979, 445–60.

Khilnani, N.M. "Political and Constitutional Developments in Greece," *Journal of Constitutional and Parliamentary Studies* [New Delhi], 14, No. 2, April-June 1980, 136–63.

Kitsikis, Dimitri. "Greek Communists and the Karamanlis Government," *Problems of Communism*, 26, No. 1, January-February 1977, 42–56.

"KKE Issues Election Program Declaration for 1981," Foreign Broadcast Information Service, *Daily Report: Western Europe*, 7, No. 142 (FBIS-WEU-81-142), July 24, 1981, S1–S6.

Kohler, Beate. *Political Forces in Spain, Greece, and Portugal.* London: Butterworth Scientific, 1982.

Koumoulides, John T.A. (ed.). *Greece in Transition: Essays in the History of Modern Greece, 1821-1914.* London: Zeno, 1977.

Kourvetaris, George A., and Betty A. Dobratz. "Political Clientelism in Athens, Greece: A Three-Paradigm Approach to Political Clientelism," *East European Quarterly*, 18, No. 1, March 1984, 35–59.

Kousoulas, D.G. "Greece." Pages 481–83 in Richard F. Staar (ed.), *Yearbook on International Communist Affairs.* Stanford: Hoover Institution Press, 1984.

Larrabee, F. Stephen. "Dateline Athens: Greece for the Greeks," *Foreign Policy*, No. 45, Winter 1981–82, 158–74.

Legg, Keith. "Greece (Elliniki Demokratia)." Pages 379–93 in George E. Delury (ed.), *World Encyclopedia of Political Systems and Parties.* New York: Facts on File, 1983.

Loulis, John C. "Greeks Distrust a Party Bearing No Ideas," *Wall Street Journal*, September 5, 1984, 33.

―――. "New Democracy: The New Face of Conservatism." Pages 49–83 in Howard R. Penniman (ed.), *Greece at the Polls: The National Elections of 1974 and 1977.* Washington: American Enterprise Institute for Public Policy Research, 1981.

―――. "Papandreou's Foreign Policy," *Foreign Affairs*, 63, No. 2, Winter 1984–85, 375–91.

Lyrintzis, Christos. "Political Parties in Post-Junta Greece: A Case of 'Bureaucratic Clientelism'?" *West European Politics* [London], 7, No. 2, April 1984, 99–118.

―――. "The Rise of PASOK: The Greek Election of 1981," *West European Politics* [London], 5, No. 3, July 1982, 308–13.

McNeill, William H. *The Metamorphosis of Greece since World War II.* Chicago: University of Chicago Press, 1978.

Macridis, Roy C. "Elections and Political Modernization in Greece." Pages 1–20 in Howard R. Penniman (ed.), *Greece at the Polls: The National Elections of 1974 and 1977.* Washington: American Enterprise Institute for Public Policy Research, 1981.

_____. *Greek Politics at a Crossroads: What Kind of Socialism?* Stanford: Hoover Institution Press, 1984.

Mavrogordatos, George T. "The Emerging Party System." Pages 70–94 in Richard Clogg (ed.), *Greece in the 1980s.* New York: St. Martin's Press, 1983.

_____. "The Greek Party System: A Case of 'Limited but Polarised Pluralism'?" *West European Politics* [London], 7, No. 4, October 1984, 156–69.

Milligan, Stephen. "Survey: Greece," *Economist* [London], 284, No. 7244, July 3, 1982, 1–18 (supplement).

Mouzelis, Nicos P. "Class and Clientelistic Politics: The Case of Greece," *Sociological Review* [Staffordshire, England], 26, No. 3, August 1978, 471–97.

_____. *Modern Greece: Facets of Underdevelopment.* New York: Holmes and Meier, 1978.

_____. "On the Greek Elections," *New Left Review* [London], No. 108, March–April 1978, 59–76.

"New Democracy Government Issues Program Statement," Foreign Broadcast Information Service, *Daily Report: Western Europe*, 7, No. 139 (FBIS-WEU-81-139), July 21, 1981, S2–S4.

Papandreou, Nick. "Decentralization in Greece." (Research paper.) Princeton: Princeton University, n. d.

"Papandreou Addresses PASOK Congress, 10 May [1984]," Foreign Broadcast Information Service, *Daily Report: Western Europe*, 7, No. 95 (FBIS-WEU-84-095), May 15, 1984, S1–S6.

"Papandreou Opens PASOK Election Campaign," Foreign Broadcast Information Service, *Daily Report: Western Europe*, 7, No. 171 (FBIS-WEU-81-170), September 2, 1981, S1–S6.

Papayannakis, Michalis. "The Crisis in the Greek Left." Pages 130–59 in Howard R. Penniman (ed.), *Greece at the Polls: The National Elections of 1974 and 1977.* Washington: American Enterprise Institute for Public Policy Research, 1981.

Parker, Mushtak. "Greece: A Greek Policy Path That Leads Nowhere," *Arabia: The Islamic World Review* [East Burnham, Bucks, England], 4, No. 41, January 1985, 21–22.

"Part Two of PASOK Government Policy Declaration [To Vima 12 July]," Foreign Broadcast Information Service, *Daily*

*Report: Western Europe,* 7, No. 136 (FBIS-WEU-81-136), July 16, 1981, SA–S15.

"Part Three of PASOK Government Policy Declaration," Foreign Broadcast Information Service, *Daily Report: Western Europe,* 7, No. 140 (FBIS-WEU-81-140), July 22, 1981, S3–S22.

"Part Four of PASOK Government Policy Declaration [To Vima 26 July]," Foreign Broadcast Information Service, *Daily Report: Western Europe,* 7, 145 (FBIS-WEU-81-145), July 29, 1981, S2–S10.

"Part Five of PASOK Government Policy Declaration [To Vima 26 July]," Foreign Broadcast Information Service, *Daily Report: Western Europe,* 7, 146 (FBIS-WEU-81-146), July 30, 1981, S4–S15.

"PASOK Policy Declaration: Papandreou Statement," Foreign Broadcast Information Service, *Daily Report: Western Europe,* 7, No. 132 (FBIS-WEU-81-132), July 10, 1981, S1–S14.

Penniman, Howard R. (ed.). *Greece at the Polls: The National Elections of 1974 and 1977.* Washington: American Enterprise Institute for Public Policy Research, 1981.

Randal, Jonathan C. "Shift Favors U.S., Say Greeks: Communists Called Losers in Elimination of Karamanlis," *Washington Post,* March 12, 1985, A12.

Rigos, John. "Greek Socialists Play for More U.S. Aid in Talks on American Military Bases," *Christian Science Monitor,* March 1, 1983, 7.

Rusinow, Dennison I. *The Cyprus Deadlock: Forever or Another Day?* (American Universities Field Staff. Fieldstaff Reports. Europe, No. 11.) Hanover, New Hampshire: AUFS 1981.

"Socialist Government Takes Power: Decisive Electoral Victory for Mr. Papandreou," *Greece: A Record of Current Events* [Athens], 7, No. 5, September-October 1981, 1–3.

Stokes, Lee. "Greek Vote on President Inconclusive," *Miami Herald,* March 18, 1985, 6B.

*Threat in the Aegean: There Are No Differences Between Greece and Turkey. There Are Only Turkish Designs on Greece.* n. pl.: Journalists' Union of the Athens Daily Newspapers, n. d.

Tsoucalas, Constantine. "On the Problem of Political Clientalism in Greece in the Nineteenth Century," *Journal of the Hellenic Diaspora,* 5, Nos. 1–2, Spring-Summer 1978, 5–15.

United States. Congress. 98th, 1st Session. House of Representatives. Committee on Foreign Affairs. Subcommittee on Europe and the Middle East. *Developments in Europe, August 1983.* Washington: GPO, August 1983.

United States. Department of State. *Country Reports on Human Rights Practices for 1984.* (Report submitted to United States Congress, 99th, 1st Session, Senate, Committee on Foreign Relations, and House of Representatives, Committee on Foreign Affairs.) Washington: GPO, February 1985.

United States. Department of State. Bureau of Public Affairs. *Background Notes: Greece.* (Department of State publication, No. 8198.) Washington: GPO, February 1982.

Vegleris, Phaedo. "Greek Electoral Law." Pages 21–48 in Howard R. Penniman (ed.), *Greece at the Polls: The National Elections of 1974 and 1977.* Washington: American Enterprise Institute for Public Policy Research, 1981.

Veremis, Thanos M. "The Union of the Democratic Center." Pages 84–104 in Howard R. Penniman (ed.), *Greece at the Polls: The National Elections of 1974 and 1977.* Washington: American Enterprise Institute for Public Policy Research, 1981.

Williams, Allan (ed.). *Southern Europe Transformed: Political and Economic Change in Greece, Italy, Portugal, and Spain.* London: Harper and Row, 1984.

Woodhouse, C.M. *Karamanlis: The Restorer of Greek Democracy.* London: Oxford University Press, 1982.

(Various issues of the following publications were also used in the preparation of this chapter: *Athens News* [Athens], November 1984-March 1985; *Christian Science Monitor,* January 1978-April 1985; *Deadline Data,* January 1980-June 1984; *Economist* [London], January 1978-April 1985; *Financial Times* [London], January 1980-April 1985; Foreign Broadcast Information Service, *Daily Report: Western Europe,* January 1980-April 1985; *Greece: The Week in Review,* December 1984-April 1985; *Greece Today* [Athens], 1983-84; *Keesing's Contemporary Archives* [London], January 1978-January 1985; *New York Times,* January 1978-April 1985; and *Washington Post,* January 1978-April 1985.)

**Chapter 5**

Alford, Jonathan. *Greece and Turkey: Adversity in Alliance.* (Adelphi Library series, No. 12.) London: Gower, 1984.

Borowiec, Andrew. *The Mediterranean Feud.* New York: Praeger, 1983.

Brown, James. "Greek Civil-Military Relations," *Armed Forces and Society,* 6, Spring 1980, 389-413.

Couloumbis, Theodore A. *The United States, Greece, and Turkey: The Troubled Triangle.* New York: Praeger, 1983.

Couloumbis, Theodore A., John A. Petropulos, and Harry J. Psomiades. *Foreign Interference in Greek Politics: An Historical Perspective.* New York: Pella, 1976.

Danopoulos, Constantine P. "The Greek Military Regime (1967-1974) and the Cyprus Question—Origins and Goals," *Journal of Political and Military Sociology,* 10, Fall 1982, 257–73.

──────. "Military Professionalism and Regime Legitimacy in Greece, 1967-1974," *Political Science Quarterly,* 98, No. 3, Fall 1983, 485–506.

"Defense Industry in Greece," *Journal of Defense and Diplomacy,* 2, No. 10, October 1984, 24–28.

Dimitras, Panayote Elias. "Greece: A New Danger," *Foreign Policy,* No. 58, Spring 1985, 134–50.

Felton, John. "Capitol Hill Provides a Forum for Turkish-Greek Differences," *Congressional Quarterly,* December 15, 1984, 3098–3105.

Flume, Wolfgang. "Military Assistance Within the Alliance," *NATO's Sixteen Nations* [Amstelveen, Netherlands], 29, No. 5, September-October 1984, 54–63.

Giacomo, Carol. "The Disagreeing Democracies," *Journal of Defense and Diplomacy,* 2, No. 10, October 1984, 19–22.

Greece. National Statistical Service. *Statistical Yearbook of Greece, 1982.* Athens: 1983.

Grimmett, Richard F. "United States Military Installations in Greece." (Library of Congress Congressional Research Service, No. 84-24-F.) 1984.

Howarth, H.M.F. "Greece's Growing Defense Industry," *International Defense Review* [Geneva], 17, No. 9, September 1984, 1287–96.

Janke, Peter. *Guerrilla and Terrorist Organizations: A World Directory and Bibliography.* New York: Macmillan, 1983.

Kourvetaris, George A. "Greek Service Academies: Patterns in

Recruitment and Organization Change." Pages 113–39 in Gwyn Harries-Jenkins and Jacques van Doorn (eds.), *The Military and the Problem of Legitimacy*, 2. Beverly Hills: Sage, 1976.

Kourvetaris, George A., and Betty A. Dobratz. "Public Opinion and Civil-Military Relations in Greece since 1974," *Journal of Strategic Studies* [London], No. 4, March 1981, 71–84.

Larrabee, F. Stephen. "Dateline Athens: Greece for the Greeks," *Foreign Policy*, No. 45, Winter 1981-82, 158–74.

Luttwak, Edward. *Coup d'État: A Practical Handbook*. Cambridge: Harvard University Press, 1979.

*The Military Balance, 1984-1985*. London: International Institute for Strategic Studies, 1984.

Munir, Metin. "The Aegean Conflict: Is Reconciliation Possible?" *Middle East* [London], No. 24, October 1976, 8–12.

NATO Information Service. *NATO Handbook*. Brussels: 1983.

_____. The North Atlantic Treaty Organisation: Facts and Figures. Brussels: 1981.

Oliver, E. Eugene. *Greece: A Study of the Educational System of Greece and a Guide to the Academic Placement of Students in Educational Institutions in the United States*. Washington: American Association of Collegiate Registrars and Admissions Officers, 1982.

Pappas, Nicos. "The Importance of the Hellenic Navy in Southern Europe Operations," *NATO's Fifteen Nations* [Amstelveen, Netherlands], 27, No. 2, 1982, 48–50.

Roubatis, Yiannis P. "The United States and the Operational Responsibilities of the Greek Armed Forces, 1947-1987," *Journal of the Hellenic Diaspora*, 6, No. 1, Spring 1979, 39–57.

Rusinow, Dennison I. *The Cyprus Deadlock: Forever or Another Day?* (American Universities Field Staff. Fieldstaff Reports. Europe, No. 11.) Hanover, New Hampshire: AUFS, 1981.

Salvy, Robert. "Modernizing the Greek Armed Forces," *International Defense Review* [Geneva], 15, No. 9, September 1982, 1258–60.

Schwab, Peter, and George D. Frangos. *Greece under the Junta*. New York: Facts on File, 1970.

Simpsas, Marcos-Marios. "The Hellenic Navy: Past and Present," *NAVY International* [Haslemere, Surrey, England], July 1983, 418–22.

Stavrianos, Leften S. *The Balkans since 1453*. New York: Holt, Rinehart and Winston, 1965.

Szulc, Tad. "Greece vs. Turkey: NATO's Unruly Two," *New Republic*, November 27, 1976, 14–16.

United States. Arms Control and Disarmament Agency. *World Military Expenditures and Arms Transfers, 1972-1982*. Washington: 1984.

United States. Congress. 94th, 1st Session. House of Representatives, Committee on Foreign Affairs. *Greece and Turkey: Some Military Implications Related to NATO and the Middle East*. Washington: GPO, February 28, 1975.

United States. Congress. 96th, 2d Session. Senate. Committee on Foreign Relations. *Turkey, Greece, and NATO: The Strained Alliance*. Washington: GPO, March 1980.

United States. Congress. 97th, 2d Session. Senate. Committee on Foreign Relations. *NATO Today: The Alliance in Evolution*. Washington: GPO, April 1982.

United States. Congress. 98th, 1st Session. House of Representatives. Committee on Foreign Affairs. Subcommittee on Europe and the Middle East. *Developments in Europe, August 1983*. Washington: GPO, August 1983.

_____. *Human Rights in Cyprus, Greece, and Turkey*. Washington: GPO, April 1983.

_____. *U.S. Interests in the Eastern Mediterranean: Turkey, Greece and Cyprus*. Washington: GPO, June 1983.

United States. Congress. 98th, 1st Session. Senate. Committee on Foreign Relations. *U.S. Security Assistance to NATO's Southern Flank*. Washington: GPO, April 1984.

United States. Congress. 98th, 2d Session. Senate. Committee on Foreign Relations. *Security and Development Assistance*. (Hearings.) Washington: GPO, 1984.

United States. Department of State. *Country Reports on Human Rights Practices for 1984*. (Report submitted to United States Congress, 99th, 1st Session, Senate, Committee on Foreign Relations, and House of Representatives, Committee on Foreign Affairs.) Washington: GPO, February 1985.

Veremis, Thanos M. "Greece and the Southern Region: Defense of a Critical Region," *NATO's Sixteen Nations* [Amstelveen, Netherlands], 28, No. 3, June-July 1983, 68–72.

_____. *Greek Security: Issues and Politics*. (Adelphi Papers, No. 179.) London: International Institute for Strategic Studies, 1982.

_____. "Some Observations on the Greek Military in the Inter-War Period, 1918-1935," *Armed Forces and Society*, 4, No. 3, May 1978, 527–41.

Weinberger, Caspar. *Report on Allied Contributions to the Common Defense.* Washington: Department of Defense, 1984.

Wilson, Andrew. *The Aegean Dispute.* (Adelphi Papers, No. 155.) London: International Institute for Strategic Studies, Winter 1979-80.

Xydis, Stephen G. "Coups and Countercoups in Greece, 1967-1973 (with postscript)," *Political Science Quarterly*, 89, No. 3, Fall 1974, 507–38.

Zaharopoulos, George. "Politics and the Army in Post-War Greece." Pages 17–35 in Richard Clogg and George Yannopoulos (eds.), *Greece under Military Rule.* New York: Basic Books, 1972.

Zais, Melvin, "NATO's Southeastern Flank," *Strategic Review*, 5, Spring 1977, 45–51.

(Various issues of the following publication were also used in the preparation of this chapter: *Jane's Defence Weekly* [London], 1984-85.)

# Glossary

bilateral clearing account arrangement—Trade arrangement governing barter transactions between governments. In a clearing agreement two countries decide on the kinds and quantities of goods they can obtain from each other. During the period covered by the agreement (usually one year) an accounting is made, and any imbalances are made up either through a hard-currency payment or through the issuance of a credit against the next year's clearing account.

drachma—The national currency, consisting of 100 leptas. In March 1975 the drachma was first floated; from 1953 to 1975 it had been pegged at Dr30 per US$1. Since 1980 it has steadily depreciated even with 15.5 percent devaluation in January 1983. The number of drachmas per US$1 averaged Dr42.6 in 1980, Dr55.4 in 1981, Dr66.8 in 1982, Dr88.1 in 1983, Dr112.7 in 1984, and Dr129.3 in January 1985.

flags of convenience—Refers to the practice of registering vessels under other countries' flags in order to minimize taxes, wages, or avoid specific regulatory laws. Liberia and Panama have been among the most attractive countries for such registration.

gross domestic product (GDP)—The total value of all final (consumption and investment) goods and services produced by an economy in a given period, usually one year.

gross national product (GNP)—The GDP (q.v.) plus income from overseas investments minus earnings of foreign investors in the home economy.

International Monetary Fund (IMF)—Established along with the World Bank (q.v.) in 1945, the IMF is a specialized agency affiliated with the United Nations and is responsible for stabilizing international exchange rates and payments. The main business of the IMF is the provision of loans to its members (including industrialized and developing countries) when they experience balance of payments difficulties. These loans frequently carry conditions that require substantial internal economic adjustments by the recipients, most of which are developing countries.

Organisation for Economic Co-operation and Development (OECD)—Established in 1961 to replace the Organisation for European Economic Co-operation, the OECD is an international organization composed of the industrialized market economy countries (24 full members as of 1985). It seeks to promote economic and social welfare in member countries as well as in developing countries by providing a forum in which to formulate and coordinate policies designed to this end.

World Bank—Informal name used to designate a group of three affiliated international institutions: the International Bank for Reconstruction and Development (IBRD), the International Development Association (IDA), and the International Finance Corporation (IFC). The IBRD, established in 1945, has the primary purpose of providing loans to developing countries for productive projects. The IDA, a legally separate loan fund but administered by the staff of the IBRD, was set up in 1960 to furnish credits to the poorest developing countries on much easier terms than those of conventional IBRD loans. The IFC, founded in 1956, supplements the activities of the IBRD through loans and assistance designed specifically to encourage the growth of productive private enterprises in the less developed countries. The president and certain senior officers of the IBRD hold the same positions in the IFC. The three institutions are owned by the governments of the countries that subscribe their capital. To participate in the World Bank group, member states must first belong to the International Monetary Fund (IMF—*q.v.*).

# Published Country Studies

## (Area Handbook Series)

| | | | | |
|---|---|---|---|---|
| 550–65 | Afghanistan | | 550–151 | Honduras |
| 550–98 | Albania | | 550–165 | Hungary |
| 550–44 | Algeria | | 550–21 | India |
| 550–59 | Angola | | 550–154 | Indian Ocean |
| 550–73 | Argentina | | 550–39 | Indonesia |
| | | | | |
| 550–169 | Australia | | 550–68 | Iran |
| 550–176 | Austria | | 550–31 | Iraq |
| 550–175 | Bangladesh | | 550–25 | Israel |
| 550–170 | Belgium | | 550–182 | Italy |
| 550–66 | Bolivia | | 550–69 | Ivory Coast |
| | | | | |
| 550–20 | Brazil | | 550–177 | Jamaica |
| 550–168 | Bulgaria | | 550–30 | Japan |
| 550–61 | Burma | | 550–34 | Jordan |
| 550–83 | Burundi | | 550–56 | Kenya |
| 550–50 | Cambodia | | 550–81 | Korea, North |
| | | | | |
| 550–166 | Cameroon | | 550–41 | Korea, South |
| 550–159 | Chad | | 550–58 | Laos |
| 550–77 | Chile | | 550–24 | Lebanon |
| 550–60 | China | | 550–38 | Liberia |
| 550–63 | China, Republic of | | 550–85 | Libya |
| | | | | |
| 550–26 | Colombia | | 550–172 | Malawi |
| 550–91 | Congo | | 550–45 | Malaysia |
| 550–90 | Costa Rica | | 550–161 | Mauritania |
| 550–152 | Cuba | | 550–79 | Mexico |
| 550–22 | Cyprus | | 550–76 | Mongolia |
| | | | | |
| 550–158 | Czechoslovakia | | 550–49 | Morocco |
| 550–54 | Dominican Republic | | 550–64 | Mozambique |
| 550–52 | Ecuador | | 550–35 | Nepal, Bhutan and Sikkim |
| 550–43 | Egypt | | 550–88 | Nicaragua |
| 550–150 | El Salvador | | 550–157 | Nigeria |
| | | | | |
| 550–28 | Ethiopia | | 550–94 | Oceania |
| 550–167 | Finland | | 550–48 | Pakistan |
| 550–155 | Germany, East | | 550–46 | Panama |
| 550–173 | Germany, Fed. Rep. of | | 550–156 | Paraguay |
| 550–153 | Ghana | | 550–185 | Persian Gulf States |
| | | | | |
| 550–87 | Greece | | 550–42 | Peru |
| 550–78 | Guatemala | | 550–72 | Philippines |
| 550–174 | Guinea | | 550–162 | Poland |
| 550–82 | Guyana | | 550–181 | Portugal |
| 550–164 | Haiti | | 550–160 | Romania |

| 550–84 | Rwanda | 550–89 | Tunisia |
| 550–51 | Saudi Arabia | 550–80 | Turkey |
| 550–70 | Senegal | 550–74 | Uganda |
| 550–180 | Sierra Leone | 550–97 | Uruguay |
| 550–184 | Singapore | 550–71 | Venezuela |
| | | | |
| 550–86 | Somalia | 550–57 | Vietnam, North |
| 550–93 | South Africa | 550–55 | Vietnam, South |
| 550–95 | Soviet Union | 550–183 | Yemens, The |
| 550–179 | Spain | 550–99 | Yugoslavia |
| 550–96 | Sri Lanka (Ceylon) | 550–67 | Zaire |
| | | | |
| 550–27 | Sudan | 550–75 | Zambia |
| 550–47 | Syria | 550–171 | Zimbabwe |
| 550–62 | Tanzania | | |
| 550–53 | Thailand | | |
| 550–178 | Trinidad and Tobago | | |